P9-EDP-140

SHAKESPEARE:

HIS

LIFE, ART, AND CHARACTERS.

WITH

AN HISTORICAL SKETCH OF THE ORIGIN AND GROWTH
OF THE DRAMA IN ENGLAND.

FOURTH EDITION, REVISED.

BY

THE REV. H. N. HUDSON, LL.D.

VOLUME I.

GINN AND COMPANY
BOSTON · NEW YORK · CHICAGO · LONDON
ATLANTA · DALLAS · COLUMBUS · SAN FRANCISCO

825.6

The Athenæum Press
GINN AND COMPANY · PRO-
PRIETORS · BOSTON · U.S.A.

TO

MR. JOSEPH BURNETT,

OF SOUTHBOROUGH, MASS.

SIR:

The Memories of a Friendship running, I believe, without interruption through a period of more than five-and-twenty years, prompt the inscribing of these volumes to you.

H. N. HUDSON.

BOSTON, January 1, 1872.

CONTENTS.

LIFE OF SHAKESPEARE.

SHAKESPEARE,* by general suffrage, is the greatest name in literature. There can be no extravagance in saying, that to all who speak the English language his genius has made the world better worth living in, and life a nobler and diviner thing. And even among those who do not "speak the tongue that Shakespeare spake," large numbers are studying the English language mainly for the purpose of being at home with him. How he came to be what he was, and to do what he did, are questions that can never cease to be interesting, wherever his works are known, and men's powers of thought in any fair measure developed. But Providence has left a veil, or rather a cloud, about his history, so that these questions are not likely to be satisfactorily answered.

The first formal attempt at an account of Shakespeare's life was made by Nicholas Rowe, and the result thereof

* Much discussion has been had in our time as to the right way of spelling the Poet's name. The few autographs of his that are extant do not enable us to decide positively how he wrote his name; or rather they show that he had no one constant way of writing it. But the *Venus and Adonis* and the *Lucrece* were unquestionably published by his authority, and in the dedications of both these poems the name is printed "Shakespeare." The same holds in all the quarto issues of his plays where the author's name is given, with the one exception of *Love's Labour's Lost*, which has it "Shakespere"; as it also holds in the folio. And in very many of these cases the name is printed with a hyphen, "Shake-speare," as if on purpose that there might be no mistake about it. All which, surely, is or ought to be decisive as to how the Poet willed his name to be spelt in print. Inconstancy in the spelling of names was very common in his time.

published in 1709, ninety-three years after the Poet's death. Rowe's account was avowedly made up, for the most part, from traditionary materials collected by Betterton the actor, who made a visit to Stratford expressly for that purpose. Betterton was born in 1635, nineteen years after the death of Shakespeare; became an actor before 1660, retired from the stage about 1700, and died in 1710. At what time he visited Stratford is not known. It is to be regretted that Rowe did not give Betterton's authorities for the particulars gathered by him. It is certain, however, that very good sources of information were accessible in his time: Judith Quiney, the Poet's second daughter, lived till 1662; Lady Barnard, his granddaughter, till 1670; and Sir William Davenant, who in his youth had known Shakespeare, was manager of the theatre in which Betterton acted.

After Rowe's account, scarce any thing was added till the time of Malone, who by a learned and most industrious searching of public and private records brought to light a considerable number of facts, some of them very important, touching the Poet and his family. And in our own day Mr. Collier has followed up the inquiry with very great diligence, and with no inconsiderable success; though, unfortunately, much of the matter supplied by him has been discredited as unauthentic, by those from whom there is in such cases no appeal. Lastly, Mr. Halliwell has given his intelligent and indefatigable labours to the same task, and made some valuable additions to our stock.

The lineage of WILLIAM SHAKESPEARE, on the paternal side, has not been traced further back than his grandfather. The name, which in its composition smacks of brave old knighthood and chivalry, was frequent in Warwickshire from an early period.

The father of our Poet was JOHN SHAKESPEARE, who is found living at Stratford-on-Avon in 1552. He was most likely a native of Snitterfield, a village three miles from Stratford; as we find a Richard Shakespeare living there in 1550, and occupying a house and land owned by Robert Arden, the maternal grandfather of our Poet. This appears from a deed executed July 17, 1550, in which Robert Arden conveyed certain lands and tenements in Snitterfield, described as being "now in the tenure of one Richard Shakespeare," to be held in trust for three daughters "after the death of Robert and Agnes Arden."

An entry in a Court Roll, dated April, 1552, ascertains that John Shakespeare was living in Stratford at that time. And an entry in the Bailiff's Court, dated June, 1556, describes him as "John Shakespeare, of Stratford in the county of Warwick, *glover*." In 1558, the same John Shakespeare, and four others, one of whom was Francis Burbadge, then at the head of the corporation, were fined four pence each "for not keeping their gutters clean."

There is ample proof that at this period his affairs were in a thriving condition. In October, 1556, he became the owner of two copyhold estates, one of them consisting of a house with a garden and a croft attached to it, the other of a house and garden. As these were estates of inheritance, the tenure was nearly equal to freehold; so that he must have been pretty well-to-do in the world at the time. For several years after, his circumstances continued to improve. Before 1558, he became the owner, by marriage, of a farm at Wilmecote, consisting of fifty-six acres, besides two houses and two gardens; moreover, he held, in right of his wife, a considerable share in a property at Snitterfield. Another addition to his property was made in 1575,—a freehold estate, bought for the sum of £40, and described as consisting of "two houses, two gardens, and two orchards, with their appurtenances."

Several other particulars have been discovered, which go to ascertain his wealth as compared with that of other Stratford citizens. In 1564, the year of the Poet's birth, a malignant fever, called the plague, invaded Stratford. Its hungriest period was from the last of June to the last of December, during which time it swept off two hundred and thirty-eight persons out of a population of about fourteen hundred. None of the Shakespeare family are found among its victims. Large draughts were made upon the charities of the town on account of this frightful visitation. In August, the citizens held a meeting in the open air, from fear of infection, and various sums were contributed for the relief of the poor. The High-Bailiff gave 3 *s.* 4 *d.*, the head-alderman 2 *s.* 8 *d.*; John Shakespeare, being then only a burgess, gave 12 *d.*; and in the list of burgesses there were but two who gave more. Other donations were made for the same cause, he bearing a proportionable share in them.

We have seen that in June, 1556, John Shakespeare was termed a glover. In November of the same year he is found bringing an action against one of his neighbours for unjustly detaining a quantity of barley; which naturally infers him to have been more or less engaged in agricultural pursuits. It appears that at a later period agriculture was his main pursuit, if not his only one; for the town records show that in 1564 he was paid three shillings for a piece of timber; and we find him described in 1575 as a "yeoman." Rowe gives a tradition of his having been "a considerable dealer in wool." It is nowise unlikely that such may have been the case. The modern divisions of labour and trade were then little known and less regarded; several kinds of business being often carried on together, which are now kept distinct; and we have special proof that gloves and wool were apt to be united as articles of trade.

I must next trace, briefly, the career of John Shakespeare as a public officer in the Stratford corporation. After holding several minor offices, he was in 1558, and again in 1559, chosen one of the four constables. In 1561, he was a second time made one of the four affeerors, whose duty it was to determine the fines for such offences as had no penalties prescribed by statute. The same year, 1561, he was chosen one of the chamberlains of the borough, a very responsible office, which he held two years. Advancing steadily in the public confidence, he became an alderman in 1565; and in 1568 was elected Bailiff, the highest honour the corporation could bestow. He held this office a year. The series of local honours conferred upon him ended with his being chosen head-alderman in 1571; which office also he held a year. The rule being "once an alderman always an alderman," unless positive action were taken to the contrary, he retained that office till 1586, when, for persevering non-attendance at the meetings, he was deprived of his gown.

After all these marks of public consequence, the reader may be surprised to learn that John Shakespeare, the father of the world's greatest thinker and greatest poet, could not write his name! Such was undoubtedly the fact; and I take pleasure in noting it, as showing, what is too apt to be forgotten in these bookish days, that men may know several things, and may have witty children, without being initiated in the mysteries of pen and ink. In the borough records for 1565 is an order signed by nineteen aldermen and burgesses, calling upon John Wheler to undertake the office of Bailiff. Of these signers thirteen are markmen, and among them are the names of George Whately, then Bailiff, Roger Sadler, head-alderman, and John Shakespeare. So that there was nothing remarkable in his not being able to wield a pen. As Bailiff of Stratford, he was *ex officio* a justice of the peace; and two warrants are extant, granted by him in December, 1568, for the arrest of John Ball and Richard Walcar on account of debts; both of them bearing witness that "he had a mark to himself, like an honest, plain-dealing man." Several other cases in point are met with at later periods; some of which show that his wife stood on the same footing with him in this respect. In October, 1579, John and Mary Shakespeare executed a deed and bond for the transfer of their interest in certain property; both of which are subscribed with their several marks, and sealed with their respective seals.

John Shakespeare's good fortune seems to have reached its height about the year 1575, after which time we meet with many clear tokens of his decline. It is not improbable that his affairs may have got embarrassed from his having too many irons in the fire. The registry of the Court of Record, from 1555 to 1595, has a large number of entries respecting him, which show him to have been engaged in a great variety of transactions, and to have had more litigation on his hands than would now be thought either creditable or safe. But, notwithstanding his decline of fortune, we have proofs as late as 1592 that he still retained the confidence and esteem of his fellow-citizens. From that time forward, his affairs were doubtless taken care of by one who, as we shall see hereafter, was much interested not to let them suffer, and also well able to keep them in good trim. He was buried September 8, 1601; so that, supposing him to have reached his majority when first heard of in 1552, he must have passed the age of threescore and ten.

On the maternal side, our Poet's lineage was of a higher rank, and may be traced further back. His mother was Mary Arden, a name redolent of old poetry and romance. The family of Arden was among the most ancient in Warwickshire. Their history, as given by Dugdale, spreads over six centuries. Sir John Arden was squire of the body to Henry the Seventh; and he had a nephew, the son of a younger brother, who was page of the bedchamber to the same monarch. These were at that time places of considerable service and responsibility; and both the uncle and the nephew were liberally rewarded by their royal master. By conveyances dated in December, 1519, it appears that Robert Arden then became the owner of houses and land in Snitterfield. Other purchases by him of lands and houses are recorded from time to time. The Poet's maternal grandfather, also named Robert, died in 1556. In his will, dated November 24th, and proved December 17th, of that year, he makes special bequests to his "youngest daughter Mary," and also appoints her and another daughter, named Alice, "full executors of this my last will and testament." On the whole, it is evident enough that he was a man of good landed estate. Both he and Richard Shakespeare appear to have been of that honest and substantial old English yeomanry, from whose better-than-royal stock and lineage the great Poet of Nature might most fitly fetch his life and being. Of the Poet's grandmother on either side we know nothing whatever.

Mary Arden was the youngest of seven children, all of them daughters. The exact time of her marriage is uncertain, no registry of it having been found. She was not married at the date of her father's will, November, 1556. Joan, the first-born of John and Mary Shakespeare, was baptized in the parish church of Stratford-on-Avon, September 15, 1558. We have seen that at this time John Shakespeare was well established and thriving in business, and was making good headway in the confidence of the Stratfordians, being one of the constables of the borough. On the 2d of December, 1562, while he was chamberlain, his second child was christened Margaret. On the 26th of April, 1564, was baptized "WILLIAM, son of John Shakespeare." The birth is commonly thought to have taken place on the 23d, it being then the usual custom to present infants at the Font the third day after their birth; but we have no certain information whether it was observed on this august occasion. We have seen that throughout the following Summer the destroyer was busy in Stratford, making fearful spoil of her sons and daughters; but it spared the babe on whose life hung the fate of English literature. Other children were added to the family, to the number of eight, several of them dying in the mean time. On the 28th of September, 1571, soon after the father became head-alderman, a fourth daughter was baptized Anne. Hitherto the parish register has known him only as John Shakespeare: in this case it designates him "*Master* Shakespeare." Whether *Master* was a token of honour not extended to any thing under an ex-bailiff, does not appear; but in all cases after this the name is written with that significant prefix.

Nothing further is heard of Mrs. Mary Shakespeare till her death in 1608. On the 9th of September, that year, the parish register notes the burial of "Mary Shakespeare, widow," her husband having died seven years before. That she had in a special degree the confidence and affection of her father, is apparent from the treatment she received in his will. It would be very gratifying, no doubt, perhaps very instructive also, to be let into the domestic life and character of the Poet's mother. That both her nature and her discipline entered largely into his composition, and had much to do in making him what he was, can hardly be questioned. Whatsoever of woman's beauty and sweetness and wisdom was expressed in her life and manners could not but be caught and repeated in his susceptive and fertile mind. He must have grown familiar with the noblest parts of womanhood somewhere; and I can scarce conceive how he should have learned them so well, but that the light and glory of them beamed upon him from his mother. At the time of her death, the Poet was in his forty-fifth year, and had already produced those mighty works which were to fill the world with his fame. For some years she must in all likelihood have been more or less under his care and protection; as her age, at the time of her death, could not well have been less than seventy.

And here I am minded to notice a point which, it seems to me, has been somewhat overworked within the last few years. Gervinus, the German critic, thinks — and our Mr. White agrees with him — that Shakespeare acquired all his best ideas of womanhood after he went to London, and conversed with the ladies of the city. And in support of this notion they cite the fact — for such it is — that the women of his later plays are much superior to those of his earlier ones. But are not the *men* of his later plays quite as much superior to the men of his first? Are not his later plays as much better *every way*, as in respect of the female characters? The truth seems to be, that Shakespeare saw more of great and good in both man and woman, as he became older and knew them better; for he was full of intellectual righteousness in this as in other things. And in this matter it may with something of special fitness be said that a man finds what he brings with him the faculty for finding. Shakespeare's mind did not stay on the surface of things. Probably there never was a man more alive to the presence of humble, modest worth. And to his keen yet kindly eye the plain-thoughted women of his native Stratford may well have been as pure, as sweet, as lovely, as rich in all the inward graces which he delighted to unfold in his female characters, as any thing he afterwards found among the fine ladies of the metropolis; albeit I mean no disparagement to these latter; for the Poet was by the best of all rights a gentleman, and the ladies who pleased him in London doubtless had sense and womanhood enough to recognize him as such. At all events, it is reasonable to suppose that the foundations of his mind were laid before he left Stratford, and that the gatherings of the boy's eye and heart were the germs of the man's thoughts.

We have seen our Poet springing from what may be justly termed the best vein of old English life. At the time of his birth, his parents, considering the purchases previously made by the father, and the portion inherited by the mother, must have been tolerably well off. Malone, reckoning only the bequests specified in her father's will, estimated Mary Shakespeare's fortune to be not less than £110. Later researches have brought to light considerable items of property that were unknown to Malone. Supposing her fortune to have been as good as £150 then, it would go nearly if not quite as far as $5000 in our time. So that the Poet passed his boyhood in just about that medium state between poverty and riches which is accounted most favourable to health of body and mind.

At the time when his father became High-Bailiff the Poet was in his fifth year; old enough to understand something of what would be said and done in the home of an English magistrate, and to take more or less interest in the duties, the hospitalities, and perhaps the gayeties incident to the headship of the borough. It would seem that the Poet came honestly by his inclination to the Drama. During his term of office, John Shakespeare is found acting in his public capacity as a patron of the stage. The chamberlain's accounts show that twice in the course of that year money was paid to different companies of players; and these are the earliest notices we have of theatrical performances in that ancient town. The Bailiff and his son William were most likely present at those performances. From that time forward, all through the Poet's youth, probably no year passed without similar exhibitions at Stratford. In 1572, however, an act was passed for restraining itinerant players, whereby, unless they could show a patent under the great seal, they became liable to be proceeded against as vagabonds, for performing without a license from the local authorities. Nevertheless, the chamberlain's accounts show that between 1569 and 1587 no less than ten distinct companies performed at Stratford under the patronage of the corporation. In 1587, five of those companies are found performing there; and within the period just mentioned the Earl of Leicester's men are noted on three several occasions as receiving money from the town treasury. In May, 1574, the Earl of Leicester obtained a patent under the great seal, enabling his players, James Burbadge and four others, to exercise their art in any part of the kingdom except London. In 1587, this company became "The Lord Chamberlain's servants"; and we shall in due time find Shakespeare belonging to it. James Burbadge was the father of Richard Burbadge, the greatest actor of that age. The family was most likely from Warwickshire, and perhaps from Stratford, as we have already met with the name in that town. Such were the opportunities our embryo Poet had for catching the first rudiments of the art in which he afterwards displayed such learned mastery.

The forecited accounts have an entry, in 1564, of two

shillings "paid for defacing image in the chapel." Even then the excesses generated out of the Reformation were invading such towns as Stratford, and waging a "crusade against the harmless monuments of the ancient belief; no exercise of taste being suffered to interfere with what was considered a religious duty." In these exhibitions of strolling players this spirit found matter, no doubt, more deserving of its hostility. While the Poet was yet a boy, a bitter war of books and pamphlets had begun against plays and players; and the Stratford records inform us of divers attempts to suppress them in that town; but the issue proves that the Stratfordians were not easily beaten from that sort of entertainment, in which they evidently took great delight.

We have seen that both John and Mary Shakespeare, instead of writing their name, were so far disciples of Jack Cade as to use the more primitive way of making their mark. It nowise follows from this that they could not read; neither have we any certain evidence that they could. Be this as it may, there was no good reason why their children should not be able to say, "I thank God, I have been so well brought up, that I can write my name." A Free-School had been founded at Stratford by Thomas Jolyffe in the reign of Edward the Fourth. In 1553, King Edward the Sixth granted a charter, giving it a legal being, with legal rights and duties, under the name of "The King's New School of Stratford-upon-Avon." What particular course or method of instruction was used there, we have no certain knowledge; but it was probably much the same as that used in other like schools of that period; which included the elementary branches of English, and also the rudiments of classical learning.

Here it was, no doubt, that Shakespeare acquired the "small Latin and less Greek" which Ben Jonson accords to him. What was "small" learning in the eyes of such a scholar as Jonson, may yet have been something handsome in itself; and his remark may fairly imply that the Poet had at least the regular free-school education of the time. Honourably ambitious, as his father seems to have been, of being somebody, it is not unlikely that he may have prized learning the more for being himself without it. William was his oldest son; when his tide of fortune began to ebb, the Poet was in his fourteenth year, and, from his native qualities of mind, we cannot doubt that, up to that time at least, "all the learnings that his *town* could make him the receiver of he took, as we do air, fast as 'twas ministered, and in his Spring became a harvest."

The honest but credulous gossip Aubrey, who died about 1700, states, on the authority of one Beeston, that "Shakespeare understood Latin pretty well, for he had been in his younger years a schoolmaster in the country." The statement may fairly challenge some respect, inasmuch as persons of the name of Beeston were connected with the stage before Shakespeare's death and long afterwards. And it is not unlikely that the Poet may, at some time, have been an assistant teacher in the free-school at Stratford. Nor does this conflict with Rowe's account, which states that John Shakespeare kept William at the free-school for some time; but that straitness of circumstances and need of help forced him to withdraw his son from the school. Though writing from tradition, Rowe was evidently careful, and what he says agrees perfectly with what later researches have established respecting John Shakespeare's course of fortune. He also tells us that the Poet's father "could give him no better education than his own employment." John Shakespeare, as we have seen, was so far occupied with agriculture as to be legally styled a "yeoman." Nor am I sure but the ancient functions of an English yeoman's oldest son might be a better education for what the Poet afterwards accomplished than was to be had at any free-school or university in England. His large and apt use of legal terms and phrases has induced many good Shakespearians learned in the law to believe that he must have been for some time a student of that noble science. It is indeed difficult to understand how he could have spoken as he often does, without some study in the law; but, as he seems thoroughly at home in the specialties of many callings, it is possible his knowledge in the law may have grown from the large part his father had, either as magistrate or as litigant, in legal transactions. I am sure he either studied divinity or else had a strange gift of knowing it without studying it; and his ripeness in the knowledge of disease and of the healing art is a standing marvel to the medical faculty.

Knight has speculated rather copiously and romantically upon the idea of Shakespeare's having been a spectator of the more-than-royal pomp and pageantry with which the Queen was entertained by Leicester at Kenilworth in 1575. Stratford was fourteen miles from Kenilworth, and the Poet was then eleven years old. That his ears were assailed and his imagination excited by the fame of that magnificent display cannot be doubted, for all that part of the kingdom was laid under contribution to supply it, and was resounding with the noise of it; but his father was not of a rank to be summoned or invited thither, nor was he of an age to go thither without his father. Positive evidence either way on the point there is none; nor can I discover any thing in his plays that would fairly infer him to have drunk in the splendour of that occasion, however the fierce attractions thereof may have kindled a mind so brimful of poetry and life. The whole matter is an apt theme for speculation, and for nothing else.

The gleanings of tradition apart, the first knowledge that has reached us of the Poet, after his baptism, has reference to his marriage. Rowe tells us that "he thought fit to marry while he was very young," and that "his wife was the daughter of one Hathaway, said to have been a substantial yeoman in the neighbourhood of Stratford." These statements are borne out by later disclosures. The marriage took place in the Fall of 1582, when the Poet was in his nineteenth year. On the 28th of November, that year Fulk Sandels and John Richardson subscribed a bond whereby they became liable in the sum of £40, to be forfeited to the Bishop of Worcester in case there should be found any lawful impediment to the marriage of William Shakespeare and Anne Hathaway, of Stratford; the object being to procure such a dispensation from the Bishop as would authorize the ceremony after once publishing the banns. The original bond is preserved at Worcester, with the marks and seals of the two bondsmen affixed, and also bearing a seal with the initials R. H., as if to show that some legal representative of the bride's father, Richard Hathaway, was present and consenting to the act. There was nothing peculiar in the transaction; the bond is just the same as was usually given in such cases, and several others like it are to be seen at the office of the Worcester registry.

The parish books all about Stratford and Worcester have been ransacked, but no record of the marriage has been discovered. The probability is, that the ceremony took place in some one of the neighbouring parishes where the registers of that period have not been preserved.

Anne Hathaway was of Shottery, a pleasant village situate within an easy walk of Stratford, and belonging to the same parish. No record of her baptism has come to light, but the baptismal register of Stratford did not begin till 1558. She died on the 6th of August, 1623, and the inscription on her monument gives her age as sixty-seven years. Her birth, therefore, must have been in 1556, eight years before that of her husband.

From certain precepts, dated in 1566, and lately found among the papers of the Stratford Court of Record, it appears that the relations between John Shakespeare and Richard Hathaway were of a very friendly sort. Hathaway's will was made September 1, 1581, and proved July 19, 1582, which shows him to have died a few months before the marriage of his daughter Anne. The will makes good what Rowe says of his being "a substantial yeoman." He appoints Fulk Sandels one of the supervisors of his will, and among the witnesses to it is the name of William Gilbert, then curate of Stratford. One item of the will is: "I owe unto Thomas Whittington, my shepherd, £4 6 *s.* 8 *d.*" Whittington died in 1601; and in his will he gives and bequeaths "unto the poor people of Stratford 40 *s.* that is in the hand of Anne Shakespeare, wife unto Mr. William Shakespeare." The careful old shepherd had doubtless placed the money in Anne Shakespeare's hand for safe keeping, she being a person in whom he had confidence.

The Poet's match was evidently a love-match: whether the love was of that kind which forms the best pledge of wedded happiness, is another question. It is not unlikely that the marriage may have been preceded by the ancient ceremony of troth-plight, or *handfast*, as it was sometimes called; like that which almost takes place between Florizel and Perdita in *The Winter's Tale*, and quite takes place between Olivia and Sebastian in *Twelfth Night*. The custom of troth-plight was much used in that age, and for a long time after. In some places it had the force and effect of an actual marriage. Serious evils, however, sometimes grew out of it; and the Church of England did wisely, no doubt, in uniting the troth-plight and the marriage in one and the same ceremony. Whether such solemn betrothment had or had not taken place between William Shakespeare and Anne Hathaway, it is certain from the parish register that they had a daughter, Susanna, baptized on the 26th of May, 1583.

Some of the Poet's later biographers and critics have supposed he was not happy in his marriage. Certain passages of his plays, especially the charming dialogue between the Duke and the disguised Viola in Act ii., scene 4, of *Twelfth Night*, have been cited as involving some reference to the Poet's own case, or as having been suggested by what himself had experienced of the evils resulting from the wedlock of persons "misgraffed in respect of years." There was never any thing but sheer conjecture for this notion. Rowe mentions nothing of the kind; and we may be sure that his candour would not have spared the Poet, had tradition offered him any such matter. As for the passages in question, I know no reason for excepting them from the acknowledged purity and disinterestedness of the Poet's representations; where nothing is more remarkable, or more generally commended, than his singular aloofness of self, his perfect freedom from every thing bordering upon egotism.

Our Mr. White is especially hard upon the Poet's wife, worrying up the matter against her, and fairly tormenting the poor woman's memory. Now the facts about the marriage are just precisely as I have stated them. I confess they are not altogether such as I should wish them to have been; but I can see no good cause why prurient inference or speculation should busy itself in going behind them. If, however, conjecture must be at work on those facts, surely it had better run in the direction of charity, especially as regards the weaker vessel. I say weaker vessel, because in this case the man must in common fairness be supposed to have had the advantage at least as much in natural strength of understanding as the woman had in years. And as Shakespeare was, by all accounts, a very attractive person, it is not quite clear why she had not as good a right to lose her heart in his company as he had to lose his in hers. Probably she was as much smitten as he was; and we may well remember in her behalf, that love's "favourite seat is feeble woman's breast"; especially as there is not a particle of evidence that her life after marriage was ever otherwise than clear and honourable. And indeed it will do no hurt to remember in reference to them both, how

"'Tis affirmed
By poets skilled in Nature's secret ways,
That Love will not submit to be controlled
By mastery."

In support of his view, Mr. White urges, among other things, that most foul and wicked fling which Leontes, in his mad rapture of jealousy, makes against his wife, in Act

i. scene 2, of *The Winter's Tale.* He thinks the Poet could not have written that and other strains of like import, but that he was stung into doing so by his own bitter experience of "sorrow and shame"; and the argument is that, supposing him to have had such a root of bitterness in his life, he must have been thinking of that while writing those passages. The obvious answer is, To be sure, he must have been thinking of that; but then he must have known that others would think of it too; and a reasonable delicacy on his part would have counselled the withholding of any thing that he was conscious might be applied to his own domestic affairs. Sensible men do not write in their public pages such things as would be almost sure to breed or foster scandal about their own names or their own homes. The man that has a secret cancer on his person will naturally be the last to speak of cancers in reference to others. I can hardly think Shakespeare was so wanting in a sense of propriety as to have written the passages in question, but that he knew no man could say he was exposing the foulness of his own nest. So that my inferences in the matter are just the reverse of Mr. White's. As for the alleged need of personal experience in order to the writing of such things, why should not this hold just as well in regard, for instance, to Lady Macbeth's pangs of guilt? Shakespeare's prime characteristic was, that he knew the truth of Nature in all such things without the help of personal experience.

Mr. White presumes, moreover, that Anne Shakespeare was a coarse, low, vulgar creature, such as, the fascination of the honeymoon once worn off, the Poet could not choose but loath and detest; and that his betaking himself to London was partly to escape from her hated society. This, too, is all sheer conjecture, and rather lame at that. That Shakespeare was more or less separated from his wife for a number of years, cannot indeed be questioned; but that he ever found or ever sought relief or comfort in such separation, is what we have no warrant for believing. It was simply forced upon him by the necessities of his condition. The darling object of his London life evidently was, that he might return to his native town, with a handsome competence, and dwell in the bosom of his family; and the yearly visits, which tradition reports him to have made to Stratford, look like any thing but a wish to forget them or be forgotten by them. From what is known of his subsequent life, it is certain that he had, in large measure, that honourable ambition, so natural to an English gentleman, of being the founder of a family; and as soon as he had reached the hope of doing so, he retired to his old home, and there set up his rest, as if his best sunshine of life still waited on the presence of her from whose society he is alleged to have fled away in disappointment and disgust.

To Anne Hathaway, I have little doubt, were addressed, in his early morn of love, three sonnets playing on the author's name, which are hardly good enough to have been his work at any time; certainly none too good to have been the work of his boyhood. And I have met with no conjecture on the point that bears greater likelihoods of truth, than that another three, far different in merit, were addressed, much later in life, to the same object. The prevailing tone and imagery of them are such as he would hardly have used but with a woman in his thoughts; they are full-fraught with deep personal feeling, as distinguished from exercises of fancy; and they speak, with unsurpassable tenderness, of frequent absences, such as, before the Sonnets were printed, the Poet had experienced from his wife. I feel morally certain that she was the inspirer of them. I can quote but a part of them:

"How like a Winter hath my absence been
From thee, the pleasure of the fleeting year!
What freezings have I felt, what dark days seen,
What old December's bareness everywhere!
For Summer and his pleasures wait on thee,
And, thou away, the very birds are mute.

"From you I have been absent in the Spring,
When proud-pied April, dress'd in all his trim,

Hath put a spirit of youth in every thing,
That heavy Saturn laugh'd and leap'd with him:
Yet nor the lays of birds, nor the sweet smell
Of different flowers in odour and in hue,
Could make me any Summer's story tell,
Or from their proud lap pluck them where they grew:
Nor did I wonder at the lily's white,
Nor praise the deep vermilion in the rose;
They were but sweet, but figures of delight,
Drawn after you; you pattern of all those.
Yet seem'd it Winter still, and, you away,
As with your shadow I with these did play."

And I am scarcely less persuaded that a third cluster, of nine, had the same source. These, too, are clearly concerned with the deeper interests and regards of private life; they carry a homefelt energy and pathos, such as argue them to have had a far other origin than in trials of art; they speak of compelled absences from the object that inspired them, and are charged with regrets and confessions, such as could only have sprung from the Poet's own breast:

"Alas! 'tis true I have gone here and there,
And made myself a motley to the view;
Gor'd mine own thoughts, sold cheap what is most dear,
Made old offences of affections new:
Most true it is, that I have look'd on truth
Askance and strangely.

"O, for my sake do you with Fortune chide,
The guilty goddess of my harmful deeds,
That did not better for my life provide,
Than public means, which public manners breeds.
Thence comes it that my name receives a brand,
And almost thence my nature is subdu'd
To what it works in, like the dyer's hand.

"Accuse me thus: That I have scanted all
Wherein I should your great deserts repay;
Forgot upon your dearest love to call,
Whereto all bonds do tie me day by day;
That I have frequent been with unknown minds,
And given to time your own dear-purchas'd right."

It will take more than has yet appeared, to convince me, that when the Poet wrote these and other similar lines his thoughts were travelling anywhere but home to the bride of his youth and mother of his children.

I have run ahead of my theme; but it may as well be added, here, that Francis Meres, writing in 1598, speaks of the Poet's "sugared Sonnets among his private friends"; which indicates the purpose for which they were written. None of them had been printed when this was said of them. They were first collected and published in 1609; the collection being arranged, I think, in "most admirable disorder," so that it is scarce possible to make head or tail to them.

On the 2d of February, 1585, two more children, twins, were christened in the parish church as "Hamnet and Judith, son and daughter to William Shakespeare." We hear of no more children being added to the family. I must again so far anticipate as to observe, that the son Hamnet was buried in August, 1596, being then in his twelfth year. This is the first severe home-stroke known to have lighted on the Poet.

Tradition has been busy with the probable causes of Shakespeare's going upon the stage. Several causes have been assigned; such as, first, a natural inclination to poetry and acting; second, a deer-stealing frolic, which resulted in making Stratford too hot for him; third, the pecuniary embarrassments of his father. It is not unlikely that all these causes, and perhaps others, may have concurred in prompting the step.

For the first, we have the testimony of Aubrey, who was at Stratford probably about the year 1680. He was an arrant and inveterate hunter after anecdotes, and seems to have caught up, without sifting, whatever quaint or curious matter came in his way. So that no great reliance can attach to what he says, unless it is sustained by other authority. But in this case his words sound like truth, and are supported by all the likelihoods that can grow from what we should presume to have been the Poet's natural turn of mind. "This William," says he, "being inclined naturally to poetry and acting, came to London, I guess, about eighteen, and was an actor in one of the playhouses, and did act exceedingly well. He began early to make essays in dramatic poetry, which at that time was very low, and his plays took well. He was a handsome, well-shaped man, very good company, and of a very ready and pleasant smooth wit. Ben Jonson and he did gather humours of men daily wherever they came."

This natural inclination, fed by the frequent theatrical performances at Stratford, would go far, if not suffice of itself, to account for the Poet's subsequent course of life. Before 1586, no doubt, he was well acquainted with some of the players, with whom we shall hereafter find him associated. In their exhibitions, rude as these were, he could not but have been a greedy spectator and an apt scholar. Thomas Greene, a fellow-townsman of his, was already one of their number. All this might not indeed be enough to draw him away from Stratford; but when other reasons came, if others there were, for leaving, these circumstances would hold out to him an easy and natural access and invitation to the stage. Nor is there any extravagance in supposing that, by 1586, he may have taken some part as actor or writer, perhaps both, in the performances of the company which he afterwards joined.

The deer-stealing matter as given by Rowe is as follows: That Shakespeare fell into the company of some wild fellows who were in the habit of stealing deer, and who drew him into robbing a park owned by Sir Thomas Lucy, of Charlecote, near Stratford. That, being prosecuted for this, he lampooned Sir Thomas in some bitter verses; which made the Knight so sharp after him, that he had to steal himself off and take shelter in London.

Several have attempted to refute this story; but the main substance of it stands approved by too much strength of credible tradition to be easily overthrown. And it is certain from public records that the Lucys had great power at Stratford, and were not seldom engaged in disputes with the corporation. Mr. Halliwell met with an old record entitled "the names of them that made the riot upon Master Thomas Lucy, Esquire." Thirty-five inhabitants of Stratford, chiefly tradespeople, are named in the list, but no Shakespeares among them.

Knight, over-zealous in the Poet's behalf, will not allow any thing to be true that infers the least moral blemish in his life: he therefore utterly discredits the story in question, and hunts it down with arguments more ingenious than sound. In writing biography, special-pleading is not good; and I would fain avoid trying to make the Poet out any better than he was. Little as we know about him, it is evident enough that he had his frailties, and ran into divers faults, both as a poet and as a man. And when we hear him confessing, as in a passage already quoted, "Most true it is, that I have looked on truth askance and strangely"; we may be sure he was but too conscious of things that needed to be forgiven; and that he was as far as any one from wishing his faults to pass for virtues. Deer-stealing, however, was then a kind of fashionable sport, and whatever might be its legal character, it was not morally regarded as involving any criminality or disgrace. So that the whole thing may be justly treated as a mere youthful frolic, wherein there might indeed be some indiscretion, and a deal of vexation to the person robbed, but no stain on the party engaged in it.

The precise time of the Poet's leaving Stratford is not known; but we cannot well set it down as later than 1586. His children, Hamnet and Judith, were born, as I have said, in the early part of 1585; and for several years before that time his father's affairs were drooping. The prosecutions of Sir Thomas Lucy, added to his father's straitness of means, may well have made him desirous of quitting Stratford; while the meeting of inclination and opportunity in his acquaintance with the players may have determined him where to go, and what to do. The company were already in a course of thrift; the demand for their labours was growing; and he might well see, in their fellowship, a chance of retrieving, as he did retrieve, his father's fortune.

Of course there need be no question that Shakespeare held at first a subordinate rank in the theatre. Dowdal, writing in 1693, tells us "he was received into the playhouse as a servitor"; which probably means that he started as an apprentice to some actor of standing, — a thing not unusual at the time. It will readily be believed that he could not be in such a place long without recommending himself to a higher one. As for the well-known story of his being reduced to the extremity of "picking up a little money by taking care of the gentlemen's horses that came to the play," I cannot perceive the slightest likelihood of truth in it. The first we hear of it is in *The Lives of the Poets*, written by a Scotchman named Shiels, and published under the name of Cibber, in 1753. The story is there said to have passed through Rowe in coming to the writer. If so, then Rowe must have discredited it, else, surely, he would not have omitted so remarkable a passage. Be that as it may, the station which the Poet's family had long held at Stratford, and the fact of his having influential friends at hand from Warwickshire, are enough to stamp it as an arrant fiction.

We have seen that the company of Burbadge and his fellows held a patent under the great seal, and in 1587 took the title of "The Lord Chamberlain's Servants." Eleven years before this time, in 1576, they had started the Blackfriars theatre, so named from a monastery that had formerly stood on or near the same ground. Hitherto the several bands of players had made use of halls, or temporary erections in the streets or the inn-yards, stages being set up, and the spectators standing below, or occupying galleries about the open space. In 1577, two other playhouses were in operation; and still others sprang up from time to time. The Blackfriars and some others were without the limits of the corporation, in what were called "the Liberties." The

Mayor and Aldermen of London were from the first decidedly hostile to all such establishments, and did their best to exclude them the City and Liberties; but the Court, many of the chief nobility, and, which was still more, the common people favoured them. The whole mind indeed of Puritanism was utterly down on stage-plays of all sorts and in every shape. But it did not go to work the right way: it should have stopped off the demand for them. This, however, it could not do; for the Drama was at that time, as it long had been, an intense national passion: the people would have plays, and could not be converted from the love of them.

From what we shall presently see, it would be unreasonable not to suppose, that by the year 1590 the Poet was well started in his dramatic career; and that the effect of his cunning labours was beginning even then to be felt by his senior fellows in that line. Allowing him to have entered the theatre in 1586, when he was twenty-two years of age, he must have made good use of his time, and worked onwards with surprising speed, during those four years; though whether he got ahead more by his acting or his writing, we have no certain knowledge. In tragic parts, none of the company could shine beside the younger Burbadge; while Greene, and still more Kempe, another of the band, left small chance of distinction in comic parts. Aubrey, as before quoted, tells us that Shakespeare "was a handsome, well-shaped man," which is no slight matter on the stage; and adds, "He did act exceedingly well." Rowe "could never meet with any further account of him this way, than that the top of his performance was the Ghost in his own *Hamlet*." But this part, to be fairly dealt with, requires an actor of no mean powers; and as Burbadge is known to have played the Prince, we may presume that "the Majesty of buried Denmark" would not be cast upon very inferior hands. That the Poet was master of the theory of acting, and could tell, none better, how the thing ought to be done, is evident enough from Hamlet's instructions to the players. But it nowise follows that he could perform his own instructions.

Let us see now how matters stood some two years later. One of the most popular and most profligate playwriters of that time was Robert Greene, who, having been reduced to beggary, and forsaken by his companions, died miserably at the house of a poor shoemaker, in September, 1592. Shortly after he died, his *Gratsworth of Wit* was given to the public by Henry Chettle. Near the close of this tract, Greene makes an address "to those gentlemen his *quondam* acquaintance, who spend their wits in making plays," exhorting them to desist from such pursuits. One of those "gentlemen" was Christopher Marlowe, distinguished alike for poetry, profligacy, and profanity; the others were Thomas Lodge and George Peele. Greene here vents a deal of fury against the players, alleging that they have all been beholden to him, yet have now forsaken him; and from thence inferring that the three worthies whom he is exhorting will fare no better at their hands. After which he goes on thus: "Yes, trust them not; for there is an upstart crow beautified with our feathers, that, with his 'tiger's heart wrapt in a player's hide,' supposes he is as well able to bombast out a blank-verse as the best of you; and, being an absolute *Johannes Fac-totum*, is in his own conceit the only Shake-scene in a country."

Here the spiteful fling at Shakespeare is unmistakable, and nobody questions that he is the "Shake-scene" of the passage. The terms of the allusion yield conclusive evidence as to how the Poet stood in 1592. Though sneered at as a player, it is plain that he was already throwing the other playwriters into the shade, and making their labours cheap. Blank-verse was Marlowe's special forte, and some of his dramas show no little skill in the use of it, though the best part of that skill was doubtless caught from Shakespeare; but here was "an upstart" from the country who was able to rival him in his own line. Moreover, this Shake-scene was a Do-all, a *Johannes Fac-totum*, who could turn his hand to any thing; and his readiness to undertake what none others could do so well naturally drew upon him the imputation of conceit from those who envied his rising, and whose lustre was growing dim in his light.

It appears that both Shakespeare and Marlowe were offended at the liberties thus taken with them. For, before the end of that same year, Chettle published a tract entitled *Kind Heart's Dream*, wherein we have the following: "With neither of them that take offence was I acquainted; and with one of them [Marlowe] I care not if I never be: the other I did not so much spare as since I wish I had; because myself have seen his demeanour no less civil than he excellent in the quality he professes: besides, divers of worship have reported his uprightness of dealing, which argues his honesty, and his facetious grace in writing, that approves his art."

On the whole, we can readily pardon the malice of Greene's assault for the sake of this tribute, which it was the means of drawing forth, to Shakespeare's character as a man and his cunning as a poet. The words "excellent in the quality he professes," refer most likely to the Poet's acting; while the term *facetious* is used, apparently, not in the sense it now bears, but in that of *felicitous* or *happy*, as was common at that time. So it seems that Shakespeare already had friends in London, some of them "worshipful," too, who were strongly commending him as a poet, and who were prompt to remonstrate with Chettle against the mean slur cast upon him.

This naturally starts the inquiry, what dramas the Poet had then written, to earn such praise. Greene speaks of him as "beautified with our feathers." Probably there was at least some plausible colour of truth in this charge. The charge, I have no doubt, refers mainly to the Second and Third Parts of *King Henry the Sixth.* The two plays on which these were founded were published, respectively, in 1594 and 1595, their titles being, *The First Part of the Contention betwixt the two famous Houses of York and*

Lancaster, and *The True Tragedy of Richard, Duke of York*. In the form there given, the plays have, as Mr. White has clearly shown, along with much of Shakespeare's work, many unquestionable marks of Greene's hand. All those marks, however, were disciplined out of them, as they have come down to us in Shakespeare's works. There can be no doubt, then, that Greene, and perhaps Marlowe also, had a part in them as they were printed in 1594 and 1595, though no author's name was then given. Now it was much the custom at that time for several playwrights to work together. Of this we have many well-authenticated instances. The most likely conclusion, therefore, is, that these two plays in their original form were the joint workmanship of Shakespeare, Greene, and Marlowe. Perhaps, however, there was a still older form of the plays, written entirely by Marlowe and Greene; which older form Shakespeare, some time before Greene's death, may have taken in hand, and recast, retaining more or less of their matter, and working it in with his own nobler stuff; for this was often done also. Or, again, it may be that, before the time in question, Shakespeare, not satisfied to be joint author with them, had rewritten the plays, and purged them of nearly all matter but what he might justly claim as his own; thus making them as we now have them.

As regards the occasion of Greene's assault, it matters little which of these views we take, as in either case his charge would have some apparent ground of truth. It is further probable that the same course of remark would apply more or less to *The Taming of the Shrew*, and perhaps also to *Titus Andronicus*, and the original form of *Pericles*. At all events, I have no doubt that these five plays, together with the First Part of *King Henry the Sixth*, *The Comedy of Errors*, *The Two Gentlemen of Verona*, and *Love's Labour's Lost*, in its first form, were all written before the time of Greene's death. Perhaps the first shape, also, of *Romeo and Juliet* should be added to this list.

My reasons for this opinion are too long to be stated

here: I can but observe that in these plays, as might be expected from one who was modest and wished to learn, we have much of imitation as distinguished from character, though of imitation surpassing its models. And it seems to me that no fair view can be had of the Poet's mind, no justice done to his art, but by carefully discriminating in his work what grew from imitation, and what from character. For he evidently wrote very much like others of his time, before he learned to write like himself; that is, it was some time before he found, by practice and experience, his own strength; and meanwhile he relied more or less on the strength of custom and example. Nor was it till he had surpassed others in *their* way, that he hit upon that more excellent way in which none could walk but he.

It has been quite too common to speak of Shakespeare as a miracle of spontaneous genius, who did his best things by force of instinct, not of art; and that, consequently, he was nowise indebted to time and experience for the reach and power which his dramas display. This is an "old fond paradox" which seems to have originated with those who could not conceive how any man could acquire intellectual skill without scholastic advantages; forgetting, apparently, that several things, if not more, may be learned in the school of Nature, provided one have an eye to read her "open secrets" without "the spectacles of books." This notion has vitiated a good deal of Shakespearian criticism. Rowe had something of it. "Art," says he, "had so little, and Nature so large a share in what Shakespeare did, that, for aught I know, the performances of his youth were the best." I think decidedly otherwise; and have grounds for doing so which Rowe had not, in what has since been done towards ascertaining the chronology of the Poet's plays.

It would seem from Chettle's apology, that Shakespeare was already beginning to attract liberal notice from that circle of brave and accomplished gentlemen which adorned the state of Queen Elisabeth. Among the "divers of worship," first and foremost stood, no doubt, the high-souled, the generous Southampton, then in his twentieth year. Henry Wriothesley, the third Earl of Southampton, was but eight years old when his father died: the Southampton estates were large; during the young Earl's minority his interests were in good hands, and the revenues accumulated; so that on coming of age he had means answerable to his dispositions. Moreover, he was a young man of good parts, of studious habits, of cultivated tastes, and withal of a highly chivalrous and romantic spirit: to all which he added the honour of being the early and munificent patron of Shakespeare. In 1593, the Poet published his *Venus and Adonis*, with a modest and manly dedication to this nobleman, very different from the usual high-flown style of literary adulation then in vogue; telling him, "If your Honour seem but pleased, I account myself highly praised, and vow to take advantage of all idle hours, till I have honoured you with some graver labour." In the dedication, he calls the poem "the first heir of my invention." Whether he dated its birth from the writing or the publishing, does not appear: probably it had been written some time; possibly before he left Stratford. This was followed, the next year, by his *Lucrece*, dedicated to the same nobleman in a strain of more open and assured friendship: "The warrant I have of your honourable disposition, not the worth of my untutored lines, makes it assured of acceptance. What I have done is yours, what I have to do is yours."

It was probably about this time that the event took place which Rowe heard of through Sir William Davenant, that Southampton at one time gave the Poet a thousand pounds, to enable him to go through with a purchase which he knew him to be desirous of making. Rowe might well scruple, as he did, the story of so large a gift, — equal to nearly $30,000 in our time; but the fact of his scruples being overruled shows that he had strong grounds for the statement. The sum may indeed have been exaggerated; but all we know of the Earl assures us that he could not but wish to make a handsome return for the *Venus and*

Adonis; and that whatever of the kind he did was bound to be something rich and rare; while it was but of a piece with his approved nobleness of character, to feel more the honour he was receiving than that he was conferring by such an act of generosity. Might not this be what Shakespeare meant by "the *warrant* I have of your honourable disposition"? That the Earl was both able and disposed to the amount alleged, need not be scrupled: the only doubt has reference to the Poet's occasions. Let us see, then, what these may have been.

In December, 1593, Richard Burbadge, who, his father having died or retired, was then the leader of the Blackfriars company, signed a contract for the building of the Globe theatre, in which Shakespeare is known to have been a large owner. The Blackfriars was not accommodation enough for the company's uses, but was entirely covered-in, and furnished suitably for the Winter. The Globe, made larger, and designed for Summer use, was a round wooden building, open to the sky, with the stage protected by an overhanging roof. All things considered, then, it is not incredible that the munificent Earl may have bestowed even as large a sum as a thousand pounds, to enable the Poet to do what he wished towards the new enterprise.

The next authentic notice we have of Shakespeare is a public tribute of admiration from the highest source that could have yielded any thing of the sort at that time. In 1594, Edmund Spenser published his *Colin Clout's Come Home again*, which has these lines:

> "And there, though last not least, is Ætion:
> A gentler Shepherd may nowhere be found;
> Whose Muse, full of high thought's invention,
> Doth, like himself, heroically sound."

This was Spenser's delicate way of suggesting the Poet's name. Ben Jonson has a like allusion in his lines,—"To the Memory of my beloved Mr. William Shakespeare":

> "In each of which he seems to *shake a lance*
> As brandish'd at the eyes of ignorance."

There can be little doubt, though we have no certain knowledge on the point, that by this time the Poet's genius had sweetened itself into the good graces of Queen Elisabeth; as the irresistible compliment paid her in a *A Midsummer-Night's Dream* could hardly have been of a later date. It would be gratifying to know by what play he made his first conquest of the Queen. That he did captivate her, is told us in Ben Jonson's poem just quoted:

"Sweet swan of Avon, what a sight it were
To see thee in our waters yet appear;
And make those flights upon the banks of Thames
That so did take Eliza and our James!"

King John, *King Richard the Second*, *King Richard the Third*, *A Midsummer-Night's Dream*, and the original form of *All's Well that Ends Well*, were, no doubt, all written before the Spring of 1596. So that these five plays, and perhaps one or two others, in addition to the ten mentioned before, may by that time have been performed in her Majesty's hearing, "as well for the recreation of our loving subjects as for our solace and pleasure."

Aubrey tells us that Shakespeare "was wont to go to his native country once a year." We now have better authority than Aubrey for believing that the Poet's heart was in "his native country" all the while. No sooner is he well established at London, and in receipt of funds to spare from the demands of business, than we find him making liberal investments amidst the scenes of his youth. Some years ago, Mr. Halliwell discovered in the Chapter-House, Westminster, a document which ascertains that in the Spring of 1597 Shakespeare bought of William Underhill, for the sum of £60, the establishment called "New Place," described as consisting of "one messuage, two barns, and two gardens, with their appurtenances." This was one of the best dwelling-houses in Stratford, and was situate in one of the best parts of the town. Early in the sixteenth century it was owned by the Cloptons, and called "the great house." It was in one of the gardens belonging to this house that the

Poet was believed to have planted a mulberry-tree. New Place remained in the hands of Shakespeare and his heirs till the Restoration, when it was repurchased by the Clopton family. In the Spring of 1742, Garrick, Macklin, and Delane were entertained there by Sir Hugh Clopton, under the Poet's mulberry-tree. About 1752, the place was sold to the Rev. Francis Gastrell, who, falling out with the Stratford authorities in some matter of rates, demolished the house, and cut down the tree; for which his memory has been visited with exemplary retribution.

We have other tokens of the Poet's thrift about this time. One of these is a curious letter, dated January 24, 1598, and written by Abraham Sturley, an alderman of Stratford, to his brother-in-law, Richard Quiney, who was then in London on business for himself and others. Sturley, it seems, had learned that "our countryman, Mr. Shakespeare," had money to invest, and so was for having him urged to buy up certain tithes at Stratford, on the ground that such a purchase "would advance him indeed, and would do us much good"; the meaning of which is, that the Stratford people were in want of money, and were looking to Shakespeare for a supply.

Another token of like import is a letter written by the same Richard Quiney, whose son Thomas afterwards married the Poet's youngest daughter. The letter was dated, "From the Bell, in Carter-lane, the 25th October, 1598," and addressed, "To my loving good friend and countryman, Mr. Wm. Shakespeare." The purpose of the letter was to solicit a loan of £30 from the Poet on good security. No private letter written by Shakespeare has been found; and this is the only one written *to* him that has come to light. How the writer's request was answered we have no certain information; but we may fairly conclude the answer to have been satisfactory, because on the same day Quiney wrote to Sturley, and in Sturley's reply, dated November 4, 1598, which is also extant, the writer expresses himself much comforted at learning that "our countryman, Mr. Wm. Shak., would procure us money."

The earliest printed copies of Shakespeare's plays, known in our time, are *Romeo and Juliet*, *King Richard the Second*, and *King Richard the Third*, which were published separately in 1597. Three years later there was another edition of *Romeo and Juliet*, "newly corrected, augmented, and amended." In 1598, two more, the First Part of *King Henry the Fourth* and *Love's Labour's Lost*, came from the press. The author's name was not given in any of these issues except *Love's Labour's Lost*, which was said to be "newly corrected and augmented." *King Richard the Second* and *King Richard the Third* were issued again in 1598, and the First Part of *King Henry the Fourth* in 1599; and in all these cases the author's name was printed in the title-page. The Second Part of *King Henry the Fourth* was most likely written before 1598, but we hear of no edition of it till 1600.

Francis Meres has the honour of being the first critic of Shakespeare that appeared in print. In 1598, he put forth a book entitled *Palladis Tamia, Wit's Treasury*, which has the following: "As Plautus and Seneca are accounted the best for comedy and tragedy among the Latins; so Shakespeare among the English is the most excellent in both kinds for the stage." The writer then instances twelve of the Poet's dramas by title, in proof of his point. His list, however, contains none but what I have already mentioned, except *The Merchant of Venice*. Taking all our sources of information together, we find at least eighteen of the plays written before 1598, when the Poet was thirty-four years of age, and had probably been in the theatre about twelve years.

Shakespeare was now decidedly at the head of the English Drama; moreover, he had found it a low, foul, disreputable thing, chiefly in the hands of profligate adventurers, and he had lifted it out of the mire, breathed strength and sweetness into it, and made it clean, fair, and honourable, a structure all alive with beauty and honest delectation. Such being the case, his standing was naturally firm and secure; he had little cause to fear rivalry; he could well afford to be generous; and any play that had his approval would be likely to pass. Ben Jonson, whose name has a peculiar right to be coupled with his, was ten years younger than he, and was working with that learned and sinewy diligence which marked his character. We have it on the sound authority of Rowe, that Shakespeare lent a helping hand to honest Ben, and on an occasion that does credit to them both. "Mr. Jonson," says he, "who was at that time altogether unknown to the world, had offered one of his plays to the players, in order to have it acted; and the persons into whose hands it was put, after having turned it carelessly and superciliously over, were just upon returning it to him, with an ill-natured answer that it would be of no service to their company, when Shakespeare luckily cast his eye upon it, and found something in it so well, as to engage him first to read it through, and afterwards to recommend Mr. Jonson and his writings to the public."

Some attempts have been made to impugn this account, but the result of them all has been rather to confirm it. How nobly the Poet's gentle and judicious act of kindness was remembered, is shown by Jonson's superb verses, some of which I have quoted, prefixed to the folio of 1623; enough of themselves to confer an immortality both on the writer and on the subject of them.

In 1599, we find a coat of arms granted to John Shakespeare, by the Herald's College, in London. The grant was made, no doubt, at the instance of his son William. The matter is involved in a good deal of perplexity; the claims of the son being confounded with those of the father, in order, apparently, that out of the two together might be made a good, or at least a plausible, case. Our Poet, the son of a glover, or a yeoman, had evidently set his heart on being heralded into a gentleman; and, as his profession of actor stood in the way, the application was made in his father's name. The thing was started as early as 1596, but so much question was had, so many difficulties raised, concerning it, that the Poet was three years in working it through. To be sure, such heraldic gentry was of little worth in itself, and the Poet knew this well enough; but then it assured a certain very desirable social standing, and therefore, as an aspiring member of society, he was right in seeking it.

In the year 1600, five more of his plays were published in as many quarto pamphlets. These were, *A Midsummer-Night's Dream*, *The Merchant of Venice*, *Much Ado about Nothing*, the Second Part of *King Henry the Fourth*, and *King Henry the Fifth*. It appears, also, that *As You Like It* was then written; for it was entered at the Stationers' for publication, but was locked up from the press under a "stay." *The Merry Wives of Windsor* was probably then in being also, though not printed till 1602. And a recent discovery ascertains that *Twelfth Night* was played in February, 1602. The original form of *Hamlet*, too, is known to have been written before 1603. Adding, then, the six plays now heard of for the first time, to the eighteen mentioned before, we have twenty-four plays written before the Poet had finished his thirty-eighth year.

The great Queen died on the 24th of March, 1603. We have abundant proof that she was, both by her presence and her purse, a frequent and steady patron of the Drama, especially as its interests were represented by "the Lord Chamberlain's servants." Everybody, no doubt, has heard the tradition of her having been so taken with Falstaff in *King Henry the Fourth*, that she requested the Poet to continue the character through another play, and to represent him in love; whereupon he wrote *The Merry Wives of Windsor*. Whatever embellishments may have been added, there is nothing incredible in the substance of the tradition; while the approved taste and judgment of this female king, in matters of literature and art, give it strong likelihoods of truth.

Elizabeth knew how to unbend in such noble delectations without abating her dignity as a queen, or forgetting her duty as the mother of her people. If the patronage of King James fell below hers in wisdom, it was certainly not lacking in warmth. One of his first acts, after reaching London, was to order out a warrant from the Privy Seal for the issuing of a patent under the Great Seal, whereby the Lord Chamberlain's players were taken into his immediate patronage under the title of "The King's Servants." The instrument names nine players, and Shakespeare stands second in the list. Nor did the King's patent prove a mere barren honour: many instances of the company's playing at the Court, and being well paid for it, are on record.

The Poet evidently was, as indeed from the nature of his position he could not but be, very desirous of withdrawing from the stage; and had long cherished, apparently, a design of doing so. In several passages of his Sonnets, two of which I have already quoted, he expresses, in very strong and even pathetic language, his intense dislike of the business, and his grief at being compelled to pursue it. At what time he carried into effect his purpose of retirement is not precisely known; nor can I stay to trace out the argument on that point. The probability is, that he ceased to be an actor in the Summer of 1604. The preceding year, 1603, Ben Jonson's *Sejanus* was brought out at the Blackfriars, and one of the parts was sustained by Shakespeare. After this we have no note of his appearance on the stage; and there are certain traditions inferring the contrary.

In 1603, an edition of *Hamlet* was published, though very different from the present form of the play. The next year, 1604, the finished *Hamlet* was published; the title-page containing the words, "enlarged to almost as much again as it was." Of *Measure for Measure* we have no well-authenticated notice during the Poet's life; though there is a record, which has been received as authentic, of its having been acted at Court on the 26th of December, 1604. That record, however, has lately been discredited. Of *Timon of Athens* and *Julius Cæsar* we have no express contemporary notice at all, authentic or otherwise. Nor have we any of *Troilus and Cressida* till 1609, in which year a stolen edition of it was published. Nevertheless, I have no doubt that these plays were all written, though perhaps not all in their present shape, before the close of 1604. Reckoning, then, the four last named, we have twenty-eight of the plays written when the Poet was forty years of age, and had probably been at the work about eighteen years. Time has indeed left few traces of the process; but what a magnificent treasure of results! If Shakespeare had done no more, he would have stood the greatest intellect of the world. How all alive must those eighteen years have been with intense and varied exertion! His quick discernment, his masterly tact, his grace of manners, his practical judgment, and his fertility of expedients, would needs make him the soul of the establishment; doubtless the light of his eye and the life of his hand were in all its movements and plans. Besides, the compass and accuracy of information displayed in his writings prove him to have been, for that age, a careful and voluminous student of books. Portions of classical and of continental literature were accessible to him in translations. Nor are we without strong reasons for believing that, in addition to his "small Latin and less Greek," he found or made time to form a tolerable reading acquaintance with Italian and French. Chaucer, too, "the day-star," and Spenser, "the sunrise," of English poetry, were pouring their beauty round his walks. From all these, and from the growing richness and abundance of contemporary literature, his all-gifted and all-grasping mind no doubt greedily took in and quickly digested whatever was adapted to please his taste, or enrich his intellect, or assist his art.

I have mentioned the Poet's purchase of New Place at Stratford in 1597. Thenceforward he kept making other investments from time to time, some of them pretty large, the records of which have lately come to light. It appears by a subsidy roll of 1598, that he was assessed on property valued at £5 13 *s.* 4 *d.*, in the parish of St. Helen's, Bishopsgate, London. In May, 1602, was executed a deed of conveyance whereby he became the owner of a hundred and seven acres of arable land in the town of Old Stratford, bought of William and John Combe for the sum of £320. In September following, a copyhold house in Walker-street, near New Place, was surrendered to him by Walter Getley. This property was held under the manor of Rowington: the transfer took place at the court-baron of the manor; and it appears that the Poet was not present at the time; there being a proviso, that the property should remain in the hands of the Lady of the manor till the purchaser had done suit and service in the court. One Philip Rogers, it seems, had several times bought malt of Shakespeare to the amount of £1 15 *s.* 10 *d.*; and in 1604 the Poet, not being able to get payment, filed in the Stratford Court of Record a declaration of suit against him; which probably had the desired effect, as nothing more is heard of it. This item is interesting, as it shows the Poet engaged in other pursuits than those relating to the stage. We have seen how, in 1598, Alderman Sturly was for "moving him to deal in the matter of our tithes." This was a matter wherein much depended on good management; and, as the town had a yearly rent from the tithes, it was for the public interest to have them managed well; and the moving of Shakespeare to deal in the matter sprang most likely from confidence in his practical judgment and skill. The tithes of "corn, grain, blade, and hay," and also those of "wool, lamb, hemp, flax, and other small and privy tithes," in Stratford, Old Stratford, Welcombe, and Bishopton, had been leased in 1544 for the term of ninety-two years. In July, 1605, the unexpired term of the lease, thirty-one years, was bought in by Shakespeare for the sum of £440. In the indenture of conveyance, he is styled "William Shakespeare, of Stratford-upon-Avon, *Gentleman.*"

These notices enable us to form some tolerable conjecture as to how the Poet was getting on at the age of forty. Such details of business may not seem very appropriate in a *Life* of the greatest of poets; but we have clear evidence that he took a lively interest in them, and was a good hand at managing them. He had learned by experience, no doubt, that "money is a good soldier, and will on"; and that, "if money go before, all ways do lie open." And the thing carries this benefit, if no other, that it tells us a man may be something of a poet without being either above or below the common affairs of life.

A pretty careful investigation of the matter has brought good judges to the conclusion, that in 1608 the Poet's income could not have been less than £400 a year. This, for all practical purposes, would be equivalent to some $12,000 in our time. The Rev. John Ward, who became vicar of Stratford in 1662, noted in his *Diary*, that Shakespeare, after his retirement, "had an allowance so large that he spent at the rate of £1,000 a year, as I have heard." The honest and cautious man did well to add, "as I have heard." That the Poet kept up a liberal establishment, and was fond of entertaining his neighbours, and still more his old associates, we can well believe; but that he had £1,000 a year to spend, or would have spent it if he had, is not credible.

Some question has been made whether Shakespeare was a member of the celebrated convivial club established by Sir Walter Raleigh, and which held its meetings at the Mermaid tavern. We have nothing that directly certifies his membership of that choice institution; but there are several things inferring it so strongly as to leave no reasonable doubt on the subject. His conversations certainly ran in that circle of wits some of whom are directly known to have belonged to it; and among them all there is not one whose then acknowledged merits gave him a better title to its privileges. It does not indeed necessarily follow from his facility and plenipotence of wit in writing, that he could shine at those extempore "flashes of merriment that were wont to set the table on a roar." But, besides the natural inference that way, we have the statement of honest old Aubrey, that "he was very good company, and of a very ready and pleasant smooth wit." Francis Beaumont, who was a prominent member of that jovial senate, and to whom Shirley applies the fine hyperbolism that "he talked a comedy," was born in 1586, and died in 1615. I cannot doubt that he had our Poet, among others, in his eye, when he wrote those celebrated lines to Ben Jonson:

> "Methinks the little wit I had is lost
> Since I saw you; for wit is like a rest
> Held up at tennis, which men do the best
> With the best gamesters. What things have we seen
> Done at the Mermaid! heard words that have been
> So nimble, and so full of subtile flame,
> As if that every one from whence they came
> Had meant to put his whole wit in a jest,
> And had resolv'd to live a fool the rest
> Of his dull life."

In further token of Shakespeare's having belonged to this merry parliament of genius, I must quote from Dr. Thomas Fuller, who, though not born till 1608, was acquainted with some of the old Mermaid wits. In his *Worthies of Warwickshire*, he winds up his account of the Poet thus: "Many were the wit-combats betwixt him and Ben Jonson; which two I behold like a Spanish great galleon and an English man-of-war. Master Jonson, like the former, was built far higher in learning; solid, but slow, in his performances: Shakespeare, with the English man-of-war, lesser in bulk, but lighter in sailing, could turn with all tides, tack about, and take advantage of all winds, by the quickness of his wit and invention."

The Poet kept up his interest in the affairs of the company, and spent more or less of his time in London, after ceasing to be an actor. We have several subsequent notices of his being in the metropolis on business, one of which is a deed of conveyance, executed in March, 1613, and transferring to him and three others a house with a small piece of land for £140; £80 being paid down, and the rest left on bond and mortgage. The deed bears the Poet's signature, which shows him to have been in London at the time. The vicar, from whose *Diary* I have already quoted, notes further that Shakespeare "frequented the plays all his younger time, but in his elder days he lived at Stratford, and supplied the stage with two plays every year." That the writer's information was in all points literally correct, is not likely; but there is no doubt that the Poet continued to write for the stage after his retirement from it.

Of the nine plays still to be accounted for, *Macbeth* was played at the Globe in 1610, though probably written some time before; *King Lear* was acted at Whitehall in December, 1606, and three editions of it were issued in 1608; *Antony and Cleopatra* was entered at the Stationers' in 1608; *Cymbeline* was performed some time in the Spring of 1611, and *The Winter's Tale* in May the same year; *King Henry the Eighth* is not heard of till the burning of the Globe theatre in 1613, when it is described as "a new play." Of *Coriolanus* we have no notice whatever till after the Poet's death; while of *Othello* and *The Tempest* we have no well-authenticated notices during his life; though there is a record, which has generally passed for authentic, noting them to have been acted at Court, the former on the 1st of November, 1604, and the latter on the 1st of November, 1611: but that record, as in the case of *Measure for Measure*, has lately been pronounced spurious by the highest authority.

It would seem that after the year 1609, or thereabouts, the Poet's reputation did not mount any higher during his life. A new generation of dramatists was then rising into favour, who, with some excellences derived from him, united gross vices of their own, which however were well adapted to captivate the popular mind. Moreover, King James himself, notwithstanding his liberality of patronage, was essentially a man of loose morals and low tastes; and his taking to Shakespeare at first probably grew more from the public voice, or perhaps from Southampton's influence, than from his own preference. Before the Poet's death, we may trace the beginnings of that corruption which, rather stimulated than discouraged by Puritan bigotry and fanaticism, reached its height some seventy years later; though its course was for a while retarded by King Charles the First, who, whatever else may be said of him, was unquestionably a man of as high and elegant tastes in literature and art as England could boast of in his time.

Shakespeare, however, was by no means so little appreciated in his time as later generations have mainly supposed. No man of that age was held in higher regard for his intellectual gifts; none drew forth more or stronger tributes of applause. Kings, princes, lords, gentlemen, and, what is probably still better, common people, all united in paying homage to his transcendent genius. The noble lines, already referred to, of Ben Jonson, — than whom few men, perhaps none, ever knew better how to judge and how to write on such a theme, — indicate how he struck the scholarship of the age. And from the scattered notices of his contemporaries we get, withal, a very complete and very exalted idea of his personal character as a man; although, to be sure, they yield us few facts in regard to his personal history or his actual course of life. How dearly he was held by those who knew him best, is well shown by a passage of Ben Jonson, written long after the Poet's death, and not published till 1640. Honest Ben had been charged with malevolence towards him, and he repelled the charge thus: "I lov'd the man, and do honour his memory, on this side idolatry, as much as any. He was indeed honest, and of an open and free nature; had an excellent phantasy, brave notions, and gentle expressions."

I cannot dwell much on the particulars of the Poet's latter years; a few, however, must be added touching his family.

On the 5th of June, 1607, his eldest daughter, Susanna, then in her twenty-fifth year, was married to Mr. John

Hall, of Stratford, styled "gentleman" in the parish register, and afterwards a practising physician of good standing. The February following, Shakespeare became a grandfather; Elizabeth, the first and only child of John and Susanna Hall, being baptized the 17th of that month. It is supposed, and apparently with good reason, that Dr. Hall and his wife lived in the same house with the Poet; she was evidently deep in her father's heart; she is said to have had something of his mind and temper; the house was large enough for them all; nor are there wanting signs of entire affection between Mrs. Hall and her mother. Add to all this the Poet's manifest fondness for children, and his gentle and affable disposition, and we have the elements of a happy family and a cheerful home, such as might well render a good-natured man impatient of the stage. Of the moral and religious tenour of domestic life at New Place we are not permitted to know: at a later period the Shakespeares seem to have been not a little distinguished for works of piety and charity.

On the 10th of February, 1616, the Poet saw his youngest daughter, Judith, married to Thomas Quiney, of Stratford, vintner and wine-merchant, whose father had been High-Bailiff of the town. From the way Shakespeare mentions this daughter's marriage portion in his will, which was made the 25th of March following, it is evident that he gave his sanction to the match. Which may be cited as argument that he had not himself experienced any such evils, as some have alleged, from the woman being older than the man; for his daughter had four years the start of her husband; she being at the time of her marriage thirty-one, and he twenty-seven.

Shakespeare was still in the meridian of life. There was no special cause, that we know of, why he might not live many years longer. It were vain to conjecture what he would have done, had more years been given him; possibly, instead of augmenting his legacy to us, he would have recalled and suppressed more or less of what he had written as our inheritance. For the last two or three years, at least, he seems to have left his pen unused; as if, his own ends once achieved, he set no value on that mighty sceptre with which he since sways so large a portion of mankind. That the motives and ambitions of authorship had little to do in the generation of his works, is evident from the serene carelessness with which he left them to shift for themselves; tossing these wonderful treasures from him as if he thought them good for nothing but to serve the hour. Still, to us, in our ignorance, his life cannot but seem too short. For aught we know, Providence, in its wisdom, may have ruled not to allow the example of a man so gifted living to himself.

Be that as it may, WILLIAM SHAKESPEARE departed this life on the 23d of April, 1616. Two days after, his remains were buried beneath the chancel of Trinity Church, in Stratford. The burial took place on the day before the anniversary of his baptism; and it has been commonly believed that his death fell on the anniversary of his birth. If so, he had just entered his fifty-third year.

The Poet's will bears date March 25, 1616. I must notice one item of it: "I give unto my wife the second-best bed, with the furniture." As this is the only mention made of her, the circumstance was for a long time regarded as betraying a strange indifference, or something worse, on the testator's part, towards his wife. And on this has hung the main argument that the union was not a happy one. We owe to Mr. Knight an explanation of the matter; which is so simple and decisive, that we can but wonder it was not hit upon before. Shakespeare's property was mostly freehold; and in all this the widow had what is called the right of dower fully secured to her by the ordinary operation of English law. The Poet was lawyer enough to know this. As for "the second-best bed," this was doubtless the very thing which a loving and beloved wife would naturally prize above any other article of furniture in the establishment.

From the foregoing sketch it appears that the materials for a biography of Shakespeare are scanty indeed, and, withal, rather dry. Nevertheless, there is enough, I think, to show, that in all the common dealings of life he was eminently gentle, candid, upright, and judicious; open-hearted, genial, and sweet, in his social intercourses; among his companions and friends, full of playful wit and sprightly grace; kind to the faults of others, severe to his own; quick to discern and acknowledge merit in another, modest and slow of finding it in himself: while, in the smooth and happy marriage, which he seems to have realized, of the highest poetry and art with systematic and successful prudence in business affairs, we have an example of compact and well-rounded practical manhood, such as may justly engage our admiration and respect.

I have spoken somewhat as to the motive and purpose of his intellectual labour. It was in and for the theatre that his multitudinous genius was developed, and his works produced; there Fortune, or rather Providence, had cast his lot. Doubtless it was his nature, in whatever he undertook, to do his best. As an honest and true man, he would, if possible, make the temple of the Drama a noble, a beautiful, and glorious place; and it was while working quietly and unobtrusively in furtherance of this end, — building better than he knew, — that he approved himself the greatest, wisest, sweetest of men.

ORIGIN AND GROWTH OF THE DRAMA IN ENGLAND.

THE ENGLISH DRAMA, as we have it in Shakespeare. was the slow growth of several centuries. Nor is it clearly traceable to any foreign source: it was an original and independent growth, the native and free product of the soil. This position is very material in reference to the subject of structure and form; as inferring that the Drama in question is not amenable to any ancient or foreign jurisdiction; that it has a life and spirit of its own, is to be viewed as a thing by itself, and judged according to the peculiar laws under which it grew and took its shape; in brief, that it had just as good a right to differ from any other Drama as any other had from it.

The ancient Drama, that which grew to perfection, and, so far as is known, had its origin, in Greece, is universally styled the Classic Drama. By what term to distinguish the modern Drama of Europe, writers are not fully agreed. Within a somewhat recent period, it has received from high authorities the title of the Romantic Drama. A more appropriate title, as it seems to me, suggested by its Gothic original, and used by earlier authorities, is that of the Gothic Drama. Such, accordingly, is the term by which it will be distinguished in these pages. The fitness of the name, I think, will readily be seen from the fact that the thing was an indigenous and self-determined outgrowth from the Gothic mind under Christian culture. And the term naturally carries the idea, that the Drama in question stands on much the same ground relatively to the Classic Drama as is commonly recognized in the case of Gothic and Classic architecture; which may help us to realize how each Drama forms a distinct species, and lives free of the other, so that any argument or criticism from the ancient against the modern is wholly irrelevant.

The Gothic Drama, as it fashioned itself in different nations of modern Europe, especially in England and Spain, where it grew up independently, has certain diversities. Upon the nature and reason of these I cannot enlarge. Suffice it to say that they do not reach beyond points of detail; their effect thus being to approve the strength of the common principles that underlie and support them. These principles cover the whole ground of difference from the Classic Drama. The several varieties, therefore, of the Gothic Drama may be justly regarded as bearing concurrent testimony to a common right of freedom from the jurisdiction of ancient rules.

Of the rise and progress of the Drama in England, my limits will permit only a brief sketch, not more than enough to give a general idea on the subject.

In England, as in the other Christian nations where it had any thing of originality, the Drama was of ecclesiastical origin, and for a long time was used only as a means of diffusing a knowledge of the leading facts and doctrines of Christianity as then understood and received. Of course, therefore, it was in substance and character religious, or was meant to be so, and had the Clergy for its authors and founders. But I cannot admit the justice of Coleridge's remark on the subject. "The Drama," says he, "recommenced in England, as it first began in Greece, in religion. The people were unable to read; the Priesthood were unwilling that they should read; and yet their own interest compelled them not to leave the people wholly ignorant of the great events of sacred history."

Surely, it is of consequence to bear in mind that at that time "the people" had never been able to read; printing had not been heard of in Europe; books were multiplied with great difficulty, and could not be had but at great expense: so that it was impossible the people should be able to read; and while there was an impossibility in the way, it is not necessary to impute an unwillingness. Nor is there any good reason for supposing that the Priesthood, in their simplicity of faith, were then at all apprehensive or aware of any danger in the people being able to read. Probably they worked as honest men with the best means they could devise; endeavouring to clothe the most needful of all instruction in such forms, and mould it up with such arts of recreation and pleasure, as might render it interesting and attractive to the popular mind. In all which they seem to have merited any thing but an impeachment of their motives. However, the point best worth noting here is the large share those early dramatic representations had in shaping the culture of Old England, and in giving to the national mind its character and form. And perhaps later ages, and ourselves as the children of a later age, are more indebted to those rude labours of the Clergy in the cause of religion than we are aware, or might be willing to acknowledge.

MIRACLE-PLAYS.

In its course through several ages the Drama took different forms from time to time, as culture advanced. The earliest form was in what are called Plays of Miracles, or Miracle-Plays. These were mostly founded on events of Scripture, though the apocryphal gospels and legends of saints and martyrs were sometimes drawn upon for subjects or for embellishments. In these performances no regard was paid to the rules of natural probability; for, as the operation of supernatural power was assumed, this was held a sufficient ground or principle of credibility in itself. Hence, indeed, the name Marvels, Miracles, or Miracle-Plays, by which they were commonly known.

Our earliest instance of a Miracle-Play in England was

near the beginning of the twelfth century. Matthew Paris, in his *Lives of the Abbots*, written as early as 1240, informs us that Geoffrey, Abbot of St. Albans, while yet a secular person brought out the Miracle-Play of *St. Catharine* at Dunstaple; and that for the needed decorations he obtained certain articles "from the Sacristy of St. Albans." Geoffrey, who was from the University of Paris, was then teaching a school at Dunstaple, and the play was performed by his scholars. Warton thinks this was about 1110: but we learn from Bulæus that Geoffrey became Abbot of St. Albans in 1119; and all that can with certainty be affirmed is, that the performance was before he assumed a religious habit. Bulæus also informs us that the thing was not then a novelty, but that it was customary for teachers and scholars to get up such exhibitions.

Our next information on the subject is from Fitzstephen's *Life of Thomas à Becket*, as quoted by Stowe. Becket died in 1170, and the *Life* was probably written about twelve years later. After referring to the public amusements of ancient Rome, Fitzstephen says: "In lieu of such theatrical shows and performances, London has plays of a more sacred kind, representing the miracles which saints have wrought, or the sufferings and constancy of martyrs."

It appears that about the middle of the next century itinerant actors were well known; for one of the regulations found in the *Burton Annals* has the following, under date 1258: "Actors may be entertained, not because they are actors, but because of their poverty; and let not their plays be seen nor heard, nor the performance of them allowed in the presence of the Abbot or the monks." The Clergy differed in opinion as to the lawfulness of such exhibitions; and in an Anglo-French poem written about this time they are sharply censured, and the using of them is restricted to certain places and persons. An English paraphrase of this poem was made by Robert Brunne in 1303; who specifies what pastimes are allowed to "a clerk of order," declaring it lawful for him to perform Miracle-Plays of the birth and resurrection of Christ in churches, but a sin to witness them "on the highways or greens." He also reproves the practice, then not uncommon, of aiding in such performances by lending horses or harness from the monasteries, and especially declares it sacrilege if a priest or clerk lend the hallowed vestments for that purpose.

The dogma of transubstantiation was particularly fruitful of such exhibitions. The festival of *Corpus Christi*, designed for the furthering of this dogma, was instituted by Pope Urban IV. in 1264. Within a few years from that date, Miracle-Plays were annually performed at Chester during Whitsuntide: they were also introduced at Coventry, York, Durham, Lancaster, Bristol, Cambridge, and other towns; so that the thing became a sort of established usage throughout the kingdom. A considerable variety of subjects, especially such as relate to the Incarnation, the Passion, and the Resurrection, was embraced in the plan of these exhibitions; the purpose being to extend an orthodox belief in those fundamentals of the faith.

A very curious specimen of the plays that grew out of the *Corpus-Christi* festival was lately discovered in the library of Trinity College, Dublin, the manuscript being, it is said, as old as the reign cf Edward IV., who died in 1483. It is called *The Play of the Blessed Sacrament*, and is founded on a miracle alleged to have been wrought in the forest of Arragon, in 1461. In form it closely resembles the Miracle-Plays founded on Scripture, the Saviour being one of the characters, the others being five Jews, a bishop, a priest, a merchant, and a physician and his servant. The merchant, having the key of the church, steals the Host, and sells it to the Jews, who promise to turn Christians in case they find its miraculous powers verified. They put the Host to various tests. Being stabbed with their daggers, it bleeds, and one of the Jews goes mad at the sight. They next attempt nailing it to a post, when one of them has his hand torn off; whereupon the physician and his man come in to dress the wound, but after a long comic scene are driven out as quacks. The Jews then proceed to boil the Host, but the water forthwith turns blood-red. Finally, they cast it into a heated oven, which presently bursts asunder, and an image of the Saviour rises and addresses the Jews, who make good their promise on the spot. The merchant confesses his theft, declares his penitence, and is forgiven, under a strict charge never again to buy or sell. The whole winds up with an epilogue from the bishop, enforcing the moral of the play, which turns on the dogma of transubstantiation.

There are three sets of Miracle-Plays extant, severally known as the Towneley, Coventry, and Chester Collections; the first including thirty plays, the second forty-two, and the third twenty-four. Some of the manuscripts are thought to be as old as the time of Henry VI., who died in 1471. The three sets have all been recently printed by the Shakespeare Society. The Towneley set most likely belonged to Widkirk Abbey: at what time they grew into use there and at Coventry is not certainly known. At Chester the plays were probably first acted in 1268; after which time they were repeated yearly, with some interruptions, till 1577. And we have conclusive evidence that such exhibitions formed a regular part of English life in the reign of Edward III., which began in 1327. For Chaucer alludes to "plays of miracles" as things of common occurrence; and in *The Miller's Tale* he makes it a prominent feature of the parish clerk, "that jolly was and gay," that he performed in them. And in 1378, which was the first year of Richard II., the choristers of St. Paul's, London, petitioned the King to prohibit some ignorant persons from acting plays founded on Scripture, as conflicting with the interest of the Clergy, who had incurred expense in getting up a set of plays on similar subjects. Stowe informs us, also, that in 1409 there was a great play in London, "which lasted eight days, and was of matter from the creation of the world."

As to the general character of the plays, this will best

appear by brief analyses of some of them. The Towneley set being the most ancient, my first specimens will be from that.

The first play of the series includes the creation, the revolt of Lucifer and his adherents, and their expulsion from Heaven. It opens with a short address from the Deity, who then begins the creation, and, after a song by the cherrubim, descends from the throne, and retires; Lucifer usurps it, and asks his fellows how he appears. The good and bad angels have different opinions about that; but the Deity soon returns, and ends the dispute by casting the rebels with their leader out of Heaven. Adam and Eve are then created, and Satan winds up the piece with a speech venting his envy of their happiness in Eden.

The second play relates to the killing of Abel, and is opened by Cain's ploughboy with a sort of prologue in which he warns the spectators to be silent. Cain then enters with a plough and team, and quarrels with the boy for refusing to drive the team. Presently Abel comes in, and wishes Cain good-speed, who meets his kind word with an unmentionable request. The murder then proceeds, and is followed by the cursing of Cain; after which he calls the boy, and gives him a beating. Cain owns the murder, and the boy counsels flight, lest the bailiffs catch him. Next we have a course of buffoonery: Cain makes a mock proclamation in the King's name, the boy repeats it blunderingly after him, and is then sent off with the team; and the piece closes with a speech by Cain to the spectators, bidding them farewell.

The third of the series is occupied with the Deluge. After a lamentation by Noah on the sinfulness of the world, God is introduced repenting that he made man, telling Noah how to build the Ark, and blessing him and his. Noah's wife is an arrant shrew, and they fall at odds in the outset, both of them swearing by the Virgin Mary. Noah begins and finishes the Ark on the spot; then tells his spouse what is coming, and invites her on board: she stoutly refuses to embark, which brings on another flare-up; he persuades her with a whip; she wishes herself a widow, and the same to all the wives in the audience; he exhorts all the husbands to break in their wives betimes: at length harmony is restored by the intervention of the sons; all go aboard, and pass three hundred and fifty days talking about the weather; a raven is sent out, then a dove, and they debark.

Two plays of the set are taken up with the adoration of the shepherds; and the twelfth is worthy of special notice as being a piece of broad comedy approaching to downright farce, with dashes of rude wit and humour. The three shepherds, after talking awhile about their shrewish wives, are on the point of striking up a song, when an old acquaintance of theirs named Mak, whose character is none of the best, comes among them. They suspect him of meditating some sly trick; so, on going to bed, they take care to have him lie between them, lest he play the wolf among their woolly subjects. While they are snoring, he steals out, helps himself to a fat sheep, and makes off. His wife, fearing he may be snatched up and hanged, suggests a scheme, which is presently agreed upon, that she shall make as if she had just been adding a member to the family, and that the sheep shall be snugly wrapped up in the cradle. This done, Mak hastens back, and resumes his sleeping-place. In the morning the shepherds wake much refreshed, but Mak feigns a crick in the neck; and, while they are walking to the fold, he whips away home. They soon miss the sheep, suspect Mak, and go to his cottage: he lets them in, tells them what his wife has been doing, and begs them not to disturb her; and, as the least noise seems to pain her, they are at first deceived. They ask to see the child; he tells them the child is asleep, and will cry badly if waked; still they insist; pull up the covering of the cradle, and know their sheep by the ear-mark; but the wife assures them it is a child, and that evil spirits have transformed it into what they see. They are not to be duped again; beat

Mak till they are tired, then lie down to rest; the star in the East appears, and the angel sings the *Gloria in Excelsis;* whereupon they proceed to Bethlehem, find the infant Saviour, and give him, the first "a bob of cherries," the second a bird, the third a tennis-ball.

The Chester and Coventry plays, for the most part, closely resemble the Towneley series, both in the subjects and the manner of treating them. A portion, however, of the Coventry set, from the eighth to the fifteenth, inclusive, deserve special notice, as they show the first beginnings or buddings of a higher dramatic growth, which afterwards resulted in what are called Moral-Plays. For instance, Contemplation, who serves as speaker of prologues, and moralizes the events, is evidently an allegorical personage, that is, an abstract idea personified, such as afterwards grew into general use, and gave character to stage performances. And we have other like personages, Verity, Justice, Mercy, and Peace.

The eighth play represents Joachim grieving that he has no child, and praying that the cause of his grief may be removed: Anna, his wife, heartily joins with him, taking all the blame of their childlessness to herself. In answer to their prayers, an angel announces to them the birth of a daughter who shall be called Mary. Then follows the presentation of Mary, and, after an interview between her and the bishop, Contemplation informs the audience that fourteen years will elapse before her next appearance, and promises that they shall soon see "the Parliament of Heaven." Next we have Mary's betrothment. The bishop summons the males of David's House to appear in the temple, each bringing a white rod; he being divinely assured that the man whose rod should bud and bloom was to be the husband of Mary. Joseph, after a deal of urging, offers up his rod, and the miracle is at once apparent. When asked if he will be married to the maiden, he deprecates such an event with all his might, and pleads his old age in bar of it; nevertheless the marriage proceeds. Some while after,

Joseph informs the Virgin that he has hired "a pretty little house" for her to live in, and that he will "go labouring in far country" to maintain her. Then comes the Parliament of Heaven. The Virtues plead for pity and grace to man; Verity objects, urging that there can be no peace made between sin and the law; this calls forth an earnest prayer from Mercy in man's behalf; Justice takes up the argument on the other side; Peace answers in a strain that brings them all to accord. The Son then raises the question how the thing shall be done. Verity, Justice, Mercy, and Peace having tried their wit, and found it unequal to the cause, a council of the Trinity is held, when the Son offers to undertake the work by assuming the form of a man; the Father consents, and the Holy Ghost agrees to co-operate. Gabriel is then sent to salute Mary and make known to her the decree of the Incarnation.

Joseph is absent some months. On his return he is in great affliction, and reproaches Mary, but, an angel explaining the matter to him, he makes amends. The bishop holds a court, and his officer summons to it a large number of people, all having English names, and tells the audience to "ring well in their purse"; which shows that money was collected for the performance. Mary is brought before the court, to be tried for naughtiness, and Joseph also for tamely bearing it. His innocence is proved by his drinking, without harm, a liquid which, were he guilty, would cause spots on his face. Mary also drinking of the same, unhurt, one of the accusers affirms that the bishop has changed the draught, but is cured of his unbelief by being forced to drink what is left. The fifteenth play relates to the nativity. Joseph, it seems, is not yet satisfied of Mary's innocence, and his doubts are all removed in this manner: Mary, seeing a tall tree full of ripe cherries, asks him to gather some for her; he replies that the father of her child may help her to them; and the tree forthwith bows down its top to her hand. This is soon followed by the Saviour's birth.

Besides the three sets of Miracle-Plays in question, there are other specimens, some of which seem to require notice. Among these are three, known as the Digby Miracle-Plays, on the Conversion of St. Paul. One of the persons is Belial, whose appearance and behaviour are indicated by the stage-direction, "Enter a Devil with thunder and fire." He makes a soliloquy in self-glorification, and then complains of the dearth of news: after which we have the stage-direction, "Enter another Devil called Mercury, coming in haste, crying and roaring." He tells Belial of St. Paul's conversion, and declares his belief that the Devil's reign is about to end; whereat Belial is in stark dismay. They then plot to stir up the "Jewish Bishops" in the cause, and soon after "vanish away with a fiery flame and a tempest."

A Miracle-Play relating to Mary Magdalen is remarkable as having required four scaffolds for the exhihition; Tiberius, Herod, Pilate, and the Devil having each their several stations; and one of the directions being, "Enter the Prince of Devils on a stage, and Hell underneath the stage." Mary lives in a castle inherited from her father, who figures in the opening of the play as King Cyrus. A ship owned by St. Peter is brought into the space between the scaffolds, and Mary and some others make a long voyage in it. Of course St. Peter's ship represents the Catholic Church. The heroine's castle is besieged by the Devil with the Seven Deadly Sins, and carried; Luxury takes her to a tavern where a gallant named Curiosity treats her to "sops and wine." The process of Mary's repentance and amendment is carried through in due order. Tiberius makes a long speech glorifying himself; a parasite named Serybil flatters him on his good looks, and he in return blesses Serybil's face, which was probably carbuncled as richly as Corporal Bardolph's. Herod makes his boast in similar style, and afterwards goes to bed. The devils, headed by Satan, perform a mock pagan mass to Mahound, which is the old name for Mohammed. The three Kings of the

World, the Flesh, and the Devil figure in the play, but not prominently. A Priest winds up the performance, requesting the spectators not to charge its faults on the poet.

Here, again, we have allegorical personages, as Lechery, Luxury, and Curiosity, introduced along with concrete particular characters of Scripture. This is carried still further in another play of a later date, called the *Life and Repentance of Mary Magdalen*, where we have divers personifications of abstract ideas, such as Law, Faith, Pride, Cupidity, and Infidelity; the latter being much the same as the Vice or Iniquity who figured so largely in Moral-Plays. Infidelity acts as the heroine's paramour, and assumes many disguises, to seduce her into all sorts of vice, wherein he is aided by Pride, Cupidity, and Carnal-concupiscence. When she has reached the climax of sin, he advises her "not to make two hells instead of one," but to live merrily in this world, since she is sure of perdition in the next; and his advice succeeds for a while. On the other hand, Law, Faith, Repentance, Justification, and Love strive to recover her, and the latter half of the play is taken up with this work of benevolence. At last, Christ expels the seven devils, who "roar terribly"; whereupon Infidelity and his companions give her up. The piece closes with a dialogue between Mary, Justification, and Love, the latter two rejoicing over the salvation of a sinner.

This play was printed in 1567, and is described in the title-page, as "not only godly, learned, and fruitful, but also well furnished with pleasant mirth and pastime, very delectable for those which shall hear or read the same: Made by the learned clerk, Lewis Wager." It bears clear internal evidence of having been written after the Reformation; and the prologue shows that it was acted by itinerant players, and had been performed "at the university."

Four Miracle-Plays have come down to us, which were written by Bishop Bale, and printed on the Continent in 1538. The most notable point concerning them is their being the first known attempt to use the stage in furtherance of the Reformation. One of them is entitled *Christ's Temptation.* It opens with Christ in the wilderness, faint through hunger; and His first speech is meant to refute the Romish doctrine of the efficacy of fasting. Satan joins Him in the disguise of a hermit, and the whole temptation proceeds according to Scripture. In one of his arguments, Satan vents his spite against "false priests and bishops," but plumes himself that "the Vicar of Rome" will worship and serve him. Bale wrote several plays in a different line, of one of which I have given some account in another place.*

The Miracle-Play of *King Darius* is scarce worth notice, save that Iniquity with his wooden dagger has a leading part in the action. He, together with Importunity and Partiality, has several contests with Equity, Charity, and Constancy: for a while he has the better of them; but at last they catch him alone, each in turn threatens him with sore visitings, and then follows the direction, "Here somebody must cast fire to Iniquity"; who probably had some fireworks about his person, to explode for the amusement of the audience, as he went out.

Hitherto we have met with nothing that can be regarded as portraiture of individual character, unless somewhat of the sort be alleged in the case of Mak the sheep-stealing rogue. The truth is, character and action, in the proper sense of the terms, were hardly thought of in the making of Miracle-Plays; the work aiming at nothing higher than a literal or mechanical reflection of facts and events; sometimes relieved indeed with certain generalities of popular humour and satire, but without any contexture of individual traits. The piece next to be noticed deserves remark, as indicating how, under the pressure of general dramatic improvement, Miracle-Plays tried to rise above their proper sphere, and still retain their proper form.

The History of Jacob and Esau, probably written as early as 1557, and printed in 1568, is of very regular con-

* See the chapter on *King John*, vol. ii., pages 10 and 11.

struction, having five Acts, which are duly subdivided into scenes. Besides the Scripture characters, are Ragau, Esau's servant; Mido, a boy who leads blind Isaac; Hanan and Zethar, two of his neighbours; Abra, a girl who assists Rebecca; and Debora, an old nurse. Esau and his servant Ragau set forth together on a hunt. While they are gone, Rebecca urges Jacob to secure his brother's birthright. Esau returns with a raging appetite, and Jacob demands his birthright as the condition of relieving him with a mess of rice pottage; he consents, and Ragau laughs at his stupidity, while Jacob, Rebecca, and Abra sing a psalm of thanksgiving. These things occupy the first two Acts; in the third, Esau and his man take another hunt. The blessing of Jacob takes place in the fourth Act; Rebecca tasking her cookery to the utmost in dressing a kid, and succeeding in her scheme. In the last Act, Esau comes back, and learns from his father what has occurred in his absence. The plot and incidents are managed with considerable propriety; the characters are discriminated with some art; the comic portions show some neatness of wit and humour.

In the Interlude of *Godly Queen Esther*, printed in 1561, we have a Miracle-Play going still further out of itself. One of the characters is named Hardy-dardy, who, with some qualities of the Vice, foreshadows the Jester, or professional Fool, of the later Drama; wearing motley, and feigning weakness or disorder of intellect, to the end that his wit may run more at large, and strike with the better effect. Hardy-dardy offers himself as a servant to Haman; and after Haman has urged him with sundry remarks in dispraise of fools, he sagely replies, that "some wise man must be fain sometime to do on a fool's coat." Besides the Scripture characters, the play has several allegorical personages, as Pride, Ambition, and Adulation, who make their wills, bequeathing all their bad qualities to Haman, and thereby ruin him.

Of all the persons who figured in the Miracle-Plays, Herod, the slayer of the Innocents, appears to have been the greatest popular favourite. We hear of him as early as the time of Chaucer, who says of the parish clerk, Absolon,

> "Sometime, to show his lightness and maistrie,
> He plaieth Herode on a scaffold hie."

From that time onwards, and we know not how long before, he was a sort of staple character, no set of Miracle-Plays being regarded as complete without him. And he was always represented as an immense swearer and braggart and swaggerer, evermore ranting and raving up and down the stage, and cudgelling the spectators' ears with the most furious bombast and profanity. Thus, in one of the Chester series:

> "For I am king of all mankind;
> I bid, I beat, I loose, I bind:
> I master the Moon: Take this in mind,
> That I am most of might.
> I am the greatest above degree,
> That is, that was, or ever shall be:
> The Sun it dare not shine on me,
> An I bid him go down."

Thus, too, in one of the Coventry series:

> "Of beauty and of boldness I bear evermore the bell;
> Of main and of might I master every man;
> I ding with my doughtiness the Devil down to Hell;
> For both of Heaven and of Earth I am king certain."

Termagant, the supposed god of the Saracens, was another staple character in the Miracle-Plays; who is described by John Florio as "a great boaster, quarreller, killer, tamer or ruler of the universe, the child of the earthquake and of the thunder, the brother of death." That Shakespeare himself had suffered under the monstrous din of these "strutting and bellowing" stage-thumpers is shown by Hamlet's remonstrance with the players: "O, it offends me to the soul, to hear a robustious periwig-pated fellow tear a passion to rags, to very tatters, to split the ears of the groundlings: I would have such a fellow whipped for o'erdoing Termagant; it out-herods Herod: pray you, avoid it."

Thus much must suffice by way of indicating, in a general sort, the character of those primitive sprouts and upshoots of the Gothic Drama in England. Their rudeness of construction, their ingrained coarseness of style,their puerility, their obscenity, and indecency, according to our standard, are indescribable. Their quality in these respects could only be shown by specimens, and these I have not room to produce, nor would it be right or decent to do so, if I had.

But what strikes us, perhaps, still more offensively in those old religious plays, is the irreverent and shocking familiarity everywhere used with the sacredest persons and things of the Christian Faith. The awfullest and most moving scenes and incidents of the Gospel history, such as the Last Supper and the Crucifixion, were treated with what cannot but seem to us the most shameless and most disgusting profanity: the poor invention of the time was racked to the uttermost, to harrow the audience with dramatic violence and stress; and it seems to us impossible but that all the solemnity of the matter must have been defeated by such coarseness of handling.

But, indeed, we can hardly do justice either to the authors or the audiences of those religious comedies; there being an almost impassable gulf fixed between their modes of thought and ours. The people were then just emerging from the thick darkness of Gothic barbarism into what may be termed the border-land of civilization. As such, their minds were so dominated by the senses, that they could scarce conceive of any beings much more than one grade above themselves. A sort of infantile unconsciousness, indeed, had possession of them; so that they were really quite innocent of the evils which we see and feel in what was so entertaining to them. Hence, as Michelet remarks, "the ancient Church did not scruple to connect whimsical dramatic rites with the most sacred doctrines and objects."

So that the state of mind from which and for which those old plays were produced goes far to explain and justify what we are apt to regard as a shocking contradiction between the subject-matter and the treatment. The truth is, such religious farces, with all their coarse trumperies and comicalities and sensuous extravagances, were in perfect keeping with the genius of an age when, for instance, a transfer of land was not held binding without the delivery of a clod. And so, what Mr. John Stuart Mill describes as "the childlike character of the religious sentiment of a rude people, who know terror, but not awe, and are often on the most intimate terms of familiarity with the objects of their adoration," makes it conceivable how that which seems to us the most irreverent handling of sacred things, may notwithstanding have been, to the authors and audiences in question, but the natural issue of such religious thoughts and feelings as they had or were capable of having. At all events, those exhibitions, so revolting to modern taste and decorum, were no doubt in most cases full of religion and honest delectation to the simple minds who witnessed them. Moreover, rude and ignorant as the Miracle-Plays were in form, coarse and foul as they were in language and incident, they nevertheless contained the germ of that splendid dramatic growth with which the literature and life of England were afterwards enriched and adorned.

Before leaving this branch of the subject, perhaps I ought to add something further as to the part which was taken by the Clergy in those old stage exhibitions. The register of the Guild of *Corpus Christi* at York, which was a religious fraternity, mentions, in 1408, books of plays, various banners and flags, beards, vizards, crowns, diadems, and scaffolds, belonging to the society; which shows that its members were at that time concerned in the representation of Miracle-Plays. It appears that a few years afterwards these performances, because of certain abuses attending them, were discontinued: but in 1426 William Melton, a friar who is called "a professor of holy pageantry," preached several sermons in favour of them; and the result was, that they were then made annual, suitable measures being taken for preventing the former disorders. But the best evidence as to the share the Clergy had in the representations is furnished by the account-book of Thetford Priory from 1461 to 1540; which contains numerous entries of payments to players; and in divers cases expressly states that members of the convent assisted in the performances. These were commonly held twice or three times a year; in 1531 there were five repetitions of them; after which time there are but three entries of plays wherein the members participated with the common actors; the old custom being broken up most likely by the progress of the Reformation.

The practice in question, however, was by no means universal. We learn from Stowe that in 1391 and 1409, plays were acted in London by the parish clerks. In cities and large towns, these performances were generally in the hands of the trade fraternities or guilds. Our information touching the *Corpus Christi* plays at Coventry extends from 1416 to 1590; during which period there is no sign of the Clergy having any part in them. The records of Chester also show that the whole business was there managed by laymen. And in 1487 a Miracle-Play on the descent of Christ into Hell was acted before Henry the Seventh by the charity boys of Hyde Abbey and St. Swithin's Priory. Long before this date, acting was taken up as a distinct profession, and regular companies of actors were formed.

That churches and chapels of monasteries were at first, and for a long time after, used as theatres, is very certain. The Anglo-French poem already referred to informs us that Miracle-Plays were sometimes performed in churches and cemeteries, the Clergy getting them up and acting in them. And Burnet tells us that Bishop Bonner as late as 1542 issued an order to his clergy, forbidding "all manner of common plays, games, or interludes to be played, set forth, or declared within their churches and chapels." Nor was the custom wholly discontinued till some time after that; for in 1572 was printed a tract which has a passage inferring that churches were still sometimes used for such purposes.

When plays were performed in the open air, temporary scaffolds or stages were commonly erected for the purpose; though in some cases the scaffold was set on wheels, so as to be easily moved from one part of the town to another. It appears that the structure used at Chester had two stages, one above the other; the lower being closed in, to serve as a dressing-room for the actors, while the performance was on the upper stage where it could be seen by all the spectators. Sometimes the lower stage seems to have been used for Hell, the devils rising out of it, or sinking into it, as occasion required. In some plays, however, as we have seen in that of *Mary Magdalen*, more than one scaffold was used; and certain stage-directions in the Towneley and Coventry plays infer that two, three, and even four scaffolds were erected round a centre, the actors going from one to another across the intervening space, as the scene changed, or their several parts required.

MORAL-PLAYS.

The purpose of the Miracle-Plays was to inculcate, in a popular way, what may be termed the theological verities; at first they took their substance and form solely with a view to this end, the securing of an orthodox faith being then looked upon as the all-important concern. In course of time, the thirst for novelty and variety drew them beyond their original sphere of revealed religion into that of natural ethics. By degrees, allegorical personages came, as we have seen, to be more or less mixed up with Scripture characters and events; the aim being to illustrate and enforce the virtues that refer directly to the practical conduct of life. The new-comers kept encroaching more and more: invited in as auxiliaries, they remained as principals; and at last quite superseded and replaced the original tenants. Hence there grew into use a different style or order of workmanship, a distinct class of symbolical or allegorical dramas; that is, dramas made up entirely of abstract ideas personified. These, from their structure and purpose, are properly termed MORAL-PLAYS. We shall see hereafter that much the same process of transition was repeated in the gradual rising of genuine Comedy and Tragedy out of the allegorical dramas.

In Miracle-Plays the Devil of course made a legitimate part of the representation. He was endowed in large measure with a biting, caustic humour, and with a coarse, scoffing, profane wit; therewithal he had an exaggerated grotesqueness of look and manner, such as to awaken mixed emotions of fear, mirth, and disgust. In these qualities of mind and person, together with the essential malignity of which they are the proper surface and outside, we have the germs of both Comedy and Tragedy. For the horrible and the ridiculous easily pass into each other, they being indeed different phases of the same thing. Accordingly, the Devil, under one name or another, continued to propagate himself on the stage long after his original co-actors had withdrawn.

On the other hand, a personage called Iniquity, Vice, or some such name, was among the first characters to take stand in Moral-Plays, as a personification of the evil tendencies in man. And the Vice thus originating from the moral view of things was a sort of natural counterpart to that more ancient impersonation of evil which took its origin from the theological sphere. The Devil, being the stronger principle, naturally had use for the Vice as his agent or factor. Hence we may discover in these two personages points of mutual sympathy and attraction; and, in fact, it was in and through them that the two species of drama met and coalesced.

In Moral-Plays the Devil and the Vice, or at least one of them, almost always bore a leading part, though not always under those names. Most commonly the two were retained together; there are cases however of each figuring apart from the other. And no pains were spared to give the Devil as hideous an aspect as possible: he was made an out-and-out monster in appearance, all hairy and shaggy, with a "bottle nose" and an "evil face," having horns, hoofs, and a long tail; so that the sight had been at once loathsome and ludicrous, but for the great strength and quickness of wit, and the fiendish, yet merry and waggish malignity, which usually marked his conversation. Sometimes, however, he was endowed with a most protean versatility of mind and person, so that he could walk abroad as "plain devil," scaring all he met, or steal into society as a prudent counsellor, a dashing gallant, or whatever else would best work out his ends.

As for the Vice, he commonly acted the part of a broad, rampant jester and buffoon, full of mad pranks and mischief-making, liberally dashed with a sort of tumultuous, swaggering fun. He was arrayed in fantastic garb, with something of drollery in its appearance, so as to aid the comic effect of his action, and armed with a dagger of lath, perhaps as symbolical that his use of weapons was but to the end of provoking his own defeat. Therewithal he was vastly given to cracking ribald and saucy jokes with and upon the Devil, and treating him in a style of coarse familiarity and mockery; and a part of his ordinary business was to bestride the Devil, and beat him till he roared, and the audience roared with him; the scene ending with his being carried off to Hell on the Devil's back. Much of the old custom in these two personages is amusingly set forth in Ben Jonson's *Staple of News*, where, at the end of each Act, we have some imaginary spectators commenting on the performance. At the end of the first Act, one of them expressing a fear that the play has no Fool in it, as the Vice was often called, Gossip Tattle delivers herself thus: "My husband, Timothy Tattle, God rest his poor soul! was wont to say there was no play without a Fool and a Devil in't; he was for the Devil still, God bless him! The Devil for his money, he would say; I would fain see the Devil." It being asked, "But was the Devil a proper man?" Gossip Mirth replies, "As fine a gentleman of his inches as ever I saw trusted to the stage or anywhere else; and loved the commonwealth as well as ever a patriot of them all: he would carry away the Vice on his back, quick, to Hell, wherever he came, and reform abuses." Again, at the end of the second Act, the question being put, "How like you the Vice in the play?" Widow Tattle complains, "But here is never a fiend to carry him away. Besides, he has never a wooden dagger! I would not give a rush for a Vice that has not a wooden dagger, to snap at everybody he meets." Whereupon Mirth observes, "That was the old way, gossip, when Iniquity came in, like Hocus-Pocus, in a juggler's jerkin, with false skirts, like the knave of clubs." *

The most ancient specimen of a Moral-Play known to have survived dates as far back as the reign of Henry VI., which closed in 1461. It is entitled *The Castle of Perseverance*, and is opened by Mundus, Belial, and Caro descanting on their several gifts: Humanum Genus, who represents mankind, then announces himself, just born, and naked; while he is speaking Good Angel and Bad Angel appear on his right and left, each claiming him as a follower. He prefers Bad Angel, who leads him straight to Mundus; the latter orders his friends Voluptas and Stultitia to take him in hand. Detractio, who calls himself Backbiter, is also made one of his train, and procures him the acquaintance of Avaritia, by whom he is introduced to the other Deadly Sins: not long after, he meets with Luxuria, and falls in love with her. At all this Bad Angel exults, but Good Angel mourns, and sends Confessio to Humanum Genus, who repels him at first, as having come too soon. However, Confessio at last reclaims him; he asks where he can live in safety, and is told, in the Castle of Perseverance: so, thither he goes, being at that time "forty Win-

* Shakespeare has several allusions to this old stage custom. See the author's Harvard Edition of Shakespeare, vol. v. page 222, note 17; also, vol ix. pages 202, 203, notes 8 and 9.

ters old." The Seven Cardinal Virtues there wait upon him with their respective counsels. Belial, after having beaten the Seven Deadly Sins for letting him escape, heads them in laying siege to the Castle; but he appeals to "the Duke that died on rood" to defend him, and the assailants retire discomfited, being beaten "black and blue" by the roses which Charity and Patience hurl against them. As he is now grown "hoary and cold," Avaritia worms in under the walls, and induces him to quit the Castle. No sooner has he got well skilled in the lore of Avaritia, than Garcio, who stands for the rising generation, demands all his wealth, alleging that Mundus has given it to him. Presently Mors comes in for *his* turn, and makes a speech extolling his own power; Anima also hastens to the spot, and invokes the aid of Misericordia: notwithstanding, Bad Angel shoulders the hero, and sets off with him for the infernal regions. Then follows a discussion in Heaven, Mercy and Peace pleading for the hero, Verity and Justice against him: God sends for his soul; Peace takes it from Bad Angel, who is driven off to Hell; Mercy presents it to Heaven; and "the Father sitting in judgment" pronounces sentence, which unfolds the moral of the performance.

This analysis shows that the piece partakes somewhat the character of a Miracle-Play. A list of the persons is given at the end; also a rude sketch of the scene, showing a castle in the centre, with five scaffolds for Deus, Belial, Mundus, Caro, and Avaritia. Bad Angel is the Devil of the performance: there is no personage answering to the Vice.

The next piece to be noticed bears the title of *Mind, Will, and Understanding.* It is opened by Wisdom, who represents the Second Person of the Trinity; Anima soon joins him, and they converse upon heavenly love, the seven sacraments, the five senses, and reason. Mind, Will, and Understanding then describe their several qualities; the Five Wits, attired as virgins, go out singing; Lucifer enters "in a Devil's array without, and within as proud as a gallant," that is, with a gallant's dress under his proper garb;

relates the creation of Man, describing Mind, Will, and Understanding as the three properties of the soul, which he means to assail and corrupt. He then goes out, and presently returns, succeeds in the attempt, and makes an exulting speech, at the close of which "he taketh a shrewd boy with him, and goeth his way crying"; probably snatching up a boy from the audience, — an incident designed to "bring down the house." Lucifer having gone out, his three victims appear in gay apparel; they dismiss Conscience; Will dedicates himself to lust; all join in a song, and then proceed to have a dance. First, Mind calls in his followers, Indignation, Sturdiness, Malice, Hastiness, Wreck, and Discord. Next, Understanding summons his adherents, Wrong, Slight, Doubleness, Falseness, Ravin, and Deceit. Then come the servants of Will, named Recklessness, Idleness, Surfeit, Greediness, Spouse-breach, and Fornication. The minstrels striking up a hornpipe, they all dance together till a quarrel breaks out among them, when the eighteen servants are driven off, their masters remaining alone on the stage. Just as these are about to withdraw for a carouse, Wisdom enters: Anima also reappears, "in most horrible wise, fouler than a fiend," and presently gives birth to six of the Deadly Sins; whereupon she perceives what a transformation has befallen her, and Mind, Will, and Understanding learn that they are the cause of it. They having retired, Wisdom opens his mouth in a long speech; after which the three dupes of Lucifer return, renounce their evil ways, and Anima is made happy in their reformation.

These two pieces have come down to us only in manuscript. *A Goodly Interlude of Nature* is a Moral-Play written by Henry Medwall, chaplain to Archbishop Morton, which has descended to us in print. It is in two parts, and at the end of the first part we learn that it was played before Morton himself, who became Primate in 1486, and died in 1500. Like the two foregoing specimens, it was meant to illustrate the strife of good and evil in man.

There are several other pieces in print dating from about the same period. One of them, printed in 1522, and entitled *The World and the Child*, represents man in the five stages of infancy, — boyhood, youth, maturity, and infirmity. Another of them, called *Hick Scorner*, deserves mention chiefly as being perhaps the earliest specimen of a Moral-Play in which some attempt is made at individual character. The piece is somewhat remarkable, also, in having been such a popular favourite, that the phrase "Hick Scorner's jests" grew into use as a proverb, to signify the profane scurrility with which certain persons treated the Scriptures in the reign of Elizabeth.

"*The Necromancer*, written by Master Skelton, Laureate," came from the press in 1504, having been played before the King at Woodstock on Palm Sunday. The piece is now lost; but a copy was seen by Warton, who gave an account of it. As the matter is very curious, I must add a few of its points. The persons are a Conjurer, the Devil, a Notary Public, Simony, and Avarice. The plot is the trial of Simony and Avarice, the Devil being the judge, and the Notary serving as assessor. The Conjurer has little to do but open the subject, evoke the Devil, and summon the court. The prisoners are found guilty, and ordered off straight to Hell: the Devil kicks the Conjurer for waking him too early in the morning; and Simony tries to bribe the Devil, who rejects her offer with indignation. The last scene presents a view of Hell, and a dance between the Devil and the Conjurer; at the close of which the former trips up his partner's heels, and disappears in fire and smoke.

Another piece of Skelton's entitled *Magnificence*, and designed to expose the vanity of worldly grandeur, has survived in print. Magnificence, the hero, being eaten out of substance by his friends and retainers, falls into the hands of Poverty and Adversity: in this state he meets with Despair and Mischief, who furnish him with a knife and halter; he is about killing himself, when Good-hope steps in and stays his arm; Redress, Circumspection, and Perseverance then take him in hand, and wean him from his former passion. The most note-worthy feature of the thing is, that comic incident and dialogue are somewhat made use of, to diversify and enliven the serious parts; which shows the early disposition to weave tragedy and comedy together in one dramatic web.

The play of *Every-man*, printed some time before 1531, opens with a soliloquy by the Deity, lamenting that the people forsake Him for the Seven Deadly Sins. He then summons Death, and sends him after Every-man, who stands for the human race. Death finds him, delivers the message, and tells him to bring his account-book; but allows him to prove his friends. First, he tries Fellowship, who, though ready to murder any one for his sake, declines going with him on his long journey. Next, he tries Kindred, who excuses himself as having "the cramp in his toe." Then he applies to Riches, who also gives him the cold shoulder. At last he resorts to Good-deeds, whom he finds too weak to stand; but she points him to the blank in his book of works. However, she introduces him to Knowledge, who takes him to Confession: there he meets with Strength, Discretion, Beauty, and Five Wits, who undertake to go with him. Arriving at the brink of the grave, he calls on his friends to enter it with him. First, Beauty refuses, then Strength, then Discretion, then Five Wits; even Knowledge deserts him; Good-deeds alone having the virtue to stick by him.

Considering the ecclesiastical origin of the English Drama, it had been something wonderful if, when controversies arose, different sides had not used it in furtherance of their views. In the reign of Henry the Eighth, Bishop Bale, as we have seen, wrote Miracle-Plays for the avowed purpose of advancing the Reformation; and his plays were printed on the Continent in 1538. This, no doubt, was because a royal proclamation had been set forth some years before, forbidding any plays to be performed, or any books printed, in the English tongue, touching matters then in controversy, unless the same had been first allowed by public authority. The King, however, was not at all averse to the stage being used against the Reformers; the purpose of that measure being, so far as regarded plays, to prevent any using of them on the other side.

This is most aptly shown in a notable event that happened in November, 1527. Catholic Europe had just been scandalized beyond measure by the course of Charles the Fifth, who had made war on the Pope, and had actually captured the city of Rome; and who, moreover, was then holding the children of Francis the First as prisoners in Spain. King Henry was mightily stirred up against the Emperor on this account, and was for going into a mortal buffeting with him in behalf of the Holy See. The arrival of a French Embassy at the English Court was the occasion of the event referred to. The Ambassadors were entertained with great splendour by the King at Greenwich; a part of the entertainment being a Moral-Play in Latin, performed by the boys of St. Paul's School. The principal characters were as follows: Religio, Ecclesia, and Veritas, like three widows, in garments of silk, and suits of lawn and cypress; Heresy and False Interpretation, like sisters of Bohemia, apparelled in silk of divers colours; the heretic Luther, like a party friar, in russet damask and black taffety; Luther's wife, like a frau of Spiers, in red silk; Peter, Paul, and James, in habits of white sarcenet, and three red mantles; a Cardinal in his apparel; the Dauphin and his brother, in coats of velvet embroidered with gold; three Germans, in apparel all cut and holed in silk; Lady Peace, in apparel white and rich; Lady Quietness and Dame Tranquillity. The subject of the play was the captivity of the Pope and the oppression of the Church. St. Peter put Cardinal Wolsey in authority to free the Pope and restore the Church; and by his intercession the Kings of England and France took part together, and got the Pope delivered. Then the French King's children complained to the Cardinal that the

Emperor kept them as hostages, and desired him to work for their deliverance, and he effected this also.

This matter is so very curious in several respects, that I give it with more than usual fulness. Only three years later, King Henry himself was quarrelling with the same Pope, and the Emperor was acting as the Pope's champion.

In 1543, an Act of Parliament was passed for the restraining of dramatic performances. The preamble states that divers persons, intending to subvert the true and perfect doctrine of Scripture, have presumed to use in that behalf not only sermons and arguments, but printed books, plays, and songs; and the body of the statute enacts that no person shall play in interludes, sing, or rhyme any matter contrary to the Church of Rome; the penalty being a fine of £10 and three months' imprisonment for the first offence; for the second, forfeiture of all goods, and perpetual imprisonment.

When Edward the Sixth came to the throne, in 1547, legislation took a new turn, and the Act of 1543 was repealed. There arose, however, so great an excess on the part of printers and players, that in 1552 a strong proclamation was issued, forbidding them to print or play any thing without a special license under the sign manual, or under the hands of six of the Privy Council, the penalty being imprisonment without bail, and fine at the King's pleasure.

Soon after the accession of Mary, in 1553, was set forth a proclamation against "busy meddlers in matter of religion, and for redress of preachers, printers, and players"; the intent of which was to prevent the printing or playing of any thing adapted to further the Reformation. The thing seems to have been effectual for more than two years, after which further measures were found necessary. But all would not do; the restraints kept giving way. In 1557, "certain naughty plays" broke loose even in London; and the Lord Mayor was called upon by the Court to discover and arrest the players, and "to take order that no play be made henceforth within the city, except the same be first seen, and the players authorized." Nevertheless Mary was far from discouraging plays and players: on the contrary, she kept up the theatrical establishment of her father to the full. The old Miracle-Plays, being generally of the right Roman Catholic stamp, were revived under the patronage of the Court. In 1556, the play of *Christ's Passion* was presented at the Greyfriars in London, before the Lord Mayor, the Privy Council, and many of the nobility. The next year it was repeated at the same place; and also, on the feast of St. Olave, the miraculous life of that Saint was performed as a stage-play in the church dedicated to him.

Elizabeth succeeded to the crown, November 17, 1558; and in May following she issued a proclamation forbidding any plays or interludes to be performed in the kingdom without special license from the local magistrates; and also ordering that none should be so licensed, wherein either matters of religion or of State were handled. This was probably deemed necessary in consequence of the strong measures which had lately been used for putting down all plays that smacked of the Reformation.

The Moral-Play of *Lusty Juventus*, printed some time after 1551, is full of shots against what are called the superstitions of Rome. Its arguments and positions are exceedingly scriptural, chapter and verse being quoted or referred to with all the exactness of a theological treatise. And the tenets of the new "gospellers" are as openly maintained as those of Rome are impugned. Juventus, the hero, who is bent on going it while he is young, starts out in quest of his companions, to have a merry dance: Good Counsel meets him, warns him of the evil of his ways, and engages him on the spot in a prayer for grace to aid him in his purpose of amendment. Just at this moment Knowledge comes up, and prevails on him to spend his time chiefly in hearing sermons and reading the Scriptures. This puts the Devil in great alarm; he has a soliloquy on the subject, then calls in Hypocrisy, and sets him to work in the cause.

While Juventus is on his way to "hear a preaching," Hypocrisy encounters him, argues with him against forsaking the traditions of his fathers, and diverts him from his purpose. Some while after, Good Counsel finds him in the lowest state of debauchery, and reclaims him; and God's Merciful Promises undertakes to procure his pardon.

The Longer Thou Livest the More Fool Thou Art is the title of a piece probably written early in Elizabeth's reign. Moros, the hero, is represented as an ignorant and vicious fool, thinking of nothing but ballads and songs, and constantly singing scraps of them. Discipline finds him venting this humour, and reproves him; Piety and Exercise add their efforts to reform him, but discover him to be as much knave as fool. The two latter hold him while Discipline lays on the whip, till he affects contrition; but he is soon wheedled into a relapse by Idleness, Incontinence, and Wrath, who, however, profess to hold him in contempt. Wrath gives him the Vice's sword and dagger, and they all promise him the society of Nell, Nan, Meg, and Bess. Fortune then endows him with wealth; he takes Impiety, Cruelty, and Ignorance into his service; Impiety stirs him up against "these new fellows," that is, the Protestants, and he vows to "hang, burn, and kill" them without remorse. When they are gone, People enters, complaining of the hero's cruelty and oppression, but runs off in a fright as soon as he returns. God's Judgment then comes and strikes him down; Confusion follows; they strip off his "goodly gear," and put on him a fool's coat. Being required by Confusion to go with him he replies, —

> " If it please the Devil me to have,
> Let him carry me away on his back."

We are left to infer that Confusion, who is the Devil of the piece, takes him at his word.

The Marriage of Wit and Science is the earliest known instance of a Moral-Play regularly distributed into five Acts, and these again into scenes. The allegory is quite elaborate and wire-drawn; and the piece has something of humour in the matter, and of melody in the versification. *Like Will to Like, Quoth the Devil to the Collier*, printed in 1568, has some rude approaches to individual character; which is my reason for noticing it. Nichol Newfangle, though in fact the hero, enacts the Vice, and is armed with the wooden dagger; among his friends are Ralph Royster, Tom Tosspot, Philip Fleming, Pierce Pickpurse, and Cuthbert Cutpurse, who have some lines of individual peculiarity. To these are added several allegorical personages, as Good Fame, Severity, Virtuous Life, and Honour. Lucifer also figures in the piece; Newfangle claims him as godfather, and is at last carried off by him. *The Conflict of Conscience* is worthy of notice as being one of the earliest germinations of the Historical Drama. The hero, though called Philologus, is avowedly meant for Francis Speira, an Italian lawyer, who, it is said, "forsook the truth of God's Gospel, for fear of the loss of life and worldly goods." The characters of the piece are partly historical, partly allegorical.

If *The Conflict of Conscience* deserves mention as an approach to Tragedy, *Tom Tiler and his Wife* equally deserves it as an early sprout of Comedy. It contains a mixture of allegorical and individual persons, the latter, however, taking the chief part of the action. Tom Tiler has a spouse named Strife, who is not only a great scold, but hugely given to drinking with Sturdy and Tipple. Tiler meets his friend Tom Tailor, an artificer of shreds and patches, and relates his sufferings. Tailor changes clothes with him; in this disguise goes to Strife as her husband, and gives her such a drubbing that she submits. Tiler then resumes his own clothes, goes home, and pities his wife, who, ignorant of the trick, vows she will never love him again: to appease her, he unwarily owns up; whereupon she snatches a stick, and belabours him till he cries out for life; and she declares that Tailor had better eaten her than beaten her. Tiler flies to his friend Tailor, and tells him what has happened; Tailor then falls to beating him; and the lady, coming up just at the time, goes to playing her batteries on them both, until Patience arrives and restores harmony all round, charming the discontent out of Tiler, and the fury out of Strife.

Jack Juggler, "a new interlude for children to play," is somewhat remarkable, not only in that it carries still higher the effort at individual character, but as being one of the oldest pieces founded on a classic original; the author claiming, in his prologue, to have taken "Plautus' first comedy" as his model. Master Bongrace sends his lacquey Jenkin to Dame Coy, his lady-love; but Jenkin loiters to play at dice and steal apples. Jack Juggler, who enacts the Vice, watches him, gets on some clothes just like his, and undertakes to persuade him "that he is not himself, but another man." The task proves too much, till he brings fist-arguments to bear; when Jenkin gives up the point, and makes a comical address to the audience, alleging certain reasons for believing that he is not himself. The humour of the piece turns mainly on this doubt of his identity.

We have many other specimens in the class of Moral-Plays; but, as they are all cast in much the same mould, any further dwelling upon them would accomplish little towards illustrating the progress of the Drama.

COMEDY AND TRAGEDY.

We have seen how the old Miracle-Plays gradually gave way to Moral-Plays, first borrowing some of their materials, then thrown into the background, and finally quite displaced by them. Yet both these forms of the Drama were radically different from Comedy and Tragedy in the proper sense of these terms: there was very little of character or of human blood in them; and even that little was rather forced in by external causes than a free outgrowth from the genius of the thing. The first, in their proper idea and original plan, were but a mechanical collocation of the events of Scripture and old legend, carried on by a sort of personal representatives; the second, a mere procession of abstract ideas rudely and inartificially personified, with something of fantastical drapery thrown around them. So that both alike stood apart from the vitalities of nature and the abiding interests of thought, being indeed quite innocent of the knowledge of them.

Of course it was impossible that such things, themselves the offspring of darkness, should stand the light. None but children in mind could mistake them for truth, or keep up any real sympathy with such unvital motions. Precluded from the endless variety of individual nature and character, they could not but run into great monotony: in fact, the whole thing was at best little more than a repetition of one fundamental air under certain arbitrary variations. As the matter shown was always much the same, the interest had to depend chiefly on the manner of showing it; and this naturally generated a cumbrous and clumsy excess of manner; unless indeed the thing drew beyond itself; while in doing this it could scarce fail to create a taste that would sooner or later force it to withdraw from the scene.

Accordingly, Moral-Plays, as we have seen, began, early in their course, to deviate into veins foreign to their original design: points of native humour and wit, and lines of personal interest were taken in to diversify and relieve the allegorical sameness; and these grew more and more into the main texture of the workmanship. As the new elements gained strength, much of the old treasure proved to be mere refuse and dross; as such it was discarded; while so much of sterling wealth as had been accumulated was sucked in, retained, and carried up into the supervening growth.

The beginnings, then, of English Comedy and Tragedy were made long before these appeared in distinct formation. And the first known hand that drew off the elements of Comedy, and moulded them up by themselves, was John Heywood, who belonged to the theatrical and musical establishment of Henry the Eighth. His pieces, however, have not the form of regular comedies. He called them Interludes, a name in use many years before, and probably adopted by him as indicating the purpose to which he designed them, of filling the gaps or intervals of banquets and other entertainments. They are short, not taking much more time than a single act in an ordinary comedy. Yet they have the substance of comedy, in that they give pictures of real life and manners, containing much sprightliness of dialogue, and not a little of humour and character, and varied with amusing incident and allusion drawn fresh from the writer's observation, with the dews of nature upon them.

Heywood's earliest piece, printed in 1533, is entitled *A merry Play between the Pardoner and the Friar, the Curate and Neighbour Pratt.* A Pardoner and a Friar have each got leave of the Curate to use his church, the one to exhibit his relics, the other to preach a sermon. The Friar comes first, and is about to begin his preachment, when the other enters and disturbs him: each wants to be heard first; and, after a long trial which has the stronger lungs, they fall into a regular performance of mutual kicking and cuffing. The Curate, aroused to the spot by the noise, endeavours to part them; failing of this, he calls in Neighbour Pratt, and then seizes the Friar, leaving Pratt to manage the other, the purpose being to put them both in the stocks. But they get the worst of it altogether; so that they gladly come to terms, allowing the Pardoner and Friar quietly to depart. As a sample of the incidents, I may add that the Friar, while his whole sermon is against covetousness, harps much on the voluntary poverty of his order, and then gives notice of his intention to take up a collection. In a like satirical humour, the Pardoner is made to exhibit some laughable relics, such as "the great toe of the Holy Trinity," and the "blessed jaw-bone" of all the saints in the Calendar. Of course his purpose also is to bless money into his purse.

Another of Heywood's pieces, also printed in 1533, is

called *A merry Play between John the Husband, Tib the Wife, and Sir John the Priest.* Here the comic vein runs out even more freely than in the former piece, and has quite as much relish of home-made observation. Still another of Heywood's pieces, also full of broad fun, and equally smacking of real life, is called *The Four Ps;* while a fourth, called *The Play of the Weather*, has something the character of a Moral-Play, the Vice figuring in it under the name of Merry Report.—Thus much must suffice for indicating the steps taken by Heywood in the direction of genuine Comedy.

An anonymous interlude called *Thersites*, and written in 1537, deserves mention as the oldest dramatic piece in English, with characters purporting to be borrowed from secular history. The piece, however, has nothing of historical matter but the names: it is merely a piece of broad comedy in the vein of English life and manners.

The oldest known specimen of a regular English comedy is *Ralph Roister Doister*, written as early as 1551. It was the work of Nicholas Udall, a name distinguished in the early literature of the Reformation; who, in 1534, was appointed Head-Master of Eton, then famous for teaching the classics, became Prebendary of Windsor in 1551, was afterwards made Head-Master of Westminster School, and died in 1556.

In his prologue the author refers to Plautus and Terence as his models. The play is in five Acts, which are subdivided into scenes; the scene is in London, the persons and manners all English. The hero and heroine are Ralph Roister Doister and Dame Custance, a widow; in the train of the former are Matthew Merrygreek and Harpax; of the latter, Truepenny her man, Madge Mumblecrust her nurse, Tibet Talkapace, and Annot Alyface. The play is opened by Matthew, who enters singing, and expounds his mind in a soliloquy, dilating on his patron's qualities and his own. Presently Ralph comes in talking to himself, and calls on Matthew for counsel and help, as he is dying for love of a lady whose name he does not at first remember, and who, he hears, is engaged to a merchant named Goodluck. Matthew stuffs him with the assurance that his figure is such as no woman can resist, and that the people go into raptures over him as he passes in the streets; all which he greedily swallows. Next, we have a scene of Madge, Tibet, and Annot at their work, praising their good fare, rallying each other, and singing snatches of song: Ralph overhears them, and takes joy to think how happy he shall live with a wife who keeps such servants; strikes up an acquaintance with them, and, after divers comic passages, leaves with Madge a letter for her mistress. The next day Dobinet Doughty comes from Goodluck with a ring and token, which Madge refuses to deliver, she having been scolded for taking Ralph's letter. He tells the servants he is a messenger from their lady's intended husband, but does not mention his name: they are delighted at the prospect of such a change in the family, and almost fall at strife for the honour of carrying the presents to their mistress, who, however, sharply reproves them for taking such things without knowing whence they come.

In the third Act Matthew is sent to reconnoitre, when he learns that the lady's hand is already engaged, and that she has not even read Ralph's letter. Returning, he tells Ralph she will have nothing to do with him, and how she abuses him with opprobrious terms; which puts him to dying for love right on the spot; and Matthew, to help on the joke, calls in the parish clerk and others to sing a mock requiem. As Ralph does not succeed in dying, Matthew counsels him to put on a bold face, and claim the lady's hand in person, after treating her to a serenade. He agrees to this, and while the serenade is in progress the lady enters; he declares his passion; she rejects him with scorn, and returns his letter unread; whereupon Matthew reads it in her hearing, but so varies the pointing as to turn the sense all upside down; and Ralph denies it to be his. As soon as she has left them, Matthew goes to refreshing him again with extravagant praise of his person, wishing himself a woman for his sake, and advising him to hold off awhile, as this will soon bring her to terms. Ralph consents to try this course, and swears vengeance against the scrivener who copied his letter; but in the scrivener's reading it is found all right, and Matthew is seen to be the true culprit.

In the fourth Act Sim Suresby comes from Goodluck to salute the lady on his master's return from a voyage; while they are talking, Ralph arrives with Matthew, and addresses her as his spouse; whereupon Sim, thinking them married, goes to inform his master what seems to have happened in his absence. The lady, full of grief and anger at this staining of her good name, calls on her man and maids to drive out Ralph and Matthew, who quickly retreat, but threaten to return. Matthew now contrives to let the lady know that he has joined with Ralph only to make fun of him. In due time, Ralph comes back armed with kitchen utensils and a popgun, and attended by Matthew and Harpax. The issue of the scrape is, that the lady and her maids beat off the assailants with mop and broom; Matthew managing to have all his blows light on Ralph.

The fifth Act opens with the arrival of Goodluck and his man Sim, both persuaded of the lady's infidelity. She proceeds to welcome him with much affection, but he draws back, and calls for an explanation: she protests her innocence, and refers him to her friend Tristram Trusty. This brings about the conclusion, the wedding of Goodluck and Custance being appointed, and Ralph and Matthew being invited to it.

The piece, its date considered, is certainly one of no little merit: it has considerable wit and humour, in which there is nothing coarse or vulgar; the dialogue abounds in variety and spirit, and the characters are well discriminated and life-like. The idea of Merrygreek was evidently caught from the old Vice; but his love of sport and mischief is without malignity, and the interest of his part is in the character, not in the trimmings. The play is written in lines of unequal length, and with nothing to mark them as verse but the rhymes.

Misogonus, a piece which has lately come to light, appears from internal evidence to have been written about 1560. The scene is laid in Italy, but the manners and allusions are English, while the persons have Greek and Roman names significant of their tempers or positions. Here, again, the characterization is diversified and sustained with no little skill, while many of the incidents and situations are highly diverting. Perhaps the most noteworthy feature of the play is Cacurgus, a specimen of the professional domestic Fool that succeeded the old Vice. And he is one of the most remarkable instances of his class that have survived; there being no other play of so early a date wherein the part is used with so much skill. Before his master, who is the hero, Cacurgus commonly affects the simpleton, but at other times is full of versatile shrewdness and waggish mischief. He is usually called, both by himself and others, Will Summer; as though he were understood to model his action after the celebrated court Fool of Henry the Eighth.

An analysis of the plot would occupy too much space; besides, the piece, with all its merit, does not really offer much towards illustrating the matter of dramatic progress: it only shows that the spirit of improvement was alive in more minds than one. Perhaps I ought to add, that the events of the play extend over a considerable period of time; yet the unity of action is so well maintained, that the diversities of time do not press upon the thoughts. On the whole, it is clear that even at that date the principles of the Gothic Drama were vigorously at work, preparing that magnificent fruitage of art which came to full harvest, ere she who then sat on the English throne was taken to her rest.

Hitherto we have met with no instance of regular tragedy, which was in England of later growth than comedy; though we have seen that some beginnings of tragedy were made in the older species of drama. *The Tragedy of Gorboduc*, or, as it is sometimes called, *Of Ferrex and Porrex*, is on several accounts deserving of special attention. It was acted before the Queen at Whitehall, by gentlemen of the Inner Temple, in January, 1562; and was printed in 1565, the title-page informing us that three Acts were written by Thomas Norton, and the last two by Thomas Sackville. Norton made and published a translation of Calvin's *Institutes*, which went through five editions during his lifetime. Sackville, afterwards Earl of Dorset, succeeded Burghley as Lord Treasurer in 1599, which office he held till his death, in 1608; and was eulogized by divers pens, Lord Bacon's being one, for his eloquence, his learning, his charity, and integrity.

Warton's statement of the plot is brief and accurate, as follows: "Gorboduc, a king of Britain about six hundred years before Christ, made in his lifetime a division of his kingdom to his two sons Ferrex and Porrex. The two young princes within five years quarrelled for universal sovereignty. A civil war ensued, and Porrex slew his elder brother Ferrex. Their mother, Videna, who loved Ferrex best, revenged his death by entering Porrex's chamber in the night, and murdering him in his sleep. The people, exasperated at the cruelty and treachery of this murder, rose in rebellion, and killed both Gorboduc and Videna. The nobility then assembled, collected an army, and destroyed the rebels. An intestine war commenced between the chief lords; the succession of the crown became uncertain and arbitrary, for want of a lineal royal issue; and the country, destitute of a king, and wasted by domestic slaughter, was reduced to a state of the most miserable desolation."

Each Act of the tragedy is preceded by a dumb-show significant of what is forthcoming, and the first four are followed by choruses, moralizing the events. But the most notable fact about it is, that all except the choruses is in blank-verse; in which respect it was a great and noble innovation. And the versification runs abundantly smooth; beyond which little can be said in its favour; though that was a good deal for the time. With considerable force of thought and language, the speeches are excessively formal, stately, and didactic; every thing is told, nothing represented; the dialogue is but a series of studied declamation, without any pulses of life, or any relish of individual traits; in brief, all is mere State rhetoric speaking in the same vein, now from one mouth, now from another. From the subject-matter, the unities of time and place are necessarily disregarded, while there is no continuity of action or character to lift it above the circumscriptions of sense. The Acts and scenes follow one another without any innate principle of succession: there is nothing like an organic composition of the parts, no weaving of them together by any law of dramatic sequence and development. Still, the piece marks an era in the English Drama. In the single article of blank-verse, though having all the monotony of the most regular rhyming versifier, it did more for dramatic improvement than, perhaps, could have been done in a century without that step being taken.

The Supposes, translated from the Italian of Ariosto by George Gascoigne, and acted at Gray's Inn in 1566, is chiefly remarkable as being the oldest extant play in English prose. *Jocasta*, also acted at Gray's Inn the same year, is the second known play in blank-verse. It was avowedly taken from Euripides, but can hardly be called a translation, since it makes "many omissions, retrenchments, and transpositions"; though the main substance of the original is retained.

The example of making English plays out of Italian novels appears to have been first set, unless the lost play of *Romeo and Juliet* should be excepted, in 1568, when the tragedy of *Tancred and Gismunda* was performed before Elizabeth at the Inner Temple. It was the work of five persons, each contributing an Act, and one of them being Christopher Hatton, afterwards known as Elizabeth's "dancing Chancellor." Except in the article of blank-verse, the writers seem to have taken *Gorboduc* as their model; each Act beginning with a dumb-show, and ending with a chorus. The play was founded on one of Boccaccio's tales, an English version of which had recently appeared in *The Palace of Pleasure.*

The accounts of the revels from 1568 to 1580 furnish the titles of fifty-two dramas performed at Court, none of which have survived. Of these fifty-two pieces, judging by the titles, eighteen were on classical subjects; twenty-one on subjects from modern history, romance, and other tales; while seven may be classed as comedies, and six as Moral-Plays. It is to be noted, also, that at this time the Master of the Revels was wont to have different sets of players rehearse their pieces before him, and then to choose such of them as he judged fit for royal ears; which infers that the Court rather followed than led the popular taste.

This may probably be taken as a fair indication how far the older species of drama still kept its place on the stage. Moral-Plays lingered in occasional use till long after this period; and we even hear of Miracle-Plays performed now and then till after the death of Elizabeth. And this was much more the case, no doubt, in the country towns and villages than in the metropolis, as the growing life of thought could not but beat lustiest at the heart; and of course all the rest of the nation could not bridle Innovation, spurred as she was by the fierce competition of wit in London.

Certain parts, however, of the Moral-Plays had vigour enough, it appears, to propagate themselves into the drama of comedy and tragedy after the main body of them had been withdrawn. An apt instance of this is furnished in *A Knack to know a Knave*, entered at the Stationers' in 1593, but written several years before. It was printed in 1594, the title-page stating that it had been "acted sundry times by Edward Alleyn and his company," and that it contained "Kempe's applauded merriments of the men of Gotham." *

The play is made up partly of allegorical personages, partly of historical; the chief of the latter being King Edgar, St. Dunstan, Ethenwald, Osrick, and his daughter Alfrida. From reports of Alfrida's beauty, Edgar gets so enamoured of her, that he sends Ethenwald, Earl of Cornwall, to court her for him. The Earl, being already in love with the lady, wants to court her for himself. Introduced by her father, his passion gets the better of his commission; he woos and wins her, and has her father's consent. On his return, he tells Edgar she will do very well for an earl, but not for a king: Edgar distrusts his report, and goes to see for himself, when Ethenwald tries to pass off the kitchen-maid as Alfrida: the trick is detected, Dunstan counsels forgiveness, and Edgar generously renounces his claim. There is but one scene of "Kempe's applauded merriments," and this consists merely of a blundering dispute, whether a mock petition touching the consumption of ale shall be presented to the King by a cobbler or a smith.

As to the allegorical persons, it is worth noting that several of these have individual designations, as if the author had some vague ideas of representative character, — that is, persons standing for classes, yet clothed with individuality, — but lacked the skill to work them out. Such is the Bailiff of Hexham, who represents the iniquities of local magistrates. He has four sons, — Walter, representing the frauds of farmers; Priest, the sins of the clergy; Coney-catcher, the tricks of cheats; and Perin, the vices of courtiers. Besides these, we have Honesty, whose business it is to expose crimes and vices. The Devil makes his appearance several times, and, when the old Bailiff dies, carries

* Alleyn, the founder of Dulwich College, was the leading actor of the Lord Admiral's company; and, after the death of Tarlton in 1588, Kempe, who at a later period was of the same company with Shakespeare, bore the palm as an actor of comic parts.

him off. At last, Honesty exposes the crimes of all classes to the King, who has justice done on their representatives.—The piece is in blank-verse, and in respect of versification shows considerable improvement on the specimens hitherto noticed.

SHAKESPEARE'S CONTEMPORARIES.

TOUCHING the general state of the Drama a few years before Shakespeare took hold of it, our information is full and clear, not only in the specimens that have survived, but in the criticisms of contemporary writers. A good deal of the criticism, however, is so mixed up with personal and polemical invective, as to be unworthy of much credit. George Whetstone, in the dedication of his *Promos and Cassandra*, published in 1578, tells us: "The Englishman in this quality is most vain, indiscreet, and out of order. He first grounds his work on impossibilities; then in three hours he runs through the world, marries, makes children men, men to conquer kingdoms, murder monsters, and bringeth gods from Heaven, and fetcheth devils from Hell. And, that which is worst, many times, to make mirth, they make a clown companion with a king; in their grave counsels they allow the advice of Fools; yea, they use one order of speech for all persons, — a gross indecorum." — In 1581, Stephen Gosson published a tract in which he says: "Sometimes you shall see nothing but the adventures of an amorous knight, passing from country to country for the love of his lady, encountering many a terrible monster made of brown paper; and at his return so wonderfully changed, that he cannot be known but by some posy in his tablet, or by a broken ring, or a handkerchief, or a piece of cockle-shell." And in another part of the same tract he tells us that "*The Palace of Pleasure*, *The Ethiopian History*, *Amadis of France*, and *The Round Table*, comedies in Latin, French, Italian, and Spanish, have been thoroughly ransacked, to furnish the play-houses in London." Which shows very clearly what direction the public taste was then taking. The matter and method of the old dramas, and all "such musty fopperies of antiquity," would no longer do: there was an eager though ignorant demand for something wherein the people might find or fancy themselves touched by the real currents of nature. And, as prescription was thus set aside, and art still ungrown, the materials of history and romance, foreign tales and plays, any thing that could furnish incidents and a plot, were blindly pressed into the service.

Whatever discredit may attach to the foregoing extracts on the score of prejudice or passion, nothing of the sort can hold in the case of Sir Philip Sidney, whose *Defence of Poesy*, though not printed till 1595, must have been written before 1586, in which year the author died. "Our tragedies and comedies," says he, "are not without cause cried out against, observing rules neither of honest civility nor skilful poetry. You shall have Asia of the one side, and Afric of the other, and so many other under-kingdoms, that the player, when he comes in, must ever begin with telling where he is, or else the tale will not be conceived. Now you shall have three ladies walk to gather flowers, and then we must believe the stage to be a garden: by-and-by we hear news of a shipwreck in the same place; then we are to blame if we accept it not for a rock. Upon the back of that, comes out a hideous monster with fire and smoke, and then the miserable beholders are bound to take it for a cave; while in the mean time two armies fly in, represented with four swords and bucklers, and then what hard heart will not receive it for a pitched field? Now, of time they are much more liberal; for ordinary it is, that two young princes fall in love; after many traverses she is delivered of a fair boy; he is lost, groweth a man, falleth in love, and all this in two hours' space: which how absurd it is in sense, even sense may imagine, and art hath taught, and all ancient examples justified. But, besides these gross absurdities, all their plays be neither right tragedies nor right comedies, mingling kings and clowns, not because the matter so carrieth it, but thrust in the clown by head and shoulders, to play a part in majestical matters with neither decency nor discretion."

From all which it is evident enough that very little if any heed was then paid to dramatic propriety and decorum. It was not *merely* that the unities of place and time were set at nought, but that events and persons were thrown together without *any* order or law; unconnected with each other save to the senses, while at the same time according to sense they were far asunder. It is also manifest that the principles of the Gothic Drama in respect of general structure and composition, in disregard of the minor unities, and in the free blending and interchange of the comic and tragic elements, were thoroughly established; though not yet moulded up with sufficient art to shield them from the just censure and ridicule of sober judgment and good taste. Here was a great work to be done; greater than any art then known was sufficient for. Without this, any thing like an original or national drama was impossible. Sir Philip saw the chaos about him; but he did not see, and none could foresee, the creation that was to issue from it. He would have spoken very differently, no doubt, had he lived to see the intrinsic relations of character and passion, the vital sequence of mental and moral development, set forth in such clearness and strength, the whole fabric resting on such solid grounds of philosophy, and charged with such cunning efficacies of poetry, that breaches of local and chronological succession either pass without notice, or are noticed only for the gain of truth and nature that is made through them. For the laws of sense hold only as the thoughts are absorbed in what is sensuous and definite; and the very point was, to lift the mind above this by working on its imaginative forces, and penetrating it with the light of relations more inward and essential.

At all events, it was by going ahead, and not by retreating, that modern thought was to find its proper dramatic expression. The foundation of principles was settled, and stood ready to be built upon whenever the right workman should come. Moreover public taste was sharp for something warm with life, so much so indeed as to keep running hither and thither after the shabbiest semblances of it, but still unable to rest with them. The national mind, in discarding, or rather outgrowing the older species of drama, had worked itself into contact with Nature. And it was the uncritical, popular, living, practical mind that was to give the law in this business: nothing was to be achieved either by the word or the work of those learned folk who would not be pleased unless they could parse their pleasure by the rules of ancient grammar. But to reproduce nature in mental forms requires great power of art, much greater, perhaps, than minds educated amidst works of art can well conceive.

Which brings me to the matter of Shakespeare's SENIOR CONTEMPORARIES. For here, again, the process was gradual. Neither may we affirm that nothing had yet been done towards organizing the collected materials. But the methods and faculties of art were scattered here and there; different parts of the thing had been worked out severally; and it yet remained to draw and knit them all up together. It is difficult, perhaps impossible, to determine exactly by whom the first steps were taken in this work. But all that was done of much consequence, Shakespeare apart, may be found in connection with the three names of George Peele, Robert Greene, and Christopher Marlowe.

PEELE took his first degree at Oxford in 1577, and became Master of Arts in 1579. Soon after this, he is supposed to have gone to London as a literary adventurer. Dissipation and debauchery were especially rife at that time among the authors by profession, who hung in large numbers upon the metropolis, haunting its taverns and ordinaries; and it is but too certain that Peele plunged deeply into the vices of his class.

His first dramatic work, *The Arraignment of Paris*, was printed in 1584, the title-page stating that it had been played before the Queen by the children of her chapel. The piece is vastly superior to any thing known to have preceded it. It is avowedly a pastoral drama, and sets forth a whole troop of gods and goddesses; with nothing that can properly be called delineation of character. The plot is simply this: Juno, Pallas, and Venus get at strife who shall have the apple of discord which Até has thrown among them, with directions that it be given to the fairest. As each thinks herself the fairest, they agree to refer the question to Paris, the Trojan shepherd, who, after mature deliberation, awards the golden ball to Venus. An appeal is taken: he is arraigned before Jupiter in a synod of the gods for having rendered a partial and unjust sentence; but defends himself so well, that their godships are at a loss what to do. At last, by Apollo's advice, the matter is referred to Diana, who, as she wants no lovers, cares little for beauty. Diana sets aside all their claims, and awards the apple to Queen Elizabeth; which verdict gives perfect satisfaction all round.

The piece displays fair gifts of poetry; it abounds in natural and well-proportioned sentiment; thoughts and images seem to rise up fresh from the writer's observation, and not merely gathered at second hand; a considerable portion is in blank-verse, but the author uses various measures, in all which his versification is graceful and flowing.

The Battle of Alcazar, written as early as 1589, but not printed till 1594, is a strange performance, and nearly as worthless as strange; full of tearing rant and fustian; while the action, if such it may be called, goes it with prodigious license, jumping to and fro between Portugal and Africa without remorse. I have some difficulty in believing the piece to be Peele's: certainly it is not in his vein, nor, as to that matter, in anybody's else; for it betrays at every step an ambitious imitation of Marlowe, wherein, as usually happens, the faults of the model are exaggerated, and the virtues not reached. Peele could hardly have been cast into such an ecstasy of disorder, but from a wild attempt to rival the author of *Tamburlaine*, which is several times referred to in the piece.

King Edward the First, printed in 1593, and probably written later than the preceding, is much better every way. But its chief claim to notice is as an early attempt in the Historical Drama, which Shakespeare brought to such perfection. The character of Edward is portrayed with considerable spirit and truth to history, and is perhaps Peele's best effort in that line. On the other hand, Queen Elinor of Castile is shockingly disfigured, and this, not only in contempt of history, which might be borne with if it really enriched the scene, but to the total disorganizing of the part itself; the purpose being, no doubt, to gratify the bitter national antipathy to the Spaniards. Peele seems to have been incapable of the proper grace and delectation of comedy: nevertheless the part of Prince Lluellen, of Wales, and his adherents, who figure pretty largely, and sometimes in the disguise of Robin Hood and his merry men, shows something of comic talent, and adds to the entertainment of the piece. The other comic portions have nothing to recommend them.

The Old Wives' Tale, printed in 1595, is little worth mention save as having probably contributed somewhat to one of the noblest and sweetest poems ever written. — Two brothers are wandering in quest of their sister, whom Sacrapant, an enchanter, has imprisoned: they call her name, and Echo replies; whereupon Sacrapant gives her a potion that induces self-oblivion. His magical powers depend on a wreath which encircles his head, and on a light enclosed in glass which he keeps hidden under the turf. The brothers afterwards meet with an old man, also skilled in magic, who enables them to recover their sister. A Spirit in the likeness of a young page comes to Sacrapant, tears off his wreath, and kills him. Still the sister remains enchanted, and cannot be released till the glass is broken and the light extinguished; which can only be done by a Lady who is neither maid, wife, nor widow. The Spirit blows a magical horn, and the Lady appears, breaks the glass, and puts out the light. A curtain being then withdrawn discovers the sister asleep; she is disenchanted, joins her brothers, and the Spirit vanishes. — The resemblance to Milton's *Comus* need not be pointed out. The difference of the two pieces in all points of execution is literally immense; Peele's work in this case being all steeped in meanness and vulgarity, without a touch of truth, poetry, or wit.

The Love of King David and Fair Bethseba is commonly regarded as Peele's masterpiece. And here, again, we breathe the genuine air of nature and simplicity. The piece is all in blank-verse, which, though wanting in variety, is replete with melody; and it has passages of tenderness and pathos such as to invest it with an almost sacred charm. There is perhaps a somewhat too literal adherence to the Scripture narrative, and very little art used in the ordering and disposing of the materials, for Peele was neither strong nor happy in the gift of invention; but the characters generally are seized in their most peculiar traits, and presented with a good degree of vigour and discrimination; while at the same time their more prominent features are not worked into disproportion with the other parts.

Peele's contributions to the Drama were mainly in the single article of poetry: here his example was so marked, that it was bound to be respected and emulated by all who undertook to work in the same field. In the development of character, and in the high art of dramatic composition and organization, he added very little; his genius being far unequal to this high task, and his judgment still more so. And his efforts were probably rendered fitful and unsteady by vicious habits; which may explain why it was that he who could do so well sometimes did so meanly. Often, no doubt, when reduced to extreme shifts, he patched up his matter loosely and trundled it off in haste, to replenish his wasted means, and start him on a fresh course of riot and debauchery.

Greene, inferior to Peele as a whole, surpassed him however in fertility and aptness of invention, in quickness and luxuriousness of fancy, and in the right seizing and placing of character, especially for comic effect. In his day he was vastly notorious both as a writer and a man; — a cheap counterfeit of fame which he achieved with remarkable ease, and seems not to have coveted any thing better. He took his first degree at Cambridge in 1578, proceeded Master of Arts in 1583, and was incorporated at Oxford in 1588; after which he was rather fond of styling himself "Master of Arts in both Universities." Soon after 1585, if not before, he betook himself to London, where he speedily sank into the worst type of a literary adventurer. Thenceforth his life seems to have been one continual spasm, plunging hither and thither in transports of wild profligacy and repentance. He died in 1592, eaten up with diseases purchased by sin.

Much of Greene's notoriety during his lifetime grew from his prose writings, which, in the form of tracts, were rapidly thrown off, and were well adapted both in matter and style to catch a loud but transient popularity. One of them had the honour of being laid under contribution for *The Winter's Tale.* In these pieces, generally, the most striking features are a constant affecting of the euphuistic style which John Lily had rendered popular, and a certain incontinence of metaphors and classical allusions, the issue of a full and ready memory unrestrained by taste or judgment; the writer galloping on from page to page with unflagging volubility, himself evidently captivated with the rolling sound of his own sentences. Still, his descriptions often have a warmth and height of colouring that could not fail to take prodigiously in an age when severity or delicacy of taste was none of the commonest. Several of his prose pieces are liberally interspersed with passages of poetry, in which he uses a variety of measures, and most of them with an easy, natural skill, while his cast of thought and imagery shows him by no means a stranger to the springs of poetic sweetness and grace, though he never rises to any thing like grandeur.

The History of Orlando Furioso was acted as early as 1591, and probably written some time before. The plot was partly founded on Ariosto's romance, partly invented by Greene himself. The action, or what stands for such, is conducted with the wildest license, and shows no sense or idea of dramatic truth, but only a prodigious straining after stage effect; the writer trying, apparently, how many men of different nations, European, African, and Asiatic, he could huddle in together, and how much love, rivalry, and fighting he could put them through in the compass of five Acts. As for the fury of Orlando, it is as far from the method of madness as from the logic of reason; being none other than the incoherent jargon of one endeavouring to talk stark nonsense.

Alphonsus, King of Arragon, belongs, by internal marks, to about the same period as the preceding, but is not known to have been printed till 1597. Each Act opens with a chorus by Venus. Medea, also, is employed to work enchantments, and raises Homer's Calchas, who comes forth "clad in a white surplice and a cardinal's mitre." This play, too, is crammed from first to last brimful of tumult and battle; the scene changing between Italy and Turkey with admirable lawlessness; and Christians of divers nations, Turks, and a band of Amazonian warriors, bestriding the stage with their monstrous din.

Both of these pieces are mainly in blank-verse, with a frequent interspersing of couplets. In the latter piece, allusion is made to "the mighty Tamburlaine," thus indicating the height which Greene was striving to reach, if not surpass. In fact, both pieces have plenty of Marlowe's thunder, but none of his lightning. Even the blank-verse reads like that of one accustomed to rhyme, and unable to get out of his wonted rut. And the versification runs, throughout, in a stilted monotony, the style being made thick and turgid with high-sounding epithets; while we have a perfect flux of learned impertinence. As for truth, nature, character, poetry, we look for them in vain; though there is much, in the stage noise and parade, that might keep the multitude from perceiving the want of them.

In *The Scottish History of James the Fourth*, probably written some time after the two preceding, the author seems to have got convinced that imitation of Marlowe was not his line, and that he could do best by working his own native vein: accordingly, considerable portions of it are in prose and rhyme; while the style throughout is disciplined into a tolerable degree of sobriety and simplicity. Though purporting to be a history, it has scarce any thing of historical matter. It opens with a comic scene betwixt Oberon, King of Fairies, and Bohan, an old Scottish lord, who, disgusted with the vices of Court, city, and country, has withdrawn from the world with his two sons, Slipper and Nano, turned Stoic, lives in a tomb, and talks broad Scotch. King Oberon has nothing in common with the fairy king of *A Midsummer Night's Dream*, except the name. The main plot of the drama is as follows:

King James marries Dorothea, the daughter of Arius, King of England. Before the wedding is fairly over, he falls in love with Ida, the Countess of Arran's daughter, makes suit to her, and is rejected with horror. He then sets himself to work to get rid of his Queen, turns away from his old counsellors, and gives his ear to an unscrupulous parasite named Ateukin. Through his influence, the King forms a scheme for assassinating the Queen; who gets information of the plot, disguises herself in male attire, and escapes, with Nano in her company. The parasite's agent overtakes her, finds out who she is, fights with her, and leaves her for dead. During the fight, Nano runs for help, and soon returns with Sir Cuthbert Anderson, who takes her to his house, where her wounds are healed, both Sir Cuthbert and his wife supposing her all the while to be a man. Meanwhile Ida gives herself in marriage to Lord Eustace, with whom she has suddenly fallen in love upon his asking her hand. The King now begins to be devoured by compunctions on account of the Queen, believing her to be dead. The King of England also gets intelligence how his daughter has been treated, and makes war on her husband. When they are on the eve of a decisive battle, Dorothea makes her appearance, to the astonishment of all the parties: she pleads tenderly for her repentant husband, and a general reconciliation takes place; Ateukin and his abettors being delivered over to their deserts.

This play has something of what may not unworthily be called character. The parts of Ida and the Queen are not without delicacy and pathos, showing that the author was not far from some right ideas of what womanhood is. Ateukin's part, too, is very well conceived and sustained, though the qualities of a parasite are made rather too naked and bald, as would naturally result from the writer's ambition being stronger than his love of nature and truth. The comic portions are much beyond any thing we have met with in that line, since *Ralph Roister Doister* and *Misogonus*. The versification is endurably free from gas, and the style in many parts may be pronounced rather tight and sinewy.

Friar Bacon and Friar Bungay was printed in 1594, but acted as early as 1591. The hero is Edward, Prince of Wales, afterwards King Edward the First; the heroine, Margaret, a keeper's daughter, known as "the fair maid of Fressingfield." The Prince, who is out on a hunting excursion with Lacy and several other friends, and Ralph Simnel, the Court Fool, meets with Margaret, and his fancy is at once smitten with her, while she has no suspicion who he is. At Ralph's suggestion, he sends Lacy, in the disguise of a farmer's son, to court Margaret for him, and sets out on a visit to Friar Bacon at Oxford, to learn from the conjurer how his suit is going to speed. Lacy thinks the Prince's aim is not to wed the girl, but to entrap and beguile her; besides, his own heart is already interested; so he goes to courting her in good earnest for himself. Meanwhile the Prince with his company, all disguised, arrives at Friar Bacon's; and, through the conjurer's art, learns what Lacy is doing. Soon after, he comes upon Lacy, poniard in hand, meaning to kill him on the spot. Margaret, being present, intercedes for her lover, and takes all the blame of his course to herself. The Prince then lays siege to her in person, but she vows she will rather die with Lacy than divorce her heart from his, and finally reminds him of his own princely honour; whereupon he frankly resigns her to his rival's hand.

Among other entertainments of the scene, we have a trial of national skill between Bacon and Bungay on one side, and Vandermast, a noted conjurer from Germany, on the other. First, Bungay tries his art, and is thoroughly baffled by the German; then Bacon takes Vandermast in hand, and outconjures him all to nothing. Bacon has a servant named Miles, who, for his ignorant blundering in a weighty matter, is at last carried off by one of his master's devils. The last scene is concerned with the marriage of Prince Edward and Elinor of Castile, and is closed by Bacon with a grand prophecy touching Elizabeth.

Here, again, we have some fair lines of characterization, especially in the Prince, Lacy, Margaret, and Ralph. The heroine is altogether Greene's masterpiece in female character; she exhibits much strength, spirit, and sweetness of composition; in fact, she is not equalled by any woman of the English stage till we come to Shakespeare, whom no one has ever approached in that line. It scarce need be said that the play is quite guiltless of any thing worthy to be named *dramatic composition*. But it has a good deal of dramatic poetry, that would be almost charming, had not Shakespeare spoilt every thing of the kind that was done before he taught men how to do it.

The comedy of *George a Greene, the Pinner of Wakefield*, printed in 1599, is ascribed to Greene, but, it seems to me, not on very strong grounds. I can hardly believe it his; certainly the style and versification are much better than in any other of his plays; nor does it show any thing of that incontinence of learning which he seems to have been unable to restrain. The blank-verse, too, is far unlike Greene's anywhere else.

The story of the piece is quite entertaining in itself, and is set forth with a good deal of vivacity and spirit. Among the characters are King Edward of England, King James of Scotland, the Earl of Kendall, with other lords, and Robin Hood. George a Greene is the hero; who, what with his wit, and what with his strength, gets the better of all the other persons in turn. Withal he is full of high and solid manhood, and his character is drawn with more vigour and life than any hitherto noticed. The piece opens with the Earl of Kendall and his adherents in rebellion against the State. The Earl sends Sir Nicholas Mannering to Wakefield, to demand provision for his camp. Sir Nicholas enters the town, and shows his commission: the magistrates are at a loss what to do, till the hero comes amongst them, outfaces the messenger, tears up his commission, makes him eat the seals, and sends him back with an answer of defiance.

Greene was concerned, along with Thomas Lodge, in writing another extant play, entitled *A Looking-Glass for London and England.* This is little better than a piece of stage trash, being a mixture of comedy, tragedy, and Miracle-Play; an Angel, a Devil, and the Prophet Hosea taking part in the action. The verse parts are in Greene's puffiest style, the prose parts in his filthiest.

Greene probably wrote divers other plays, but none others have survived that are known to be his.

Marlowe, the greatest of Shakespeare's senior contemporaries, was baptized in St. George's church, Canterbury, on the 26th of February, 1564, just two months before the baptism of Shakespeare. He took his first degree at Cambridge in 1583, became Master of Arts in 1587, and was soon after embarked among the worst literary adventurers in London, living by his wits, and rioting on the quick profits of his pen. His career was brief, but fruitful, — fruitful in more senses than one. He was slain by one Francis Archer in a brawl, on the 1st of June, 1593.

His first dramatic work was *Tamburlaine the Great*, in two parts; printed in 1590, but written before 1588. In this work, what Ben Jonson describes as "Marlowe's mighty line" is out in all its mightiness. The lines, to be sure, have a vast amount of strut and swell in them, but then they also have a good deal of real energy and force. Marlowe has had much praise, perhaps more than his due, as the introducer of blank-verse on the public stage; it being alleged that the previous use of it was only in what may be called private theatricals. Be that as it may, he undoubtedly did much towards *fixing* it as the habit of English dramatic poetry. *Tamburlaine* had a sudden, a great, and long-continued popularity. And its success may have been partly owing to its faults, inasmuch as the public ear, long used to rhyme, needed some compensation in the way of grandiloquent stuffing, which was here supplied in abundance.

The scene of these two plays, which are substantially one, takes in the whole period of time from the hero's first conquest till his death; so that the action ranges at large over divers kingdoms and empires. Except the hero, there is little really deserving the name of characterization, this being a point of art which Marlowe had not yet reached, and which he never attained but in a moderate degree, taking Shakespeare as the standard. But the hero is drawn with grand and striking proportions, and perhaps seems the larger, that the bones of his individuality stand out in undue prominence; the author lacking that balance of powers which is requisite, to produce the symmetry and roundness met with in the higher forms of Nature. And he knew not, apparently, how to express the hero's greatness *in word*, but by making him bethump the stage with tempestuous verbiage; which, to be sure, is not the style of greatness at all, but only of one trying to be great, and *trying* to be so, because he is not so. For to talk big is the instinct of ambitious littleness. But Tamburlaine is also represented *in act* as a most magnanimous prodigy: amidst his haughtiest strides of conquest, we have strains of gentleness mingling with his iron sternness; and he everywhere appears lifted high with generous passions and impulses: if he regards not others, he is equally ready to sacrifice himself, his ease, pleasure, and even life, in his prodigious lust of glory.

As to the rest, this drama consists rather of a long series of speeches than any genuine dialogue. And the persons all speak from one brain, the hero talking just like the others, only more so; as if the author had no way to discriminate character but by different degrees of the same thing: in which respect the work has often reminded me of divers more civilized stage preparations, such as Addison's *Cato*, Young's *Revenge, et id genus omne*. For the proper constituent of dramatic dialogue is, that the persons strike fire out of each other by their sharp collisions of thought, so that their words relish at once of the individual speaking and the individual spoken to. Moreover the several parts of this work are not moulded together in any thing like vital unity; the materials seem bundled up arbitrarily, and for stage effect, instead of being assorted on any principle of organic coherence; every thing thus going by the author's will, not by any law of reason or art. But this is a high region, from which there was in that age but one man big enough to be seen; so it 's no use speaking of the rest. Therewithal the work affects us, throughout, as a dead-level of superlatives; everywhere we have nearly the same boisterous wind of tragical storm-and-stress: so that the effect is much like that of a picture all foreground, with no perspective, no proportionateness of light and shade, to give us distinct impressions.

The Jew of Malta shows very considerable advance towards a chaste and sober diction, but not much either in development of character or composition of parts. Barabas the Jew is a horrible monster of wickedness and cunning, yet not without strong lines of individuality. The author evidently sought to compass the effect of tragedy by accumulation of murders and other hellish deeds; which shows that he had no steady ideas as to wherein the true secret of tragic terror lies: he here strives to reach it by overfilling the senses; whereas its proper method stands in the joint working of the moral and imaginative powers, which are rather stifled than kindled by causing the senses to "sup full of horrors." The piece, however, abounds in quick and caustic wit; in some parts there is a good share of dialogue as distinguished from speech-making; and the versification is far more varied and compact than in *Tamburlaine.* Still the work, as a whole, shows little that can properly be called dramatic power as distinguished from the general powers of rhetoric and wit.

The Tragical History of Doctor Faustus, probably written before 1590, exhibits Marlowe in a higher vein of workmanship. I think it must be acknowledged that he here wields the right elements and processes of tragic effect with no ordinary subtlety and power. Faustus, the hero, is a mighty necromancer, who has studied himself into direct communion with preternatural beings, and beside whom Friar Bacon sinks into a tame forger of bugbears. A Good Angel and a Bad Angel figure in the piece, each trying to win Faustus to his several way. Lucifer is ambitious to possess "his gorious soul," and the hero craves Lucifer's aid, that he may work wonders on the Earth. At his summons, Mephistophilis, who acts as Lucifer's prime minister, visits him to negotiate an arrangement. I must quote a brief passage from their interview:

"*Faust.* Tell me, what is that Lucifer thy lord?
Meph. Arch-regent and commander of all spirits.
Faust. Was not that Lucifer an angel once?
Meph. Yes, Faustus, and most dearly lov'd of God.
Faust. How comes it, then, that he is Prince of Devils?

Meph. O, by aspiring pride and insolence !
For which God threw him from the face of Heaven.
Faust. And what are you that live with Lucifer ?
Meph. Unhappy spirits that fell with Lucifer,
And are for ever damn'd with Lucifer.
Faust. Where are you damn'd ?
Meph. In Hell.
Faust. How comes it, then, that thou art out of Hell
Meph. *Why, this is Hell, nor am I out of it :*
Think'st thou that I, who saw the face of God,
And tasted the eternal joys of Heaven,
Am not tormented with ten thousand hells
In being depriv'd of everlasting bliss ?
O Faustus, leave these frivolous demands,
Which strike a terror to my fainting soul.
Faust. What ! is great Mephistophilis so passionate
For being deprivéd of the joys of Heaven ?
Learn thou of Faustus manly fortitude,
And scorn those joys thou never shalt possess.
Go, bear these tidings to great Lucifer:
Seeing Faustus hath incurr'd eternal death,
Say, he surrenders up to him his soul,
So he will spare him four-and-twenty years,
Letting him live in all voluptuousness ;
Having thee ever to attend on me,
To give me whatsoever I shall ask,
To tell me whatsoever I demand,
To slay mine enemies, and aid my friends,
And always be obedient to my will."

This passage, especially the hero's cool indifference in questioning about things which the fiend shudders to consider, has often struck me as not altogether unworthy to be thought of in connection with Milton.

The result of the interview is, that Faustus makes a compact with Lucifer, draws blood from his own arm, and with it writes out a deed of gift, assuring his soul and body to the fiend at the end of twenty-four years. Thenceforth he spends his time in exercising the mighty spells and incantations thus purchased: he has the power of making himself invisible, and entering whatsoever houses he lists; he passes from kingdom to kingdom with the speed of thought;

wields the elements at will, and has the energies of Nature at his command; summons the Grecian Helen to his side for a companion; and holds the world in wonder at his acts. Meanwhile the knowledge which Hell has given him of Heaven haunts him; he cannot shake off the thought of what the awful compact binds him to; repentance carries on a desperate struggle in him with the necromantic fascination, and at one time fairly outwrestles it; but he soon recovers his purpose, renews his pledge to Lucifer, and finally performs it.

This feature of the representation suggests a great thought, perhaps I should say, principle of man's moral being, which Shakespeare has more than once worked upon with surpassing effect. For it is remarkable that, in *Macbeth*, the thinking of the Weird Sisters (and he cannot choose but think of them) fires the hero's moral and imaginative forces into convulsive action, and thus causes him to shrink back from the very deed to which the prophetic greetings stimulate him. So, again, in *Hamlet*, the intimations of the Ghost touching "the secrets of its prison-house" kindle the hero full of "thoughts beyond the reaches of his soul," which entrance him in meditation, unstring his resolution, and render him morally incapable of the office to which that same Ghost has called him.

The Jew of Malta has divers passages in a far higher and richer style of versification than any part of *Tamburlaine*. The author's diction has grown more pliant and facile to his thought; consequently it is highly varied in pause and movement; showing that in his hand the noble instrument of dramatic blank-verse was fast growing into tune for a far mightier hand to discourse its harmonies upon. I must add that considerable portions both of this play and the preceding are meant to be comical. But the result only proves that Marlowe was incapable of comedy. No sooner does he attempt the comic vein than his whole style collapses into mere balderdash. In fact, though plentifully gifted with wit, there was not a particle of real humour in him; none of that subtle and perfusive essence out of which the true comic is spun; for these choice powers can hardly live but in the society of certain moral elements that seem to have been left out of his composition.

Edward the Second, probably the latest, certainly much the best, of Marlowe's dramas, was printed in 1598. Here, for the first time, we meet with a genuine specimen of the English Historical Drama. The scene covers a period of twenty years; the incidents pass with great rapidity, and, though sometimes crushed into indistinctness, are for the most part well used both for historic truth and dramatic effect; and the dialogue, generally, is nervous, animated, and clear. In the great article of character, too, this play has very considerable merit. The King's insane dotage of his favourites, the upstart vanity and insolence of Gaveston, the artful practice and doubtful virtue of Queen Isabella, the factious turbulence of the nobles, irascible, arrogant, regardless of others' liberty, jealous of their own, sudden of quarrel, eager in revenge, are all depicted with a goodly mixture of energy and temperance. Therewithal the versification moves, throughout, with a freedom and variety, such as may almost stand a comparison with Shakespeare in what may be called his earlier period; as when, for instance, *King Richard the Second* was written. It is probable, however, that by this time, if not before, Marlowe had begun to feel the power of that music which was to charm him, and all others of the time, out of audience and regard. For we have very good evidence, that before Marlowe's death Shakespeare had far surpassed all of that age who had ever been competent to teach him in any point of dramatic workmanship.

Marlowe is of consequence, *mainly*, as one of the first and greatest improvers of dramatic poetry in so far as relates to diction and metrical style; which is my reason for emphasizing his work so much in that regard. But, as this is a virtue much easier felt than described, I can best show what it is, by giving a taste of it; which however must be brief:

"*Edw.* What, Lord Arundel, dost thou come alone?
Arun. Yea, my good lord, for Gaveston is dead.
Edw. Ah, traitors! have they put my friend to death?
Tell me, Arundel, died he ere thou cam'st,
Or didst thou see my friend to take his death?
Arun. Neither, my lord; for, as he was surpris'd,
Begirt with weapons and with enemies round,
I did your Highness' message to them all,
Demanding him of them, entreating rather,
And said, upon the honour of my name,
That I would undertake to carry him
Unto your Highness, and to bring him back.
Edw. And, tell me, would the rebels deny me that?
Spen. Proud recreants!
Edw. Yea, Spenser, traitors all!
Arun. I found them at the first inexorable:
The Earl of Warwick would not bide the hearing;
Mortimer hardly; Pembroke and Lancaster
Spake least; and when they flatly had denied,
Refusing to receive me pledge for him,
The Earl of Pembroke mildly thus bespake:
'My lords, because our sovereign sends for him,
And promiseth he shall be safe return'd,
I will this undertake, to have him hence,
And see him redeliver'd to your hands.'
Edw. Well, and how fortunes it that he came not?
Spen. Some treason or some villainy was cause.
Arun. The Earl of Warwick seiz'd him on the way;
For, being deliver'd unto Pembroke's men,
Their lord rode home, thinking the prisoner safe;
But, ere he came, Warwick in ambush lay,
And bare him to his death, and in a trench
Strake off his head, and march'd unto the camp.
Spen. A bloody part, flatly 'gainst law of arms!
Edw. O, shall I speak, or shall I sigh, and die?
Spen. My lord, refer your vengeance to the sword
Upon these barons; hearten up your men;
Let them not unreveng'd murder your friends;
Advance your standard, Edward, in the field,
And march to fire them from their starting-holes.
Edw. I will have heads and lives for him as many

As I have manors, castles, towns, and towers! —
Treacherous Warwick! traitorous Mortimer!
If I be England's king, in lakes of gore
Your headless trunks, your bodies will I trail,
That you may drink your fill, and quaff in blood,
And stain my royal standard with the same;
You villains that have slain my Gaveston! —
And, in this place of honour and of trust,
Spenser, sweet Spenser, I adopt thee here;
And merely of our love we do create thee
Earl of Gloucester and Lord Chamberlain.
Spen. My lord, here is a messenger from the barons,
Desires access unto your Majesty.
Edw. Admit him.
Herald. Long live King Edward, England's lawful lord!
Edw. So wish not they, I wis, that sent thee hither."

This, to be sure, does not read much like, for instance, Hotspur's speech, beginning,

"O, then the earth shook to see the heavens on fire,"

nor is there any thing in Marlowe that does. In the passage quoted, however, (and there are many more like it,) we have the rhymeless ten-syllable iambic verse as the basis; but this is continually diversified, so as to relieve the ear and keep it awake, by occasional spondees, dibrachs, anapests, and amphibrachs, and by the frequent use of trochees in all parts of the verse, but especially at the beginning, and by a skilful shifting of the pause to any part of the line. It thus combines the natural ease and variety of prose with the general effect of metrical harmony, so that the hearing does not surfeit nor tire. As to the general *poetic* style of the performance, the kindling energy of thought and language that often beats and flashes along the sentences, there is much both in this and in *Faustus* to justify the fine enthusiasm of Drayton:

"Next, Marlowe, bathéd in the Thespian springs,
Had in him those brave translunary things
That the first poets had: his raptures were
All air and fire, which made his verses clear;
For that fine madness still he did retain
Which rightly should possess a poet's brain."

Before leaving the subject, I must notice a remark by Charles Lamb, — the dear, delightful Charley. "The reluctant pangs," says he, "of abdicating royalty in Edward furnished hints which Shakespeare scarce improved in his *Richard the Second;* and the death-scene of Marlowe's king moves pity and terror beyond any scene, ancient or modern, with which I am acquainted." Both the scenes in question have indeed great merit, but this praise seems to me far beyond the mark. Surely, there is more of genuine, pity-moving pathos in the single speech of York, — "As in a theatre the eyes of men," etc., — than in all Marlowe's writings put together. And as to the moving of terror, there is, to my mind, nothing in *Edward the Second* that comes up to *Faustus;* and there are a dozen scenes in *Macbeth*, any one of which has more of the terrific than the whole body of *Faustus*. And in the death-scene of Edward, it can hardly be denied that the senses are somewhat overcrammed with images of physical suffering, so as to give the effect rather of the horrible than the terrible.

Others, again, have thought that Marlowe, if he had lived, would have made some good approach to Shakespeare in tragic power. A few years more would no doubt have lifted him to very noble things, that is, provided his powers could have been kept from the eatings and cripplings of debauchery; still, any approach to that great Divinity of the Drama was out of the question for him. For, judging from his life and works, the moral part of genius was constitutionally defective in him; and, with this so defective, the intellectual part cannot be truly itself; and his work must needs be comparatively weak in those points of our being which it touches, because it does not touch them all: for the whole must be moved at once, else there can be no great moving of any part. No, no! there was not, there could not have been in Marlowe, great as he was, a tithe of Shakespeare, for tragedy, nor any thing else. To go no further, he was, as we have seen, destitute of humour; the powers of comedy evidently had no place in him; and these powers are indispensable to the production of high tragedy: a position affirmed as long ago as the days of Plato; sound in the reason of the thing; and, above all, made good in the instance of Shakespeare; who was *Shakespeare*, mainly because he had *all* the powers of the human mind in harmonious order and action, and *used* them all, explicitly or implicitly, in every play he wrote.

Shakespeare had one or two other senior contemporaries of whom I must say a few words, though it is not likely that they contributed much, if any thing, towards preparing him. John Lily, born in 1554, and Master of Arts in 1576, has considerable wit, some poetry; withal a certain crisp, clever, conceited mannerism of style, which caused him to be spoken of as "eloquent and witty"; but nothing that can be properly termed dramatic talent. His persons all speak in precisely the same vein, being indeed but so many empty figures or puppets, reflecting or propagating the motions of the author himself. His dramatic pieces, of which we have nine, seven in prose, one in rhyme, and one in blank-verse, seem to have been designed for Court entertainments, but were used more or less on the public stage, chiefly by the juvenile companies. They are all replete with that laboured affectation of fine writing which was distinguished at the time as Euphuism. One of his main peculiarities stands in using, for images and illustrations, certain imaginary products of a sort of artificial nature, which he got up especially for that purpose; as if he could invent better materials for poetic imagery than ancient Nature had furnished! Still, it is not unlikely that we owe to him somewhat of the polish and flexibility of the Shakespearian dramatic diction: that he could have helped the Poet in any thing beyond mere diction it were absurd to suppose.

I have already spoken of Thomas Lodge as joint author with Greene of a good-for-nothing play. We have one other play by him, entitled *The Wounds of Civil War*, and having for its subject "the true tragedies of Marius and Sylla," written before 1590, but not printed till 1594. It is in blank-verse; which however differs from the most regular rhyming ten-syllable verse in nothing but the lack of consonous endings. — Lodge is chiefly memorable in that one of his prose pieces was drawn upon for Shakespeare's *As You Like It.*

We have now reached the time when Shakespeare's hand had learnt its cunning, so far at least as any previous examples could teach it. Perhaps I ought to add, as showing the prodigious rush of life and thought towards the drama in that age, that, besides the authors I have mentioned, Henslowe's *Diary* supplies the names of thirty other dramatists, most of whom have propagated some part of their workmanship down to our time. In the same document, during the twelve years beginning in February, 1591, we have the titles recorded of no less than two hundred and seventy pieces, either as original compositions, or as revivals of older plays. As all these entries have reference only to Henslowe's management; and as, during that period, except for some short intervals, he was concerned with the affairs of but a single company; we may thence conceive how vastly fertile the age was in dramatic production.

After all, it is hardly possible for us to understand how important a part dramatic exhibitions played in the life of "merry England in the olden time." From a very early period, the interest in them was deep, general, and constant; it grew with the growth of civilization; it became complicated with all the mental, moral, and social habitudes of the people; and, in fact, whatever "seed-points of light" got planted in the popular mind had no way but to organize themselves into that shape. Those old plays, such as they were, with their rude, bold attempts to combine religion and mirth, instruction and sport, may almost be described as having been the nerves upon which the whole mental character of the nation formed itself. The spirit which began so early to work in them kept on asserting itself more and more strongly from age to age, till the Drama became emphatically a popular passion; as indeed must always be the case before any thing deserving the name of a National Drama can possibly arise. And it is quite surprising how long this spirit, so universal and so intense, was restrained from putting on so much of institutional form and expression as is implied in having buildings erected or adapted for its special use and service. For we have thus far heard of nothing in the character of temples provided for the liturgies of the Dramatic Art.

The spirit in question, however, did at last reach such a measure of strength, that it could no longer be restrained from issuing in a provision of that sort. The play-house known as the *Blackfriars* was established in 1576, and was owned and run by the company to which Shakespeare afterwards belonged. Two others, called *The Theatre* and *The Curtain*, were probably started about the same time, as we find them in operation in 1577. Before the end of the century, the city and suburbs of London had at least eight more in full blast. And there were, besides, ever so many strolling companies of players carrying the mysteries of their craft into nearly all parts of the kingdom. So that the Drama may well be judged to have been, in the Poet's time, decidedly a great institution. In fact, it was a sort of fourth estate of the realm; nearly as much so, indeed, as the Newspaper Press is in our time. Practically, the Government was vested in King, Lords, Commons, and Dramatists, including in the latter both writers and actors; the Poet thus having far more reason than now exists for making Hamlet say to the old statesman, "After your death you were better have a bad epitaph, than their ill report while you live."

The foregoing review, brief and inadequate as it is, may answer the purpose of imparting some just notion of the growth and progress of the English Drama till it reached the eve of its maturity. The allegorical drama had great influence, no doubt, in determining the scope and quality of the proper drama of comedy and tragedy; since, by its long discipline of the popular mind in abstract ideas, or in the generalized forms of ethical thought, it did much towards forming that public taste which required and prompted the drama to rise above a mere geography of facts into the empyrean of truth; and under the instructions of which Shakespeare learned to make his persons embodiments of general nature as well as of individual character. For the excellences of the Shakespearian Drama were probably owing as much to the mental preparation of the time as to the powers of the individual man. He was in demand before he came; and it was that preexisting demand that taught and enabled him to do what he did. If it was the strength of his genius that lifted him to the top of the heap, it was also the greatness of the heap that enabled him to reach and maintain that elevation. For it is a great mistake to regard Shakespeare as standing alone, and working only in the powers of his individual mind. In fact, there never was any growth of literature or art that stood upon a wider basis of collective experience, or that drew its form and substance from a larger or more varied stock of historical preparation.*

* Since the passage in the text was written, I have met with some well-drawn remarks of a like drift in Froude's *History of England*, Chapter I.: "The chroniclers have given us many accounts of the masques and plays which were acted in the Court, or in the castles of the noblemen. Such pageants were but the most splendid expression of a taste which was national and universal. As in ancient Greece, generations before the rise of the great dramas of Athens, itinerant companies wandered from village to village, carrying their stage furniture in their little carts, and acted in their booths and tents the grand stories of the mythology; so in England the mystery-players haunted the wakes and fairs, and in barns or taverns, tap-rooms, or in the farm-house kitchen, played at saints and angels, and transacted on their petty stage the entire drama of the Christian Faith. We allow ourselves to think of Shakespeare or of Raphael or of Phidias as having accomplished their work by the power of their own individual genius; but greatness like

Dryden, in one of his occasional pieces, represents the Poet's ghost as saying,

> "Untaught, unpractis'd, in a barbarous age,
> I found not, but created first, the stage";

and such has been the common belief. But the saying is far from true; and Shakespeare's ghost must have sipped large draughts of Lethe, to be capable of speaking thus. For, though the least that he did is worth more than all that was done before him, and though his poorest performances surpass the best of his models; it is nevertheless certain that his task was but to continue and perfect what was already begun. Not only were the three forms of comedy, history, and tragedy in use on the English stage, but the elements of these were to some extent blended in the freedom and variety of the Gothic Drama. The usage also of dramatic blank-verse stood up inviting his adoption; though no one before or since has come near him in the mastery of its capabilities; his genius being an inexhaustible spring of both mental and verbal modulation. Nor can all this be justly regarded as any alleviation of his task, or any abatement of his fame. For, to work thus with materials and upon models already prepared, without being drawn down to their level and subdued to their quality, requires, if possible, a higher order and exercise of

theirs is never more than the highest degree of an excellence which prevails widely round it, and forms the environment in which it grows. No single mind in single contact with the facts of nature could have created out of itself a Pallas, a Madonna, or a Lear: such vast conceptions are the growth of ages, the creations of a nation's spirit; and artist and poet, filled full with the power of that spirit, have but given them form, and nothing more than form. Nor would the form itself have been attainable by any isolated talent. No genius can dispense with experience; the aberrations of power, unguided or ill-guided, are ever in proportion to its intensity, and life is not long enough to recover from inevitable mistakes. Noble conceptions already existing, and a noble school of execution, which will launch mind and hand at once upon their true courses, are indispensable to transcendent excellence; and Shakespeare's plays were as much the offspring of the long generations who had pioneered his road for him as the discoveries of Newton were the offspring of those of Copernicus."

power than to strike out in a way and with a stock entirely new. And so the absorbing, quickening, creative efficacy of Shakespeare's genius is best seen in this, that, taking the Drama as it came to his hand, a thing of unsouled forms and lack-lustre eyes, all brainless and meaningless, he at once put a spirit into it, tempered its elements in the proportions of truth, informed its shapes with grace and virtue, and made it all alive, a breathing, speaking, operative power. Thus his work naturally linked in with the whole past; and in his hands the collective thought and wisdom of ages were smelted out of the earth and dross wherein they lay imbedded, and wrought into figures of undecaying beauty.

It is indeed true that the Drama shot ahead with amazing rapidity as soon as it came to feel the virtue of Shakespeare's hand. We have nothing more dreary, dismal, and hopeless than the course of the English Drama down to his time. The people would have dramatic entertainments, and hundreds of minds, apparently, were ever busy furnishing them wooden things in dramatic form. And so, century after century, through change after change, the work of preparation went on, still scarce any progress, and no apparent result, nothing that could live, or was worth keeping alive. It seemed as if no rain would ever fall, no sun ever shine, to take away the sterility of the land. Yet all of a sudden the Drama blazed up with a splendor that was to illuminate and sweeten the ages, and be at once the delight and the despair of other nations and future times. All this, too, came to pass in Shakespeare! and, which is more, the process ended with him! It is indeed a singular phenomenon, and altogether the most astonishing that the human mind has produced.

Yet even here we should be careful of attributing too much to the genius of the individual man. It was rather the genius of the age and nation springing into flowerage through him, — a flowerage all the larger and more eloquent for the long delay, and the vast accumulation of force. For it is remarkable that when the Warwickshire peasant entered upon his work, with the single exception of Chaucer, not one good English book had been written. Yet he was far from being alone in thus beginning and perfecting the great workmanship which he took in hand. Before *Hamlet*, *Othello*, and *The Tempest* were written, Romantic Poetry had done its best in Spenser, Philosophical Divinity in Hooker, Civil and Moral Discourse in Bacon. All these alike are unapproached and unapproachable in their several kinds. We have nothing more tuneable and melodious than Spenser's verse; no higher and nobler eloquence than Hooker's prose; no practical wisdom of deeper reach or more attractive garb than Bacon's *Essays*. Yet they did not learn their cunning from Shakespeare, nor did Shakespeare learn his cunning from them. The language was then just ripe for the uses of such minds; it had the wealth of much learning incorporated with it, yet had not been cast into rigidity nor dressed into primness by a technical and bookish legislation; it had gone on for centuries gathering in and assimilating stores from Nature and from Religion; it was rich with the life of a nation of brave, free, honest, full-souled, and frank-hearted men; it was at once copious, limber, and sinewy, capable alike of expressing the largest and the subtlest thought, the deepest and strongest passion, the most tender and delicate feeling; wit could sport itself for ever, humour could trim its raciest issues, imagination could body forth its sweetest and awfullest visions, in the furnishings of the English tongue. And so these four great thinkers found it equal, apparently, to all their thoughts and powers. They were all, though each in a different sort, its masters, not its slaves. They used it, but they did not make it. And the thought which they found it capable of expressing must have pre-existed in some form, else the language could not have stood ready, as it did, for their use. The truth seems to be that, for reasons which we cannot fathom, and in ways past our finding out, the time had now come, the mental life of the nation was fully grown to a head, so as to express itself in several forms at the same time; and Shakespeare, wise, true, and mighty beyond his thought, became its organ of dramatic utterance; which utterance remains, and will remain, a treasury of everlasting sweetness and refreshment to mankind.

SHAKESPEARE'S ART.

NATURE AND USE OF ART.

TRANQUILLITY ! the sovereign aim wert thou
In heathen schools of philosophic lore ;
Heart-stricken by stern destiny of yore,
The Tragic Muse thee serv'd with thoughtful vow ;
And what of hope Elysium could allow
Was fondly seiz'd by Sculpture, to restore
Peace to the Mourner. But when He who wore
The crown of thorns around His bleeding brow
Warm'd our sad being with celestial light,
Then Arts which still had drawn a softening grace
From shadowy fountains of the Infinite,
Commun'd with that Idea face to face ;
And move around it now as planets run,
Each in its orbit round the central Sun." — WORDSWORTH.

ART is in its proper character the solidest and sincerest expression of human thought and feeling. To be much within and little without, to do all for truth, nothing for show, and to express the largest possible meaning with the least possible stress of expression, — this is its first law.

Thus artistic virtue runs down into one and the same root with moral righteousness. Both must first of all be genuine and sincere, richer and better at the heart than on the surface; as always having it for their leading aim to recommend themselves to the perfect Judge; that is, they must seek the praise of God rather than of men: for, indeed, whatsoever studies chiefly to please men will not please them long, but will soon be openly or secretly repudiated by them; whereas, "when a man's ways are pleasing unto the Lord, he maketh even his enemies to be at peace with him."

Such is the right form, such the normal process, of what may be called intellectual and artistic righteousness. A soul of perfect veracity lies at the bottom of the thing, and is the source and the life of all that is good and beautiful in it. And the work, like Nature herself, does not strike excitingly, but "melts into the heart"; it therefore wears well, and don't wear out. Every thing is done "in simple and pure soul," and without any thought, on the doer's part, of the figure he is making; and when he turns from the beauty he should express to his own beauty of expression, his work becomes false. And it may be justly affirmed that perfection of workmanship in Art is where the senses are touched just enough, and in just the right way, to kindle the mind; and this too without making the mind distinctly conscious of being kindled; for when the soul is moved perfectly both in kind and degree, self-consciousness is lost in the interest of that which moves it.

Hence it is that all deep and earnest feeling, all high and noble thought so naturally puts on a style of modesty and reserve. It communicates itself, not by verbal emphasis or volume, but by a sort of blessed infection too subtile and too potent for words to convey. Volubility strangles it; and it is felt to be insincere when it grows loquacious. A wordy grief is merely a grief from the throat outwards: "the grief that does not speak," this it is that "whispers the o'erfraught heart, and bids it break." And the truly eloquent speaker or writer is not he who says a multitude of fine things in finely turned language and figures, which is very easily done, but he who says just the right things, and says them in the fewest, simplest, and aptest words. As for the speaker who lives, not in the inspiration of his theme, but in the display of his eloquence, we may rest assured that he will never say any thing worth hearing: his work will naturally turn all to mere elocution; which may be described as the art of pronouncing nothing in such a way as to make it pass for something grand.

Thus there appears to be a profound natural sympathy or

affinity between the forces of religion and the forms of Art. Therefore it is that the higher efficacies of Christian culture and the deeper workings of religious thought and emotion have instinctively sought to organize and enshrine themselves in artistic creations; no other mode or power of expression being strong enough to hold them, or inclusive enough to contain them. It is in such works as the ancient marvels of ecclesiastical building that the Christian mind has found its most fitting and most operative eloquence.

What was the motive-principle, what the inspiring power, of those architectural wonders that transport the impress of mediæval piety across the ocean of so many centuries? Wordsworth, referring to some of the English cathedrals, says, —

> "They dreamt not of a perishable home,
> Who thus could build."

And, sure enough, we may well deem that nothing less than the most intense and burning conceptions of eternity could have inspired the souls of men and made them strong enough to project and accomplish those stupendous structures which, in their silent majesty and awe-inspiring suggestiveness, are the most persuasive and the most unanswerable preachers of Christianity that the Church of two thousand years has produced. "They builded better than they knew." And what are all the sermons and theologies of that time in comparison with those great old monuments of Christian Art? "The immortal mind craves objects that endure." And immortality itself, the spirit of celestial order, a beauty that awes while it charms, and chastens while it kindles, are imaged in the aspect and countenance of those structures. And it is remarkable that nothing has come down to us touching the persons of those grand old builders, not even their names. It seems indeed as if their great souls had been so possessed by the genius that stirred within them, so entranced in the contemplation of their religious ideals, as to leave no room for any self-regarding thoughts; so that we know them only as a band of anonymous immortals.

> "They were pedants who could speak:
> Grander souls have passed unheard;
> Such as found all language weak;
> Choosing rather to record
> Secrets before Heaven, than break
> Faith with Angels by a word."

Now it is the nature of Christian meaning thus embodied to penetrate and pervade the depths of the mind without agitating its surface; and when the effect is greatest, then it is that the mind is least conscious of it: it is a silent efficacy that "sweetly creeps into the study of imagination," and charms its way into "the eye and prospect of the soul" by delicacy of touch and smoothness of operation. Such art is of course in no sort an intellectual gymnastic. It is as complex and many-sided as our nature itself; and the frame of mind from which it proceeds, and which it aims to inspire, is that calmness wherein is involved a free and harmonious exercise of the whole man; sense, intellect, and heart moving together in sympathy and unison: in a word, it is the fitting expression of

> "That monumental grace
> Of Faith, which doth all passions tame
> That reason *should* control;
> And shows in the untrembling frame
> A statue of the soul."

From such workmanship, every thing specially stimulant of any one part of the mind, every thing that ministers to the process of self-excitation, every thing that fosters an unhealthy consciousness by untuning the inward harmonies of our being, every thing that appeals to the springs of vanity and self-applause, or invites us to any sort of glass-gazing pleasure, — every such thing is, by an innate law of the work, excluded. So that here we have the right school of moral healthiness, a moral digestion so perfect as to be a secret unto itself. The intelligence, the virtue, the piety, that grows by such methods, is never seen putting on airs, or feeding on the reflection of its own beauty; but evermore breathes freely and naturally, as in communion with the proper sources of its life.

Works of Art, then, above all other productions of the mind, must have solidity and inwardness, that essential retiring grace which seems to shrink from the attention it wins, that style of power held in reserve which grows upon acquaintance, that suggestive beauty, "part seen, imagined part," which does not permit the beholder to leave without a silent invitation to return. And in proportion as the interest of such works depends on novelty, or stress of manner, or any strikingness of effect, as if they were ambitious to make themselves felt, and apprehensive of not being prized at their worth; in the same proportion their tenure of interest is naturally short, because they leave the real springs of thought untouched.

This, to be sure, holds more or less true of all the forms of mental production; but its truth is more evident and more self-approving in the sphere of Art than in the others. Hence the common saying, that poetry, for instance, must be very good indeed, else it is good for nothing. And men of culture and judgment in that line naturally feel, in general, that a work of art which is not worth seeing many times is not worth seeing at all; and if they are at first taken with such a work, they are apt to be ashamed of it afterwards, and to resent the transient pleasure they found in it, as a sort of fraud upon them. In other words, Art aspires to interest *permanently*, and even to be more interesting the more it is seen; and when it does not proceed in the order of this "modest charm of not too much," this remoteness of meaning where far more is inferred than is directly shown, there we may be sure the vital principle of the thing is wanting.

Allston, the distinguished painter-artist, is said to have had an intense aversion to all "eccentricity in Art." He might well do so; and, being a philosopher of Art as well as an artist, he had no difficulty in knowing that his aversion was founded in truth, and was fully justified by the reason of the thing. For the prime law of Art, as is implied in what I have been saying, is to produce the utmost possible of *silent* effect; and to secure this end *truth* must be the all-in-all of the artist's purpose, — a purpose too inward and vital, perhaps, for the subject to be distinctly conscious of it; which is the right meaning of *artistic inspiration.* But eccentricity in Art aims, first and last, at *sensible* effect; to appease an eager, prurient curiosity is its proper motive-spring; and it is radically touched with some disease, perhaps an itch of moral or intellectual or emotional demonstrativeness; and so it naturally issues in a certain *plurisy* of style, or some self-pleasing crotchet or specialty of expression, — something which is striking and emphatic, and which is therefore essentially disproportionate and false. In a word, there is a fatal root of insincerity in the thing. For instance, if one were to paint a tree in the brilliancy of full-bloom, or a human face in the liveliest play of soul, I suppose the painting might be set down as a work of eccentricity; for, though such things are natural in themselves, they are but transient or evanescent moods of Nature; and a painting of them has not that calmness and purity of truth and art on which the mind can repose:

"Soft is the music that would charm for ever."

Moreover a work of art, as such, is not a thing to be learnt or acquired, as formal knowledge is acquired: it is rather a presence for the mind to commune with, and drink in the efficacy of, with an "eye made quiet by the power of Beauty." Nor is such communion by any means unfruitful of mental good: on the contrary, it is the right force and food of the soundest and healthiest inward growth; and to be silent and secret is the character of every process that is truly vital and creative. It is on this principle that Nature, when conversed with in the spirit of her works, acts "as a teacher of truth through joy and through gladness, and as a creatress of the faculties by a process of smoothness and delight"; and we gather in the richer intellectual harvest from such converse when the mind is too intent on Nature's forms to take any thought of its gatherings. We cannot truly live with her without being built up in the best virtues of her life. It is a mighty poor way of growing wise, when one loves to see

> "Each little drop of wisdom as it falls
> Into the dimpling cistern of his heart."

And so the conversing rightly with works of art may not indeed be very available for showing off in recitation: it is all the better for that, inasmuch as its best effect must needs be too deep for the intellectual consciousness to grasp: because the right virtue of Art lies in a certain self-withdrawing power which catches the mind as from a distance, and cheats the forces of self-applause into abdication through intentness of soul. All which infers, moreover, that a full appreciation of any true work of art cannot be extemporized; for such a work has a thousand meanings, which open out upon the eye gradually, as the eye feeds and grows and kindles up to them: its virtue has to *soak* into the mind insensibly; and to this end there needs a long, smooth, quiet fellowship.

PRINCIPLES OF ART.

The several forms of Art, as Painting, Sculpture, Music, Architecture, the Poem, the Drama, all have a common root, and proceed upon certain common principles. The faculties which produce them, the laws that govern them, and the end they are meant to serve, in short their source, method, and motive, are at bottom one and the same. Art, therefore, is properly and essentially *one:* accordingly I take care to use the phrase *several forms of Art*, and not *several arts.* This identity of life and law is perhaps most apparent in the well-known fact that the several forms of Art, wherever they have existed at all, and in any character of originality, have all had a religious origin; have sprung up and taken their growth in and for the service of religion. The earliest poems everywhere were sacred hymns and songs, conceived and executed in recognition and honour of the Deity. Grecian sculpture, in all its primitive and progressive stages, was for the sole purpose of making statues of the gods; and when it forsook this purpose, and sophisticated itself into a preference of other ends, it went into a decline. The Greek architecture, also, had its force, motive, and law in the work of building religious temples and shrines. That the Greek Drama took its origin from the same cause, is familiar to all students in dramatic history. And I have already shown that the Gothic Drama in England, in its upspring and through its earlier stages, was entirely the work of the Christian Church, and was purely religious in its purpose, matter, and use. That the same holds in regard to our modern music, is too evident to need insisting on: it all sprang and grew in the service of religion; religious thought and emotion were the shaping and informing spirit of it. I have often thought that the right use of music, and perhaps that which drew it into being, could not be better illustrated than in "the sweet Singer of Israel," who, when the evil spirit got into King Saul, took harp and voice, and with his minstrelsy charmed it out. Probably, if David had undertaken to argue the evil spirit out, he would have just strengthened the possession; for the Devil was then, as now, an expert logician, but could not stand a divine song.

Thus the several forms of Art have had their source and principle deep in man's religious nature: all have come into being as so many projections or outgrowths of man's religious life. And it may well be questioned whether, without the motives and inspirations of religion, the human soul ever was, or ever can be, strong and free enough to produce any shape of art. In other words, it is only as the mind stands dressed in and for religion that the Creative Faculty of Art gets warmed and quickened into operation. So that religion is most truly the vivifying power of Art in all its forms; and all works of art that do not proceed from a religious life in the mind are but imitations, and can never be any thing more. Moreover the forms of Art have varied in mode, style, and character, according to the particular genius and spirit of the religion under which they grew. There is a most intimate correspondence between the two. This is manifestly true of the old Egyptian and Grecian art. And it is equally true of Christian art, save as this has been more or less modified by imitation of those earlier works, and in so far as this imitative process has got the better of original inspiration, the result has always been a falling from the right virtue of Art. For the Christian mind can never overtake the Greek mind in that style of Art which was original and proper to the latter. Nothing but the peculiar genius of the Greek mythology could ever freely and spontaneously organize or incarnate itself in a body of that shape. The genius of Christianity requires and naturally prompts a different body. Nor can the soul of the latter ever be made to take on the body of the former, but under the pressure of other than the innate and organic law of the thing. For every true original artist is much more possessed by the genius of his work than possessing it. Unless, indeed, a man be inspired by a power stronger than his individual understanding or any conscious purpose, his hand can never reach the cunning of any process truly creative. And so in all cases the temper and idiom of a people's religious culture will give soul and expression to their art; or, if they have no religious culture, then there will not be soul-power enough in them to produce any art at all.*

* On this subject Schlegel has some of the wisest and happiest sayings that I have met with. For example: "All truly creative poetry must proceed from the inward life of a people, and from religion, the root of that life." And again: "Were it possible for man to renounce all religion, including that which is unconscious, or independent of the will, he would become a mere surface without any internal substance. When this centre is disturbed, the whole system of the mental faculties and feelings takes a new shape." Once

As I am on the subject of Art considered as the offspring of Religion or the religious Imagination, I am moved to add a brief episode in that direction. And I the rather do so, forasmuch as Artistic Beauty is commonly recognized as among the greatest educational forces now in operation in the Christian world. On this point a decided reaction has taken place within my remembrance. The agonistic or argumentative modes, which were for a long time in the ascendant, and which proceeded by a logical and theological presentation of Christian thought, seem to have spent themselves, insomuch as to be giving way to what may be called the poetical and imaginative forms of expression. It is not my purpose to discuss whether the change be right or for the better, but merely to note it as a fact; for such I think it clearly is. I presume it will be granted, also, that as a general thing we need to have our places of worship and our religious services made far more beautiful than they are; and that indeed we cannot have too much of beauty in them, so that beauty be duly steeped in the grace and truth of Christian inspiration. But Art has its dangers here as well as its uses: especially it is apt to degenerate from a discipline of religious virtue into a mere relaxation, losing the severity that elevates and purifies, in what is merely pretty or voluptuous or pleasing. It is therefore of the utmost consequence what style of beauty we cultivate, and how the tastes of people are set in this matter.

more, speaking of the Greeks: "Their religion was the deification of the powers of Nature and of earthly life; but this worship, which, among other nations, clouded the imagination with hideous shapes, and hardened the heart to cruelty, assumed among the Greeks a mild, a grand, and a dignified form. Superstition, too often the tyrant of the human faculties, here seems to have contributed to their freest development. It cherished the arts by which itself was adorned, and its idols became the models of beauty But, however highly the Greeks may have succeeded in the Beautiful and even in the Moral, we cannot concede any higher character to their civilization than that of a refined and ennobling sensuality Of course this must be understood generally. The conjectures of a few philosophers, and the irradiations of poetical inspiration, constitute an occasional exception. Man can never altogether turn aside his thoughts from infinity, and some obscure recollections will always remind him of the home he has lost."

Now Christianity is indeed a great "beauty-making power"; but the Beauty which it makes and owns is a presence to worship in, not a bauble to play with, or a show for unbaptized entertainment and pastime. It cannot be too austerely discriminated from mere ornament, and from every thing approaching a striking and sensational character. Its right power is a power to chasten and subdue. And it is never good for us, especially in our religious hours, to be charmed without being at the same time chastened. Accordingly the highest Art always has something of the terrible in it, so that it awes you while it attracts. The sweetness that wins is tempered with the severity that humbles; the smile of love, with the sternness of reproof. And it is all the more beautiful in proportion as it knows how to bow the mind by the austere and hushing eloquence of its forms. And when I speak of Art, or the creation of the Beautiful, as the highest and strongest expression of man's intellectual soul, I must be understood to mean this order of the Beautiful: for indeed the beauty (if it be not a sin to call it such) that sacrifices or postpones truth to pleasure is not good;

> "And that which is not good is not delicious
> To a well-govern'd and wise appetite."

In all our use of Art, therefore, it stands us much in hand to know that true Beauty is indeed an awful as well as a pleasant thing; and that men are not in a good way when they have ceased to feel that it is so. Nor can I deem our case a very hopeful one when we surrender ourselves to that style of beauty which pleases without chastening the soul. For it is but too certain that when Art takes to gratifying such an unreligious taste, and so works its forces for the pleasing of men without touching them with awe, it becomes no better than a discipline of moral enervation. Perhaps this same law would silence much of the voluble rhetoric with which a certain school of writers are wont to discourse of the great Miracle of Beauty which has been given to men in the life and character of the blessed Saviour. For I must needs think that, if they duly felt the awfulness of that Beauty, their fluency would be somewhat repressed; and that their eloquence would be better if they feared more and flourished less.

But the point which these remarks are chiefly meant to enforce is, that there is no true beauty of Art but what takes its life from the inspirations of religious awe; and that even in our highest intellectual culture the intellect itself will needs be demoralized, unless it be toned to order by a supreme reference to the Divine will. There is no true school of mental health and vigour and beauty, but what works under the presidency of the same chastening and subduing power. Our faculties of thought and knowledge must be held firmly together with a strong girdle of modesty, else they cannot possibly thrive; and to have the intellect "undevoutly free," loosened from the bands of reverence, is a sure pledge and forecast of intellectual shallowness and deformity.*

* Since this was written, I have met with some capital remarks, closely bordering upon the topic, in Mr. J. C. Shairp's *Studies in Poetry and Philosophy*, a book which I cannot but regard as one of the choicest contributions to the literature of our time. The passage is in his essay on *The Moral Dynamic*, near the end:

"There are things which, because they are ultimate ends in themselves, refuse to be employed as means, and, if attempted to be so employed, lose their essential character. Religion is one, and the foremost of these things. Obedience, conformity of the finite and the imperfect will of man to the infinite and perfect will of God, this, which is the essence of religion, is an end in itself, the highest end which we can conceive. It cannot be sought as a means to an ulterior end without being at once destroyed. This is an end, or rather the end in itself, which culture and all other ends by right subserve. And here in culture, as in pleasure, the great ethic law will be found to hold, that the abandoning of it as an end, in obedience to a higher, more supreme aim, is the very condition of securing it. Stretch the idea of culture, and of the perfection it aims at, wide as you will, you cannot, while you make it your last end, rise clear of the original self-reference that lies at its root; this you cannot get rid of, unless you go out of culture, and beyond it, abandoning it as an end, and sinking it into what it really is, — a means, though perhaps the highest means, towards full and perfect duty. *No one ever really became beautiful by aiming at beauty. Beauty comes, we scarce know how, as an emanation from sources deeper than itself.* If culture, or rather the ends of culture, are to be healthy and natural growths, they must come unconsciously, as results

It were something beside my purpose to unfold and illustrate in detail the common principles of Art: I shall but endeavour to do this so far as may be needful for a due understanding of those principles as we have them embodied in the Shakespearian Drama.

The first of those principles, as I am to view them, is what I know not better how to designate than by the term *Solidarity.* By which I mean that the several parts of a given work must all stand in mutual sympathy and intelligence; or that the details must not only have each a force and meaning of their own, but must also be helpful, directly or remotely, to the force and meaning of the others; all being drawn together and made to coalesce in unity of effect by some one governing thought or paramount idea. This gives us what the philosophers of Art generally agree in calling an *organic structure;* that is, a structure in which an inward vital law shapes and determines the outward form; all the parts being, moreover, assimilated and bound each to each by the life that builds the organiza-

of conformity to the will of God, sought not for any end but itself." — "It cannot indeed be denied that these two, culture or the love of beauty, religion or the love of godliness, appear in individuals, in races, in ages, as rival, often as conflicting, forces. The votary of beauty shrinks from religion as something stern and ungenial, the devout Puritan discards beauty as a snare; and even those who have hearts susceptible of both find that a practical crisis will come when a choice must be made whether of the two they will serve. The consciousness of this disunion has of late years been felt deeply, and by the most gifted minds. Painful often has the conflict been, when the natural love of beauty was leading one way, loyalty to that which is higher than beauty called another, and no practical escape was possible, except by the sacrifice of feelings which in themselves were innocent and beautiful. Only in recent times have we begun to feel strongly that both are good, that each without the other is so far imperfect, and that some reconciliation, if it were possible, is a thing to be desired. Violent has been the reaction which this new consciousness has created. In the recoil from what they call Puritanism, or religion without culture, many have given themselves up to culture without religion, or, at best, with a very diluted form of religion. They have set up for worship the golden calf of art, and danced round it to the pipe which the great Goethe played. They have promulgated what they call the gospel of art, — as Carlyle says, the windiest gospel ever yet preached, which never has saved and never will save any man from moral corruption."

tion, and so rendered mutually aidant, and at the same time conducive to the well-being of the whole. In a word, they must all have a purpose and a truth in common as well as each a truth and purpose of its own.

To illustrate this in a small instance, and perhaps the more intelligible for being small. — Critics had been wont to speak lightly, not to say sneeringly, of the Sonnet, as being but an elaborate trifle that cost more than it came to. Wordsworth undertook to vindicate the thing from this unjust reproach, as he considered it; and to that end he wrote the following:

"Scorn not the Sonnet; Critic, you have frown'd,
Mindless of its just honours: with this key
Shakespeare unlock'd his heart; the melody
Of this small lute gave ease to Petrarch's wound;
A thousand times this pipe did Tasso sound;
With it Camöens sooth'd an exile's grief;
The Sonnet glitter'd a gay myrtle leaf
Amid the cypress with which Dante crown'd
His visionary brow; a glow-worm lamp,
It cheer'd mild Spenser, call'd from Faery-land
To struggle through dark ways; and, when a damp
Fell round the path of Milton, in his hand
The Thing became a trumpet; whence he blew
Soul-animating strains, — alas, too few!"

Now, here we have a place for every thing, and every thing in its place. There is nothing irrelevant, nothing ajar. The parts are not only each true and good and beautiful in themselves, but each is helpful to the others, and all to the author's purpose: every allusion, every image, every word, tells in furtherance of his aim. There need nothing be added, there must nothing be taken away. The argument at every step is clear and strong. The thing begins, proceeds, and ends, just as it ought; you cannot change a word in it without injuring it: the understanding, the imagination, the ear, are all satisfied with the result. And the specimen is itself a full triumph of the Sonnet, from the intellectual truth and beauty and sweetness which are here put into it. So that, what with the argument, and what with the example, the vindication of the Sonnet is perfect. Accordingly, I believe no one has spoken lightly of the thing since that specimen was given to the public.

Many have written poetry, and good poetry too, who, notwithstanding, have not written, and could not write, a Poem. But this sonnet is, in its measure, a genuine poem; and as such I am willing to bear the responsibility of pronouncing it faultless. Wordsworth could do the Sonnet completely, and did it so in many instances: and he could do more than this; in several of his longer pieces the workmanship is perhaps equally faultless; as, for instance, in *Laodamia* and the *Ode to Duty*, which, to my sense, are perfect poems in their kind. But to do thus through so complex and multitudiuous a work as our higher specimens of the Gothic Drama, is a very different matter, — a thing far beyond the power of a Wordsworth. To combine and carry on together various distinct lines of thought, and various individual members of character, so that each shall constantly remember and respect the others, and this through a manifold, diversified, and intricate course of action; to keep all the parts true to the terms and relations of organic unity, each coming in and stopping just where it ought, each doing its share, and no more than its share, in the common plan, so as not to hinder the life or interfere with the rights of the others; to knit them all together in a consistent and harmonious whole, with nothing of redundancy or of deficiency, nothing "overdone or come tardy off," — the members, moreover, all mutually interacting, all modifying and tempering one another; — this is a task which it is given to few to achieve. For the difficulty of the work increases in a sort of geometrical ratio with the number and greatness of the parts; and when we come to such a work as *Hamlet* or *Cymbeline* or *King Lear*, few of us have heads long enough and strong enough to measure the difficulty of it.

Such, then, in my reckoning, is the first principle, I will not say of artistic perfection, but of all true excellence in Art. And the same law, which thus requires that in a given work each earlier part shall prepare for what comes after, and each later part shall finish what went before, holds with equal force in all the forms of Art; for whether the parts be rendered or delivered in space, as in Painting and Architecture, or in time, as in Music, a Poem, or a Drama, makes no difference in this respect.

The second principle of Art which I am to consider is *Originality*. And by this I do not mean novelty or singularity, either in the general structure or in the particular materials, but something that has reference to the method and process of the work. The construction must proceed from the heart outwards, not the other way, and proceed in virtue of the inward life, not by any surface aggregation of parts, or by any outward pressure or rule. In organic nature, every plant, and every animal, however cast in the mould of the species, and so kept from novelty or singularity, has an individual life of its own, which life is and must be original. It is a development from a germ; and the process of development is vital, and works by selection and assimilation of matter in accordance with the inward nature of the thing. And so in Art, a work, to be original, must grow from what the workman has inside of him, and what he sees of Nature and natural fact around him, and not by imitation of what others have done before him. So growing, the work will, to be sure, take the specific form and character; nevertheless it will have the essence of originality in the right sense of the term, because it will have originated from the author's mind, just as the offspring originates from the parent. And the result will be, not a showy, emphatic, superficial virtue, which is indeed a vice, but a solid, genuine, substantive virtue; that is, the thing will be just what it seems, and will mean just what it says. Moreover the greatness of the work, if it have any, will be more or less hidden in the order and temperance and harmony of the parts; so that the work will keep growing larger and richer to you as you become familiar with it: whereas in case of a thing made in the unoriginal way, at a distance it will seem larger than it is, and will keep shrinking and dwarfing as you draw nearer to it; and perhaps, when you get fairly into it, it will prove to be no substance at all, but only a mass of shining vapour; or, if you undertake to grasp it, your hand will just close through it, as it would through a shadow.*

All this, however, is nowise to be understood as inferring that a great original artist must be an independent or isolated growth, without parents and brethren, and the natural aids and inspirations of society. This never was and never can be. Art-life must be had in common, or not at all. In this, as in other things, many minds must grow up together, else none can grow up. And no form of Art ever grew to perfection, or any thing near it, but that it was and long had been matter of strong national passion,

* This law of originality I have never seen better stated than by Coleridge, in a passage justifying the form of Shakespeare's dramas against a mode of criticism which has now, happily, gone out of use. "The true ground," says he, "of the mistake lies in the confounding mechanical regularity with organic form. The form is mechanic, when on any given material we impress a pre-determined form, not necessarily arising out of the properties of the material; as when to a mass of wet clay we give whatever shape we wish it to retain when hardened. The organic form, on the other hand, is innate; it shapes, as it develops, itself from within, and the fulness of its development is one and the same with the perfection of its outward form. Such as the life is, such is the form. Nature, the prime genial artist, inexhaustible in diverse powers, is equally inexhaustible in forms: each exterior is the physiognomy of the being within, — its true image reflected and thrown out from the concave mirror." — With this may well be coupled Schlegel's remarks on the same point: "Form is mechanical when it is impressed upon any piece of matter by an outward operation, as an accidental addition without regard to the nature of the thing; as, for example, when we give any form at pleasure to a soft mass, to be retained after induration. Organic form on the contrary, is innate; it unfolds itself from within, and attains its determinate character along with the full development of the germ. Such forms are found in Nature universally, wherever living powers are in action. And in Art, as well as in Nature, the supreme artist, all genuine forms are organic, that is, are determined by the quality of the work. In short, the form is no other than a significant exterior, the physiognomy of a thing, — when not defaced by disturbing accidents, the *speaking* physiognomy, — which bears true witness of its hidden essence."

or of a free and vigorous public spirit. Men are not kindled to such a height without many convergent rays of fellowship. In other words, before excellence of Art in any kind can come, there has to be a large and long preparation, and this not only in the spiritual culture and development of the people, but also in the formal order and method of the thing. Accordingly great artists, so far as the history of the matter is known, have always lived and worked in successions and clusters, each adding something, till at length a master mind arose, and gathered the finer efficacies of them all into one result. This is notoriously true of Greek, Venetian, Florentine, and Gothic Art: Phidias, Sophocles, Titian, and Raphael had each many precursors and companions. The fact indeed is apt to be lost sight of, because the earlier and inferior essays perish, and only the finished specimens survive; so that we see them more or less isolated; whereas in truth their origin and growth were social, the fruit of a large intellectual partnership and co-operation. — It is on the same principle that nothing truly excellent either in the minds or the characters of men is reached without much of "ennobling impulse from the Past"; and that they who live too much in the present miss the right food of human elevation, contented to be, perhaps proud of being the vulgar things they are, because ignorant of what has been before them. It is not that the present age is worse than former ages; it may even be better as a whole: but what is bad or worthless in an age dies with the age; so that only the great and good of the Past touches us; while of the present we are most touched by that which is little and mean.

The third principle of Art, as I am taking them, is *Completeness*. A work of art must have within itself all that is needful for the due understanding of it, *as Art;* so that the beholder will not have to go outside or beyond the work itself to learn what it means; that is, provided he have the corresponding faculties alive within him, so as to be capable of its proper force. For, if the work speaks through form and colour, there must be, in answering measure, a natural or an instructed eye; if sound is its organ, there must be a natural or an instructed ear; if its speech is verbal, there must be, besides a natural or an instructed taste, a sufficient knowledge also of the language in which it is written. All this of course. But, apart from this, the work must be complete in and of itself, so as to be intelligible without a commentary. And any work which requires a sign or a showman to tell the beholder what it is, or to enable him to take the sense and virtue of it, is most certainly a failure.

In all this, however, I am speaking of the work simply as art, and not as it is or may be something else. For works of art, in many cases, are or have a good deal besides that. And in connection with such a work there may arise various questions, — of antiquity, philology, local custom and allusion; in what place and at what time it was done; whence, how, and why it came to be as it is; where the author got any hints or materials for it, and what of antecedent or contemporary history may be gathered from it. All this is legitimate and right in its place, but has nothing to do with the character and meaning of the thing as a work of art, in which respect it must know its cue without a prompter, and be able to tell its own tale. That which holds the mirror up to nature must not need another mirror to discover or interpret its reflection to us. For instance, a building, as a building, looks to certain practical ends and uses; and, before we can rightly understand the order and reason of it, we must know from other sources the ends and uses for which it was designed: but in so far as it is architecture, in so far as it is truly imaginative, and embodies the author's intellectual soul, it must be able to express its own meaning, so that we can understand and feel it without any thing but what comes directly from the work itself. But perhaps the point may be better illustrated in the case of an historical drama, which may be viewed either as history or as art: and, to determine its merit as history, we must go to other sources; but, for ascertaining its merit as art, the work must itself give us all the knowledge we need: so that the question of its historic truth is distinct and separate from the question of its artistic truth: it may be true as history, yet false as art; or it may be historically wrong, yet artistically right; true to nature, though not true to past fact: and, however we may have to travel abroad in the historical inquiry, the virtue of the work as art must be ascertainable directly from the thing itself. This, then, is what I mean by artistic completeness; that quality in virtue of which a work justifies itself, without foreign help, by its own fulness and clearness of expression.

The fourth and last principle that I am to consider is *Disinterestedness.* This is partly an intellectual, but more a moral quality. Now one great reason why men fail so much in their mental work is because they are not willing to see and to show things as they are, but must still be making them as they would have them to be. Thus from self-love or wilfulness or vanity they work their own humours and crotchets and fancies into the matter, or overlay it with some self-pleasing quirks of peculiarity. Instead of this, the artist must lose himself, his personal aims, interests, passions, and preferences, in the enthusiasm and inspiration of his work, in the strength, vividness, and beauty of his ideas and perceptions, and must give his whole mind and soul to the task of working these out into expression. To this end, his mind must live in constant loving sympathy and intercourse with Nature; he must work close to her life and order; must study to seize and reproduce the truth of Nature just precisely as it is, and must not think to improve her or get ahead of her; though, to be sure, out of the materials she offers, the selection and arrangement must be his own; and all the strength he can put forth this way will never enable him to come up to her stern, honest, solid facts. So, for instance, the highest virtue of good writing stands in saying a plain thing in a plain way. And in all art-work the first requisite is, that a man have, in the collective sense and reason of mankind, a firm foothold for withstanding the shifting currents and fashions and popularities of the day. The artist is indeed to work in free concert with the imaginative soul of his age: but the trouble is, that men are ever mistaking some transient specialty of mode for the abiding soul; thus tickling the folly of the time, but leaving its wisdom untouched.

If, therefore, a man goes to admiring his own skill, or airing his own powers, or imitating the choice touches of others, or heeding the breath of conventional applause; if he yields to any strain of self-complacency, or turns to practising smiles, or to taking pleasure in his self-begotten graces and beauties and fancies; — in this giddy and vertiginous state he will be sure to fall into intellectual and artistic sin. The man, in such a case, is no more smitten with a genuine love of Art than Malvolio was with a genuine love of Virtue: like that hero of conceit, he is merely "sick of self-love, and tastes with a distempered appetite." And his giddiness of self-love will take from him the power of seeing things as they are; and because he sees them as they are not, therefore he will think he sees them better than they are. A man cannot find Nature by gazing in a looking-glass; and it is vanity or some undisinterested force, and not any inspiration of truth or genius, that puts a man upon doing so. And, in the condition supposed, the mind becomes a prism to sophisticate and falsify the light of truth into striking and brilliant colours, instead of being a clear and perfect lens to concentrate that light in its natural whiteness and purity. For, assuredly, the proper worth, health, strength, virtue, joy, and life of Art is to be the interpreter and discoverer of Truth, to "feel the soul of Nature, and see things as they are"; and when, instead of this, it turns to glorifying its own powers and achievements, or sets up any end apart from such discovery and interpretation, it becomes sickly, feeble, foolish, frivolous, vicious, joyless, and moribund; and meanness, cruelty, sensuality, impiety, and irreligion are the companions of it.

It is indeed true that an artist may find one of the main

spurs to his art-work in the needs, duties, and affections of his earthly being. The support of himself, of his wife, or her whom he wishes to be his wife, of his children, his parents, or remoter kin; the desire of being independent, of having the respect of society, or of doing the charities of a Christian; an honest, manly yearning after fame, an ambition to achieve something that "the world will not willingly let die," — all these, and yet others, may justly be among the determining motives of his pursuit, and the thought of them may add fresh life and vigour to his efforts: nevertheless he will not succeed, nor deserve to succeed, in his art, except he have such an earnest and disinterested love for it, and such a passion for artistic truth, as will find the work its own exceeding great reward. In a word, his heart and soul must be in it *as an end*, and not merely or chiefly as a means. However prudence may suggest and shape his plans, love must preside over the execution; and here, as elsewhere,

> "Love's not love
> When it is mingled with respects that stand
> Aloof from the entire point."

These four, then, are, in my account, essential principles of Art, and the only ones which it lies within my purpose to consider; namely, Solidarity, Originality, Completeness, and Disinterestedness. And to the attaining of these there needs, especially, three things in the way of faculty, — high intellectual power, great force of will, and a very tender heart; — a strong head to perceive and grasp the truth of things, a strong will to select and order the materials for expressing it, and a strong heart, which is tenderness, to give the work a soul of beauty and sweetness and amiability. As a man combines all these strengths, and as, moreover, through the unifying power of imagination, he pours the united life and virtue of them all into his work; so will his worth and honour stand as an artist. For whence should the noblest fruitage of human thought and culture grow, but from the noblest parts and attributes of manhood, moving together in perfect concert and reciprocity?

DRAMATIC COMPOSITION.

Shakespeare's dramas — not all of them indeed, but those which were written after he reached what may be called his mastership — are in the highest sense of the term Works of Art, and as such embody to the full the principles set forth in the preceding section. In this general survey of his workmanship, I propose to consider, first, his Dramatic Architecture or Composition.

I have remarked in a previous chapter,* that in Shakespeare's time, and for several ages before, the Drama was a national passion in England, nearly all classes of people being pervaded by it. And yet, strange to say, this passion, notwithstanding the great frequency and variety of dramatic exhibitions, never came to any sound fruitage of Art, till the work fell into Shakespeare's hands. Moreover the tide of patriotic feeling, or the passion of nationality, which had for centuries been growing in strength, intelligence, and manliness, was then at its height, the people of all sorts being possessed with a hearty, honest English enthusiasm and national pride. And this passion was inextricably bound up with traditions of the past and with the ancient currents of the national life. Therewithal this deep, settled reverence for what was then "Old England," while it naturally drew into the mind the treasured riches of many foregoing ages, was at the same time strangely combined with a very bold and daring spirit of progress and improvement. Men seem indeed to have been all the more open to healthy innovation for being thus firmly rooted in the ground of prescription. The public mind received what was new the more freely because it loved the old. So that hope and anticipation walked with the bolder pace, inasmuch as memory and retrospection were still their cherished companions. In a word, men's tenacity of the past gave them the larger and brighter vision of the future. Because

* Page 120 of this volume.

they had no mind to forsake the law of their fathers, or to follow the leading of "sages undevoutly free," therefore they were able to legislate the better for their children, and felt the less of danger in true freedom of thought.

It was natural, perhaps inevitable, that those two passions thus coexisting should somehow work together, and at least endeavour to produce a joint result. And so it was in fact. Historical plays, or things purporting to be such, were highly popular: the public taste evidently favoured, not to say demanded them; and some of Shakespeare's earliest essays were undoubtedly in that line. There are many clear evidences to this point. For instance, Thomas Nash, in his *Pierce Penniless*, 1592, speaks of certain plays "wherein our forefathers' valiant acts, that have been long buried in rusty brass and worm-eaten books, are revived, and they themselves raised from the grave of oblivion, and brought to plead their aged honours in open presence." And again: "How would it have joyed brave Talbot, the terror of the French, to think that, after he had lain two hundred years in the tomb, he should triumph again on the stage; and have his bones new-embalmed with the tears of ten thousand spectators at least, — at several times, — who, in the tragedian that represents his person, behold him fresh-bleeding!" From these passages it is clear that historical plays on English subjects were strong in the public interest and patronage. And I have no doubt that the second passage quoted refers to Shakespeare's First Part of *King Henry the Sixth.* And it might well be that the popular mind should take special delight in entertainments where, to the common interest of dramatic exhibitions was added the further charm of national feeling and recollection, and where a large patriotism, "looking before and after," would find itself at home.

The Historical Drama, then, grew up simultaneously with Comedy and Tragedy, and established itself as a coördinate branch of the Gothic Drama in England. Now this circumstance could not be without great influence in determining the whole scope and character of the English Drama in all its varieties. The natural effect was to make them all more or less historical in method and grain. For the process generated, and could not fail to generate, corresponding modes and habits of thought in dramatic composition; and these would needs go with the writers into whatever branch of the Drama they might take in hand. Because modes and habits of thought are not things that men can put off and on for different subjects and occasions. What they learn to practise in one field of labour transfers itself with them, whether they will or no, to other fields. Their way of viewing things, nay, their very faculties of vision, catch the temper and drift of what they work in; which drift and temper cleave to them in spite of themselves, and unconsciously shape all their movements of thought; so that, change their matter as they may, their mind still keeps the same. Accordingly, even when Shakespeare does not deal specifically with the persons and events of history; when he fetches his incidents and characters from the realms of imagination; still his workmanship is historical in its spirit and method; proceeding according to the *laws*, even while departing from the *matter*, of history; so that we have pure creations formed upon the principles, and in the order and manner, of historical dramas.

The practical consequences of all this were both manifold and strongly marked. The Drama thus cut itself loose and swung clean away from the narrow circle of myths and legends, where the ancients had fixed it, and ranged at large in all the freedom and variety of historical representation. It took on all the compass, amplitude, and expansiveness of the Homeric Epos. The stereotyped sameness and confinement of the Greek stage were necessarily discarded, and the utmost breadth of matter and scope, compatible with clearness of survey, became the recognized freehold of Dramatic Art.*

* At this time the Drama was recognized throughout Europe as the poetic form most suitable to modern times and races. As it occupied the *place* of the

So that, as I have before observed, the English Drama was, in the largest sense, a national growth, and not the work of any individual. Neither was it a sudden growth, as indeed nothing truly national ever can be: like the English State, it was the slow, gradual, silent production of centuries, — the result of the thoughts of many minds in many ages. The whole platform, and all that relates to the formal construction of the work, were fixed before Shakespeare put his hand to it: what remained for him to do, and what he was supremely gifted for doing, was to rear a grand and beautiful fabric on the basis and out of the materials already prepared. And where I like best to contemplate the Poet is, not in the isolation of those powers which lift him so far above all others, but as having the mind of the nation, with its great past and greater present, to back him up. And it seems to me, his greatness consisted very much in that, as he had the gift, so he surrendered himself to the high task, of reproducing in artistic immortality the beatings of old England's mighty heart. He therefore did not go, nor needed he, to books to learn what others had done: he just sucked in without stint, and to the full measure of his angelic capacity, the wisdom and the poetry that lived on the lips, and in the thoughts, feelings, sentiments, and manners of the people. What he thus sucked in, he

epic poem, and did not merely, like the ancient drama, stand *side by side* with it, so, along with the office of replacing it, it inherited also the task of showing itself capable of managing, like the epopee, any matter however extended. The materials presented to it were not common property, like the many well-known myths of antiquity, handed down in a ready-made poetical form; but they were those rudiments formed in the religious dramas, those Mysteries founded on vast actions, and those historical subjects, which required a whole cycle of pieces for the mastering of the huge matter. The things of the world had become complicated and manifold: the variety of men, their nature, their passions, their situations, their mutually-contending powers, would not submit, in dramatic representation, to be limited to a simple catastrophe: a wider horizon must be drawn; the actions must be represented throughout their course; the springs of action must be more deeply searched. Thus Art was put to the work of setting forth the utmost fulness of matter in a corresponding form, which, however, according to Aristotle's law, must not be extended so far as to preclude an easy survey. — GERVINUS.

purged from its drossy mixtures, replenished with fresh vitality, and then gave it back clothed in the grace and strength of his own clear spirit. He told the nation better — O how much better! — than any other could, just what it wanted to hear, — the very things which its heart was swelling with; only it found not elsewhere a tongue to voice them, nor an imagination to body them forth.*

Thus the time and the man were just suited to each other; and it was in his direct, fearless, whole-hearted sympathy with the soul of the time that the man both lost himself and found his power: which is doubtless one reason why we see so little of him in what he wrote. So that the

* The times, far from being a hindrance to a great poet, were, indeed, from fortunate local and national conditions, the most propitious that modern times could offer. In a few points they might be prejudicial to Shakespeare's poetry, but on the whole he had cause to bless his happy star. The conflict with scholastic philosophy and religious fanaticism was not indeed over; yet Shakespeare came at a precious moment of mental freedom, *after* the struggle with Popery, and *before* that with the Puritans. He could thus in his poetry give to the age the basis of a natural mode of feeling, thought, and life, upon which Art prospers in its purest form. In many respects the age itself was in this favourable to the Poet. It maintained a happy medium between crudeness and a vitiated taste: life was not insipid and colourless, as it is nowadays: men still ventured to appear what they were; there was still poetry in reality. Our German poets, in an age of rouge and powder, of hoops and wigs, of stiff manners, rigid proprieties, narrow society, and cold impulses, had indescribable trouble in struggling out of this dulness and deformity, which they had first to conquer in themselves before they could discern and approve what was better. In Shakespeare's time, nature was still alive: the age was just halting on the threshold of these distorted views of false civilization; and if our Poet had to combat against the first approaches of the disease, he was yet sound and free from it himself. He had the immense advantage of being at one with his age, and not at odds with it. When he sought materials for his poetry, he did not need, like our painters, to dive into past worlds, restore lost creeds, worship fallen gods, and imitate foreign works of art: from his national soil he drew the power which makes his poetry unrivalled. The age favoured him from another side also. He appeared at that auspicious period when the Drama had in England already obtained acceptance and love; when the sympathy of the people was most alive; and when, on the other hand, the public were not yet corrupted with oversensibility. He took that in hand which most actively engaged the spirit of the people; and he carried it through progressive steps to a consummation beyond which there was nothing possible but retrogression. — GERVINUS.

work could not possibly have been done anywhere but in England, — the England of Spenser and Raleigh and Bacon; nor could it have been done there and then by any man but Shakespeare. In his hand what had long been a national passion became emphatically a National Institution: how full of life, is shown in that it has ever since refused to die. And it seems well worth the while to bring this clearly into view, inasmuch as it serves to remove the subject upon deeper and broader principles of criticism than have commonly stood uppermost in the minds of the Poet's critics.

Properly speaking, then, it was the mind and soul of old England that made the English Drama as we have it in Shakespeare: her life, genius, culture, spirit, character, built up the work, and built themselves into the work, at once infusing the soul and determining the form. Of course, therefore, they ordered and shaped the thing to suit their own purpose, or so as to express freely and fitly their proper force and virtue; and they did this in wise ignorance, or in noble disregard, of antecedent examples, and of all formal and conventional rules. In other words, they were the *life* of the thing; and that life organized its body, as it needs must do, according to its innate and essential laws.*

Which naturally starts the question, how or why the Shakespearian Drama came to take on a form so very different from that of the Classic Drama. This question has been partly disposed of already, in speaking of the freedom and

* A Poet! — He hath put his heart to school,
Nor dares to move unpropp'd upon the staff
Which Art hath lodg'd within his hand, — must laugh
By precept only, and shed tears by rule.
Thy Art be Nature! the live current quaff,
And let the groveller sip his stagnant pool,
In fear that else, when Critics grave and cool
Have kill'd him. Scorn should write his epitaph.
How doth the Meadow-flower its bloom unfold?
Because the lovely little flower is free
Down to its root, and in that freedom bold;
And so the grandeur of the Forest-tree
Comes not by casting in a formal mould,
But from its *own* divine vitality. WORDSWORTH.

variety which the historical branch imported into the sphere of dramatic production. Still it may be asked how, if the Classic form is right, as all admit it to be, can we avoid concluding the Shakespearian form to be wrong? The answer of course is, that the form differs, and ought to differ, just as much as the life does; so that both forms may be right, or at least equally so. Formerly it was the custom to censure the Poet greatly, if not to condemn him utterly, because, in his dramatic workmanship, he did not observe what are called the Minor Unities, that is, the Unities of Time and Place. The controversy indeed is now all out of date, and there need not a word be said by way of answering or refuting that old objection: no interest attaches to the question, nor is it worth considering at all, save as it may yield light and illustration in the philosophy of Art, and in the general matter of art criticism. On this account, it may be worth the while to look a little further into the reason of the difference in question.

I have already said that religion or religious culture has always been the originating and shaping spirit of Art. There is no workmanship of Art in which this holds more true than in the English Drama. Now the religious culture of Christian England was essentially different from that of Classic Greece; the two being of quite diverse and incommunicable natures; so that the spirit of the one could not possibly live in the dramatic form of the other. In other words, the body of the Classic Drama was not big enough nor strong enough to contain the soul of Christian England. The thing could no more be, except in a purely mechanical and arbitrary way, than an acorn could develop itself into a violet, or the life of an eagle build itself into the body of a trout, or the soul of a horse put on the organism of a dove. Moreover the Greek religion was mythical or fabulous, and could nowise stand the historic method: the Christian religion is historical both in origin and form; as such it has a natural sympathy and affinity with the historic method, the hardest facts being more in keeping with its spirit than the most beautiful and ingenious fables and myths. Not indeed but that Christianity has its own ideal, or rather its sphere of ideality, and this in a much higher and purer kind than any mythology ever had; but its nature is to idealize from fact; its ideality is that of the waking reason and the ruling conscience, not that of the dreaming fancy and the dominating senses; and even in poetry its genius is to "build a princely throne on humble truth": it opens to man's imaginative soul the largest possible scope, — "Beauty, a living Presence, surpassing the most fair ideal forms which craft of delicate spirits hath composed from earth's materials"; a world where imagination gathers fresh life and vigour from breathing the air of reason's serenest sky, and where it builds the higher and nobler, that it rests on a deep and solid basis of humility, instead of "revolving restlessly" around its own airy and flitting centre. The Shakespearian Drama works in the order and spirit of this principle; so that what the Poet creates is in effect historical, has the solidity and verisimilitude of Fact, and what he borrows has all the freedom and freshness of original creation. Therewithal he often combines the two, or interchanges them freely, in the same work; where indeed they seem just as much at home together as if they were twins; or rather each is so attempered to the other, that the two are vitally continuous.

But let us note somewhat further the difference of structure. Now the Classic Drama, as we have it in Sophocles, though exquisitely clear and simple in form, and austerely beautiful withal, is comparatively limited in its scope, with few characters, little change of scene, no blending or interchanging of the humourous and the grave, the tragic and the comic, and hardly exceeding in length a single Act of the Shakespearian Drama. The interest all, or nearly all, centres in the catastrophe, there being only so much of detail and range as is needful to the evolving of this. Thus the thing neither has nor admits any thing like the complexity and variety, the breadth, freedom, and massiveness, of Shakespeare's workmanship. There is timber enough and life enough in one of his dramas to make four or five Sophoclean tragedies; and one of these might almost be cut out of *Hamlet* without being missed. Take, for instance, the *Œdipus at Colonos* of Sophocles and *King Lear*, each perhaps the most complex and varied work of the author. The Greek tragedy, though the longest of the author's pieces, is hardly more than a third the length of *King Lear*. The former has no change of scene at all; the first Act of the other has five changes of scene. The Sophoclean drama has eight characters in all, besides the Chorus; *King Lear* has twenty characters, besides the anonymous persons. To be sure, quantity in such things is no measure of strength or worth; but when we come to wealth, range, and amplitude of thought, the difference is perhaps still greater.

And so, generally, the Classic Drama, like the Classic Architecture, is all light, graceful, airy, in its form; whereas the Gothic is in nature and design profound, solemn, majestic. The genius of the one runs to a simple expressiveness; of the other to a manifold suggestiveness. That is mainly statuesque, and hardly admits any effect of background and perspective; this is mainly picturesque, and requires an ample background and perspective for its characteristic effect. There the mind is drawn more to objects; here, more to relations. The former, therefore, naturally detaches things as much as possible, and sets each out by itself in the utmost clearness and definiteness of view; while the latter associates and combines them in the largest possible variety consistent with unity of interest and impression, so as to produce the effect of indefiniteness and mystery. Thus a Shakespearian drama is like a Gothic cathedral, which, by its complexity of structure, while catching the eye would fain lift the thoughts to something greater and better than the world, making the beholder feel his littleness, and even its own littleness, in comparison of what it suggests. For, in this broad and manifold diversity struggling up into unity, we may recognize the awe-inspiring grandeur and vastness of the Gothic Architecture, as distinguished from the cheerful, smiling beauty of the Classic. Such is the difference between the spirit of Classic Art and the spirit of Gothic Art.*

Now, taking these two things together, namely, the historic spirit and method, and also the breadth and amplitude of matter and design, both of which belong to the Gothic Drama, and are indeed of its nature; — taking these together, it cannot but be seen, I think, that the work must have a much larger scope, a far more varied and expansive scene, than is consistent with the Minor Unities. If, for example, a man would *represent* any impressive course or body of historical events, the historic order and process of the thing plainly necessitate a form very different from that of the Classic Drama: the work must needs use considerable diversity of time and place, else narrative and description will have to be substituted, in a great measure, for representation; that is, the right dramatic form must be sacrificed to what, after all, has no proper coherence or consanguinity with the nature and genius of the work. As to which of the two is better in itself, whether the austere

* Schlegel has a passage that hits the core of the matter: "Rousseau recognized the contrast in Music, and showed that rhythm and melody was the ruling principle of ancient as harmony is of modern music. On the imaging arts, Hemsterhuys made this ingenious remark, that the ancient painters were perhaps too much of sculptors, modern sculptors too much of painters. This touches the very point of difference; for the spirit of collective ancient art and poetry is plastic, as that of the modern is picturesque." And again: "The Pantheon is not more different from Westminster Abbey or the Church of St. Stephen at Vienna than the structure of a tragedy of Sophocles from a drama of Shakespeare. The comparison between these two wonderful productions of poetry and architecture might be carried still further." Coleridge also has some very choice remarks on the subject: "I will note down the fundamental characteristics which contradistinguish the ancient literature from the modern generally, but which more especially appear in prominence in the tragic drama. The ancient was allied to statuary, the modern refers to painting. In the first there is a predominance of rhythm and melody; in the second, of harmony and counterpoint. The Greeks idolized the finite, and therefore were masters of all grace, elegance, proportion, fancy, dignity, majesty, — of whatever, in short, is capable of being definitely conveyed by defined forms and thoughts; the moderns revere the infinite, and affect the indefinite as a vehicle of the infinite; hence their passions, their obscure hopes and fears, their wandering through the unknown, their grander moral feelings, their more august conception of man as man, their future rather than their past, — in a word, their sublimity."

and simple beauty of the Sophoclean tragedy, or the colossal grandeur and massiveness of such a drama as *King Lear*, this is not for me to say: for myself, however, I cannot choose but prefer the latter; for this too has a beauty of its own; but it is indeed an *awful* beauty, and to my sense all the better for being so. Be this as it may, it is certain that the human mind had quite outgrown the formal limitations of the Classic Drama.*

But what are the conditions of building, in right artistic order, a work of such vastness and complexity? As the mind is taken away from the laws of time and place, it must be delivered over to the higher laws of reason. So that the work lies under the necessity of proceeding in such a way as to make the spectator live in his imagination, not in his senses, and even his senses must, for the time being, be made imaginative, or be ensouled. That is, instead of the formal or numerical unities of time and place, we must have the unities of intellectual time and intellectual space: the further the artist departs from the local and chronological succession of things, the more strict and manifest must be their logical and productive succession. Incidents and characters are to be represented, not in the order of sensible juxtaposition or procession, but in that of cause and effect, of principle and consequence. Whether, therefore, they stand ten minutes or ten months, ten feet or ten miles, asunder, matters not, provided they are really and evidently

* Two thousand years lie between Shakespeare and the flourishing period of the ancient tragedy. In this interval Christianity laid open unknown depths of mind: the Teutonic race, in their dispersion, filled wide spaces of the Earth; the Crusaders opened the way to the East, voyages of discovery revealed the West and the form of the whole globe; new spheres of knowledge presented themselves; whole nations and periods of time arose and passed away; a thousand forms of life, public and private, religious and political, had come and gone; the circle of views, ideas, experiences, and interests was immensely enlarged, the mind thereby made deeper and broader, wants increased, passions more various and refined, the conflict of human endeavours more diversified and intricate, the resources of the mind immeasurable; all in a way quite foreign to the childish times of antiquity. This abundance of external and internal material streamed into the sphere of Art on all sides: poetry could not resist it without injury, and even ruin. — GERVINUS.

united in this way; that is, provided the unities of action and interest are made strong enough and clear enough to overcome the diversities of time and place. For, here, it is not *where* and *when* a given thing happened, but how it was produced, and why, whence it came and whither it tended, what caused it to be as it was, and to do as it did, that we are mainly concerned with.

The same principle is further illustrated in the well-known nakedness of the Elizabethan stage in respect of furniture and scenic accompaniment. The weakness, if such it were, appears to have been the source of vast strength. It is to this poverty of the old stage that we owe, in part, the immense riches of the Shakespearian Drama, since it was thereby put to the necessity of making up for the defect of sensuous impression by working on the rational, moral, and imaginative forces of the audience. And, undoubtedly, the modern way of glutting the senses with a profusion of showy and varied dress and scenery has struck, as it must always strike, a dead palsy on the legitimate processes of Gothic Art. The decline of the Drama began with its beginning, and has kept pace with its progress. So that here we have a forcible illustration of what is often found true, that men cannot get along because there is nothing to hinder them. For, in respect of the moral and imaginative powers, it may be justly affirmed that we are often assisted most when *not* assisted, and that the right way of helping us on is by leaving us unhelped. That the soul may find and use her wings, nothing is so good as the being left where there is little for the feet to get hold of and rest upon.

To answer fully the conditions of the work, to bring the Drama fairly through the difficulties involved therein, is, it seems to me, just the greatest thing the human intellect has ever done in the province of Art. Accordingly I place Shakespeare's highest and most peculiar excellence in the article of Dramatic Composition. He it was, and he alone, that accomplished the task of *organizing* the English

Drama. Among his predecessors and senior contemporaries there was, properly speaking, no dramatic artist. What had been done was not truly Art, but only a preparation of materials and a settlement of preliminaries. Up to his time, there was little more than the elements of the work lying scattered here and there, some in greater, some in less perfection, and still requiring to be gathered up and combined in right proportions, and under the proper laws of dramatic life. Take any English drama written before his, and you will find that the several parts do not stand or draw together in any thing like organic consistency: the work is not truly a *concrescence* of persons and events, but only, at the best, a mere succession or aggregation of them; so that, for the most part, each would both be and appear just as it does, if detached from the others, and viewed by itself. Instead, therefore, of a vital unity, like that of a tree, the work has but a sort of aggregative unity, like a heap of sand.

Which may in some fair measure explain what I mean by dramatic composition. For a drama, regarded as a work of art, should be in the strictest sense of the term a *society;* that is, not merely a numerical collection or juxtaposition, but a living contexture, of persons and events. For men's natures do not, neither can they, unfold themselves severally and individually; their development proceeds from, through, and by each other. And, besides their individual circulations, they have a common circulation; their characters interpenetrating, more or less, one with another, and standing all together in mutual dependence and support. Nor does this vital coherence and reciprocity hold between the several characters merely, but also between these, taken collectively, and the various conditions, objects, circumstances, and influences, amidst which they have grown. So that the whole is like a large, full-grown tree, which is in truth made up of a multitude of little trees, all growing from a common root, nourished by a common sap, and bound together in a common life.

Now in Shakespeare's dramas — I do not say all of them, for some were but his apprentice-work, but in most of them — the several parts, both characters and incidents, are knit together in this organic way, so as to be all truly members one of another. Each needs all the others, each helps all the others, each is made what it is by the presence of all the others. Nothing stands alone, nothing exists merely for itself. The persons not only have each their several development, but also, besides this, and running into this, a development in common. In short, their whole transpiration proceeds by the laws and from the blood of mutual membership. And as each lives and moves and has his being, so each is to be understood and interpreted, with reference, explicit or implicit, to all the others. And there is not only this coherence of the characters represented, one with another, but also of them all with the events and circumstances of the representation. It is this coefficient action of all the parts to a common end, this mutual participation of each in all, and of all in each, that constitutes the thing truly and properly a work of art.

So then a drama may be fitly spoken of as an *organic* structure. And such it must be, to answer the conditions of Art. Here we have a thing made up of divers parts or elements, with a course or circulation of mutual reference and affinity pervading them all, and binding them together, so as to give to the whole the character of a multitudinous unit; just as in the illustration, before used, of a large tree made up of innumerable little trees. And it seems plain enough that, the larger the number and variety of parts embraced in the work, or the more diversified it is in matter and movement, the greater the strength of faculty required for keeping every thing within the terms of Art; while, provided this be done, the grander is the impression produced, and the higher is the standing of the work as an intellectual achievement of man.

This, then, as before observed, is just the highest and hardest part of dramatic creation: in the whole domain of literary workmanship there is no one thing so rarely attained, none that so few have been found capable of attaining, as this. And yet in this Shakespeare was absolutely — I speak advisedly — without any teacher whatever; not to say, what probably might be said without any hazard, that it is a thing which no man or number of men could impart. The Classic Drama, had he been ever so well acquainted with it, could not have helped him here at all, and would most likely have been a stumbling-block to him. And, in my view of the matter, the most distinguishing feature of the Poet's genius lies in this power of broad and varied combination; in the deep intuitive perception which thus enabled him to put a multitude of things together, so that they should exactly fit and finish one another. In some of his works, as *Titus Andronicus*, *The Comedy of Errors*, and the three Parts of *King Henry the Sixth*, though we have, especially in the latter, considerable skill in individual character, — far more than in any English plays preceding them, — there is certainly very little, perhaps nothing, that can be rightly termed dramatic composition. In several, again, as *The Two Gentlemen of Verona*, *Love's Labour's Lost*, and *King John*, we have but the beginnings and first stages of it. But in various others, as *The Tempest*, *The Merchant of Venice*, *As You Like It*, *King Henry the Fourth*, *Hamlet*, *Macbeth*, *King Lear*, and *Othello*, it is found, if not in entire perfection, at least so nearly perfect, that there has yet been no criticism competent to point out the defect.

All which makes a full and conclusive answer to the charge of irregularity which has been so often brought against the Poet. To be regular, in the right sense of the term, he did not need to follow the rules which others had followed before him: he was just as right in differing from them as they were in differing from him: in other words, he stands as an original, independent, authoritative legislator in the province of Art; or, as Gervinus puts it, "he holds the place of the revealing genius of the laws of Art in the

Modern Drama"; so that it is sheer ignorance, or something worse, to insist on trying him by the laws of the ancient Tragedy. It is on this ground that Coleridge makes the pregnant remark,—"No work of true genius dares want its appropriate form, neither indeed is there any danger of this. As it must not, so genius cannot, be lawless; for it is even this that constitutes it genius,—the power of acting creatively under laws of its own origination." So that I may fitly close this branch of the subject by applying to Shakespeare a very noteworthy saying of Burke's, the argument of which holds no less true of the law-making prerogative in Art than in the State: "Legislators have no other rules to bind them but the great principles of reason and equity, and the general sense of mankind. These they are bound to obey and follow; and rather to enlarge and enlighten law by the liberality of legislative reason, than to fetter and bind their higher capacity by the narrow constructions of subordinate, artificial justice."*

* Aristotle himself was very far from setting up the form and extent of the drama of his day as a rule for all time. He declared that, "as regards the natural limit of the action, the more extended will always be the more beautiful, so long as it is easily surveyed." Shakespeare's practice is strictly correspondent to this rule. But with this rule in mind, he went to the very verge of these limits. He chose his matter as rich and full as possible; he extended its form according to its requirements, but no further: it will not be found, in any of his dramas, that the thought is exhausted before the end; that there is any superfluous extension of the form, or any needless abundance of the matter. To arrange the most ample materials in the amplest form without overstepping its fair proportions, is a task which no one has accomplished as he has done. Therein lies a large part of his artistic greatness. No poet has represented so much in so little space; none has so widely enlarged the space without exceeding the poetical limitations. In this he did not suffer himself to be perplexed by the example of the ancient tragedy. He felt that the peculiar poetic material of the new world would perish in those old forms, and that it was therefore better to mould them afresh. He knew right well that the poet's task was to represent the very substance of his times, to reflect the age in his poetry, and to give it form and stamp: he therefore created, for the enlarged sphere of life, an enlarged sphere of Art: to this end he sought, not a ready-made rule, but the inward law of the given matter,—a spirit in the things, which in the work of art shaped the form for itself. For there

CHARACTERIZATION.

I am next to consider Shakespeare's peculiar mode of conceiving and working out character; as this stands next in order and importance to the article of Dramatic Composition.

Now, in several English writers before him, we find characters discriminated and sustained with considerable judgment and skill. Still we feel a want of reality about them: they are not men and women themselves, but only the outsides and appearances of men and women; often having indeed a good measure of coherence and distinctness, but yet mere appearances, with nothing behind or beneath, to give them real substance and solidity. Of course, therefore, the parts actually represented are all that they have; they stand for no more than simply what is shown; there is nothing in them or of them but what meets the beholder's sense: so that, however good they may be to look at, they will not bear looking into; because the outside, that which is directly seen or heard, really exhausts their whole force and meaning.

Instead, then, of beginning at the heart of a character, and working outwards, these authors began at the surface, and worked the other way; and so were precluded from getting beyond the surface, by their mode of procedure. It is as if the shell of an egg should be fully formed and finished before the contents were prepared; in which case the contents of course could not be got into it. It would have to remain a shell, and nothing more: as such, it might do well enough for a show, just as well indeed as if it were full of meat; but it would not stand the weighing.

is no higher worth in a poetical work than the agreement of the form with the nature of the matter represented, and this according to its own indwelling laws, not according to external rule. If we judge Shakespeare or Homer by any such conventional rule, we may equally deny them taste and law: measured, however, by that higher standard, Shakespeare's conformity to the inner law outstrips all those regular dramatists who learned from Aristotle, not the spirit of regularity, but mechanical imitation. — Gervinus.

With Shakespeare all this is just reversed. His egg is a real egg, brimful of meat, and not an empty shell; and this, because the formation began at the centre, and the shell was formed last. He gives us, not the mere imitations or appearances of things, but the very things themselves. His characters *have* more or less of surface, but they *are* solids: what is actually and directly shown, is often the least part of them, never the whole: the rest is left to be inferred; and the showing is so managed withal as to start and propagate the inferring process in the beholder's mind.

All which clearly implies that Shakespeare conceived his persons, not from their outside, but in their rudiments and first principles. He begins at the heart of a character, and unfolds it outwards, forming and compacting all the internal parts and organs as he unfolds it; and the development, even because it is a real and true development, proceeds at every step, not by mere addition or aggregation of particulars, but by digestion and vital assimilation of all the matter that enters into the structure; there being, in virtue of the life that pervades the thing, just such elements, and just so much of them, sent to each organ, as is necessary to its formation. The result of this wonderful process is, that the characters are all that they appear to be, and a vast deal more besides: there is food for endless thought and reflection in them: beneath and behind the surface, there is all the substance that the surface promises or has room for,—an inexhaustible stock of wealth and significance beyond what is directly seen; so that the more they are looked into the more they are found to contain.

Thus there is a sort of realistic verisimilitude in Shakespeare's characters. It is as if they had been veritable living men and women, and he had seen and comprehended and delivered the whole and pure truth respecting them. Of course, therefore, they are as far as possible from being mere names set before pieces of starched and painted rhetoric, or mere got-up figures of modes and manners: they are no shadows or images of fancy, no heroes of romance, no theatrical personages at all; they have nothing surreptitious or make-believe or ungenuine about them: they do not in any sort belong to the family of poetical beings; they are not designs from works of art; nay, they are not even *designs* from nature; they are nature itself. Nor are they compilations from any one-sided or sectional view of mankind, but are cut out round and full from the whole of humanity; so that they touch us at all points, and, as it were, surround us. From all this it follows that there is no repetition among them: though there are some striking family resemblances, yet no two of them are individually alike: for, as the process of forming them was a real growth, an evolution from a germ, the spontaneous result of creative Nature working within them, so there could be no copying of one from another. Accordingly, as in the men and women of Nature's own making, different minds conceive different ideas of them, and have different feelings towards them, and even the same mind at different times: in fact, hardly any two men view them alike, or any one man for two years together; the actual changes in us being reflected and measured by correspondent *seeming* changes in them: so that a further acquaintance with them always brings advancing knowledge, and what is added still modifies what was held before. Hence even so restrained, not to say grudging, a critic as Pope was constrained to pronounce Shakespeare's characters "so much Nature herself, that it is a sort of injury to call them by so distant a name as copies of her."

> "Of Nature's inner shrine thou art the Priest,
> Where most she works when we perceive her least."

I have placed Shakespeare's power of dramatic architecture or organization at the head of his gifts and prerogatives *as an artist*. And so I suppose a just Philosophy of Art is bound to reckon it. But comparatively few men are or can be, in the fair sense of the term, philosophers of Art, as this requires a course of special training and study. But

Shakespeare is a great teacher in the School of Life as well as a great master in the School of Art. And indeed the right use of Art is nowise to serve as the raw material of philosophy, but to furnish instruction and inspiration in the truth of things; and unless it can work home to the business and bosoms of plain practical men, it might as well be struck from the roll of legitimate interests. Now, in the circle of uninspired forces, Shakespeare's art may be justly regarded as our broadest and noblest "discipline of humanity." And his characterization, not his dramatic composition, is his point of contact with us as a practical teacher. In other words, it is by his thorough *at-homeness* with human nature in the transpirations of individual character that he touches the general mind and heart. Here he speaks a language which all men of developed intelligence can understand and feel. Accordingly it is in his characters that most men place, and rightly place, his supreme excellence: here it is that his wisdom finds and grasps men *directly* as men; nor, at this point of meeting, does he leave any part of our many-sided being without its fitting portion of meat in due season; while our receptiveness is the only limit to our acquisitions.*

* Here is no stage language or manners, no standing parts, nothing that can be called ideal or favourite stage characters, no heroes of the theatre or of romance: in this active world there is nothing fantastic, nothing unsound, nothing exaggerated nor empty: neither the poet nor the actor speaks in them, but creative nature alone, which seems to dwell in and to animate these images. The forms vary, as they do in life, from the deepest to the shallowest, from the most noble to the most deformed: a prodigal dispenses these riches; but the impression is, that he is as inexhaustible as Nature herself. And not one of these figures is like another in features: there are groups which have a family likeness, but no two individuals resembling each other: they become known to us progressively, as we find it with living acquaintance: they make different impressions on different people, and are interpreted by each according to his own feelings. Hence, in the explanation of Shakespeare's characters, it would be an idle undertaking to balance the different opinions of men, or to insist arbitrarily on our own: each can only express his own view, and must then learn whose opinion best stands the test of time. For, on returning to these characters at another time, our greater ripeness and experience will ever lay open to us new features in them. Whoever has not been wrecked, with his ideals and principles, on the shore of life, whoever has not bled inwardly

"That which he hath writ
Is with such judgment labour'd and distill'd
Through all the needful uses of our lives,
That, could a man remember but his lines,
He should not touch at any serious point,
But he might breathe his spirit out of him."

Shakespeare, it is true, idealizes his characters, all of them more or less, some of them very much. But this, too, is so done from the heart outwards, done with such inward firmness and such natural temperance, that there is seldom any thing of hollowness or insolidity in the result. Except in some of his earlier plays, written before he had found his proper strength, and before his genius had got fairly disciplined into power, there is nothing ambitious or obtrusive in his idealizing; no root of falsehood in the work, as indeed there never is in any work of art that is truly worthy the name. Works of artifice are a very different sort of thing. And one, perhaps the main, secret of Shakespeare's mode in this respect is, that the ideal is so equally diffused, and so perfectly interfused with the real, as not to disturb the natural balance and harmony of things. In other words, his poetry takes and keeps an elevation at all points alike above the plane of fact. Therewithal his mass of real matter is so great, that it keeps the ideal mainly out of sight. It is only by a special act of reflection that one discovers there is any thing but the real in his workmanship; and the appreciative student, unless his attention is specially drawn to that point, may dwell with him for years without once suspecting the presence of the ideal, because in truth his mind is kindled secretly to an answering state. It is said that even Schiller at first saw nothing but realism in

with sorrow, has not suppressed holy feelings, and stumbled over the enigmas of the world, will but half understand Hamlet. And whoever has borne the sharpest pains of consciousness will understand Shakespeare's characters like one of the initiated; and to him they will be ever new, ever more admirable, ever richer in significance: he will make out of them a school of life, free from the danger of almost all modern poetry, which is apt to lead us astray, and to give us heroes of romance, instead of true men. — Gervinus.

Shakespeare, and was repelled by his harsh truth; but afterwards became more and more impressed with his ideality, which seemed to bring him near the old poets.

Thus even when Shakespeare idealizes most the effect is to make the characters truer to themselves and truer to nature than they otherwise would be. This may sound paradoxical, nevertheless I think a little illustration will make it good. For the proper idealizing of Art is a concentration of truth, and not, as is often supposed, a substitution of something else in the place of it. Now no man, that has any character to speak of, does or can show his whole character at any one moment or in any one turn of expression: it takes the gathered force and virtue of many expressions to make up any thing rightly characteristic of him. In painting, for instance, the portrait of an actual person, if the artist undertakes to represent him merely as he is at a given instant of time, he will of course be sure to misrepresent him. In such cases literal truth is essential untruth. Because the person cannot fairly deliver himself in any one instant of expression; and the business of Art is to distil the sense and efficacy of many transient expressions into one permanent one; that is, out of many passing lines and shades of transpiration the artist should so select and arrange and condense as to deliver the right characteristic truth about him. This is at least one of the ways, I think it is the commonest way, in which Shakespeare idealizes his characters; and he surpasses all other poets in the ease, sureness, and directness with which his idealizing works in furtherance of truth. It is in this sense that he idealizes from nature. And here, as elsewhere, it is "as if Nature had entrusted to him the secret of her working power"; for we cannot but feel that, if she should carry her human handiwork up to a higher stage of perfection, the result would be substantially as he gives it. Accordingly our first impression of his persons is that they are simply natural: had they been literal transcripts from fact, they would not have seemed more intensely real than they do: yet a close comparison of them with the reality of human nature discloses an ideal heightening in them of the finest and rarest quality. Even so realistic a delineation as Hostess Quickly, or the Nurse in *Romeo and Juliet*, is not an exception to this rule.

The Poet's idealizing of his characters proceeds, in part, by putting his own intellectuality into them. And the wonder is, how he could do this in so large a measure as he often does, without marring or displacing or anywise obstructing their proper individuality. For they are never any the less themselves for having so much of his intelligence in them. Nay, more; whatever may be their peculiarity, whether wit, dulness, egotism, or absurdity, the effect of that infusion is to quicken their idiom, and set it free, so that they become all the more rightly and truly themselves. Thus what he gives them operates to extricate and enfranchise their propriety, and bring it out in greater clearness and purity. His intellectuality discovers them to us just as they are, and translates their mind, or want of mind, into fitting language, yet remains so transparently clear as to be itself unseen. He tells more truth of them, or rather makes them tell more truth of themselves, in a single sentence, than, without his help, they could tell in a month. The secret of this appears to lie in sifting out what is most idiomatic or characteristic of a man, purging and depurating this of all that is uncharacteristic, and then presenting the former unmixed and free, the man of the man.

We have a very striking instance of this in *King Henry the Fifth*, where the Boy, who figures as servant to Bardolph, Pistol, and Nym, soliloquizes his judgment of those worthies: "As young as I am, I have observed these three swashers. I am boy to them all three; but they all three, though they would serve me, could not be man to me; for indeed three such antics do not amount to a man. For Bardolph, — he is white-liver'd and red-fac'd; by the means whereof 'a faces it out, but fights not. For Pistol, — he hath a killing tongue and a quiet sword; by the means whereof 'a breaks words, and keeps whole weapons. For Nym, — he hath heard that men of few words are the best men; and therefore he scorns to say his prayers, lest 'a should be thought a coward: but his few bad words are match'd with as few good deeds; for 'a never broke any man's head but his own, and that was against a post when he was drunk. They will steal any thing, and call it purchase. Bardolph stole a lute-case, bore it twelve leagues, and sold it for three half-pence. Nym and Bardolph are sworn brothers in filching; and in Calais they stole a fire-shovel: I knew by that piece of service the men would carry coals. They would have me as familiar with men's pockets as their gloves or their handkerchers: which makes much against my manhood, if I should take from another's pocket to put into mine; for it is plain pocketing-up of wrongs. I must leave them, and seek some better service: their villainy goes against my weak stomach, and therefore I must cast it up."

Here one might think the Poet must have lapsed a little from the character in making the Boy talk such a high and solid strain of intelligence: but it is not so; the Boy talks strictly in character. The intellect he shows is all truly his own too, but not his own in that space of time. He has indeed a shrewd, quick eye, and knows a thing or two; still he could not, unaided and alone, deliver so much intellect in a whole month as he here lets off in this brief speech. Shakespeare just inspires the youngster, and the effect of that inspiration is to make him so much the more himself.

But the process of the thing involves, moreover, a sort of double consciousness, which probably cannot be altogether explained. The Poet had a strange faculty, or at least had it in a strange degree, of being truly himself and truly another at one and the same time. For he does not mould a character from the outside, but is truly inside of it, nay, *is* the character for the time being, and yet all the while he continues just as much Shakespeare as if he were nothing else. His own proper consciousness, and the consciousness of the person he is representing, both of these are everywhere apparent in his characterization; both of them working together too, though in a manner which no psychology has been able to solve. In other words, Shakespeare is perfectly in his persons and perfectly out of them at the same time; has his consciousness and theirs thoroughly identified, yet altogether distinct; so that they get all the benefit of his intellect without catching the least tinge of his personality. There is the mystery of it. And the wonder on this point is greatly enhanced in his delineations of mental disease. For his consciousness takes on, so to speak, or passes into, the most abnormal states without any displacement or suspension of its normal propriety. Accordingly he explores and delivers the morbid and insane consciousness with no less truth to the life than the healthy and sound; as if in both cases alike he were inside and outside the persons at the same time. With what unexceptional mastery in Nature's hidden processes he does this, must be left till I come to the analysis of particular instances.

It is to be noted further that Shakespeare's characters, generally, are not exhibited in any one fixed state or cast of formation. There is a certain vital limberness and ductility in them, so that upon their essential identity more or less of mutation is ever supervening. They grow on and unfold themselves under our eye: we see them in course of development, in the act and process of becoming; undergoing marked changes, passing through divers stages, animated by mixed and various motives and impulses, passion alternating with passion, purpose with purpose, train of thought with train of thought; so that they often end greatly modified from what they were at the beginning; the same, and yet another. Thus they have to our minds a past and a future as well as a present; and even in what we see of them at any given moment there is involved something both of history and of prophecy.

Here we have another pregnant point of divergence from the Classic form. For, as it is unnatural that a man should continue altogether the same character, or subject to the same passion, or absorbed in the same purpose, through a period of ten years; so it is equally against nature that a man should undergo much change of character, or be occupied by many passions, or get engrossed in many purposes, the same day. If, therefore, a character is to be represented under various phases and fluctuations, the nature of the work evidently requires much length of time, a great variety of objects and influences, and, consequently, a wide range of place. Thus, in the Gothic Drama, the complexity of matter, with the implied vicissitudes of character, was plainly incompatible with the Minor Unities. On the other hand, the clearness and simplicity of design, which belong to the Classic Drama, necessarily preclude any great diversity of time and place; since, as the genius of the thing requires character to be represented mainly under a single aspect, the time and place of the representation must needs be limited correspondingly.

Again: It is admitted on all hands that in Shakespeare's works, far more than in almost any others, every thing appears to come, not from him, but from the characters; and from these too speaking, not as authors, but simply as men. The reason of which must be, that the word is just suited to the character, the character to the word; every thing exactly fitting into and filling the place. Doubtless there are many things which, considered by themselves, might be bettered; but it is not for themselves that the Poet uses them, but as being characteristic of the persons from whom they proceed; and the fact of their seeming to proceed from the persons, not from him, is clear proof of their strict dramatic propriety. Hence it is that in reading his works we think not of him, but only of what he is describing: we can hardly realize his existence, his individuality is so lost in the objects and characters he brings before us. In this respect, he is a sort of impersonal intelligence, with the power to make every thing visible but itself. Had he been merely an omniloquent voice, there could hardly have been less of subjective idiom in his deliverances. That he should have known so perfectly how to avoid giving too much or too little; that he should have let out and drawn in the reins precisely as the matter required;—this, as it evinces an almost inconceivable delicacy of mind, is also one of the points wherein his originality is most conspicuous.

Equally remarkable is the Poet's intellectual plenipotence in so ordering and moving the several characters of a play as that they may best draw out each other by mutual influences, and set off each other by mutual contrasts. The persons are thus assorted and attempered with perfect insight both of their respective natures and of their common fitness to his purpose. And not the least wonderful thing in his works is the exquisite congruity of what comes from the persons with all the circumstances and influences under which they are represented as acting; their transpirations of character being withal so disposed that the principle of them shines out freely and clearly on the mind. We have a good instance of this in Romeo's speech just before he swallows the poison; every word of which is perfectly idiomatic of the speaker, and at the same time thoroughly steeped in the idiom of his present surroundings. It is true, Shakespeare's persons, like those in real life, act so, chiefly because they are so; but so perfectly does he seize and impart the germ of a character, along with the proper conditions of its development, that the results seem to follow all of their own accord. Thus in his delineations every thing is fitted to every other thing; so that each requires and infers the others, and all hang together in most natural coherence and congruity.

To illustrate this point a little more in detail, let us take his treatment of passion. How many forms, degrees, varieties of passion he has portrayed! yet I am not aware that any instance of disproportion or unfitness has ever been successfully pointed out in his works. With but two or three exceptions at the most, so perfect is the correspondence between the passion and the character, and so freely and fitly does the former grow out of the circumstances in which the latter is placed, that we have no difficulty in justifying and accounting for the passion. The passion is thoroughly characteristic, and pervaded with the individuality of its subject. And this holds true not only of different passions, but of different modifications of the same passion; the forms of love, for instance, being just as various and distinct as the characters in which it is shown. Then too he unfolds a passion in its rise and progress, its turns and vicissitudes, its ebbings and flowings, so that we go along with it freely and naturally from first to last. Even when, as in case of Ferdinand and Miranda, or of Romeo and Juliet, he ushers in a passion at its full height, he so contrives to throw the mind back or around upon various predisposing causes and circumstances, as to carry our sympathies through without any revulsion. We are so prepared for the thing by the time it comes as to feel no abruptness in its coming. The exceptions to this, save in some of the Poet's earlier plays, are very rare indeed: the only one I have ever *seemed* to find is the jealousy of Leontes in *The Winter's Tale*, and I am by no means sure of it even there. This intuitive perception of the exact kind and degree of passion and character that are suited to each other; this quick and sure insight of the internal workings of a given mind, and of the why, the when, and the how far it should be moved; and this accurate letting-out and curbing-in of a passion precisely as the law of its individuality requires; in a word, this thorough mastery of the inmost springs and principles of human transpiration; — all this is so extraordinary, that I am not surprised to find even grave and temperate thinkers applying to the Poet such bold expressions as the instrument, the rival, the co-worker, the completer of Nature.

Nor is this the only direction in which he maintains the fitness of things: he keeps the matter right towards us as well as towards his characters. It is true, he often lays on us burdens of passion that would not be borne in any other writer. But, whether he wrings the heart with pity, or freezes the blood with terror, or fires the soul with indignation, the genial reader still rises from his pages refreshed. The reason of which is, instruction keeps pace with excitement: he strengthens the mind in proportion as he loads it. Shakespeare has been called the great master of passion: doubtless he is so; yet he is not more that than he is every thing else: for he makes us think as intensely as he requires us to feel; while opening the deepest fountains of the heart, he at the same time kindles the highest energies of the head. Nay, with such consummate art does he manage the fiercest tempests of our being, that in a healthy mind the witnessing of them is always attended by an overbalance of pleasure. With the very whirlwinds of passion he so blends the softening and assuaging influences of poetry, that they relish of nothing but sweetness and health; as in case of "the gentle Desdemona," where pathos is indeed carried to the extreme limit of endurance, so that "all for pity I could die," yet there is no breach of the rule in question. For while, as a philosopher, he surpassed all other philosophers in power to discern the passions of men; as an artist, he also surpassed all other artists in skill

> "so to temper passion, that our ears
> Take pleasure in their pain, and eyes in tears
> Both weep and smile."

Another point well worth the noting is the perfect even-handedness of Shakespeare's representations. For, among all his characters, with the single exception, perhaps, of "Prince Hal," we cannot discover from the delineation itself that he preferred any one to another; though of course we cannot conceive it possible for any man to regard, for example, Edmund and Edgar, or Iago and Desdemona, with the same feelings. It is as if the scenes of his dramas were forced on his observation against his will, himself being under a solemn oath to report the truth, the whole truth, and nothing but the truth. He thus leaves the characters to make their own impression upon us. He is their mouth-piece, not they his: what they say is never Shakespeare ventriloquizing, but is to all intents and purposes their own. With the right or wrong, the honour or shame, of their actions, he has nothing to do: that they are so, and act so, is their concern, not his; and his business is, not to reform nor deprave, not to censure nor approve them, but simply to tell the truth about them. And so, because he would not serve as the advocate of any, therefore he was able to stand as the representative of all; which is indeed his characteristic office.

Most of the many faultings of Shakespeare's workmanship on the score of taste are easily disposed of from this point. As a general thing, the blame laid upon him in this behalf belongs only to his persons, and as regards him the matter of it should rather be a theme of praise. Take, for example, the gross images and foul language used by Leontes when the rage of jealousy is on him: the matter is offensive enough certainly in itself, but it is the proper outcome of the man's character in that state of mind; that is, it is a part, and an essential part, of the truth concerning him: as the passion turns him into a brute, so he is rightly made, or rather allowed to speak a brutal dialect; and the bad taste is his, not the Poet's. That jealousy, such as that of Leontes, naturally subverts a man's understanding and manners, turns his sense, his taste, his decency all out of doors, and causes him to gloat over loathsome thoughts and fancies, — this is among the things of human nature which it would be a sin to omit in a delineation of that passion.

And so of the many absurdities and follies and obscenities which Shakespeare puts into the mouths of certain persons: for the most part, they have an ample justification in that they are characteristic of the speakers: if not beauties of art, they often have a higher beauty than art, as truths of nature; and the Poet is no more to be blamed for them than an honest reporter is for the bad taste of a speaker reported. In like sort, we have Milton's Satan satanizing thus:

> "The mind is its own place, and of itself
> Can make a Heaven of Hell, a Hell of Heaven."

I have often heard people quote this approvingly, as if they thought the better of Satan for thus declaring himself independent of God. But those words coming from Satan are a high stroke of dramatic fitness; and when people quote them with approval, this may be an argument of intellectual impiety in them, but not of Milton's agreement with them in opinion.

But do you say that Shakespeare should not have undertaken to represent any but persons of refined taste and decorous speech? That were to cut the Drama off from its proper freehold in the truth of human character, and also from some of its fruitfullest sources of instruction and wisdom: so, its office were quite another thing than "holding the mirror up to Nature." Not indeed but that Shakespeare is fairly chargeable with some breaches of good taste: these however are so few and of such a kind, that they still leave him just our highest authority in the School of Taste. Here, as elsewhere, he is our "canon of Polycletus." So Raphael made a painting of Apollo playing the fiddle on Parnassus, — a grosser breach of good taste than any thing Shakespeare ever did. And yet Raphael is the painter of the finest taste in the world! — All which just approves the old proverb, that "no man is wise at all hours": so that we may still affirm without abatement the fine saying of Schlegel, that "genius is the almost unconscious choice of the highest excellence, and, consequently, it is taste in the greatest perfection." *

* All beauty depends upon symmetry and proportion. An overgrowth that sucks out the strength of a flowering plant, and destroys its shape, may be in the oak a harmless sport of exuberance, and even an ornament to its form:

It is to be observed, also, that Shakespeare never brings in any characters as the mere shadows or instruments or appendages of others. All the persons, high and low, contain within themselves the reason why they are there and not elsewhere, why they are so and not otherwise. None are forced in upon the scene merely to supply the place of others, and so to be trifled with till the others are ready to return; but each is treated in his turn as if he were the main character of the piece. So true is this, that even if one character comes in as the satellite of another, he does so by a right and an impulse of his own: he is all the while obeying, or rather executing the law of his individuality, and has just as much claim on the other for a primary as the other has on him for a satellite; which may be aptly instanced in Justice Shallow and Justice Silence, or in Sir Toby Belch and Sir Andrew Aguecheek. The consequence is, that all the characters are developed, not indeed at equal length, but with equal perfectness as far as they go; for, to make the dwarf fill the same space as the giant were to dilute, not develop, the dwarf.

Thus much as to Shakespeare's mode of conceiving and working out character. Here, again, as in the matter of dramatic composition, we have the proper solidarity, origi-

bushes which would be a wilderness in a garden may enhance the beauty of the grander scenes of Nature. Irregularity, when isolated or taken out of its place, will always be ugly; while in its proper connection it may add to the charm by variety. The good men of Polonius's school, who cannot see beyond their beards, who never get further than such particulars as, "that is a foolish figure," — "that 's an ill phrase, a vile phrase," — "that 's good," — "this is too long," — these Hamlet sends "to the barber's with their beards" and their art criticisms; they are out of place with such a poet as Shakespeare. All the experience we have gained warns us against following their steps. The whole history of Shakespearian criticism for the last century is but a discovery of the mistakes of those who, for a century before, were thought to have discovered faults in the Poet. For numbers of the errors of taste in Shakespeare have tnrned out to be striking touches of character; the æsthetic deformities imputed to his poetry have proved the moral deformities of certain of his persons; and what had been denounced as a fault was found to be an excellence. — GERVINUS.

nality, completeness, and disinterestedness of Art, all duly and rightly maintained: that is, what was before found true in reference to all the parts of a drama viewed as a whole; the same holds, also, in regard to all the parts of an individual character considered by itself. In both these respects, and in both alike, the Poet discovers a spirit of the utmost candour and calmness, such as could neither be misled by any inward bias or self-impulse from seeing things as they are, nor swayed from reflecting them according to the just forms and measures of objective truth; while his creative forces worked with such smoothness and equanimity, that it is hardly an extravagance to describe him as another Nature. All this, however, must not be taken as applying, at least not in the full length and breadth, to what I have before spoken of as the Poet's apprentice-work. For, I repeat, Shakespeare's genius was not born full-grown, as a good many have been used to suppose. Ben Jonson knew him right well personally, and was, besides, no stranger to his method of working; and, in his noble lines prefixed to the folio of 1623, he puts this point just as, we may be sure, he had himself seen it to be true:

> "Yet must I not give Nature all; thy art,
> My gentle Shakespeare, must enjoy a part:
> For a good poet's made, as well as born;
> And such wert thou."

As to the question how far his genius went by a certain instinctive harmony and happiness of nature, how far by a process of conscious judgment and reflection, this is probably beyond the reach of any psychology to determine. From the way he often speaks of poets and poetry, of art and nature, it is evident that he was well at home in speculative and philosophical considerations of the subject. Then too the vast improvement made in some of his plays, as in *Hamlet*, upon rewriting them, shows that his greatest successes were by no means owing to mere lucky hits of instinct. On the whole, I suspect he understood the what, the how, and the why of his working as well as any first-class artist ever did. But genius, in its highest and purest instances, is a sort of unfallen intellect; so that from its pre-established harmony with the laws of mental being it goes right spontaneously. Sophocles comprehended the whole of what is meant by powerful genius working unconsciously, when he said of his great teacher, "Æschylus does what is right without knowing why." And the true secret of Shakespeare's excellence mainly lies, I take it, in a perfect co-operative union of instinct and understanding, of purpose and impulse; nature and art, inspiration and study, so working together and interpenetrating, that it is impossible to distinguish their respective shares in the joint result. And the wonder of it is, how the fruits of creative impulse could so pass through the medium of conscious reflection, as they seem to have done, and still retain all the dewy freshness of pure creative nature; insomuch that his art carries such an air of unstudied ease as gives it the appearance of perfect artlessness.*

As to the time when Shakespeare passed from the apprentice into the master, I place this in the year 1597, or

* The working together of instinct and mind in Shakespeare is not exactly wonderful in itself, but only so from the power and strength of it: in a less degree it takes place in all continued occupation among men of a healthy nature; and the brightest moments of success in any work are when the thinking mind is in unison with the instinctive feeling of the working man. It is in this unison tha. genius really displays itself, and not in the sole rule of an irregular instinct or in a state of pretended inspiration. For genius does not manifest itself in the predominance of any single power, nor is it in itself a definite faculty; but it is the harmonious combination, the united totality of all the human faculties. And if in Shakespeare's works we admire his imaginative power not without his understanding, nor both these without his sense of beauty, nor all of them without his moral sense; if we attribute all together to his genius, we must comprehend in this the union of all those faculties, and not regard it as an isolated power, which excludes judgment and reflection, and whose works do not submit to plan and rule. Much rather is the idea of rule essentially inherent to that of genius; and the whole conception of genius acting without law is the invention of pedants, which has had the sad effect of begetting that mass of false geniuses who are morally without law, and æsthetically without law, as if to entitle themselves to the name according to this convenient definition. — GERVINUS.

thereabouts, when he was thirty-two or thirty-three years old; and I take *The Merchant of Venice* and *King Henry the Fourth* as marking the clear and complete advent of the master's hand. And what I have been saying holds *altogether* true only of the plays written during his mastership. In all his earlier plays, even in *A Midsummer Night's Dream*, *King Richard the Second*, and *King Richard the Third*, probably neither the composition nor the characterization can fairly stand the test of any of the principles of Art, as I have noted them. But especially in the workmanship of that period, along with much that is rightly original, we have not a little, also, of palpable imitation. The unoriginality, however, is rather in the style than in the matter, and so will be more fitly remarked under the head of Style. Still worse, because it goes deeper, we have in those plays a want of clear artistic disinterestedness. The arts and motives of authorship are but too apparent in them; thus showing that the Poet did not thoroughly lose himself in the enthusiasm and truth of his work. In some cases, he betrays not a little sense of his own skill; at least there are plain marks of a conscious and self-observing exercise of skill. And perhaps his greatest weakness, if that word may be used of him at all, lies in a certain vanity and artifice of stage-effect, or in a sort of theatrical and dialogical intemperance, as if he were trying to shine, and pleased with the reflection of his own brilliancy. But as this too was the result of imitation, not of character, so in the earnestness of his work he soon outgrew it, working purely in the interest and from the inspiration of Nature and Truth.

Before passing on from this branch of the subject, perhaps I ought to add that Shakespeare drew largely from the current popular literature of his time. The sources from which he gathered his plots and materials will be noted pretty fully when I come to speak of particular plays. It may suffice to remark here, that there seems the more cause for dwelling on what the Poet took from other writers, in that it exhibits him, where a right-minded study should specially delight to contemplate him, as holding his unrivalled inventive powers subordinate to the higher principles of Art. He cared little for the interest of novelty, which is but a short-lived thing at the best; much for the interest of truth and beauty, which is indeed immortal, and always grows upon acquaintance. And the novel-writing of our time shows that hardly any thing is easier than to get up new incidents or new combinations of incidents for a story; and as the interest of such things turns mainly on their novelty, so of course they become less interesting the more one knows them: which order — for "a thing of beauty is a joy for ever" — is just reversed in genuine works of art. Besides, if Shakespeare is the most original of poets, he is also one of the greatest of borrowers; and as few authors have appropriated so freely from others, so none can better afford to have his obligations in this kind well known.

HUMOUR.

Shakespeare's *Humour* is so large and so operative an element of his genius, that a general review of his works would be very incomplete without some special consideration of it. And perhaps, except his marvellous duality of mind, there is nothing in his poetry of which it is more difficult to give a satisfactory account. For humour is nowise a distinct or separable thing with him, but a perfusive and permeating ingredient of his make-up: it acts as a sort of common solvent, in which different and even opposite lines of thought, states of mind, and forms of life are melted into happy reconcilement and co-operation. Through this, as a kind of pervading and essential sap, is carried on a free intercourse and circulation between the moral and intellectual parts of his being; and hence, perhaps, in part, the wonderful catholicity of mind which generally marks his representations.

It follows naturally from this that the Poet's humour is widely diversified in its exhibitions. There is indeed no part of him that acts with greater versatility. It imparts a certain wholesome earnestness to his most sportive moods, making them like the honest and whole-hearted play of childhood, than which human life has nothing that proceeds more in earnest. For who has not found it a property of childhood to be serious in its fun, innocent in its mischief, and ingenuous in its guile? Moreover it is easy to remark that, in Shakespeare's greatest dunces and simpletons and potentates of nonsense, there is something that prevents contempt. A fellow-feeling springs up between us and them; it is through our sympathetic, not our selfish emotions, that they interest us: we are far more inclined to laugh with them than at them; and even when we laugh at them we love them the more for that which is laughable in them. So that our intercourse with them proceeds under the great law of kindness and charity. Try this with any of the Poet's illustrious groups of comic personages, and it will be found, I apprehend, thoroughly true. What distinguishes us from them, or sets us above them in our own esteem, is never appealed to as a source or element of delectation. And so the pleasure we have of them is altogether social in its nature, and humanizing in its effect, ever knitting more widely the bands of sympathy.

Here we have what may be called a foreground of comedy, but the Poet's humour keeps up a living circulation between this and the serious elements of our being that stand behind it. It is true, we are not always, nor perhaps often, conscious of any stirring in these latter: what is laughable occupies the surface, and therefore is all that we directly see. But still there are deep undercurrents of earnest sentiment moving not the less really that their movement is noiseless. In the disguise of sport and mirth, there is a secret discipline of humanity going on; and the effect is all the better that it steals into us unseen and unsuspected: we know that we laugh, but we do something better than laughing without knowing it, and so are made the better by our laughter; for in that which betters us without our knowledge we are doubly benefited.

Not indeed but that Shakespeare has characters, as, for example, the Steward in *King Lear*, which are thoroughly contemptible, and which we follow with contempt. But it is to be observed that there is nothing laughable in Oswald; nothing that we can either laugh with or laugh at: he is a sort of human reptile, such as life sometimes produces, whom we regard with moral loathing and disgust, but in whose company neither mirth nor pity can find any foothold. On the other hand, the feelings moved by a Bottom, a Dogberry, an Aguecheek, or a Slender, are indeed very different from those which wait upon a Cordelia, an Ophelia, or an Imogen, but there is no essential oppugnance between them: in both cases the heart moves by the laws of sympathy; which is exactly reversed in the case of such an object as Oswald: the former all touch us through what we have in common with them; the latter touches us only through our antipathies. There is, therefore, nothing either of comic or of tragic in the part of Oswald viewed by itself: on the contrary, it runs in entire oppugnance to the proper currents of them both.

Much of what I have said touching Shakespeare's comic scenes holds true, conversely, of his tragic scenes. For it is a great mistake to suppose that his humour has its sole exercise in comic representations. It carries the power of tears as well as of smiles: in his deepest strains of tragedy there is often a subtile infusion of it, and this too in such a way as to heighten the tragic effect; we may feel it playing delicately beneath his most pathetic scenes, and deepening their pathos. For in his hands tragedy and comedy are not made up of different elements, but of the same elements standing in different places and relations: what is background in the one becomes foreground in the other; what is an undercurrent in the one becomes an uppercurrent in the other; the effect of the whole depending almost, perhaps altogether, as much on what is not directly seen as on what is. So that with him the pitiful and the ludicrous, the sublime and the droll, are like the greatness and littleness of human life: for these qualities not only coexist in our being, but, which is more, they coexist under a mysterious law of interdependence and reciprocity; insomuch that our life may in some sense be said to be great because little, and little because great.

And as Shakespeare's transports of humour draw down more or less into the depths of serious thought, and make our laughter the more refreshing and exhilarating because of what is moving silently beneath; so his tragic ecstasies take a richness of colour and flavour from the humour held in secret reserve, and forced up to the surface now and then by the superincumbent weight of tragic matter. This it is, in part, that truly makes them "awful mirth." For who does not know that the most winning smiles are those which play round a moistening eye, and tell of serious thoughts beneath; and that the saddest face is that which wears in its expression an air of remembered joy, and speaks darkly of sunshine in the inner courts of the soul? For we are so made, that no one part of our being moves to perfection unless all the other parts move with it: when we are at work, whatever there is of the playful within us ought to play; when we are at play, our working mind ought to be actively present in the exercise. It is this harmonious moving together of all the parts of our being that makes the true music of life. And to minister in restoring this "concord of a well-tuned mind," which has been broken by "discords most unjust," is the right office of Culture, and the right scope of Art as the highest organ of Culture. And in reference to this harmonious interplay of all the human faculties and sensibilities, I may not unfitly apply to Shakespeare's workmanship these choice lines from Wordsworth:

> "Brisk Youth appeared, the Morn of youth,
> With freaks of graceful folly,—

Life's temperate Noon, her sober Eve,
Her Night not melancholy;
Past, present, future, all appeared,
In harmony united,
Like guests that meet, and some from far,
By cordial love invited."

I cannot, nor need I, stay to illustrate the point in hand, at any length, by detailed reference to the Poet's dramas. This belongs to the office of particular criticism, and therefore would be something out of keeping here. The Fool's part in *King Lear* will readily occur to any one familiar with that tragedy. And perhaps there is no one part of *Hamlet* that does more to heighten the tragic effect than the droll scene of the Gravediggers. But, besides this, there is a vein of humour running through the part of Hamlet himself, underlying his darkest moods, and giving depth and mellowness to his strains of impassioned thought. And every reflecting reader must have observed how much is added to the impression of terror in the trial-scene of *The Merchant of Venice*, by the fierce jets of mirth with which Gratiano assails old Shylock; and also how, at the close of the scene, our very joy at Antonio's deliverance quickens and deepens our pity for the broken-hearted Jew who lately stood before us dressed in such fulness of terror. But indeed the Poet's skill at heightening any feeling by awakening its opposite; how he manages to give strength to our most earnest sentiments by touching some spring of playfulness; and to further our liveliest moods by springing upon us some delicate surprises of seriousness; — all this is matter of common observation.

But the Poet's humour has yet other ways of manifesting itself. And among these not the least remarkable is the subtile and delicate irony which often pervades his scenes, and sometimes gives character to whole plays, as in the case of *Troilus and Cressida*, and *Antony and Cleopatra*. By methods that can hardly be described, he contrives to establish a sort of secret understanding with the reader, so as to arrest the impression just as it is on the point of becoming tragic. While dealing most seriously with his characters, he uses a certain guile: through them we catch, as it were, a roguish twinkle of his eye, which makes us aware that his mind is secretly sporting itself with their earnestness; so that we have a double sympathy, — a sympathy with their passion and with his play. Thus his humour often acts in such a way as to possess us with mixed emotions: the persons, while moving us with their thoughts, at the same time start us upon other thoughts which have no place in them; and we share in all that they feel, but still are withheld from committing ourselves to them, or so taking part with them as to foreclose a due regard to other claims.

STYLE.

The word *style* is often used in a sense equally appropriate to all the forms of Art, — a sense having reference to some peculiar mode of conception or execution; as the Saxon, the Norman, the Romanesque style of architecture, or the style of Titian, of Raphael, of Rembrandt, of Turner, in painting. In this sense, it includes the whole general character or distinctive impression of any given workmanship in Art, and so is applicable to the Drama; as when we speak of a writer's tragic or comic style, or of such and such dramas as being in too operatic a style. The peculiarities of Shakespeare's style in this sense have been involved in the foregoing sections; so that I shall have no occasion to speak further of them in this general survey of the Poet's Art. The more restrained and ordinary meaning of the word looks merely to an author's use of language; that is, his choice and arrangement of words, the structure of his sentences, and the cast and texture of his imagery; all, in short, that enters into his diction, or his manner of conveying his particular thoughts. This is the matter now to be considered. The subject, however, is a very wide one, and naturally draws into a multitude of details; so that I can hardly do more than touch upon a few leading points, lest the discussion should quite overgrow the limits I have prescribed myself.

On a careful inspection of Shakespeare's poetry, it becomes evident that none of the epithets commonly used in regard to style, such as *plain*, *simple*, *neat*, *ornate*, *elegant*, *florid*, *figurative*, *severe*, *copious*, *sententious*, can be rightly applied to him, at least not as characteristic of him. His style is all of them by turns, and much more besides; but no one of the traits signified by those terms is so continuous or prominent as to render the term in any sort fairly discriminative or descriptive of his diction.

Under this head, then, I am to remark, first, that Shakespeare's language is as far as possible from being of a constant and uniform grain. His style seems to have been always in a sort of fluid and formative state. Except in two or three of his earliest plays, there is indeed a certain common basis, for which we have no word but *Shakespearian*, running through his several periods of writing; but upon this basis more or less of change is continually supervening. So that he has various distinct styles, corresponding to his different stages of ripeness in his work. These variations, to be sure, are nowise abrupt: the transition from one to another is gradual and insensible, proceeding by growth, not by leaps: but still, after an interval of six or seven years, the difference becomes clearly marked. It will suffice for my purpose to speak of them all under the threefold distinction of earlier, middle, and later styles. And I probably cannot do better than to take *King Richard the Second*, *As You Like It*, and *Coriolanus*, as representing, severally, those three divisions.

Shakespeare began by imitating the prevailing theatrical style of the time. He wrote in much the same way as those before and about him did, till by experience and practice he found out a better way of his own. It is even doubtful whether his first imitations surpassed his models. In *Titus*

Andronicus, the First Part of *King Henry the Sixth*, and *The Comedy of Errors*, if there be any thing of the right Shakespearian idiom, it is so overlaid by what he had caught from others as to be hardly discoverable. Accordingly those pieces seem to me little better than worthless, save as specimens of his apprentice-work. In *The Two Gentlemen of Verona*, also, *Love's Labour's Lost*, and *The Taming of the Shrew*, imitation has decidedly the upper hand; though in these plays, especially the latter, we have clear prognostics of the forthcoming dramatic divinity. From thence onward his style kept growing less imitative and more idiomatic till not the least taste or relish of the former remained. So that in this respect his course was in fact just what might be expected from a thoroughly modest, teachable, receptive, and at the same time most living, active, and aspiring mind, — a mind full indeed of native boldness, but yet restrained by judgment and good sense from the crudeness and temerity of self-will and eccentric impulse, and not trusting to its own strength till it had better reasons for doing so than the promptings of vanity and egotism.

It is to this process of imitation that the Poet's faults of style are to be mainly ascribed; though in the end it was no doubt in a great measure the source of his excellences also. For, taking his works in the order of their production, we can perceive very clearly that his faults of style kept disappearing as he became more and more himself. He advanced in the path of improvement by slow tentative methods, and was evidently careful not to deviate from what was before him till he saw unmistakably how he could do better. As he was thus "most severe in fashion and collection of himself"; so he worked in just the true way for disciplining and regulating his genius into power; and so in due time he had a good right to be "as clear and confident as Jove."

Shakespeare's faults of style, especially in his earlier plays, are neither few nor small. Among these are to be reckoned, of course, his frequent quibbles and plays upon words, his verbal conceits and affectations, his equivoques and clinches. Many of these are palpable sins against manliness; not a few of them are decidedly puerile; the results of an epidemic of trifling and of fanciful prettiness. Some critics, it is true, have strained a point, if not several points, in defence of them; but it seems to me that a fair-minded criticism has no way but to set them down as plain blemishes and disfigurements. And our right, nay, our duty to call them such is fully approved in that the Poet himself seasonably outgrew and forsook them; a comparison of his earlier and later plays thus showing that his manlier taste discarded them. They were however nowise characteristic of him: they were the fashion of the day, and were common to all the dramatic writers of the time. Nor were they by any means confined to the walks of the Drama: many men of the highest character and position both in Church and State were more or less infected with them.

It is not likely indeed that Shakespeare at first regarded these things as faults, or that he adopted them reluctantly in compliance with the popular bent, and as needful to success. In his youth he doubtless used them in good faith, and even sought for them as traits of excellence; for he himself shared to the fullest extent in the redundancy of mental life which distinguished the age, and which naturally loves to sport itself in such quirks of thought and speech. But it is manifest that he was not long in growing to distaste them, notwithstanding that he still continued occasionally to practise them. For, even in *The Merchant of Venice*, which I reckon among the last in his earlier or the first in his middle style, we find him censuring the thing while indulging it:

> "O, dear discretion, how his words are suited!
> The fool hath planted in his memory
> An army of good words; and I do know
> A many fools, that stand in better place,

Garnish'd like him, that for a tricksy word
Defy the matter."

In the case here censured, however, the thing, though a vice in itself, is no offence to good taste, and may even be justly noted as a stroke of dramatic virtue, because it is rightly characteristic of the person using it: which only makes the reproof the more pointed as aimed at the habit, then but two common in the high places of learning, of so twisting language into puns and conceits, that one could hardly come at the sense. But I can admit no such plea, when, in *King Richard the Second*, the dying Gaunt goes to punning on his name:

"Old Gaunt indeed; and gaunt in being old:
Within me grief hath kept a tedious fast;
And who abstains from meat, that is not gaunt?
For sleeping England long time have I watch'd;
Watching breeds leanness, leanness is all gaunt:
The pleasure that some fathers feed upon
Is my strict fast, — I mean my children's looks;
And therein fasting, hast thou made me gaunt:
Gaunt am I for the grave, gaunt as a grave,
Whose hollow womb inherits nought but bones."

This, notwithstanding it is defended by so sound a critic as Schlegel, seems to me a decided blot; I cannot accept it as right either in itself or on the score of dramatic fitness. Many like instances occur in *Romeo and Juliet*, *King John*, and other plays of that period; instances which I cannot help regarding not only as breaches of good taste in the speakers, but as plain faults of style in the Poet himself: the blame of them indeed properly rests with him, not with the persons; for they are out of keeping with the sentiments of the occasion, and jar on the feelings which the surrounding matter inspires; that is, they are sins against dramatic propriety, as well as against honest manliness of style: so that, however the pressure of the age may account for them, it must not be taken as excusing them; and the best we can say on this point is, that in his faults of style the Poet went with the custom and fashion of his time, while in his virtues he went quite above and beyond the time.

Near akin to these are other faults of still graver import. In his earlier plays, the Poet's style is often, not to say generally, at least in the more serious parts, rather rhetorical than rightly dramatic. The persons often lay themselves out in what may not unfairly be called speech-making. Their use of language is highly self-conscious, and abounds in marks of elaborateness, as if their mind were more intent on the figure they are making than on what they are talking about: so that the right colloquial tone is lost in a certain ambitious, oratorical, got-up manner of speech; and we feel a want of that plain, native, spontaneous talk wherein heart and tongue keep touch and time together: in short, they speak rather as authors having an audience in view than as men and women moved by the real passions and interests of life.

The reason of all this I take to be, that the Poet himself was at that time highly self-conscious in his use of language. His art was then too young to lose itself in the enthusiasm of Truth and Nature; and, as remarked before, he seems to have felt no little pleasure in the tokens of his own skill. Thus, in his earlier plays, written before he had fully found himself, the arts and motives of authorship are but too apparent: he was then, I should say, somewhat in the humour of flirting with the Muses and Graces; which, because it lacks the modesty and delicacy of genuine passion, therefore naturally runs into that excess of manner and style which is commonly called "fine writing." And it is a very note-worthy point, that when he studies most for effect, then it is that we find him least effective. But here too, as in the matter mentioned before, his fault was clearly the result of imitation, not of character. Accordingly, in the earnestness of his work, he gradually outgrew it. In the plays of his later period, the fault disappears entirely; there is not a vestige of it left: in fact, this fault is mainly revealed to us by the higher standard of judgment which his later plays supply. Here all is straightforward, genuine, natural, with no rhetorical trickeries or fineries whatever; and among all modern writers his style stands quite alone in the solid purity, directness, and inward virtue of that perfect art which not only conceals itself from others, but is even a secret unto itself; or at least is too intent on something else to be listening to the music of its own voice. For so his highest style was when, in the maturity of his power, he left the style to take care of itself, and therefore had it perfectly subordinated to his matter and thought: in other words, he always writes best when most unconscious of it, being so possessed with his theme as to take no thought of himself.

We have somewhat the same order and course of things in Burke, who may be not unfitly described as the Shakespeare of political philosophy. His treatise *On the Sublime and Beautiful* was, though in a good sense, mainly the fruit of literary ambition. There he rather sought for something to say because he wanted to speak, than spoke because he had something he wanted to say. And so he is not properly himself in that work, but only a studious, correct, and tasteful writer. When thoroughly roused and kindled in the work of defending, intrenching, and illustrating the Constitution of his country as the sacred guardian of liberty and order, he became quite another man; then it was that all the powers of his great mind were taught and inspired to act in concert and unity. As Wordsworth says of him, —

> "This is no trifler, no short-flighted wit,
> No stammerer of a minute, painfully
> Deliver'd. No! the Orator hath yok'd
> The Hours, like young Aurora, to his car:
> Thrice-welcome Presence! how can patience e'er
> Grow weary of attending on a track
> That kindles with such glory!"

The mere ambitions of authorship are not enough to make

good authors; and what Burke needed was something to lift him far above them. And when he came to grapple with the high practical questions and living interests of mankind, here he was too full of his matter, and too earnest in his cause, to observe how finely he was working; and because he was captivated by his theme, not by the figure he made in handling it, therefore he earned a prerogative place among the sons of light.

The distinction I have been remarking between Shakespeare's rhetorical and dramatic use of language, or, as I before termed it, his imitative and idiomatic style, may be better understood on comparing some brief specimens of his earlier and later workmanship. As an instance of the former, take a part of York's speech to the King, in *King Richard the Second*, ii. 1:

"I am the last of noble Edward's sons,
Of whom thy father, Prince of Wales, was first:
In war was never lion rag'd more fierce,
In peace was never gentle lamb more mild,
Than was that young and princely gentleman.
His face thou hast, for even so look'd he,
Accomplish'd with the number of thy hours;
But when he frown'd, it was against the French,
And not against his friends: his noble hand
Did win what he did spend, and not spend that
Which his triumphant father's hand had won:
His hands were guilty of no kindred's blood,
But bloody with the enemies of his kin."

No one, I think, can help feeling that this is the style of a man rather aiming at finely-turned phrases than deeply in earnest with the matter in hand; more the language of brilliant rhetoric than of impassioned thought. At all events, there is to my taste an air of falsetto about it; it seems more like the image of a painted than of a living passion. Be this as it may, the Poet's own riper style quite discredits it; though I have to confess that, but for his teachings, we might not so well have known of any thing better. Now contrast with the foregoing one of the hero's speeches in *Coriolanus*, iii. 2, where his mother urges him to play the demagogue, and practise smiles for the gaining of votes:

> "Away, my disposition, and possess me
> Some harlot's spirit! my throat of war be turn'd —
> Which quirèd with my drum — into a pipe
> Small as an eunuch's, or the virgin voice
> That babies lulls asleep! the smiles of knaves
> Tent in my cheeks; and school-boys' tears take up
> The glasses of my sight! a beggar's tongue
> Make motion through my lips; and my arm'd knees,
> Who bow'd but in my stirrup, bend like his
> That hath receiv'd an alms! — I will not do't;
> Lest I surcease to honour mine own truth,
> And by my body's action teach my mind
> A most inherent baseness."

Perhaps the Poet's different styles might be still better exemplified in passages of pathos; but here I must rest with merely referring, for instance, to York's speech in *King Richard the Second*, beginning, "As in a theatre the eyes of men," and the passage in *Macbeth* where Macduff first learns of the slaughter of his wife and children. Both are indeed very noble in their way; but I think no reader of disciplined taste can fail to see the vast superiority of the latter, and that this is owing not so much to any difference of character in the speakers as to a far higher stage of art in the Poet. I must add that the rhetorical or speech-making style appears more or less in all the plays of his first period: we find something of it even in such high specimens as *The Merchant of Venice* and *King Henry the Fourth.*

I have spoken of the fault in question as specially marking the *more serious* parts of the Poet's earlier plays. The more comic portions of the same plays are much less open to any such reproof. The Poet's style in comedy from the first ran closer to nature, and had much more of freedom, simplicity, and heartiness in its goings. The reason of this difference seems to be, that the lessons of nature in sport are more quickly learnt than those of nature in her graver moods. The child plays, the man works. And there needs a ripe soul of manhood, with much discipline besides, before a man warms into his work with the free gust and spirit of play.

In what more I have to say under this head, I shall spare further reference to the Poet's faults of imitation, and speak only of his characteristic or idiomatic traits of style.

In regard to Shakespeare's choice of words there probably need not much be said. Here the point I shall first consider is the relative proportion of Saxon and Latin words in his writing. — Students somewhat curious in this behalf have found his words of Latin derivation to average about forty per cent. This, I believe, does not greatly differ from the average used by the most select and accomplished writers of that age. I suspect that Hooker has a somewhat larger proportion of Latin words, but am not sure of it. — The English had already grown to be a learned tongue; and, which is far better, the learned portion of it had got thoroughly diffused and domesticated in the popular mind: for centuries the Saxon and Latin elements had been in process of blending and fusing together, so as to work smoothly and even lovingly side by side in the same thought; common people using both with the same easy and unstudied naturalness. Therewithal the language was then in just its freshest state of maturity; flexible to all the turns of philosophical and poetical discourse; full of vital sap and flavour; its cheeks plump and rosy, its step light and graceful, with health: pedants and grammarians had not starched and ironed it into self-conscious dignity and primness: it had not learnt the vice of putting on literary airs, and of practising before a looking-glass. Our translation of the Bible is enough of itself to prove all this, even if we had no other monuments of the fact. And the Elizabethan English was a right joyous and jolly tongue also, as became the heart of brave, honest, merry old

England; yet it was earnest and candid withal, and had in no sort caught the French disease of vanity and persiflage: it was all alive, too, with virgin sensibility and imaginative delicacy; to say nothing of how Spenser found or made it as melodious and musical as Apollo's lute.

Shakespeare has many passages, some of them running to considerable length, made up almost wholly of Saxon words. Again, he has not a few wherein the Latin largely shares. Yet I can hardly see that in either case any thing of vigour and spirit is lost. On the other hand, I can often see a decided increase of strength and grasp resulting in part from a judicious mixing and placing of the two elements. I cite a few passages in illustration; the first two being from *King Lear*, the third from *Antony and Cleopatra*:

"Mine enemy's dog,
Though he had bit me, should have stood that night
Against my fire; and wast thou fain, poor father,
To hovel thee with swine, and rogues forlorn,
In short and musty straw?"

"We two alone will sing like birds i' the cage:
When thou dost ask me blessing, I'll kneel down,
And ask of thee forgivness: so we'll live,
And pray, and sing, and tell old tales, and laugh
At gilded butterflies, and hear poor rogues
Talk of Court news; and we'll talk with them too, —
Who loses and who wins, who's in, who's out; —
And take upon 's the mystery of things,
As if we were God's spies: and we'll wear out,
In a wall'd prison, packs and sects of great ones,
That ebb and flow by th' Moon."

"Henceforth
The white hand of a lady fever thee,
Shake thou to look on't. Get thee back to Cæsar,
Tell him thy entertainment: look thou say
He makes me angry with him; for he seems
Proud and disdainful, harping on what I am,
Not what he knew I was: he makes me angry;
And at this time most easy 'tis to do't,
When my good stars, that were my former guides,

Have empty left their orbs, and shot their fires
Into th' abysm of Hell."

With these collate the following from *Troilus and Cressida* and *King Lear*, where, for aught I can see, the interweaving of Saxon and Latin words proceeds with just as much ease and happiness as the almost pure Saxon of the foregoing:

"How could communities,
Degrees in schools, and brotherhoods in cities,
Peaceful commérce from dividable shores,
The primogenity and due of birth,
Prerogative of age, crowns, sceptres, laurels,
But by degree, stand in authentic place?
Take but degree away, untune that string,
And, hark, what discord follows! each thing meets
In mere oppugnancy: the bounded waters
Should lift their bosoms higher than the shores,
And make a sop of all this solid globe:
Strength should be lord of imbecility,
And the rude son should strike his father dead:
Force should be right; or rather, right and wrong —
Between whose endless jar justice resides —
Should lose their names, and so should justice too.
Then every thing includes itself in power
Power into will, will into appetite;
And appetite, an universal wolf,
So doubly seconded with will and power,
Must make perforce an universal prey,
And last eat up himself."

"Tremble, thou wretch,
That hast within thee undivulgèd crimes,
Unwhipp'd of justice: hide thee, thou bloody hand;
Thou perjur'd, and thou simular of virtue,
That art incestuous: caitiff, to pieces shake,
That under covert and convenient seeming
Hast practis'd on man's life: close pent-up guilts,
Rive your concealing continents, and cry
These dreadful summoners grace."

Observe what a sense of muscularity this usage carries, not only in the foregoing, but also in various shorter instances:

"Stop up th' access and passage to remorse,
That no compunctious visitings of nature
Shake my fell purpose."

"This my hand will rather
The multitudinous sea incarnardine."

"What is it then to me, if impious War —
Array'd in flames, like to the Prince of Fiends —
Do, with his smirch'd complexion, all fell feats
Enlink'd to waste and desolation?"

"And other devils, that suggest by treasons,
Do botch and bungle up damnation."

It should be noted, further, that Shakespeare has many palpable Latinisms, some of them very choice too; that is, words of Latin origin used quite out of their popular English sense; such as, — "Th' *extravagant* and *erring* spirit hies to his confine," — "Upon my *secure* hour thy uncle stole," — "Rank corruption, mining all within, *infects* unseen," — and, "To *expostulate* what majesty should be, what duty is." And sometimes, not having the fear of poetical, or rather of unpoetical precisians and martinets before his eyes, he did not even scruple to naturalize words for his own use from foreign springs, such as *exsufflicate* and *deracinate*; or to coin a word, whenever the concurring reasons of sense and verse invited it; as in *fedary*, *intrinse*, *intrinsicate*, *insisture*, and various others.

As to the sources from which Shakespeare drew his choice and use of words, the most material point seems to be, that he certainly did not go to books or scholars, or to those who made language a special object of study. Yet he knew right well that this was often done; for he ridicules it deliciously in *Love's Labour's Lost*, when Sir Nathaniel the Curate says of Constable Dull, "He hath never fed of the dainties that are bred in a book; he hath not eat paper, as it were; he hath not drunk ink; his intellect is not replenished"; and again, still better, when it is said of the learned Curate and Holofernes the Schoolmaster, "They have been at a great feast of languages, and stolen the scraps";—"They have lived long in the alms-basket of words." Shakespeare did not learn his language in this way: he went right into familiar, every-day speech for his words; caught them fresh, and beating with life, from the lips of common people and intelligent men of the world, farmers, mechanics, tradesmen, and housekeepers, who used language purely as a medium, not as an object, of thought; and of professional men, as they spoke when conversing with practical things, and stirred by the motives and feelings of actual life; that is, when, however they might think as wise men do, they spoke as common people do.

Hence we find him using the special terms of the street, the farm, the garden, the shop, the kitchen, the pantry, the wine-vault, the forecastle, the counting-room, the exchange, the bower, of hunting, falconry, angling, war, and even the technical terms of the Law, of Medicine, and Divinity, all as they actually lived on the tongues of men, and just as life had steeped its sense and spirit into them. This it is, in great part, that has made him so high and so wide an authority in verbal definition: as he took the meaning of words at first hand, and so preserved them with all their native sap and juice still in them; so lexicography uses him as its best guide. Hence, too, the prodigious compass, variety, limberness, and ever-refreshing raciness of his diction: no familiarity can suck the verdure out of it: the perennial dews of nature are incorporated in its texture: so that no words but his own can fitly describe it; as when he says of Cleopatra, "Other women cloy the appetites they feed; but she makes hungry where most she satisfies." Yet there is very seldom any smack of vulgarity in his language, save when the right delineation of character orders it so: words, that are nothing but vulgar as used by vulgar minds, are somehow in his use washed clean of their vulgarity; for there was a cunning alchemy in his touch that could instantly transmute the basest materials into "something rich and strange." In this respect, Mr. White justly applies to him what Laertes says of his sister:

> "Thought and affliction, passion, Hell itself,
> She turns to favour and to prettiness."

The Poet's arrangement of words is often very peculiar, and sometimes such as to render his meaning rather obscure; not obscure, perhaps, to his contemporaries, whose apprehension was less fettered by grammatical rules; but so to us, because our wits are more tied up from nimbleness with notions of literal correctness, and with habits of mind contracted from long intercourse with parsing writers. I mean that Shakespeare often sorts and places his words in what seems to us an arbitrary manner, throwing them out, so to speak, almost at random. Here is a small instance: "At our more consider'd time, we 'll read, answer, and think upon this business." Of course, *our more consider'd time* means, when we have taken time for further consideration. So too when the King suddenly resolves on sending Hamlet to England, and on having him there put to death; fearing a popular tumult, because Hamlet is loved by the multitude, he says, "To bear all smooth and even, this sudden sending him away must seem deliberate pause"; that is, a thing that we have paused and deliberated upon. Here it would seem that the Poet, so he got the several elements of thought and the corresponding parts of expression drawn in together, cared little for the precise form and order of the latter, trusting that the hearer or reader would mentally shape and place them so as to fit the sense. But the meaning is not always so easy to come at as in these two cases. In *Macbeth*, v. 4, when others are surmising and forecasting the issue of the war, Macduff says, "Let our just censures attend the true event, and put we on industrious soldiership." He wants to have the present time all spent in doing the work, not in speculating of the issue; and his meaning is, Let us not try to judge how things are going, till the actual result enables us to judge rightly; or, Let our judgments wait till the issue is known, *that so they may be* just. In this case, the ideas signified by *judgment*, *waiting*, *result*, *known*, and *just* were all to be expressed together, and the answering parts of language are disposed in the handiest order for metre and brevity; while the relations which those parts bear to each other in the speaker's thought are to be gathered from the subject and drift of the foregoing dialogue.

As this is at times a rather troublesome feature in the Poet's style, I will add a few more instances. Thus in the same play: "This castle hath a pleasant seat: the air nimbly and sweetly recommends itself unto our gentle senses"; that is, the air *sweetens* our senses *into gentleness*, or *makes* them gentle, by its purity and pleasantness. Again: "Ere humane statute purg'd the gentle weal"; which means, ere humane laws *made* the commonwealth gentle by cleansing it from the wrongs and pollutions of barbarism. So too in *King Henry the Fifth*, when the conspiring lords find their plot detected, and hear the doom of death pronounced upon them by the King, one of them says, "And God be thankèd for prevention; which I in sufferance heartily will rejoice;" meaning, that he is thankful their murderous purpose is defeated, though it be by their death; and that he will heartily rejoice for such defeat, even while suffering the pains it involves. Again, in *King Henry the Fourth*, when Hotspur is burning to cross swords with Prince Henry in the forthcoming battle:

> "And, fellows, soldiers, friends,
> Better consider what you have to do,
> Than I, that have not well the gift of tongue,
> Can lift your blood up with persuasion."

That is, you can better kindle your spirits to the work by thinking with yourselves what is to be done, than my small power of speech can heat your courage up for the fight by any attempts at persuasion. The well-known words of Juliet — "That runaway's eyes may wink" —

come under the same class of cases; and how hard such forms of language sometimes are to understand, may be judged from the interminable discussion occasioned by that famous passage. And it must be confessed, I think, that in several cases of this kind perspicuity is not a little sacrificed to metrical convenience and verbal dispatch. But Shakespeare wrote with the stage in view, not the closet; and he doubtless calculated a good deal on the help of the actor's looks, tones, and gestures, in rendering his meaning intelligible.

As regards the other points in Shakespeare's arrangement of words, I have little more to say than that here again his practice has nothing bookish or formal about it, but draws right into life and the living speech of men. He has no settled rules, no favourite order. In this respect, as in others, language was in his hands as limber as water at the fountain. He found it full of vital flexibility, and he left it so; nay, rather made it more so. As he did not learn his craft in the little narrow world of school rhetoricians, where all goes by the cut-and-dry method, and men are taught to "laugh by precept only, and shed tears by rule," but from the spontaneous rhetoric of the great and common world; so we find him varying the order of his words with the unconscious ease of perfect freedom, and moulding his language into an endless diversity of shapes. Perhaps I cannot better express his style in this behalf than by saying that he pitches right into the matter, instead of walking or wording round it; not looking at all to the gracefulness of his attitudes or the regularity of his motions, but driving straight ahead at directness, compactness, perspicuity, and force; caring little for the grammar of his speech, so it convey his sense; and taking no thought about the facility or even possibility of parsing, but only to get the soul of his purpose into a right working body. Thus in *Cymbeline*, iii. 2, where the hard-beset Imogen is first beguiled into the hope of meeting her husband at Milford Haven:

"Then, true Pisanio, —
Who long'st, like me, to see thy lord; who long'st, —
O, let me bate, — but not like me; — yet long'st, —
But in a fainter kind; — O, not like me,
For mine's beyond beyond; — say, and speak thick, —
Love's counsellor should fill the bores of hearing
To th' smothering of the sense, — how far it is
To this same blessèd Milford: and, by th' way,
Tell me how Wales was made so happy as
T' inherit such a haven: but, first of all,
How we may steal from hence; and for the gap
That we shall make in time, from our hence-going,
And our return, t' excuse: — but, first, how get hence:
Why should excuse be born or e'er begot?
We 'll talk of that hereafter."

What a chaos of verbal confusion have we here, until we penetrate to the soul of the heroine! and then what a pavilion of life and beauty this soul organizes that chaos into! How ignorant the glorious creature is of grammar; yet how subtile and sinewy of discourse! How incorrect her placing of words, yet how transfigured with grace of feeling and intelligence! Just think into what a nice trim garden of elocution a priest of the correct and classical church, like Pope, would have dressed this free outpouring of the speaker's heart. No doubt the language would be faultlessly regular; you might analyze and parse it *currente lingua;* but how lifeless and odourless the whole thing! how all the soul of nature, which now throbs so eloquently in it, would have been dried and crimped out of it! The workmanship, in short, to borrow an illustration from Schlegel, would have been like the mimic gardens of children; who, eager to see the work of their hands, break off twigs and flowers, and stick them in the ground; which done, the childish gardener struts proudly up and down his showy beds.

Perhaps the Poet's autocratic overshooting of grammar and rhetoric is still better instanced in the same play, v. 3, where Posthumus relates the doings of old Belarius and the Princes in a certain lane. On being asked, "Where was this lane?" he replies:

"Close by the battle, ditch'd, and wall'd with turf;
Which gave advantage to an ancient soldier, —
An honest one, I warrant ; who deserv'd
So long a breeding as his white beard came to,
In doing this for 's country : athwart the lane,
He, with two striplings, — lads more like to run
The country base than to commit such slaughter ;
With faces fit for masks, or rather fairer
Than those for preservation cas'd or shame, —
Made good the passage ; cried to those that fled,
Our Britain's harts die flying, not our men."

And so on to the end of the speech; which is all, from first to last, as glorious in conception and imagery as it is reckless of rhetorical form.

I am next to say somewhat touching the Poet's sentence-building, this being a matter that rhetoricians make much of; though in this, also, I must in the outset acquit him of any practical respect for the rulings of courts rhetorical. For here, again, he has no set fashion, no preferred pattern, no oft-recurring form; nothing at all stereotyped or modish; but just ranges at large in all the unchartered freedom and versatility of the English colloquial idiom. You may find in him sentences of every possible construction; but, except in his early plays, you can hardly say that he took to any one mould of structure more than another. So that his most peculiar feature here is absence of peculiarity. Thought dominates absolutely the whole material of expression, working it, shaping it, out-and-out, as clay in the potter's hands; which has no character but what it receives from the occasion and purpose of the user. As the Poet cares for nothing but to "suit the action to the word, the word to the action," so his word takes on forms as various as the action of his persons; nay, more; is pliant to all their moods and tenses of thought, passion, feeling, and volition. Thus, in the structure of his sentences, as in other things, his language is strictly physiognomic of his matter, the speaking exterior of the inward life; which life is indeed the one sole organizing principle of it. Accordingly he has specimens of the most pithy, piercing, sententious brevity; specimens with all the ample and rich magnificence of ordered pomp; specimens of terse, restrained, yet rhythmical, and finely-modulated vigour; specimens of the most copious and varied choral harmony; specimens of the most quiet, simple, and pure-flowing melody; now a full burst of the many-voiced lordly organ, now the softest and mellowest notes of the flute. Not only these, but all the intermediate, and ever so many surrounding varieties of structure are met with in his omniformity of sentence-building. In short, the leaves of a forest are hardly more varied in figure and make than Shakespeare's sentences; so that if these were all sorted into rhetorical classes, and named, it would "dizzy the arithmetic of memory" to run through their names.

The only divisions on this score that I shall attempt to speak of are those called the Period and the Loose Sentence. Everybody knows, I presume, that in a periodic sentence, when rightly fashioned, the sense is not completed till you reach the close; so that the whole has to be formed in thought before any part is set down. The beginning forecasts the end, the end remembers the beginning, and all the intermediate parts are framed with an eye to both beginning and end. And the nearer it comes to a regular circle, the better it is held to be. This style of writing, then, may be not unfitly said to go on wheels. It is naturally rolling and high-sounding, or at least may easily be made so, and therefore is apt to be in favour with geniuses of a swelling, oratorical, and elocutionary order. Besides, it is a style easily imitated, and so is not unfavourable to autorial equality. On the other hand, the Loose Sentence begins without any apparent thought of how it is to end, and proceeds with as little apparent thought of how it began: the sense may stand complete many times before it gets through: it runs on seemingly at random, winding at its "own sweet will," though the path it holds is much nearer a straight line than a circle; and it stops, not where the starting foresaw, but where the matter so carries it. Thus it is a sort of lingual straggler, if you please, and may be said to wander with little or no conscience of the rhetorical toilet.

Shakespeare has many periodic sentences: at first he seems to have rather affected that structure: in the more serious parts of the plays written in his earlier style it is so common as to be almost characteristic of them. But, on the whole, he evidently much preferred writing in straight lines to writing in circles; and this preference grew stronger as he ripened in his art; so that in his later workmanship the periodic construction becomes decidedly rare: and the reason of his so preferring the linear to the circular structure seems to have been, not only because the former is the more natural and spontaneous way of speaking, but also because it offers far more scope for the proper freedom and variety of English colloquial speech. He has numberless sentences of exquisite beauty of structure; many indeed of the circular kind, but far more of the linear; and the beauty of the latter is purer and higher than that of the former, because it is much more unconscious and unsought, and comes along of its own accord in the undivided quest of something else: for, say what you will, the true law in this matter is just that so well stated by Professor Shairp in the passage before quoted in a note on page 138: "No one ever became really beautiful by aiming at beauty. Beauty comes, we scarce know how, as an emanation from sources deeper than itself." And so it was with Shakespeare in all respects, — I mean Shakespeare the master, not Shakespeare the apprentice, — and in none more so than in the matter of style.

Before quitting this branch of the theme, I will add a few illustrations. And I will begin with two specimens of the circular structure; the first being from the night-scene in *The Merchant of Venice*, v. 1:

> "For do but note a wild and wanton herd,
> Or race of youthful and unhandled colts,
> Fetching mad bounds, bellowing, and neighing loud,
> Which is the hot condition of their blood;
> If they but hear perchance a trumpet sound,
> Or any air of music touch their ears,
> You shall perceive them make a mutual stand,
> Their savage eyes turn'd to a modest gaze,
> By the sweet power of music."

The next is from one of Westmoreland's speeches in the Second Part of *King Henry the Fourth*, iv. 1:

> "You, Lord Archbishop, —
> Whose See is by a civil peace maintain'd;
> Whose beard the silver hand of peace hath touch'd;
> Whose learning and good letters peace hath tutor'd;
> Whose white investments figure innocence,
> The dove and very blessèd spirit of peace, —
> Wherefore do you so ill translate yourself
> Out of the speech of peace, that bears such grace,
> Into the harsh and boisterous tongue of war?"

Now for some specimens in the linear style. The first is from the courtship of Ferdinand and Miranda, *The Tempest*, iii. 1:

> "I do not know
> One of my sex; no woman's face remember,
> Save, from my glass, mine own; nor have I seen
> More that I may call men, than you, good friend,
> And my dear father: how features are abroad,
> I 'm skilless of; but, by my modesty, —
> The jewel in my dower, — I would not wish
> Any companion in the world but you;
> Nor can imagination form a shape,
> Besides yourself, to like of."

The next is from the speech of Cominius to the people on proposing the hero for Consul, in *Coriolanus*, ii. 2:

> "At sixteen years,
> When Tarquin made a head for Rome, he fought
> Beyond the mark of others: our then Dictator,
> Whom with all praise I point at, saw him fight,
> When with his Amazonian chin he drove

The bristled lips before him : he bestrid
An o'erpress'd Roman, and i' the Consul's view
Slew three opposers : Tarquin's self he met,
And struck him on his knee : in that day's feats,
When he might act the woman in the scene,
He prov'd best man i' the field, and for his meed
Was brow-bound with the oak."

The following is from the history of Posthumus given by one of the Gentlemen in *Cymbeline*, i. 1:

"The King he takes the babe
To his protection ; calls him Posthumus Leonatus ;
Breeds him, and makes him of his bed-chamber ;
Puts to him all the learnings that his time
Could make him the receiver of ; which he took,
As we do air, fast as 't was minister'd,
And in his spring became a harvest ; liv'd in Court —
Which rare it is to do — most prais'd, most lov'd ;
A sample to the youngest ; to the more mature
A glass that feated them ; and to the graver
A child that guided dotards : to his mistress,
For whom he now is banish'd, — her own price
Proclaims how she esteem'd him and his virtue ;
By her election may be truly read
What kind of man he is."

In all these three passages, the structure shapes itself from step to step as it goes on, one idea starting another, and each clause being born of the momentary impulse of the under-working vital current; which is indeed the natural way of unpremeditated, self-forgetting discourse. There is no care about verbal felicities; none for rounded adjustment of parts, or nice balancing of members, or for exactness of pauses and cadences, so as to make the language run smooth on the ear; or, if there be any care about these things, it is rather a care to avoid them. This it is that gives to Shakespeare's style such a truly organic character, in contradistinction to mere pieces of nicely-adjusted verbal joinery or cabinet-work ; so that, as we proceed, the lingual form seems budding and sprouting at the moving of the inner mental life; the thought unfolding and branching as the expression grows, and the expression growing with the growth of the thought. In short, language with him is not the dress, but the incarnation of ideas: he does not robe his thoughts with garments externally cut and fitted to them, but his thoughts robe themselves in a living texture of flesh and blood.

Hence the wonderful correspondence, so often remarked, between the Poet's style and the peculiar moods, tempers, motives, and habits of his characters, as if the language had caught the very grain and tincture of their minds. So, for instance, we find him rightly making the most glib-tongued rhetoric proceed from utter falseness of heart; for men never speak so well, in the elocutionary sense, as when they are lying; while, on the other hand, "there are no tricks in plain and simple faith." Thus, in *Macbeth*, when the murder of Duncan is first announced, we have the hero speaking of it to the Princes, when one of them asks, "What is amiss?"

> "You are, and do not know 't:
> The spring, the head, the fountain of your blood
> Is stopp'd; the very source of it is stopp'd."

Of course he words the matter so finely all because he is playing the hypocrite. Compare with this the quick honest way in which Macduff dashes out the truth: "Your royal father's murder'd." We have a still more emphatic instance of the same kind in Goneril and Regan's hollow-hearted, and therefore highly rhetorical professions of love, when the doting old King invites his three daughters to an auction of falsehood, by proposing,

> "That we our largest bounty may extend
> Where nature doth with merit challenge."

So, again in *Hamlet*, i. 2, the King opens with an elaborate strain of phrase-making, full of studied and ingenious antitheses; and he keeps up that style so long as he is using language to conceal his thoughts; but afterwards, in the same speech, on coming to matters of business, he falls at once into the direct, simple style of plain truth and intellectual manhood.

But we have a more curious illustration, though in quite another kind, in *Macbeth*, iv. 3, where Ross, fresh from Scotland, comes to Macduff in England:

> " *Macd.* Stands Scotland where it did?
> *Ross.* Alas, poor country,
> Almost afraid to know itself! it cannot
> Be call'd our mother, but our grave: where nothing,
> But who knows nothing, is once seen to smile;
> Where sighs, and groans, and shrieks that rend the air,
> Are made, not mark'd; where violent sorrow seems
> A modern ecstasy: the dead man's knell
> Is there scarce ask'd for whom; and good men's lives
> Expire before the flowers in their caps,
> Dying or e'er they sicken.
> *Macd.* O, relation
> Too nice, and yet too true!"

Here Ross's picked and precise wording of the matter shows his speech to be the result of meditated preparation; for he has come with his mind so full of what he was to say, that he could think of nothing else; and Macduff, with characteristic plainness of ear and tongue, finds it "too nice." His comment, at once so spontaneous and so apt, is a delightful touch of the Poet's art; and tells us that Shakespeare's judgment as well as his genius was at home in the secret of a perfect style; and that he understood, no man better, the essential poverty of "fine writing."

Equally apt and characteristic is another speech of Macduff's later in the same scene, after learning how "all his pretty chickens and their dam" have been put to death by the tyrant:

> "Gentle Heaven,
> Cut short all intermission; front to front
> Bring thou this fiend of Scotland and myself;
> Within my sword's length set him; if he 'scape,
> Heaven forgive him too."

Macduff is a man of great simplicity, energy, and determination of character; and here we have all these qualities boiled down to the highest intensity, as would naturally be the effect of such news on such a man. And observe how much is implied in that little word *too*, — "Heaven forgive him too." As much as to say, "Let me once but have a chance at him, if I don't kill him, then I'm as great a sinner as he, and so God forgive us both!" I hardly know of another instance of so great a volume of meaning compressed into so few words. And how like it is to noble Macduff!

I could fill many pages with examples of this perfect suiting of the style to the mental states of the dramatic speakers, but must rest with citing a few more.

Hotspur is proverbially a man of impatient, irascible, headstrong temper. See now how all this is reflected in the very step of his language, when he has just been chafed into a rage by what the King has said to him about the Scottish prisoners:

> "Why, look you, I am whipp'd and scourg'd with rods,
> Nettled, and stung with pismires, when I hear
> Of this vile politician, Bolingbroke.
> In Richard's time, — what do you call the place? —
> A plague upon 't! — it is in Glostershire; —
> 'Twas where the madcap duke his uncle kept,
> His uncle York; — where I first bow'd my knee
> Unto this king of smiles, this Bolingbroke; —
> When you and he came back from Ravenspurg. —
> Why, what a candy deal of courtesy
> This fawning greyhound then did proffer me!
> Look, *When his infant fortune came to age*,
> And, *Gentle Harry Percy*, and, *Kind cousin*, —
> O, the Devil take such cozeners!"

Hotspur's spirit is so all-for-war, that he can think of nothing else; hence he naturally scorns poetry, though his soul is full of it. But poetry is so purely an impulse with him, that he is quite unconscious of it. With Glendower, on the contrary, poetry is a purpose, and he pursues it consciously. Note, then, in iii. 1, how this poetical mood shapes and tunes his style, when he interprets his daughter's Welsh to her English husband:

> "She bids you on the wanton rushes lay you down,
> And rest your gentle head upon her lap,
> And she will sing the song that pleaseth you,
> And on your eyelids crown the god of sleep,
> Charming your blood with pleasing heaviness;
> Making such difference betwixt wake and sleep,
> As is the difference betwixt day and night,
> The hour before the heavenly-harness'd team
> Begins his golden progress in the East."

Here the whole expression seems born of melody, and the melody to pervade it as an essence. So, too, in the same scene, Mortimer being deep in the lyrical mood of honeymoon, see how that mood lives in the style of what he says about his wife's speaking of Welsh, which is all Greek to him; her tongue

> "Makes Welsh as sweet as ditties highly penn'd,
> Sung by a fair queen in a Summer's bower,
> With ravishing division, to her lute."

For another instance, take a part of the exiled Duke's speech in *As You Like It*, ii. 1:

> "Sweet are the uses of adversity,
> Which, like the toad, ugly and venomous,
> Wears yet a precious jewel in his head;
> And this our life, exempt from public haunt,
> Finds tongues in trees, books in the running brooks,
> Sermons in stones, and good in every thing."

The Duke is a thoughtful, pensive, kind-hearted man, feeling keenly the wrong that has been done him, but not at all given to cherishing a resentful temper; and here, if I mistake not, his language relishes of the benevolent, meditative, and somewhat sentimental melancholy that marks his disposition.

Still more to the point, perhaps, is the passage in *Hamlet*, iv. 5, where Ophelia so touchingly scatters out the secrets of her virgin heart: "They say the owl was a baker's daughter. — Lord, we know what we are, but we know not what we may be. — God be at your table!" And again: "I hope all will be well. We must be patient; but I cannot choose but weep, to think they should lay him i' the cold ground. My brother shall know of it; and so I thank you for your good counsel. — Come, my coach! — Good night, ladies; good night, sweet ladies; good night, good night." A poor, crazed, but still gentle, sweet-tempered, and delicate-souled girl, quite unconscious of her own distress, yet still having a dim remembrance of the great sorrows that have crazed her, — such is Ophelia here; and her very manner of speech takes the exact colour and tone of her mind.

Probably, however, the best example of all is one that I can but refer to, it being too long for quotation. It is in the second scene of *The Tempest*, where Prospero relates to his daughter the story of his past life, at the same time letting her into the fact and the reasons of what he has just been doing, and still has in hand to do. The dear wise old gentleman is here absent-minded, his thoughts being busy and very intent upon the tempest he has lately got up, and upon the incoming and forthcoming consequences of it; and he thinks Miranda is not attentive to what he is saying, because he is but half-attending to it himself. This subdued mental agitation, and wandering of his thoughts from the matter his tongue is handling, silently registers itself in a broken, disjointed, and somewhat rambling course of narrative; that is, his style runs so in sympathy with his state of mind as to be unconsciously physiognomic of it. Certainly it is among the Poet's finest instances of "suiting the word to the action"; while at the same time it perfectly remembers the "special observance" of "o'erstepping not the modesty of nature."

Since Homer, no poet has come near Shakespeare in originality, freshness, opulence, and boldness of imagery. It is this that forms, in a large part, the surpassing beauty of his poetry; it is in this that much of his finest idealizing centres. And he abounds in all the figures of speech known in formal rhetoric, except the Allegory and the Apologue. The Allegory, I take it, is hardly admissible in dramatic writing; nor is the Apologue very well suited to the place: the former, I believe, Shakespeare never uses; and his most conspicuous instance of the latter, in fact the only one that occurs to me, is that of the Belly and the Members, so quaintly delivered to the insurgent people by the juicy old Menenius in the first scene of *Coriolanus.* But, though Shakespeare largely uses all the other figures of speech, I shall draw most of what I have to say of his style in this respect, under the two heads of Simile and Metaphor, since all that can properly be called imagery is resolvable into these. Shakespeare uses both a great deal, but the Simile in a way somewhat peculiar: in fact, as it is commonly used by other poets, he does not seem to have been very fond of it; and when he admits it, he generally uses it in the most informal way possible. But, first, at the risk of seeming pedantic, I will try to make some analysis of the two figures in question.

Every student knows that the Simile may be regarded as an expanded Metaphor, or the Metaphor as a condensed Simile. Which implies that the Metaphor admits of greater brevity. What, then, is the difference?

Now a simile, as the name imports, is a comparison of two or more things, more or less unlike in themselves, for the purpose of illustration. The thing illustrated and the thing that illustrates are, so to speak, laid alongside each other, that the less known may be made more intelligible by the light of that which is known better. Here the two parts are kept quite distinct, and a sort of parallel run between them. And the actions or the qualities of the two things stand apart, each on their own side of the parallel, those of neither being ascribed to the other. In a metaphor, on the other hand, the two parts, instead of lying side by side, are drawn together and incorporated into one.

The idea and the image, the thought and the illustration, are not kept distinct, but the idea is incarnated in the image, so that the image bears the same relation to the idea as the body does to the soul. In other words, the two parts are completely identified, their qualities interfused and interpenetrating, so that they become one. Thus a metaphor proceeds by ascribing to a given object certain actions or qualities which are not literally true of that object, and which have in reference to it only the truth of analogy.

To illustrate this. When, in his sonnet composed on Westminster Bridge, Wordsworth says, "This City now doth, like a garment, wear the beauty of the morning," the language is a simile in form. If he had said, This City hath now robed herself in the beauty of the morning, it would have been in form a metaphor. On the other hand, when in the same sonnet he says, "The river glideth at his own sweet will," the language is a metaphor. If in this case he had said, The river floweth smoothly along, like a man led on by the free promptings of his own will, it would have been a simile. And so, when Romeo says of Juliet, —

> "O, she doth teach the torches to burn bright !
> Her beauty hangs upon the cheek of night,
> Like a rich jewel in an Ethiop's ear" ;

here we have two metaphors, and also one simile. Juliet cannot be said literally to teach the torches any thing; but her brightness may be said to make them, or rather the owner of them ashamed of their dimness; or she may be said to be so radiant, that the torches, or the owner of them may learn from her how torches ought to shine. Neither can it be said literally that her beauty hangs upon the cheek of night, for the night has no cheek; but it may be said to bear the same relation to the night as a diamond pendant does to the dark cheek that sets it off. Then the last metaphor is made one of the parts in a simile; what is therein expressed being likened to a rich jewel hanging in an Ethiop's ear. So, too, when Wordsworth apostrophizes Milton, —

> "Thy soul was like a Star, and dwelt apart;
> Thou hadst a voice whose sound was like the sea"; —

here we have two similes. But when he says, —

> "Unruffled doth the blue lake lie,
> The mountains looking on";

and when he says of the birds singing, —

> "Clear, loud, and lively is the din,
> From social warblers gathering in
> Their harvest of sweet lays";

and when he says of his Lucy, —

> "The stars of midnight shall be dear
> To her; and she shall lean her ear
> In many a secret place
> Where rivulets dance their wayward round,
> And beauty born of murmuring sound
> Shall pass into her face"; —

in these lines we have four pure and perfect metaphors.

Again: In *Cymbeline*, old Belarius says of the "two princely boys" that are with him, —

> "They are as gentle
> As zephyrs, blowing below the violet,
> Not wagging his sweet head; and yet as rough,
> Their royal blood enchaf'd, as the rud'st wind,
> That by the top doth take the mountain pine,
> And make him stoop to th' vale."

Here are two similes, of the right Shakespeare mintage. As metaphors from the same hand, take this from Iachimo's temptation of Imogen, "This object, which takes prisoner the wild motion of mine eye"; and this from Viola, urging Orsino's suit to the Countess, —

> "Holla your name to the reverberate hills,
> And make the babbling gossip of the air
> Cry out, *Olivia!*"

and this of Cleopatra's with the asp at her bosom, —

"Dost thou not see my baby at my breast,
That sucks the nurse asleep?"

Or, as an instance of both figures together, take the following from *King Lear*, iv. 3, where the Gentleman describes to Kent the behaviour of Cordelia on hearing of her father's condition:

"You have seen
Sunshine and rain at once; her smiles and tears
Were like: a better way, — those happy smilets
That play'd on her ripe lip seem'd not to know
What guests were in her eyes; which parted thence
As pearls from diamonds dropp'd."

Here we have two similes, in the first two and last clauses; and also two metaphors, severally conveyed in, — "That play'd on her ripe lip," and, "What guests were in her eyes." Perhaps I ought to add that a simile is sometimes merely suggested or implied; as in these lines from Wordsworth:

"What is glory? — in the socket
See how dying tapers fare!
What is pride? — a whizzing rocket
That would emulate a star.

What is friendship? — do not trust her,
Nor the vows which she has made;
Diamonds dart their brightest lustre
From a palsy-shaken head."

Thus much by way of analyzing the two figures, and illustrating the difference between them. In all these instances may be seen, I think, how in a metaphor the intensity and fire of imagination, instead of placing the two parts side by side, melts them down into one homogeneous mass; which mass is both of them and neither of them at the same time; their respective properties being so interwoven and fused together, that those of each may be affirmed of the other.

I have said that Shakespeare uses the Simile in a way

somewhat peculiar. This may require some explication.— Homer, Virgil, Dante, Spenser, Milton, and the great Italian poets of the sixteenth century, all deal largely in what may be styled full-drawn similes; that is, similes carefully elaborated through all their parts, these being knit together in a balanced and rounded whole. Here is an instance of what I mean, from *Paradise Lost*, i.:

> "As when the potent rod
> Of Amram's son, in Egypt's evil day,
> Wav'd round the coast, up call'd a pitchy cloud
> Of locusts, warping on the eastern wind,
> That o'er the realm of impious Pharaoh hung
> Like night, and darken'd all the land of Nile;
> So numberless where those bad angels seen
> Hovering on wing under the cope of Hell,
> 'Twixt upper, nether, and surrounding fires."

This may be fitly taken as a model specimen of the thing; it is severely classical in style, and is well worthy of the great hand that made it. Here is another, somewhat different in structure, and not easy to beat, from Wordsworth's *Miscellaneous Sonnets*, Part ii.:

> "Desponding Father! mark this alter'd bough,
> So beautiful of late, with sunshine warm'd,
> Or moist with dews; what more unsightly now,
> Its blossoms shrivell'd, and its fruit, if form'd,
> Invisible? yet Spring her genial brow
> Knits not o'er that discolouring and decay
> As false to expectation. Nor fret thou
> At like unlovely process in the May
> Of human life: a Stripling's graces blow,
> Fade, and are shed, that from their timely fall
> (Misdeem it not a cankerous change) may grow
> Rich mellow bearings, that for thanks shall call."

It may be worth noting, that the first member of this no less beautiful than instructive passage contains one metaphor,—"Spring her genial brow knits not"; and the second two,—"in the May of human life," and, "a Stripling's graces blow, fade, and are shed." Herein it differs from the preceding instance; but I take it to be none the worse for that.

Shakespeare occasionally builds a simile on the same plan; as in the following from *Measure for Measure*, i. 3:

"Now, as fond fathers,
Having bound up the threatening twigs of birch,
Only to stick it in their children's sight
For terror, not to use, in time the rod
Becomes more mock'd than fear'd; so our decrees,
Dead to infliction, to themselves are dead;
And liberty plucks justice by the nose;
The baby beats the nurse, and quite athwart
Goes all decorum."

But the Poet does not much affect this formal mode of the thing: he has comparatively few instances of it; while his pages abound in similes of the informal mode, like those quoted before. And his peculiarity in the use of the figure consists partly in what seems not a little curious, namely, that he sometimes begins with building a simile, and then runs it into a metaphor before he gets through; so that we have what may be termed a mixture of the two; that is, he sets out as if to form the two parts distinct, and ends by identifying them. Here is an instance from the Second Part of *King Henry the Fourth*, iv. 1:

"His foes are so enrooted with his friends,
That, plucking to unfix an enemy,
He doth unfasten so and shake a friend.
So that this land, like an offensive wife
That hath enrag'd him on to offer strokes,
As he is striking, holds his infant up,
And hangs resolv'd correction in the arm
That was uprear'd to execution."

And so in *King Henry the Fifth*, ii. 4:

"In cases of defence 'tis best to weigh
The enemy more mighty than he seems:
So the proportions of defence are fill'd;
Which of a weak and niggardly projection,

Doth, like a miser, spoil his coat with scanting
A little cloth."

Also in *Hamlet*, iv. 1:

"So much was our love,
We would not understand what was most fit;
But, like the owner of a foul disease,
To keep it from divulging, let it feed
Even on the pith of life."

And somewhat the same again in iii. 4:

"No, in despite of sense and secrecy,
Unpeg the basket on the house's top,
Let the birds fly, and, like the famous ape,
To try conclusions, in the basket creep,
And break your own neck down."

Something very like this mixing of figures occurs, also, in *Timon of Athens*, iv. 3:

"But myself,
Who had the world as my confectionary;
The mouths, the tongues, the eyes, and hearts of men
At duty, more than I could frame employment;
That numberless upon me stuck, as leaves
Do on an oak, have with one Winter's brush
Fell from their boughs, and left me open, bare
For every storm that blows."

And I suspect that certain passages, often faulted for confusion of metaphors, are but instances of the same thing, as this:

"Blest are those
Whose blood and judgment are so well commingled,
That they are not a pipe for Fortune's finger
To sound what stop she please."

This feature mainly results, no doubt, from the Poet's aptness or endeavour to make his style of as highly symbolical a character as possible without smothering the sense. And by *symbolical* I here mean the taking a representative part of a thing, and using it in such a way as to convey the sense and virtue of the whole. Metaphors are the strongest and surest mode of doing this; and so keen was the Poet's quest of this, that his similes, in the very act of forming, often become half-metaphors, as from a sort of instinct. Thus, instead of fully forming a simile, he merely *suggests* it; throwing in just enough of it to start the thoughts on that track, and then condensing the whole into a semi-metaphorical shape. Which seems to explain why it is that these suggestions of similes, notwithstanding the stereotyped censures of a too formal criticism, seldom trouble any reader who is so unsophisticated as to care little for the form, so he be sure of the substance.

The thoughtful student can hardly choose but feel that there is something peculiar in Shakespeare's metaphors. And so indeed there is. But the peculiarity is rather in degree than kind. Now the Metaphor, as before remarked, proceeds upon a likeness in the relations of things; whereas the Simile proceeds upon a likeness in the things themselves, which is a very different matter. And so surpassing was Shakespeare's quickness and acuteness of eye to discern the most hidden resemblances in the former kind, that he outdoes all other writers in the exceeding fineness of the threads upon which his metaphors are often built. In other words, he beats all other poets, ancient and modern, in constructing metaphors upon the most subtile, delicate, and unobvious analogies.

Among the English poets, Wordsworth probably stands next to Shakespeare in the frequency, felicity, originality, and strength of his metaphorical language. I will therefore quote a few of his most characteristic specimens, as this seems the fairest way for bringing out the unequalled virtue of Shakespeare's poetry in this kind.

"With heart as calm as lakes that sleep,
In frosty moonlight glistening;
Or mountain rivers, where they creep
Along a channel smooth and deep,
To their own far-off murmurs listening."

Memory.

"Leave to the nightingale her shady wood;
A privacy of glorious light is thine;
Whence thou dost pour upon the world a flood
Of harmony, with instinct more divine."

To a Skylark.

"And this huge Castle, standing here sublime,
I love to see the look with which it braves —
Cas'd in th' unfeeling armour of old time —
The lightning, the fierce wind, and trampling waves."

Peele Castle.

"Bright gem instinct with music, vocal spark;
The happiest bird that sprang out of the Ark!"

A Morning Exercise.

"One who was suffering tumult in his soul,
Yet fail'd to seek the sure relief of prayer,
Went forth, — his course surrendering to the care
Of the fierce wind, while midday lightnings prowl
Insidiously, untimely thunders growl;
While trees, dim-seen, in frenzied numbers tear
The lingering remnants of their yellow hair."

Mis. Son., Pt. ii. 15.

"So deem'd the man who fashion'd for the sense
These lofty pillars, spread that branching roof
Self-pois'd, and scoop'd into ten thousand cells,
Where light and shade repose, where music dwells
Lingering, — and wandering on as loth to die."

"But, from the arms of silence, — list, O list! —
The music bursteth into second life;
The notes luxuriate, every stone is kiss'd
By sound, or ghost of sound, in mazy strife."

Eccle. Son., Pt. iii. 43, 44.

"The towering headlands, crown'd with mist,
Their feet among the billows, know
That Ocean is a mighty harmonist."

Power of Sound.

"Whate'er
I saw, or heard, or felt, was but a stream
That flow'd into a kindred stream; a gale
Confederate with the current of the soul,
To speed my voyage."

"Past and Future are the wings
On whose support harmoniously conjoin'd
Moves the great spirit of human knowledge."

Prelude, Book vi.

"Child of loud-throated War! the mountain Stream
Roars in thy hearing; but thy hour of rest
Is come, and thou art silent in thy age."

"What art thou, from care
Cast off, — abandon'd by thy rugged Sire,
Nor by soft Peace adopted?"

"Shade of departed Power,
Skeleton of unflesh'd humanity,
The chronicle were welcome that should call
Into the compass of distinct regard
The toils and struggles of thy infant years!"

Kilchurn Castle.

"Advance, — come forth from thy Tyrolean ground,
Dear Liberty! stern Nymph of soul untam'd;
Sweet Nymph, O rightly of the mountains nam'd!
Through the long chain of Alps from mound to mound,
And o'er th' eternal snows, like Echo, bound;
Like Echo, when the hunter-train at dawn
Have rous'd her from her sleep; and forest-lawn,
Cliffs, woods, and caves her viewless steps resound,
And babble of her pastime!"

"Ye Storms, resound the praises of your King!
And ye mild Seasons — in a sunny clime,
Midway on some high hill, while father Time
Looks on delighted — meet in festal ring,
And long and loud of Winter's triumph sing!
Sing ye, with blossoms crown'd, and fruits, and flowers,
Of Winter's breath surcharg'd with sleety showers,
And the dire flapping of his hoary wing!
Knit the blithe dance upon the soft green grass;
With feet, hands, eyes, looks, lips, report your gain;
Whisper it to the billows of the main,
And to th' aerial Zephyrs as they pass,
That old decrepit Winter — *He* hath slain
That Host which render'd all your bounties vain.

Son. to Lib., Pt. ii. 10, 35.

In the foregoing passages, the imagery of course loses more or less of its force and beauty from being cut out of its proper surroundings; for Wordsworth's poetry, too, is far from being mere gatherings of finely-carved chips: as a general thing, the several parts of a poem all rightly know each other as co-members of an organic whole. Far more must this needs be the case in the passages that follow, inasmuch as these are from the most dramatic of all writing; so that the virtue of the imagery is inextricably bound up with the characters and occasions of the speakers:

"Look, love, what envious streaks
Do lace the severing clouds in yonder East:
Night's candles are burnt out, and jocund day
Stands tiptoe on the misty mountain tops."

Rom. and Jul., *iii.* 5.

"Death, that hath suck'd the honey of thy breath,
Hath had no power yet upon thy beauty:
Thou art not conquer'd; beauty's ensign yet
Is crimson in thy lips and in thy cheeks,
And death's pale flag is not advancèd there."

"Why art thou yet so fair? shall I believe
That unsubstantial Death is amorous;
And that the lean abhorrèd monster keeps
Thee here in dark to be his paramour?"

Ibid., *v.* 3.

"My gentle Puck, come hither. Thou remember'st
Since once I sat upon a promontory,
And heard a mermaid, on a dolphin's back,
Uttering such dulcet and harmonious breath,
That the rude sea grew civil at her song;
And certain stars shot madly from their spheres,
To hear the sea-maid's music."

Midsum.-Night's D., *ii.* 1.

"Rush on his host, as doth the melted snow
Upon the valleys, whose low vassal seat
The Alps doth spit and void his rheum upon."

King Henry V., *iii.* 5.

"His face is all bubukles, and whelks, and knobs, and flames o fire; and his lips plows at his nose, and it is like a coal of fire, sometimes plue, and sometimes red; but his nose is executed, and his fire is out." *Ibid.*, *iii.* 6.

"O, then th' Earth shook to see the heavens on fire,
And not in fear of your nativity.
Diseasèd Nature oftentimes breaks forth
In strange eruptions; oft the teeming Earth
Is with a kind of cholic pinch'd and vex'd
By the imprisoning of unruly wind
Within her womb; which, for enlargement striving,
Shakes the old beldame Earth, and topples down
Steeples and moss-grown towers. At your birth,
Our grandam Earth, having this distemperature,
In passion shook."

1 *King Henry IV.*, *iii.* 1.

Let heaven kiss earth! now let not Nature's hand
Keep the wild flood confin'd! let order die!
And let this world no longer be a stage
To feed contention in a lingering act;
But let one spirit of the first-born Cain
Reign in all bosoms, that, each heart being set
On bloody courses, the rude scene may end,
And darkness be the burier of the dead!"

2 *King Henry IV.*, *i* 1.

"An habitation giddy and unsure
Hath he that buildeth on the vulgar heart.
O thou fond many! with what loud applause
Didst thou beat heaven with blessing Bolingbroke,
Before he was what thou would'st have him be!
And being now trimm'd in thine own desires,
Thou, beastly feeder, art so full of him,
That thou provok'st thyself to cast him up.
So, so, thou common dog, did'st thou disgorge
Thy glutton bosom of the royal Richard;
And now thou would'st eat thy dead vomit up,
And howl'st to find it."

Ibid., *i.* 3.

"But, look, the morn, in russet mantle clad,
Walks o'er the dew of yon high eastern hill."

Hamlet, *i.* 1.

"So, haply slander—
Whose whisper o'er the world's diameter,

As level as the cannon to his blank,
Transports his poison'd shot — may miss our name,
And hit the woundless air."

Ibid., *iv.* 1.

"Thou sure and firm-set earth,
Hear not my steps, which way they walk, for fear
The very stones prate of my whereabout,
And take the present horror from the time,
Which now suits with it."

Macbeth, *ii.* 1.

"O thou day o' the world,
Chain mine arm'd neck ; leap thou, attire and all,
Through proof of harness to my heart, and there
Ride on the pants triúmphing ! "

Ant. and Cleo., *iv.* 8.

"For his bounty,
There was no Winter in 't ; an Autumn 'twas
That grew the more by reaping : his delights
Were dolphin-like ; they show'd his back above
The element they liv'd in : in his livery
Walk'd crowns and crownets."

Ibid., *v.* 2.

"The ample proposition that hope makes
In all designs begun on earth below
Fails in the promis'd largeness : checks and disasters
Grow in the veins of actions highest rear'd."

"Distinction, with a broad and powerful fan,
Puffing at all, winnows the light away."

Troil. and Cres., *i.* 3.

"Be as a planetary plague, when Jove
Will o'er some high-vic'd city hang his poison
In the sick air."

"Put armour on thine ears and on thine eyes ;
Whose proof, nor yells of mothers, maids, nor babes,
Nor sight of priests in holy vestments bleeding,
Shall pierce a jot."

"Common mother, thou,
Whose womb unmeasurable, and infinite breast,

Teems, and feeds all ; whose self-same mettle,
Whereof thy proud child, arrogant man, is puff'd,
Engenders the black toad and adder blue,
The gilded newt and eyeless venom'd worm ;
Yield him, who all thy human sons doth hate,
From forth thy plenteous bosom, one poor root ! "

"What, think'st
That the bleak air, thy boisterous chamberlain,
Will put thy shirt on warm ? will these moss'd trees,
That have outliv'd the eagle, page thy heels,
And skip where thou point'st out ? will the cold brook,
Candied with ice, caudle thy morning taste,
To cure thy o'er-night's surfeit ? "

"O thou sweet king-killer, and dear divorce
'Twixt natural son and sire ! thou bright defiler
Of Hymen's purest bed ! thou valiant Mars !
Thou ever young, fresh, lov'd, and delicate wooer,
Whose blush doth thaw the consecrated snow
That lies on Dian's lap ! thou visible god,
That solder'st-close impossibilities,
And mak'st them kiss ! that speak'st with every tongue,
To every purpose ! O thou touch of hearts !
Think, thy slave man rebels ; and by thy virtue
Set them into confounding odds, that beasts
May have the world in empire ! "

Timon of Athens, iv. 3.

Shakespeare's boldness in metaphors is pretty strongly exemplified in some of the forecited passages ; but he has instances of still greater boldness. Among these may be named Lady Macbeth's —

"Come, thick night,
And pall thee in the dunnest smoke of Hell,
That my keen knife see not the wound it makes,
Nor Heaven peep through the blanket of the dark,
To cry *Hold, hold !* "

Here "blanket of the dark" runs to so high a pitch, that divers critics, Coleridge among them, have been staggered by it, and have been fain to set it down as a corruption of the text. In this they are no doubt mistaken : the metaphor is in the right style of Shakespeare, and, with all its daring, runs in too fair keeping to be ruled out of the family. Hardly less bold is this of Macbeth's —

> "Heaven's cherubin, hors'd
> Upon the sightless couriers of the air,
> Shall blow the horrid deed in every eye,
> That tears shall drown the wind."

With these I suspect may be fitly classed, notwithstanding its delicacy, the following from Iachimo's description of Imogen, when he comes out of the trunk in her chamber:

> "The flame o' the taper
> Bows toward her; and would under-peep her lids,
> To see th' enclosèd lights, now canopied
> Under these windows, white and azure, lac'd
> With blue of heaven's own tinct."

Also this, from the soliloquy of Posthumus in repentance for the supposed death of Imogen by his order:

> "My conscience, thou art fetter'd
> More than my shanks and wrists: you good gods give me
> The penitent instrument to pick that bolt,
> Then free for ever!"

I add still another example; from one of old Nestor's speeches on the selection of a champion to fight with the Trojan hero:

> "It is suppos'd,
> He that meets Hector issues from our choice:
> And choice, being mutual act of all our souls,
> Makes merit her election; and doth boil,
> As 'twere from forth us all, a man distill'd
> Out of our virtues."

All these — and I could quote a hundred such — are, to my thinking, instances of happy and, I will add, even wise audacity: at least, if there be any overstraining of imagery, I can easily shrive the fault, for the subtile felicity involved in them. They are certainly quite at home in the millennium of poetry which Shakespeare created for us; albeit I can well remember the time when such transcendent raptures were to me as

> "Some joy too fine,
> Too subtle-potent, tun'd too sharp in sweetness,
> For the capacity of my ruder powers."

It would be strange indeed if a man so exceedingly daring did not now and then overdare. And so I think the Poet's boldness in metaphor sometimes makes him overbold, or at least betrays him into infelicities of boldness. Here are two instances, from *The Tempest*, v. 1:

> "The charm dissolves apace;
> And as the morning steals upon the night,
> Melting the darkness, so their rising senses
> Begin to chase the ignorant fumes that mantle
> Their clearer reason."

> "Their understanding
> Begins to swell; and the approaching tide
> Will shortly fill the reasonable shore
> That now lies foul and muddy."

And here is another, of perhaps still more questionable character, from *Macbeth*, i. 7:

> "His two chamberlains
> Will I with wine and wassail so convince,
> That memory, the warder of the brain,
> Shall be a fume, and the receipt of reason
> A limbeck only."

What, again, shall be said of the two following, where Coriolanus snaps off his fierce scorn of the multitude?—

> "What's the matter, you dissentious rogues,
> That, rubbing the poor itch of your opinion,
> Make yourselves scabs?"

> "So shall my lungs
> Coin words till their decay against those measles,
> Which we disdain should tetter us, yet sought
> The very way to catch them."

Either from overboldness in the metaphors, or from some unaptness in the material of them, I have to confess that my mind rather rebels against these stretches of poetical prerogative. Still more so, perhaps, in the well-known passage of *King Henry the Fifth*, iv. 3; though I am not sure but, in this case, the thing rightly belongs to the speaker's character:

> "And those that leave their valiant bones in France,
> Dying like men, though buried in your dunghills,
> They shall be fam'd; for there the Sun shall greet them,
> And draw their honours reeking up to heaven;
> Leaving their earthly parts to choke your clime,
> The smell whereof shall breed a plague in France.
> Mark, then, abounding valour in our English;
> That, being dead, like to the bullet's grazing,
> Break out into a second course of mischief,
> Killing in rélapse of mortality."

But, whatever be the right mark to set upon these and some other instances, I find but few occasions of such revolt; and my only wonder is, how any mere human genius could be so gloriously audacious, and yet be so seldom chargeable with passing the just bounds of poetical privilege.

Metaphors are themselves the aptest and clearest mode of expressing much in little. No other form of speech will convey so much thought in so few words. They often compress into a few words what would else require as many sentences. But even such condensations of meaning did not — so it appears — always answer Shakespeare's purpose: he sometimes does hardly more than *suggest* metaphors, throwing off several of them in quick succession. We have an odd instance of this in one of Falstaff's speeches, Second Part of *King Henry the Fourth*, i. 2: "Well, he may sleep in security; for he hath the horn of abundance, and the lightness of his wife shines through it: and yet cannot he see, though he have his own lantern to light him." Here we have a thick-coming series of punning metaphors, all merely suggested. So Brutus, when hunting after reasons for killing Cæsar: "It is the bright day that brings forth the adder." Here the metaphor suggested is, that the sunshine of kingly power will develop a venomous serpent in the hitherto noble Julius. So, again, Cleopatra, when Antony dies: "O, see, my women, the crown o' the earth doth melt"; — "O, wither'd is the garland of the war, the soldier's pole is fall'n"; — "Look, our lamp is spent, it 's out." And so in Macbeth's, — "The wine of life is drawn, and the mere lees is left this vault to brag of"; — "Better be with the dead than on the torture of the mind to lie in restless ecstasy"; — "Come, seeling night, scarf up the tender eye of pitiful day." Also one of the Thanes, when they are about to make their ultimate set-to against Macbeth:

> "Meet we the medicine of the sickly weal;
> And with him pour we in our country's purge
> Each drop of us."

Macbeth indeed has more of this character than any other of the Poet's dramas; he having judged, apparently, that such a style of suggested images was the best way of *symbolizing* such a wild-rushing torrent of crimes, remorses, and retributions as that tragedy consists of.

Near akin to these is a number of passages like the following from one of Antony's speeches:

> "The hearts
> That spaniel'd me at heels, to whom I gave
> Their wishes, do discandy, melt their sweets
> On blossoming Cæsar; and this pine is bark'd,
> That overtopp'd them all."

Here we have several distinct images merely suggested, and coming so thick withal, that our powers might be swamped but for the prodigious momentum or gale of thought that carries us through. I am aware that several such passages have often been censured as mere jumbles of incongruous metaphors; but they do not so strike any reader who is so unconscientious of rhetorical formalities as to care only for the meaning of what he reads; though I admit that perhaps no mental current less deep and mighty than

Shakespeare's would waft us clean over such thought-foundering passages.

There is one other trait of the Poet's style which I must briefly notice. It is the effect of some one leading thought or predominant feeling in silently modifying the language, and drawing in sympathetic words and phrases by unmarked threads of association. Thus in the hero's description of Valeria, in *Coriolanus*, v. 3:

> "The noble sister of Publicola,
> The moon of Rome ; chaste as the icicle,
> That 's curded by the frost from purest snow,
> And hangs on Dian's temple."

Here, of course, the leading thought is chastity; and observe how, as by a kind of silent sympathy, all the words and images are selected and toned in perfect unison with that thought, so that the whole may be said literally to relish of nothing else. Something of the same, though in a manner perhaps still better, because less pronounced, occurs in *As You Like It*, ii. 1, where, the exiled Duke having expressed his pain that the deer, "poor dappled fools, being native burghers of this desert city," should on their own grounds "have their round haunches gor'd," one of the attendant lords responds:

> "Indeed, my lord,
> The melancholy Jaques grieves at that.
> To-day, my Lord of Amiens and myself
> Did steal behind him, as he lay along
> Under an oak whose antique root peeps out
> Upon the brook that brawls along this wood ;
> To the which place a poor sequester'd stag,
> That from the hunter's aim had ta'en a hurt,
> Did come to languish : and indeed, my lord,
> The wretched animal heav'd forth such groans,
> That their discharge did stretch his leathern coat
> Almost to bursting ; and the big round tears
> Cours'd one another down his innocent nose
> In piteous chase ; and thus the hairy fool,
> Much markèd of the melancholy Jaques,

> Stood on th' extremest verge of the swift brook,
> Augmenting it with tears."

Here the predominant feeling of the speaker is that of kindred or half-brotherhood with the deer; and such words as *languish*, *groans*, *coat*, *tears*, *innocent*, and *hairy fool*, dropping along so quietly, impart a sort of semi-humanizing tinge to the language, so that the very pulse of his feeling seems beating in its veins.

The Poet has a great many passages from which this feature might be illustrated. And it often imparts a very peculiar charm to his poetry;—a charm the more winning, and the more wholesome too, for being, I will not say unobtrusive, but hardly perceptible; acting like a soft undertone accompaniment of music, which we are kept from noticing by the delicate concert of thought and feeling it insensibly kindles and feeds within us. Thus the Poet touches and rallies all our most hidden springs of delight to his purpose, and makes them unconsciously tributary to the refreshment of the hour; stealing fine inspirations into us, which work their effect upon the soul without prating of their presence, and not unlike the virtue that lets not the left hand know what the right hand doeth. And all this, let me tell you, is a very different thing from merely making "the sound an echo to the sense,"—as much better too as it is different.

Everybody conversant with the subject knows that an author's style, if genuine, (and it is not properly a style, but a mannerism, if ungenuine,) is a just measure of his mind, and an authentic registration of all his faculties and forces. It has indeed passed into a proverb, that "the style is the man." And there is no other English writing, probably no uninspired writing in the world, of which this is so unreservedly true as of Shakespeare's; and this, because his is the most profoundly genuine: here the style—I mean in his characteristic pieces—is all his own,—rooted perfectly in and growing entirely from the man himself, —and has no borrowed sap or flavour whatever. And as he surpasses all others alike in breadth and delicacy of perception, in sweep and subtilty of thought, in vastness of grasp and minuteness of touch, in fineness of fibre and length and strength of line; so all these are faithfully reflected in his use of language. There is none other so overwhelming in its power, none so irresistible in its sweetness. If his intellect could crush the biggest and toughest problems into food, his tongue was no less able to voice in all fitting accents the results of that tremendous digestion. Coleridge, the profoundest of critics, calls him "an oceanic mind," and this language, as expressing the idea of multitudinous unity, is none too big for him; Hallam, the severest of critics, describes him as "thousand-souled," and this has grown into common use as no more than just; another writer makes his peculiarity to consist in "an infinite delicacy of mind"; and whatsoever of truth and fitness there may be in any or all of these expressions has a just exponent in his style.

All which may suffice to explain why it is that Shakespeare's style has no imitators. He were indeed a very hardy or else a very imbecile man, who should undertake to imitate it. All the other great English poets, however, have been imitated in this respect, and some of them with no little success. Thomson's *Castle of Indolence*, for example, is an avowed imitation of Spenser; and that, I think, is Thomson's best poem. Beattie's *Minstrel*, too, is another happy imitation of the same great original. I cannot say so much for any of Milton's or Wordsworth's imitators, though both have had many of them. But no one, apparently, ever thinks of trying to tilt in Shakespeare's Titanic armour.

MORAL SPIRIT.

Much of what may need to be said on this topic will come in more fitly in speaking of particular plays and characters. A few observations of a very inclusive scope will be sufficient here.

And I will begin by saying that soundness in this respect is the corner-stone of all artistic excellence. Virtue, or the loving of worthy objects, and in a worthy manner, is most assuredly the highest interest of mankind; — an interest so vital and fundamental, that nothing which really conflicts with it, or even postpones it to any other regards, can possibly stand the test of any criticism rooted in the principles of human nature. To offend in this point is indeed to be guilty of all: things must be substantially right here, else there can be nothing right about them. So that, if an author's moral teaching or moral influence be essentially bad; or even if it be materially loose and unsound, so as to unstring the mind from thinking and doing that which is right; nay, even if it be otherwise than positively wholesome and elevating as a whole; then I more than admit that no amount of seeming intellectual or poetical merit ought to shield his workmanship from reprobation, and this too on the score of art. But then, on the other hand, I must insist that our grounds of judgment in this matter be very large and liberal; and that to require or to expect a poet to teach better morals than are taught by Nature and Providence argues either a disqualifying narrowness of mind in us, or else a certain moral valetudinarianism which poetry is not bound to respect. For a poet has a right to the benefit of being tried by the moral sense and reason of mankind: it is indeed to that seat of judgment that every great poet virtually appeals; and the verdict of that tribunal must be an ultimate ruling to us as well as to him.

But one of the first things to be considered here is the natural relation of Morality to Art. Now I believe Art cannot be better defined than as the creation or the expression of the Beautiful. And truth is the first principle of all Beauty. But when I say this, I of course imply that truth which the human mind is essentially constituted to receive as such. And in that truth the moral element holds, constitutionally, the foremost place. I mean, that the human mind draws and cannot but draw to that point, in so far as it is true to itself: for the moral consciousness is the rightful sovereign in the soul of man, or it is nothing; it cannot accept a lower seat without forfeiting all its rights, and disorganizing the whole intellectual house. So that a thing cannot be morally false and artistically true at the same time. And in so far as any workmanship sins in the former kind, just so far, whatever other elements of the Beautiful it may have, it still lacks the very bond of order which is necessary, to retain them in power; nay, the effect of those other elements is to cultivate a taste which the whole thing fails to satisfy; what of true beauty is present tends to awaken a craving for that part which is wanting.

Nor need we have any fear but that in the long run things will come right in this matter. In this, however, as in most things, truth is the daughter of time. The moral sense and reason is so strong a force in the calm and disinterested judgments of mankind, that it must and will prevail: its verdict may be some time in coming, but come it will, sooner or later, and will ultimately have things all its own way. For the æsthetic conscience is probably the most impartial and inexorable of the human powers; and this, because it acts most apart from any regards of self-interest or any apprehension of consequences. The elections of taste are in a special sort exempt both from hope of profit and from fear of punishment. And man's sense of the Beautiful is so much in the keeping of his moral reason, — secret keeping indeed, and all the surer for being secret, — that it cannot be bribed or seduced to a *constant* admiration of any beauty where the moral element is wanting, or even where it is excluded from its rightful place.

In other words, the law of goodness or of moral rectitude is so closely interwoven with the nature and truth of things, that the human mind will not set up its rest with any workmanship in Art where that law is either set at nought or discrowned. Its natural and just prerogatives will assert themselves in spite of us; and their triumph is assured the moment we go to resisting them. That which appeals merely to our sense of the Beautiful, and which has nothing to recommend it but as it touches that sense, must first of all have the moral element of beauty, and this too in the foremost place, else it stands no chance of a permanent hold upon us.

It is indeed true that works of art, or things claiming to be such, in which this law of natural proportion is not respected or not observed, may have a transient popularity and success: nay, their success may be the greater, or at least the louder and more emphatic, for that very disproportion: the multitude may, and in fact generally do, go after such in preference to that which is better. And even men not exactly of the multitude, but still without the preparation either of a natural or a truly educated taste, — men in whom the sense of beauty is outvoiced by cravings for what is sensational, and who are ever mistaking the gratification of their lower passions for the satisfaction of their æsthetic conscience; — such men may be and often are won to a passing admiration of works in which the moral law of Art is plainly disregarded: but they seldom tie up with them; indeed their judgment never stays long enough in one place to acquire any weight; and no man of true judgment in such things ever thinks of referring to their preference but as a thing to be avoided. With this spirit of ignorant or lawless admiration the novelty of yesterday is eclipsed by the novelty of to-day; other things being equal, the later instance of disproportion always outbids the earlier. For so this spirit is ever taking to things which are impotent to reward the attention they catch. And thus men of such taste, or rather such want of taste, naturally fall in with the genius of sensationalism; which, whatever form it takes on, soon wears that form out, and has no way to sustain itself in life but by continual transmigration. Wherever it fixes, it has to keep straining higher and higher: under its rule, what was exciting yesterday is dull and insipid to-day; while the excess of to-day necessitates a further excess to-morrow; and the inordinate craving which it fosters must still be met with stronger and stronger emphasis, till at last exhaustion brings on disgust, or the poor thing dies from blowing so hard as to split its cheeks.

It is for these reasons, no doubt, that no artist or poet who aims at present popularity, or whose mind is possessed with the spirit of such popularity, ever achieves lasting success. For the great majority of men at any one time have always preferred, and probably always will prefer, that which is disproportioned, and especially that which violates the law of moral proportion. This, however, is not because the multitude have no true sense of the Beautiful, but because that sense is too slow in their minds to prevent their being caught and carried away by that which touches them at lower points. Yet that sense is generally strong enough to keep them from standing to the objects of their present election; so that it is ever drawing them back one by one to the old truth from which the new falsehood withdrew them. Thus, however the popular current of the day may set, the judgment of the wise and good will ultimately give the law in this matter; and in that judgment the æsthetic and the moral conscience will ever be found to coincide. So that he who truly works upon the principle, "Fit audience let me find, though few," will in the long run have the multitude too: he will not indeed be their first choice, but he will be their last: their first will be ever shifting its objects, but their last will stand firm. For here we may justly apply the aphoristic saying of Burke: "Man is a most unwise and most wise being: the individual is foolish; the multitude is foolish for the moment, when they act without deliberation; but the species is wise."

I have said that in the legislation of Art the moral sense and reason must not only have a voice, but a prerogative voice: I have also said that a poet must not be required to teach better morals than those of Nature and Providence. Now the law of moral proportion in Art may be defeated as well by overworking the moral element as by leaving it out or by making too little of it. In other words, redundancy of conscience is quite as bad here as deficiency; in some respects it is even worse, because its natural effect is to set us on our guard against the subtle invasions of pious fraud: besides, the deficiency we can make up for ourselves, but the evil of such suspicions is not so easily cured. For of all the things that enter into human thought, I suppose morality is the one wherein we are naturally least tolerant of special-pleading; and any thing savouring of this is apt to awaken our jealousy at once; probably from a sort of instinct, that, the better the cause, the less need there is, and the more danger there is too, of acting as its attorney or advocate. And the temptation to "lie for God" is one to which professed moral teachers are so exposed, that their lessons seldom have much effect: I even suspect that, in many cases, if not in most, their moralizing is of so obtrusive a kind, that it rather repels than wins the confidence of the pupils.

Then too moral demonstrativeness is never the habit either of the best poets or of the best men. True virtue indeed is a very modest and retiring quality; and we naturally feel that they who have most of it have "none to speak of." Or, to take the same thing on another side, virtue is a law of action, and not a distinct object of pursuit: those about us may know what object we are pursuing, but the mind with which we pursue it is a secret to them; they are not obliged to know it; and when we undertake to force that knowledge upon them, then it is that they just will not receive it. They will sometimes learn it from our life, never from our lips. Thus a man's moral rectitude has its proper seat inside of him, and is then most conspicuous when it stays out of sight, and when, whatever he does and wherever he goes, he carries it with him as a thing of course, and without saying or even thinking any thing about it. It may be that our moral instincts are made to work in this way, because any ambition of conscience, any pride or ostentation of virtue, any air of moral vanity or conceit, any wearing of rectitude on the outside, as if put on for effect, or "to be seen of men," if it be not essentially fictitious and false, is certainly in the most direct course of becoming so. And how much need there still is of those eloquently silent lessons in virtue which are fitted to inspire the thing without any boasting of the name, — all this may well be judged when we consider how apt men are to build their hopes on that which, as Burke says, "takes the man from his house, and sets him on a stage, — which makes him up an artificial creature, with painted, theatric sentiments, fit to be seen by the glare of candlelight."

These positions indicate, I believe, pretty clearly the right course for poetry to pursue in order to keep the just law of moral proportion in Art. Ethical didacticism is quite out of place in workmanship of this kind. To go about moralizing as of set purpose, or to be specially dealing in formal precepts of duty, is not the poet's business. I repeat, that moral demonstrativeness and poetry do not go well together. A poet's conscience of virtue is better kept to himself, save as the sense and spirit thereof silently insinuate themselves into the shapings of his hand, and so live as an undercurrent in the natural course of truth and beauty. If he has the genius and the heart to see and to represent things just as they really are, his moral teaching cannot but be good; and the less it stands out as a special aim, the more effective it will be: but if, for any purpose, however moral, he goes to representing things otherwise than as they are, then just so far his moral teaching will miss its mark: and if he takes, as divers well-meaning persons have done, to flourishing his ethical robes in our faces, then he must be content to pass with us for something less or something more than a poet: we may still read him indeed from a mistaken sense of duty; but we shall never be drawn to him by an unsophisticated love of the Beautiful and the True.

So much for what I hold to be the natural relation of Morality to Art. And I have put the matter thus, on the well-known principle, that the moral sensibilities are the most delicate part of our constitution; that as such they require to be touched with the utmost care, or rather not to be touched directly at all; and that the thrusting of instruction upon them tends to dull and deaden, not to quicken and strengthen them. For the true virtue-making power is an inspiration, not a catechism; and the truly cunning moral teacher is he who, in the honest and free enthusiasm of moral beauty, steals that inspiration into us without our knowing it, or before we know it. The author of *Ecce Homo* tells us, and truly too, that "no heart is pure that is not passionate; no virtue is safe that is not enthusiastic." And there is probably no vainer labour than the going about to make men good by dint of moral arguments and reasoned convictions of the understanding. One noble impulse will do more towards ennobling men than a volume of ethical precepts; and there is no sure way to put down a bad passion but by planting a good one. Set the soul on fire with moral beauty, that 's the way to burn the devils out of it. So that, for making men virtuous, there is, as Gervinus says, "no more fruitless branch of literature than ethical science; except, perhaps, those dramatic moralities into whose frigid impotence poetry will always sink when it aims at direct moral teaching."

Now, I do not at all scruple to affirm that Shakespeare's poetry will stand the test of these principles better than any other writing we have outside the Bible. His rank in the School of Morals is indeed no less high than in the School of Art. He is every way as worthy to be our teacher and guide in what is morally just and noble and right as in what is artistically beautiful and true. In his workmanship the law of moral proportion is observed with a fidelity that can never be too much admired; in other words, the moral element of the beautiful not only has a place, but is in the right place, — the right place, I mean, to act the most surely and the most effectively on the springs of life, or as an inspiration of good thoughts and desires. And in the further explication or amplification of the matter I shall take for granted that the old sophism of holding Shakespeare responsible for all that is said and done by his characters is thoroughly exploded; though it is not many years since a grave writer set him down as a denier of immortality; because, forsooth, in *The Winter's Tale* he makes the rogue Autolycus say, "For the life to come, I sleep out the thought of it." This mode of judging is indeed so perverse or so ignorant, that to spend any words in refuting or reproving it would be a mere waste of breath; or, if there be any so innocent as to need help on that point, it is not to them that I write.

As to the exact features of Shakespeare's own moral character as a man; whether or how far he was himself a model of virtuous living; in what measure the moral beauty of his poetical conceptions lived in the substance of his practical conversations; the little that is known touching the facts of his life does not enable us to judge. The most we can say on this score is, that we have a few authentic notes of strong commendation, and nothing authentic whatever to set against them. Thus Chettle, in his apology, tells us that "divers of worship have reported his uprightness of dealing, which argues his honesty"; and his editors, Heminge and Condell, in their dedication claim to have no other purpose than "to keep the memory of so worthy a friend and fellow alive as was our Shakespeare." Ben Jonson, too, a pure and estimable man, who knew him well, and who was not apt to be over-indulgent in his judgments of men, speaks of him as "my beloved Shakespeare" and "my gentle Shakespeare"; and describes him as follows:

> "Look, how the father's face
> Lives in his issue, even so the race
> Of Shakespeare's mind *and manners* brightly shines
> In his well-turnèd and true-filèd lines."

These things were said some seven years after the Poet's death; and many years later the same stanch and truthful man speaks of him as "being indeed honest, and of an open and free nature." I do not now recall any other authentic testimonials to his moral character; and, considering how little is known of his life, it is rather surprising that we should have so much in evidence of his virtues as a man. But it is with what he taught, not what he practised, that we are here mainly concerned: with the latter indeed we have properly nothing to do, save as it may have influenced the former: it is enough for our purpose that he saw and spoke the right, whether he acted it or not. For, whatever his faults and infirmities and shortcomings as a man, it is certain that they did not infect his genius or taint his mind, so as to work it into any deflection from the straight and high path of moral and intellectual righteousness.

I have said that Shakespeare does not put his personal views, sentiments, and preferences, in a word, his individuality, into his characters. These stand, morally, on their own bottom; he is but the describer of them, and so is not answerable for what they do: he holds the mirror up to them, or rather to nature in them; they do not hold it up to him: we see them in what he says, but not him in what they say. And, of course, as we may not impute to him, morally, their vices, so neither have we any right to credit him, morally, with their virtues. All this, speaking generally, is true; and it implies just the highest praise that can possibly be accorded to any man as a dramatic poet. But, true as it is generally, there is nevertheless enough of exception to build a strong argument upon as to his moral principles, or as to his theory of what is morally good and noble in human character.

I have already mentioned Henry the Fifth as the one of his characters into whom the Poet throws something of his own moral soul. He delivers him both as Prince Hal and as King in such a way, that we cannot but feel he has a most warm and hearty personal admiration of the man; nay, he even discovers an intense moral enthusiasm about him: in the Choruses, where he ungirds his individual loves from the strict law of dramatic self-aloofness, and lets in a stream from his own full heart, he calls him "the mirror of all Christian kings," and ascribes to him such qualities, and in such a way, as show unequivocally his own cherished ideal of manhood, and in what course the current of his personal approval ran. Here, then, we have a trustworthy exhibit of the Poet's moral principles; here we are left in no doubt as to what moral traits of character he in heart approved, whether his own moral character exemplified them or not. What sort of a man he represents this his favorite hero to be; how modest in his greatness, how great in his modesty; how dutiful and how devout; how brave, how gentle, how generous, how affable, how humane; how full of religious fervor, yet how bland and liberal in his piety; with "a tear for pity, and a hand open as day for melting charity"; how genuine and unaffected withal these virtues grow in him; in short, how all alive he is with the highest and purest Christian *ethos* which the old "ages of faith" could breathe into a man; — all this must stand over till I come to the plays wherein he is delineated.

Something further to the same point may be gathered, not so much from the Poet's treatment of particular good characters, as from the general style of character which he evidently prefers to draw in that class, and from the peculiar complexion and grain of goodness which he ascribes to them. Antonio the Merchant, Orlando, the Sebastian of *Twelfth Night*, Horatio, Kent, Edgar, Ferdinand, Florizel,

Posthumus, Pisanio, are instances of what I mean. All these indeed differ very widely from each other as individuals; but they all have this in common, that their virtues sit easy and natural upon them, as native outgrowths, not as things put on: there is no ambition, no pretension, nothing at all boastful or fictitious or pharisaical or squeamish or *egoish* in their virtues; we never see the men hanging over them, or nursing and cosseting them, as if they were specially thoughtful and tender of them, and fearful lest they might catch cold. Then too, with all these men, the good they do, in doing it, pays itself: if they do you a kindness, they are not at all solicitous to have you know and remember it: if sufferings and hardships overtake them, if wounds and bruises be their portion, they never grumble or repine at it, as feeling that Providence has a grudge against them, or that the world is slighting them: whether they live or die, the mere conscience of rectitude suffices them, without further recompense. So that the simple happiness they find in doing what is right is to us a sufficient pledge of their perseverance in so doing. Now all this is, in its degree, just the ideal of virtue which Christian morality teaches and exemplifies. For so the right way of Christian virtue is when a man's good deeds are so much a matter of course with him, that he thinks not of himself for having done them. As bees when they have made their honey; as birds when they have carolled their hymn; as the vine when it has produced its clusters; so it is with the truly good man when he has done a good act: it suffices him that he has borne his proper fruit; and, instead of calling on others or even himself to note what he has done, he goes right on and does other good acts, just as if nothing had happened.

But if all this be true of the Poet's men, it is true in a still higher degree of his women. Here it is that the moral element of the Beautiful has its fullest and fairest expression. And I am bold to say that, next to the Christian religion, humanity has no other so precious inheritance as Shakespeare's divine gallery of Womanhood. Helena, Portia of Belmont, Rosalind, Viola, Portia of Rome, Isabella, Ophelia, Cordelia, Miranda, Hermione, Perdita, Desdemona, Imogen, Catharine of Arragon, — what a wealth and assemblage of moral beauty have we here! All the other poetry and art of the world put together cannot show such a varied and surpassing treasure of womanly excellence. And how perfectly free their goodness is from any thing like stress! How true it is in respect of their virtues, that "love is an unerring light, and joy its own security!" They are wise, witty, playful, humorous, grave, earnest, impassioned, practical, imaginative; the most profound and beautiful thoughts drop from them as things too common and familiar to be spoken with the least emphasis: they are strong, tender, and sweet, yet never without a sufficient infusion of brisk natural acid and piquancy to keep their sweetness from palling on the taste: they are full of fresh, healthy sentiment, but never at all touched with sentimentality: the soul of romance works mightily within them, yet never betrays them into any lapses from good sense, or any substitutions of feeling for duty.

Then too how nobly and serenely indifferent the glorious creatures are to the fashions and opinions and criticisms of the world! How composedly some of them walk amidst the sharpest perils and adversities, as "having the spirit to do any thing that is not foul in the truth of their spirit." Full of bitterness their cup sometimes is indeed; yet they do not mind it, — not they! — save as the welfare and happiness of others are involved in what pinches them. Several of them are represented passing through the most ticklish and trying situations in which it is possible for female modesty to be placed, — disguised in male attire and sharing as men in the conversations of men; yet so unassailable is their modesty, that they give themselves, apparently, no trouble about it. And, framed as they are, all this may well be so: for indeed such is their fear of God, or, which comes to the same thing, their fear of doing wrong, that it casts out all other fears; and so their "virtue gives herself light through darkness for to wade." Nor do we wonder that, timid maidens as they are, they should "put such boldness on"; for we see that with them

> "Mighty are the soul's commandments
> To support, restrain, or raise:
> Foes may hang upon their path, snakes rustle near,
> But nothing from their inward selves have they to fear."

It is very noteworthy, withal, how some of them are so secure in the spirit and substance of the moral law, that they do not scruple, in certain circumstances, to overrule its letter and form. Thus Isabella feigns to practise sin; and she does so as a simple act of self-sacrifice, and because she sees that in this way a good and pious deed may be done in aid of others: she shrinks not from the social imputation of wrong in that case, so her conscience be clear; and she can better brave the external finger of shame than the inward sense of leaving a substantial good undone. Helena, also, puts herself through a course of literal dishonours, and this too, with a perfect understanding of what she is about; yet she yields to no misgivings; not indeed on the ground that the end justifies the means, but because she knows that the soul of a just and honorable purpose, such as hers, will have power to redeem and even to sanctify the formal dishonours of its body. Much the same principle holds, again, in the case of Desdemona's falsehood, when, Emilia rushing into the room, and finding her dying, and asking, "Who has done this?" she sighs out, "Nobody — I myself: commend me to my kind lord." I believe no natural heart can help thinking the better of Desdemona for this brave and tender untruth, for it is plainly the unaffected utterance of a deeper truth; and one must be blind indeed not to see that the dying woman's purpose is to shield her husband, so far as she can, from the retribution which she apprehends will befall him, and the thought of which wrings her pure breast more sharply than the pangs of death.

These are plain cases of virtue tried and purified in the

straits of self-humiliation, virtue strained, as it were, through a close-knit fabric of difficulties and hardships, and triumphing over the wrongs that threaten its total defacement, and even turning its obstructions into a substance glorious as its own; that is, they are exceptional instances of a conscious departure from the letter and form of moral beauty for the fuller and clearer manifestation of its spirit and soul.

Nor are the virtues of Shakespeare's men and women the mere result of a certain felicity and harmony of nature, or the spontaneous movements of a happy instinct so strong in them that they do what is right without knowing or meaning it. No; his Henry the Fifth, and Horatio, and Kent, and Edgar, and Posthumus, his Helena, and Isabella, and Cordelia, and Hermione, and Imogen, and Catharine, are most truly "beings breathing thoughtful breath." Virtue is with them a discipline as well as a joy; a strong upright will is the backbone of it, and a healthy conscience is its keeper. They all have conscious reasons for what they do, and can state them with piercing eloquence, if occasion bids. For so the Poet, much as he delights in that fineness of nature or that innate grace which goes right of its own accord, evidently prefers, even in women, the goodness that has passed through struggles and temptations, and has its chief seat, not in impulse, but in principle, a virtue tested, and not merely instinctive: rather say, he delights most in the virtue that proceeds by a happy consent and marriage of the two. He therefore does not place his highest characters, whether men or women, in an atmosphere so pure that average mortals cannot breathe in it: he depicts their moral nature in conflict, with the powers of good and evil striving in them for the mastery; and when the former prevail, it is because they have "a strong siding champion, Conscience," to support them. Thus through their weakness the come near enough to get hold of us, while at the same time in their strength they are enough higher than we to lift us upwards.

But Shakespeare's main peculiarity as a teacher of goodness lies in this, that he keeps our moral sympathies in the right place without discovering his own. With the one exception of Henry the Fifth, we cannot perceive, from the delineation itself, whether he takes part with the good character or the bad; nevertheless he somehow so puts the matter that we cannot help taking part with the good. For I run no risk in saying there is not a single instance in his plays where the feelings of any natural-hearted reader fail to go along with those who are, at least relatively, the best. And as he does not make nor even let us see which side he is on, so of course we are led to take the right side, not because he does, but simply because it is the right side. Thus his moral lessons and inspirations affect us as coming, not from him, but from Nature herself; and so the authority they carry is not his, good as that may be, but hers, which is infinitely better. Thus he is ever appealing directly to the tribunal of our own inward moral forces, and at the same time speaking health and light into that tribunal. There need be, there can be, no higher proof of the perfect moral sanity of his genius than this. And for right moral effect it is just the best thing we can have, and is worth a thousand times more than all the ethical arguing and voting in the world. If it be a marvel how the Poet can keep his own hand so utterly unmoved by the passion he is representing, it is surely not less admirable that he should thus, without showing any compassion himself, move our compassion in just the degree, and draw it to just the place, which the laws of moral beauty and proportion require.

Herein even Milton, great and good as he unquestionably is, falls far below Shakespeare as a moral poet. Take the delineation of Satan in *Paradise Lost.* Now Milton does not leave us at all in doubt as to where his own moral sympathies go in that delineation: they are altogether on the side of God and the good Angels. And he tells us again and again, or as good as tells us, that ours ought to be there; so that there is no possibility of mistake in the matter. Notwithstanding I suspect he does not quite succeed in keeping the reader's moral sympathies there. He does indeed with me: my own feelings have somehow been so steeped in the foolish old doctrine or faith which holds obedience to be a cardinal virtue, that they have never sided with Satan in that controversy. But I believe a majority of readers do find their moral feelings rather drawing to the rebel side; this too, notwithstanding their moral judgment may speak the other way: and when the feelings and the judgment are thus put at odds, the former are pretty sure, in effect, to carry the day.

Now Milton's Satan, I think, may be not unfitly described as a highly magnified realistic freethinker. Iago and Edmund are also realistic freethinkers, the former slightly magnified, the latter unmagnified, though both may be somewhat idealized. And both of them speak and act strictly in that character. Accordingly all religion is in their account mere superstition; and they take pride in never acknowledging their Maker but to brave Him. Both exult above all things in their intellectuality; and what they have the intellect to do, that is with them the only limit to intellectual action; that is, their own will is to them the highest law: hence to ruin another by outwitting and circumventing him is their characteristic pastime; and if they can do this through his virtues, all the better. Iago's moral creed may be summed up in two of his aphoristic sayings, — "Virtue! a fig! 'tis in ourselves that we are thus or thus"; and, "Put money in thy purse"; while Edmund wants no other reason for his exploiting than that his brother is one

> "Whose nature is so far from doing harms,
> That he suspects none; on whose foolish honesty
> My practices ride easy."

The characters of the two freethinking heroes are delineated consistently throughout, in keeping with these ideas. And no one can say, no one has ever said, that the Poet discovers any the least prejudice against them, or any leanings of moral or personal sympathy towards their victims. Nothing comes from him that can be fairly construed as a hint to us against warming up to them. Nor has any one a right to say that he overdoes or overstresses their wickedness a jot: he merely shows it, or rather lets them show it, just as it is. He lends them the whole benefit of his genius for the best possible airing of their intellectual gifts and graces; all this too without swerving a hair from the line of cold, calm, even-handed justice: yet how do our feelings, how do our moral sympathies, run in these cases? I need not say they run wholly and unreservedly with the chivalrous but infirm Cassio, the honest and honour-loving Othello, the innocent though not faultless Desdemona; with the pious and unsuspecting Edgar, the erring indeed but still upright and sound-hearted Gloster. Nay, more; we would rather be in the place of the victims than of the victors: virtue wronged, betrayed, crushed, seems to us a more eligible lot than crime triumphant, prosperous, happy. — Such is the moral spirit of these great delineations.

I could easily go through all the Poet's instances of virtue and innocence in conflict or in contrast with villainy and guilt, and show that he never fails thus to keep our moral sympathies in the right place without discovering his own; that he is just as far from overdoing or overstressing the villainy of the bad as the virtue of the good; both of which fall alike under the censure of moral demonstrativeness; while, as in the two cases specified, his moral teachings, even because they thus come from Nature, not from him, therefore bring in their right hand sanctions which we cannot appeal from if we would, and would not if we could.

There is one more point on which it may be needful to say a few words. — Johnson and others have complained that Shakespeare seems to write without any moral purpose; and that he does not make a just distribution of good and evil. Both charges are strictly true; at least, so

I hope, and so I believe. As regards his seeming to write without any moral purpose, on the same principle he seems to write without any art. But who does not know that the very triumph of art lies in concealing art; that is, in seeming to write without it? And so, if the Poet writes without discovering any moral purpose, that very fact is just the highest triumph of art in the moral direction. For no one has alleged that he seems to write with an immoral purpose. Here, then, I have but to say that, with so consummate an artist as Shakespeare, if the charge is not true, it ought to be. Redundancy of conscience is indeed fatal to art; but then it is also, if not fatal, at least highly damaging to morality; "for goodness, growing to a plurisy, dies in its own too much." Verily, a moral teacher's first business is to clear his mind of cant. And so much the wise and good Dr. Johnson himself will tell us.

If, again, Shakespeare fails to make a just distribution of good and evil, so also does Providence. If, in his representations, virtue is not always crowned with visible success, nor crime with apparent defeat; if the good are often cast down, the evil often lifted up, and sometimes both cast down together; the workings of Providence in the actual treatment of men are equally at fault in that matter. Or if he makes the sun of his genius to rise on the evil and on the good, and sends the rain of his genius on the just and on the unjust, why should this be thought wrong in him, when Providence manifestly does the same?

For, explain the fact as we may, it is certain that the consummations of justice are not always experienced here. The world is full of beginnings that are to be finished elsewhere, if finished at all. Virtue often meets with very rough usage in the present order of things: poverty and want, hardship, suffering, and reproach, are often the lot of the good; while men of the opposite character have their portion carved to them out of the best that the world has to bestow. Nay, it sometimes happens that the truest, the kindest, and most upright souls are the most exposed to injuries and wrongs; their virtues being to them a kind of "sanctified and holy traitors," and the heaven within them serving to disable them from winning the prizes of earth: whereas the very unscrupulousness of the bad, their hardness of heart and unbashfulness of front build or open for them the palaces of wealth and splendour and greatness; their want of principle seems to strengthen their hands; they rise the higher, that they care not whose ruins they rise upon, and command the larger success for being reckless how they succeed.

And is a poet, who professedly aims at nothing better than a just reflection of human life and character as he finds them, is he to be blamed for faithfully holding the mirror up to facts as they are in this respect? That our Shakespeare, the mighty and the lovely, sometimes permits the good to suffer while their wrongers prosper, I thence infer, not indeed that he regarded them indifferently, but that he had a right Christian faith in a further stage of being where the present disorder of things in this point is to be rectified, and the moral discriminations of Providence consummated. His judgment clearly was, that suffering and death are not the worst things that can happen to a man here. He reverences virtue, he does not patronize it. And the virtue he has in reverence is not a hanger-on at the counters of worldly thrift. He knew right well that "the fineness of such metal is not found in Fortune's love," but rather "in the wind and tempest of her frown"; and so he paints it as a thing "that Fortune's buffets and rewards doth take with equal thanks." And, surely, what we need here is a deeper faith, a firmer trust in the government of a Being "in whose pure sight all virtue doth succeed"; yea, and perhaps succeeds most highly in those very cases where the course of things in this world fails to recognize its claims.

For so in fact it seems pretty clear that the forces of Nature have little sense or discernment of right and wrong: the sunshine and the rain are rather blindly given to favouring the good and the evil indiscriminately; the plague and the thunderbolt are strangely indifferent to moral distinctions where they strike. What of that? these things are but the under-agents of Providence in the government of the world: whereas the inward conscience of truth and right is the immediate smile of God himself; and that is the Paradise of the truly good man's soul, the very life of his life; he can live without happiness, but he cannot live without that. Shakespeare's delineations reflect, none so well, none so well as his, this great, this most refreshing article of truth; and I heartily thank him for it; yes, heartily!

So then, what though the divine Cordelia and the noble Kent die, and this too in the very sweetness and fragrance of their beauty? is it not, do we not feel that it is, better to die with them than to live with those who have caused their death? Their goodness was not acted for the sake of life, but purely for its own sake: virtue such as theirs does not make suit to Fortune's favours, nor build her trust in them; pays not her vows to time, nor is time's thrall; no! her thoughts are higher-reared; she were not herself, could she not "look on tempests, and be never shaken." And such characters as these, befall them what may, have their "exceeding great reward" in the very virtue that draws suffering and death upon them: they need nothing more, and it is their glory and immortality not to ask any thing more. And shall we pity them, or shall we blame the Poet, that their virtue is not crowned with Fortune's smiles? Nay, rather let us both pity and blame ourselves for being of so mean and miserable a spirit.

As for those poets, and those critics of poetry, who insist that in the Drama, which ought to be a just image of life as it is, there shall always be an exact fitting of rewards and punishments to moral desert; or that the innocent and the guilty, the just and the unjust, shall be perfectly discriminated in what befalls them; as for such poets and critics, I simply do not believe in them at all: their workmanship is radically both unchristian and immoral; and its moral effect, if it have any, can hardly be other than to "pamper the coward heart with feelings all too delicate for use."

Wherefore, if any students of Shakespeare are still troubled with such criticisms as the one in question, I recommend them to make a thorough study of the *Book of Job*, and not to leave it till they shall have mastered the argument of that wonderful and divine poem. They will there find that, when the good man was prosperous, the Accuser brought against him the charge, that his serving God so well was from his being sure of good pay; and that therefore he would presently give over or slack his service, if the pay should be withheld: they will also find that, when he was in affliction, his comforters sought to comfort him with the cruel reproach of having been all the while secretly a bad man, and with arguments no less cruel, that his afflictions were sent upon him as a judgment for his secret sins: and, further, they will find that, when his wife urged him to "curse God and die," her counsel proceeded upon the principle, that the evils which fall upon the upright prove the government of the world to be in the hands of a being who has no respect for the moral character of his subjects; or, in other words, the sufferings of good men are taken by her as evidence that goodness is not the law of the Divine administration.

Now, it was from such teachers as Nature and Job, and not from such as Job's Accuser and comforters and wife, that Shakespeare learnt his morality.

SHAKESPEARE'S CHARACTERS.

A MIDSUMMER-NIGHT'S DREAM.

A MIDSUMMER-NIGHT'S DREAM was registered at the Stationers' October 8, 1600, and two quarto editions of it were published in the course of that year. The play is not known to have been printed again till it reappeared in the folio of 1623, where the repetition of certain misprints shows it to have been printed from one of the quarto copies. In all three of these copies, however, the printing is remarkably clear and correct for the time, insomuch that modern editors have little difficulty about the text. Probably none of the Poet's dramas has reached us in a more satisfactory state.

The play is first heard of in the list given by Francis Meres in his *Palladis Tamia*, 1598. But it was undoubtedly written several years before that time; and I am not aware that any editor places the writing at a later date than 1594. This brings it into the same period with *King John*, *King Richard the Second*, and the finished *Romeo and Juliet*; and the internal marks of style naturally sort it into that company. Our Mr. Verplanck, however, thinks there are some passages which relish strongly of an earlier time; while again there are others that with the prevailing sweetness of the whole have such an intertwisting of nerve and vigour, and such an energetic compactness of thought and imagery, mingled occasionally with the deeper tonings of "years that bring the philosophic mind," as to argue that they were wrought into the structure of the play not long before it came from the press. The part of the Athenian lovers certainly has a good deal that, viewed by itself, would scarce do credit even to such a boyhood as Shakespeare's must have been. On the other hand, there is a large philosophy in Theseus' discourse of "the lunatic, the lover, and the poet," a manly judgment in his reasons for preferring the "tedious brief scene of young Pyramus and his love Thisbe," and a bracing freshness in the short dialogue of the chase, all in the best style of the author's second period. Perhaps, however, what seem the defects of the former, the fanciful quirks and far-fetched conceits, were wisely designed, in order to invest the part with such an air of dreaminess and unreality as would better sort with the scope and spirit of the piece, and preclude a disproportionate resentment of some naughty acts into which those love-bewildered frailties are betrayed.

There is at least a rather curious coincidence, which used to be regarded as proving that the play was not written till after the Summer of 1594. I refer to Titania's superb description, in ii. 1, of the strange misbehaviour of the weather, which she ascribes to the fairy bickerings. I can quote but a part of it:

"The seasons alter: hoary-headed frosts
Fall in the fresh lap of the crimson rose;
And on old Hiems' thin and icy crown
An odorous chaplet of sweet summer buds
Is, as in mockery, set: the Spring, the Summer,
The childing Autumn, angry Winter, change
Their wonted liveries; and the mazèd world,
By their increase, now knows not which is which:
And this same progeny of evils comes
From our debate, from our dissension."

For the other part of the coincidence, Strype in his *Annals* gives the following passage from a discourse by the Rev. Dr. King: "And see whether the Lord doth not threaten us much more, by sending such unseasonable weather and storms of rain among us; which if we will observe, and compare it with what is past, we may say that the course of nature is very much inverted. Our years are turned upside down: our Summers are no Summers; our harvests are no harvests; our seed-times are no seed-times. For a great space of time scant any day hath been seen that it hath not rained." Dyce indeed scouts the supposal that Shakespeare had any allusion to this eccentric conduct of the elements in the Summer of 1594, pronouncing it "ridiculous"; but I do not quite see it so; albeit I am apt enough to believe that most of the play was written before that date. And surely, the truth of the allusion being granted, all must admit that passing events have seldom been turned to better account in the service of poetry.

I can hardly imagine this play ever to have been very successful on the stage; and I am sure it could not be made to succeed there now. Still we are not without contemporary evidence that it had at least a fair amount of fame. And we have authentic information that it was performed at the house of Dr. John Williams, Bishop of Lincoln, on Sunday, the 27th of September, 1631. The actor of Bottom's part was on that occasion sentenced by a Puritan tribunal to sit twelve hours in the porter's room of the Bishop's palace, wearing the ass's head. This Dr. Williams was the very able but far from faultless man who was treated so harshly by Laud, and gave the King such crooked counsel in the case of Strafford, and spent his last years in mute sorrow at the death of his royal master, and had his life written by the wise, witty, good Bishop Hacket.

Some hints towards the part of Theseus and Hippolyta appear to have been taken from *The Knight's Tale* of Chaucer. The same poet's *Legend of Thisbe of Babylon*, and Golding's translation of the same story from Ovid, probably furnished the matter of the Interlude. So much as relates to Bottom and his fellows evidently came fresh from Nature as she had passed under the Poet's eye. The linking of these clowns with the ancient tragic tale of Pyramus and Thisbe, so as to draw the latter within the region of modern farce, is not less original than droll. How far it may have expressed the Poet's judgment touching the theatrical doings of the time, were perhaps a question more curious than profitable. The names of Oberon, Titania, and Robin Goodfellow were made familiar by the surviving relics of Gothic and Druidical mythology; as were also many particulars in their habits, mode of life, and influence in human affairs. Hints and allusions scattered through many preceding writers might be produced, showing that the old superstition had been grafted into the body of Christianity, where it had shaped itself into a regular system, so as to mingle in the lore of the nursery, and hold an influential place in the popular belief. Some reports of this ancient Fairydom are choicely translated into poetry by Chaucer in *The Wife of Bath's Tale.*

But, though Chaucer and others had spoken about the fairy nation, it was for Shakespeare to let them speak for themselves: until he clothed their life in apt forms, their thoughts in fitting words, they but floated unseen and unheard in the mental atmosphere of his fatherland. So that on this point there need be no scruple about receiving Hallam's statement of the matter: "*A Midsummer-Night's Dream* is, I believe, altogether original in one of the most beautiful conceptions that ever visited the mind of a poet, — the fairy machinery. A few before him had dealt in a vulgar and clumsy manner with popular superstitions; but the sportive, beneficent, invisible population of the air and earth, long since established in the creed of childhood, and of those simple as children, had never for a moment been blended with 'human mortals' among the personages of the drama." How much Shakespeare did as the friend and saviour of those sweet airy frolickers of the past from the relentless mowings of Time, has been charmingly set forth in our day in Hood's *Plea of the Midsummer Fairies.*

What, then, are the leading qualities which the Poet ascribes to these ideal or fanciful beings? Coleridge says he is "convinced that Shakespeare availed himself of the title of this play in his own mind, and worked upon it as a dream throughout." This remark no doubt rightly hits the true genius of the piece; and on no other ground can its merits be duly estimated. The whole play is indeed a sort of ideal dream; and it is from the fairy personages that its character as such mainly proceeds. All the materials of the piece are ordered and assimilated to that central and governing idea. This it is that explains and justifies the distinctive features of the work, such as the constant preponderance of the lyrical over the dramatic, and the free playing of the action unchecked by the conditions of outward fact and reality. Accordingly a sort of lawlessness is, as it ought to be, the very law of the performance. King Oberon is the sovereign who presides over the world of dreams; Puck is his prime minister; and all the other denizens of Fairydom are his subjects and the agents of his will in this capacity. Titania's nature and functions are precisely the same which Mercutio assigns to Queen Mab, whom he aptly describes as having for her office to deliver sleeping men's fancies of their dreams, those "children of an idle brain." In keeping with this central dream-idea, the actual order of things everywhere gives place to the spontaneous issues and capricious turnings of the dreaming mind; the lofty and the low, the beautiful and the grotesque, the world of fancy and of fact, all the strange diversities that enter into "such stuff as dreams are made of," running and frisking together, and interchanging their functions and properties; so that the whole seems confused, flitting, shadowy, and indistinct, as fading away in the remoteness and fascination of moonlight. The very scene is laid in a veritable dream-land, called Athens indeed, but only because Athens was the greatest beehive of beautiful visions then known; or rather it is laid in an ideal forest near an ideal Athens, — a forest peopled with sportive elves and sprites and fairies feeding on moonlight and music and fragrance; a place where Nature herself is preternatural; where everything is idealized, even to the sunbeams and the soil; where the vegetation proceeds by enchantment, and there is magic in the germination of the seed and secretion of the sap.

The characteristic attributes of the fairy people are, perhaps, most availably represented in Puck; who is apt to remind one of Ariel, though the two have little in common, save that both are preternatural, and therefore live no longer in the faith of reason. Puck is no such sweet-mannered, tender-hearted, music-breathing spirit, as Prospero's delicate prime-minister; there are no such fine interweavings of a sensitive moral soul in his nature, he has no such soft touches of compassion and pious awe of goodness, as link the dainty Ariel in so smoothly with our best sympathies. Though Goodfellow by name, his powers and aptitudes for mischief are quite unchecked by any gentle relentings of fellow-feeling: in whatever distresses he finds or occasions he sees much to laugh at, nothing to pity: to tease and vex poor human sufferers, and then to think "what fools these mortals be," is pure fun to him. Yet, notwithstanding his mad pranks, we cannot choose but love the little sinner, and let our fancy frolic with him, his sense of the ludicrous is so exquisite, he is so fond of sport, and so quaint and merry in his mischief; while at the same time such is the strange web of his nature as to keep him morally innocent. In all which I think he answers perfectly to the best idea we can frame of what a little dream-god should be.

In further explication of this peculiar people, it is to be noted that there is nothing of reflection or conscience or even of a spiritualized intelligence in their proper life: they have all the attributes of the merely natural and sensitive soul, but no attributes of the properly rational and moral soul. They worship the clean, the neat, the pretty, and the pleasant, whatever goes to make up the idea of purely sensuous beauty: this is a sort of religion with them; whatever of conscience they have adheres to this: so that herein they not unfitly represent the wholesome old notion which places cleanliness next to godliness. Every thing that is trim, dainty, elegant, graceful, agreeable, and sweet to the senses, they delight in: flowers, fragrances, dewdrops, and moonbeams, honey-bees, butterflies, and nightingales, dancing, play, and song, — these are their joy; out of these they weave their highest delectation; amid these they "fleet the time carelessly," without memory or forecast, and with no thought or aim beyond the passing pleasure of the moment. On the other hand, they have an instinctive repugnance to whatever is foul, ugly, sluttish, awkward, ungainly, or misshapen: they wage unrelenting war against bats, spiders, hedgehogs, spotted snakes, blindworms, long-legg'd spinners, beetles, and all such disagreeable creatures: to "kill cankers in the musk-rosebuds," and to "keep back the clamorous owl," are regular parts of their business. Their intense dislike of what is ugly and misshapen is the reason why they so much practise "the legerdemain of changelings," stealing away finished, handsome babies, and leaving blemished and defective ones in their stead. For the same cause they love to pester and persecute and play shrewd tricks upon decrepit old age, wise aunts, and toothless, chattering gossips, and especially such awkward "hempen home-spuns" as Bottom and his fellow-actors in the Interlude.

Thus these beings embody the ideal of the mere natural soul, or rather the purely sensuous fancy which shapes and governs the pleasing or the vexing delusions of sleep. They lead a merry, luxurious life, given up entirely to the pleasures of happy sensation, — a happiness that has no moral element, nothing of reason or conscience in it. They are indeed a sort of personified dreams; and so the Poet places them in a kindly or at least harmless relation to mortals as the bringers of dreams. Their very kingdom is located in the aromatic, flower-scented Indies, a land where mortals are supposed to live in a half-dreamy state. From thence they come, "following darkness," just as dreams naturally do; or, as Oberon words it, "tripping after the night's shade, swifter than the wandering Moon." It is their nature to shun the daylight, though they do not fear it, and to prefer the dark, as this is their appropriate work-time; but most of all they love the dusk and the twilight, because this is the best dreaming-time, whether the dreamer be asleep or awake. And all the shifting phantom-jugglery of dreams, all the sweet soothing witcheries, and all the teasing and tantalizing imagery of dream-land, rightly belong to their province.

It is a very noteworthy point that all their power or influence over the hearts and actions of mortals works through the medium of dreams, or of such fancies as are most allied to dreams. So that their whole inner character is fashioned in harmony with their external function. Nor is it without rare felicity that the Poet assigns to them the dominion over the workings of sensuous and superficial love, this being but as one of the courts of the dream-land kingdom; a region ordered, as it were, quite apart from the proper regards of duty and law, and where the natural soul of man moves free of moral thought and responsibility. Accordingly we have the King of this Fairydom endowed with the rights and powers both of the classical god of love and the classical goddess of chastity. Oberon commands alike the secret virtues of "Dian's bud" and of "Cupid's flower"; and he seems to use them both unchecked by any other law than his innate love of what is handsome and fair, and his native aversion to what is ugly and foul; that is, he owns no restraint but as he is inwardly held to apply either or both of them in such a way as to avoid all distortion or perversion from what is naturally graceful and pleasant. For everybody, I take it, knows that in the intoxications of a life of sensuous love reason and conscience have as little force as they have in a life of dreams. And so the Poet fitly ascribes to Oberon and his ministers both Cupid's delight in frivolous breaches of faith and Jove's laughter at lovers' perjuries; and this on the ground, apparently, that the doings of those in Cupid's power are as harmless and unaccountable as the freaks of a dream.

In pursuance of this idea he depicts the fairies as beings without any proper moral sense in what they do, but as having a very keen sense of what is ludicrous and absurd in the doings of men. They are careless and unscrupulous in their dealings in this behalf. The wayward follies and the teasing perplexities of the fancy-smitten persons are pure sport to them. If by their wanton mistakes they can bewilder and provoke the lovers into larger outcomes of the laughable, so much the higher runs their mirth. And as they have no fellow-feeling with the pains of those who thus feed their love of fun, so the effect of their roguish tricks makes no impression upon them: they have a feeling of simple delight and wonder at the harmless frettings and fumings which their merry mischief has a hand in bringing to pass: but then it is to be observed also, that they find just as much sport in tricking the poor lover out of his vexations as in tricking him into them; in fact, they never rest satisfied with the fun of the former so long as there is any chance of enjoying that of the latter also.

All readers of Shakespeare are of course familiar with the splendid passage in ii. 1, where Oberon describes to Puck how, on a certain occasion,

> "I heard a mermaid, on a dolphin's back,
> Uttering such dulcet and harmonious breath,
> That the rude sea grew civil at her song."

And all are no doubt aware that the subsequent lines, referring to "a fair vestal thronèd by the west," are commonly understood to have been meant as a piece of delicate flattery to Queen Elizabeth. Mr. Halpin has recently given to this famous passage a new interpretation or application, which is at least curious enough to justify a brief statement of it. In his view, "Cupid all arm'd" refers to Leicester's wooing of Elizabeth, and his grand entertainment of her at Kenilworth in 1575. From authentic descriptions of that entertainment we learn, that among the spectacles and fireworks witnessed on the occasion was one of a singing mermaid on a dolphin's back gliding over smooth water amid shooting stars. The "love-shaft" which was aimed at the "fair vestal," that is, the Priestess of Diana, whose bud has such prevailing might over "Cupid's flower," glanced off; so that "the imperial votaress passèd on, in maiden meditation, fancy-free."

Thus far, all is clear enough. But Halpin further interprets that the "little western flower" upon whom "the bolt of Cupid fell" refers to Lettice Countess of Essex, with whom Leicester carried on a secret intrigue while her husband was absent in Ireland. The Earl of Essex, on being apprised of the intrigue, set out to return the next year, but died of poison, as was thought, before he reached home. So Halpin understands the "western flower, before milk-white," that is, innocent, but "now purple with love's wound," as referring to the lady's fall, or to the deeper blush of her husband's murder. And the flower is called "love-in-idleness," to signify her listlessness of heart during the Earl's absence; as the Poet elsewhere uses similar terms of the pansy, as denoting the love that renders men pensive, dreamy, indolent, instead of toning up the soul with healthy and noble aspirations. The words of Oberon to Puck, "that very time I saw — but thou could'st not," are construed as referring to the strict mystery in which the affair was wrapped, and to the Poet's own knowledge of it, because a few years later the execution of Edward Arden, his maternal relative, was closely connected with it, and because the unfortunate Earl of Essex, so well known as for some time the Queen's favourite, and then the victim of her resentment, was the son of that Lettice, and was also the Poet's early friend and patron.

Such is, in substance, Halpin's view of the matter; which I give for what it may be worth; and freely acknowledge it to be ingenious and plausible enough. Gervinus regards it as "an interpretation full of spirit," and as "giving the most definite relation to the innermost sense of the whole piece." And I am very willing to believe that Shakespeare often took hints, perhaps something more than hints, for his poetry from the facts and doings of the time: nevertheless I rather fail to see how any real good is to be gained towards understanding the Poet from such interpretations of his scenes, or from tracing out such "definite relations" between his workmanship and the persons and particulars that may have come to his knowledge. For my own part, I doubt whether "the innermost sense" of the play is any the clearer to me for this ingenious piece of explanation.

Besides, I have yet to learn what proofs there are that the ill-fated Essex was an early patron and friend of Shakespeare. That great honour belongs to the Earls of Southampton and Pembroke. It was Lord Bacon, not Shakespeare, who enjoyed so richly the friendship and patronage of the generous Essex; and how he requited the same is known much too well for his credit. I am not unmindful that this may yield some comfort to those who would persuade us that Shakespeare's plays were written by Lord Bacon. Upon this point I have just four things to say: First, Bacon's requital of the Earl's bounty was such a piece of ingratitude as I can hardly conceive the author of *King Lear* to have been guilty of: Second, the author of Shakespeare's plays, whoever he may have been, certainly was not a scholar; he had indeed something vastly better than learning, but he had not that: Third, Shakespeare never philosophizes, Bacon never does anything else: Fourth, Bacon's mind, great as it was, might have been cut out of Shakespeare's without being missed.

Any very firm or strong delineation of character, any deep passion, earnest purpose, or working of powerful motives, would clearly go at odds with the spirit of such a performance as I have described this play to be. It has room but for love and beauty and delight, for whatever is most poetical in nature and fancy, and for such tranquil stirrings of thought and feeling as may flow out in musical expression. Any such tuggings of mind or heart as would ruffle and discompose the smoothness of lyrical division would be quite out of keeping in a course of dream-life. The characters here, accordingly, are drawn with light, delicate, vanishing touches; some of them being dreamy and sentimental, some gay and frolicsome, and others replete with amusing absurdities, while all are alike dipped in fancy or sprinkled with humour. And for the same reason the tender distresses of unrequited or forsaken love here touch not our moral sense at all, but only at the most our human sympathies; love itself being represented as but the effect of some visual enchantment, which the King of Fairydom can inspire, suspend, or reverse at pleasure. Even the heroic personages are fitly shown in an unheroic aspect: we see them but in their unbendings, when they have daffed their martial robes aside, to lead the train of day-dreamers, and have a nuptial jubilee. In their case, great care and art were required, to make the play what it has been blamed for being; that is, to keep the dramatic sufficiently under, and lest the law of a part should override the law of the whole.

So, likewise, in the transformation of Bottom and the dotage of Titania, all the resources of fancy were needed, to prevent the unpoetical from getting the upper hand, and thus swamping the genius of the piece. As it is, what words can fitly express the effect with which the extremes of the grotesque and the beautiful are here brought together? What an inward quiet laughter springs up and lubricates the fancy at Bottom's droll confusion of his two natures, when he talks, now as an ass, now as a man, and anon as a mixture of both; his thoughts running at the same time on honey-bags and thistles, the charms of music and of good dry oats! Who but Shakespeare or Nature could have so interfused the lyrical spirit, not only with, but into and through a series or cluster of the most irregular and fantastic drolleries? But indeed this embracing and kissing of the most ludicrous and the most poetical, the enchantment under which they meet, and the airy, dream-like grace that hovers over their union, are altogether inimitable and indescribable. In this singular wedlock, the very diversity of the elements seems to link them the closer, while this linking in turn heightens that diversity; Titania being thereby drawn on to finer issues of soul, and Bottom to larger expressions of stomach. The union is so very improbable as to seem quite natural: we cannot conceive how any thing but a dream could possibly have married things so contrary; and that they could not have come together save in a dream, is a sort of proof that they *were* dreamed together.

And so, throughout, the execution is in strict accordance with the plan. The play, from beginning to end, is a perfect festival of whatever dainties and delicacies poetry may command, — a continued revelry and jollification of soul, where the understanding is lulled asleep, that the fancy may run riot in unrestrained enjoyment. The bringing together of four parts so dissimilar as those of the Duke and his warrior Bride, of the Athenian ladies and their lovers, of the amateur players and their woodland rehearsal, and of the fairy bickerings and overreaching; and the carrying of them severally to a point where they all meet and blend in lyrical respondence; all this is done in the same freedom from the laws that govern the drama of character and life. Each group of persons is made to parody itself into concert with the others; while the frequent intershootings of fairy influence lift the whole into the softest regions of fancy. At last the Interlude comes in as an amusing burlesque on all that has gone before; as in our troubled dreams we sometimes end with a dream that we have been dreaming, and our perturbations sink to rest in the sweet assurance that they were but the phantoms and unrealities of a busy sleep.

Though, as I have already implied, the characterization is here quite secondary and subordinate, yet the play probably has as much of character as were compatible with so much of poetry. Theseus has been well described as a classic personage with romantic features and expression. The name is Greek, but the nature and spirit are essentially Gothic. Nor does the abundance of classical allusion and imagery in the story call for any qualification here; because whatsoever is taken is thoroughly steeped in the efficacy of the taker. This sort of anachronism, common to all modern writers before and during the age of Shakespeare, seems to have arisen in part from a comparative dearth of classical learning, which left men to contemplate the heroes of antiquity under the forms into which their own mind and manners had been cast. Thus their delineations became informed with the genius of romance; the condensed grace of ancient character giving way to the enlargement of chivalrous magnanimity and honour, with its "high-erected thoughts seated in the heart of courtesy." Such in Shakespeare's case appears to have been the no less beautiful than natural result of the small learning, so often smiled and sometimes barked at, by those more skilled in the ancient languages than in the mother-tongue of nature.

In the two pairs of lovers there are hardly any lines deep and firm enough to be rightly called characteristic. Their doings, even more than those of the other human persons, are marked by the dream-like freakishness and whimsicality which distinguish the piece. Perhaps the two ladies are slightly discriminated as individuals, in that Hermia, besides her brevity of person, is the more tart in temper, and the more pert and shrewish of speech, while Helena is of a rather milder and softer disposition, with less of confidence in herself. So too in the case of Demetrius and Lysander the lines of individuality are exceedingly faint; the former being perhaps a shade the more caustic and spiteful, and the latter somewhat the more open and candid. But there is really nothing of heart or soul in what any of them do: as we see them, they are not actuated by principle at all, or even by any thing striking so deep as motive: their conduct issues from the more superficial springs of capricious impulse and fancy, the "jugglery of the senses during the sleep of reason"; the higher forces of a mental and moral bearing having no hand in shaping their action. For the fairy influences do not reach so far as to the proper seat of motive and principle: they have but the skin-depth of amorous caprice; all the elements of character and all the vital springs of faith and loyalty and honour lying quite beyond their sphere. Even here the judgment or the genius of the Poet is very perceptible; the lovers being represented from the start as acting from no forces or inspirations too deep or strong for the powers of Fairydom to overcome. Thus the pre-condition of the two pairs in their whim-bewilderment is duly attempered to the purposed dream-play of the general action. Nor is the seeming stanchness of Hermia and Demetrius in the outset any exception to this view; for nothing is more wilful and obstinate than amorous caprice or skin-deep love during its brief tenure of the fancy.

Of all the characters in this play, Bottom descends by far the most into the realities of common experience, and is therefore much the most accessible to the grasp of prosaic and critical fingers. It has been thought that the Poet meant him as a satire on the envies and jealousies of the greenroom, as they had fallen under his keen yet kindly eye. But, surely, the qualities uppermost in Bottom the Weaver had forced themselves on his notice long before he entered the greenroom. It is indeed curious to observe the solicitude of this protean actor and critic, that all the parts of the forthcoming play may have the benefit of his execution; how great is his concern lest, if he be tied to one, the others may be "overdone or come tardy off"; and how he would fain engross them all to himself, to the end of course that all may succeed, to the honour of the stage and the pleasure of the spectators. But Bottom's metamorphosis is the most potent drawer-out of his genius. The sense of his new head-dress stirs up all the manhood within him, and lifts his character into ludicrous greatness at once. Hitherto the seeming to be a man has made him content to be little better than an ass; but no sooner is he conscious of seeming an ass than he tries his best to be a man; while all his efforts that way only go to approve the fitness of his present seeming to his former being.

Schlegel happily remarks, that "the droll wonder of Bottom's metamorphosis is merely the translation of a metaphor in its literal sense." The turning of a figure of speech thus into visible form is a thing only to be thought of or imagined; so that probably no attempt to paint or represent it to the senses can ever succeed. We can bear — at least we often have to bear — that a man should seem an ass to the mind's eye; but that he should seem such to the eye of the body is rather too much, save as it is done in those fable-pictures which have long been among the playthings of the nursery. So a child, for instance, takes great pleasure in fancying the stick he is riding to be a horse, when he would be frightened out of his wits, were the stick to quicken and expand into an actual horse. In like manner we often delight in indulging fancies and giving names, when we should be shocked were our fancies to harden into facts: we enjoy visions in our sleep, that would only disgust or terrify us, should we awake and find them solidified into things. The effect of Bottom's transformation can hardly be much otherwise, if set forth in visible, animated shape. Delightful to think of, it is scarce tolerable to look upon: exquisitely true in idea, it has no truth, or even verisimilitude, when reduced to fact; so that, however gladly imagination receives it, sense and understanding revolt at it.

Partly for reasons already stated, and partly for others that I scarce know how to state, *A Midsummer-Night's*

Dream is a most effectual poser to criticism. Besides that its very essence is irregularity, so that it cannot be fairly brought to the test of rules, the play forms properly a class by itself: literature has nothing else really like it; nothing therefore with which it may be compared, and its merits adjusted. For so the Poet has here exercised powers apparently differing even in kind, not only from those of any other writer, but from those displayed in any other of his own writings. Elsewhere, if his characters are penetrated with the ideal, their whereabout lies in the actual, and the work may in some measure be judged by that life which it claims to represent: here the whereabout is as ideal as the characters; all is in the land of dreams, — a place for dreamers, not for critics. For who can tell what a dream ought or ought not to be, or when the natural conditions of dream-life are or are not rightly observed? How can the laws of time and space, as involved in the transpiration of human character, — how can these be applied in a place where the mind is thus absolved from their proper jurisdiction? Besides, the whole thing swarms with enchantment: all the sweet witchery of Shakespeare's sweet genius is concentrated in it, yet disposed with so subtle and cunning a hand, that we can as little grasp it as get away from it: its charms, like those of a summer evening, are such as we may see and feel, but cannot locate or define; cannot say they are here, or they are there: the moment we yield ourselves up to them, they seem to be everywhere; the moment we go to master them, they seem to be nowhere.

THE MERCHANT OF VENICE.

The Merchant of Venice was registered at the Stationers' in July, 1598, but with a special proviso, "that it be not printed without license first had from the Right Honourable the Lord Chamberlain." The theatrical company to which Shakespeare belonged were then known as

"The Lord Chamberlain's Servants"; and the purpose of the proviso was to keep the play out of print till the company's permission were given through their patron. The play was entered again at the same place in October, 1600, his lordship's license having probably been obtained by that time. Accordingly two distinct editions of it were published in the course of that year. The play was never issued again, that we know of, till in the folio of 1623, where the repetition of various misprints shows it to have been reprinted from one of the quarto copies.

The Merchant of Venice also makes one in the list of Shakespeare's plays given by Francis Meres in 1598. How long before that time it was written we have no means of knowing; but, judging from the style, we cannot well assign the writing to a much earlier date; though there is some reason for thinking it may have been on the stage four years earlier; as Henslowe's *Diary* records *The Venetian Comedy* as having been originally acted in August, 1594. It is by no means certain, however, that this refers to Shakespeare's play; while the workmanship here shows such maturity and variety of power as argue against that supposal. It evinces, in a considerable degree, the easy, unlabouring freedom of conscious mastery; the persons being so entirely under the author's control, and subdued to his hand, that he seems to let them talk and act just as they have a mind to. Therewithal the style, throughout, is so even and sustained; the word and the character are so fitted to each other; the laws of dramatic proportion are so well observed; and the work is so free from any jarring or falling-out from the due course and order of art; as to justify the belief that the whole was written in the same stage of intellectual growth and furnishing.

In the composition of this play the Poet drew largely from preceding writers. Novelty of plot or story there is almost none. Nevertheless, in conception and development of character, in poetical texture and grain, in sap and flavour of wit and humour, and in all that touches the real life and virtue of the work, it is one of the most original productions that ever came from the human mind. Of the materials here used, some were so much the common stock of European literature before the Poet's time, and had been run into so many variations, that it is not easy to say what sources he was most indebted to for them. The incidents of the bond and the caskets are found separately in the *Gesta Romanorum*, an ancient and curious collection of tales. There was also an Italian novel, by Giovanni Fiorentino, written as early as 1378, but not printed till 1550, to which the Poet is clearly traceable. As nothing is known of any English translation of the novel dating as far back as his time, it seems not unlikely that he may have been acquainted with it in the original.

Such are the principal tributaries to the fund of this play. I cannot, nor need I, stay to specify the other sources to which some parts of the workmanship have been traced.

The praise of this drama is in the mouth of nearly all the critics. That the praise is well deserved appears in that, from the reopening of the theatres at the Restoration till the present day, the play has kept its place on the stage; while it is also among the first of the Poet's works to be read, and the last to be forgotten, its interest being as durable in the closet as on the boards. Well do I remember it as the very beginning of my acquaintance with Shakespeare; one of the dearest acquaintances I have ever made, and which has been to me a source of more pleasure and profit than I should dare undertake to tell.

Critics have too often entertained themselves with speculations as to the Poet's specific moral purpose in this play or that. Wherein their great mistake is the not duly bearing in mind, that the special proposing of this or that moral lesson is quite from or beside the purpose of Art. Nevertheless, a work of art, to be really deserving the name, must needs be moral, because it must be proportionable and true to Nature; thus attuning our inward forces to the voice of external order and law: otherwise it is at strife with the compact of things; a piece of dissonance; a jarring, unbalanced, crazy thing, that will die of its own internal disorder. If, then, a work be morally bad, this proves the author more a bungler than anything else. And if any one admire it or take pleasure in it, he does so, not from reason, but from something within him which his reason, in so far as he has any, necessarily disapproves: so that he is rather to be laughed at as a dunce than preached to as a sinner; though perhaps this latter should be done also.

As to the moral temper of *The Merchant of Venice*, critics have differed widely, some regarding the play as teaching the most comprehensive humanity, others as caressing the narrowest bigotries of the age. This difference may be fairly taken as an argument of the Poet's candour and evenhandedness. A special-pleader is not apt to leave the hearers in doubt on which side of the question he stands. In this play, as in others, the Poet, I think, ordered things mainly with a view to dramatic effect; though to such effect in the largest and noblest sense. And the highest praise compatible with the nature of the work is justly his, inasmuch as he did not allow himself to be swayed either way from the right measures and proportions of art. For Art is, from its very nature, obliged to be "without respect of persons." Impartiality is its essential law, the constituent of its being. And of Shakespeare it could least of all be said,

> "he narrow'd his mind,
> And to party gave up what was meant for mankind."

He represented men as he had seen them. And he could neither repeal nor ignore the old law of human nature, in virtue of which the wisest and kindest men are more or less warped by social customs and prejudices, so that they come to do, and even to make a merit of doing, some things that are very unwise and unkind; while the wrongs and insults which they are thus led to practise have the effect of goading the sufferers into savage malignity and revenge. Had he so clothed the latter with gentle and amiable qualities as to enlist the feelings all in their behalf, he would have given a false view of human nature, and his work would have lost much of its instructiveness on the score of practical morality. For good morals can never be reached by departures from truth. A rule that may be profitably remembered by all who are moved to act as advocates and special-pleaders in what they think a good cause.

The leading incidents of the play are soon told. Antonio, the Merchant, has a strange mood of sadness upon him, and a parcel of his friends are bending their wits to play it off. Among them, and dearer to him than any of the rest, is one Bassanio, a gentleman who, young and generous, has lavished his fortune. Bassanio's heart is turning towards a wealthy heiress who, highly famed for gifts and virtues, resides not many miles off; and from whose eyes he has received "fair speechless messages." But he wants "the means to hold a rival place" among her princely suitors. Antonio's wealth and credit are freely pledged to his service. His funds, however, being all embarked in ventures at sea, he tries his credit with a rich Jew, whose person he has often insulted, and whose greed his Christian liberality has often thwarted. The Jew, feigning a merry humour, consents to lend the sum, provided Antonio sign a bond authorizing him, in case of forfeiture, to cut a pound of flesh from whatever part of his body he may choose. Antonio readily agrees to this, and so furnishes his friend for the loving enterprise. Bassanio prosecutes his suit to the lady with success. But, while yet in his first transports of joy, he learns that Antonio's ventures at sea have all miscarried, and that the Jew, with malignant earnestness, claims the forfeiture. Leaving his bride the moment he has sworn the sweet oath, he hastens away, resolved to save his friend's life at the expense, if need be, of his own.

Thereupon his virgin wife forthwith gets instructions from the most learned lawyer in those parts, and, habiting herself as a doctor of laws, repairs to the trial. To divert the Jew from his purpose, she taxes her wisdom and persuasion to the utmost, but in vain: scorning the spirit of Justice, and deaf to the voice of Mercy, both of which speak with heavenly eloquence from Portia's lips; rejecting thrice the amount of the bond, and standing immoveable on the letter of the law; he pushes his revenge to the very point of making the fatal incision, when she turns the letter of the law against him, strips him of penalty, principal, and all, and subjects even his life to the mercy of the Duke. As the condition of his life, he is required to sign a deed securing all his wealth to his daughter who, loaded with his ducats and jewels, has lately eloped with another of Antonio's friends, and is staying at Portia's mansion during her absence. The play winds up with the hastening of all the parties, except the Jew, to Portia's home. When all have met, Portia announces to Antonio the safe return of his ships supposed to be lost, and surprises the fugitive lovers with the news of their good fortune.

In respect of characterization this play is exceedingly rich, and this too both in quantity and quality. The persons naturally fall into three several groups, with each its several plot and action; yet the three are skilfully complotted, each standing out clear and distinct in its place, yet so drawing in with the others, that every thing helps on every thing else; there being neither any confusion nor any appearance of care to avoid it. Of these three groups, Antonio, Shylock, and Portia are respectively the centres; while the part of Lorenzo and Jessica, though strictly an episode, seems nevertheless to grow forth as an element of the original germ; a sort of inherent superfluity, and as such essential to the well-being of the piece. But perhaps it may be better described as a fine romantic undertone accompaniment to the other parts; itself in perfect harmony with them, and therefore perfecting their harmony with each other.

In the first entry at the Stationers', the play is described as "*The Merchant of Venice*, or otherwise called *The Jew of Venice*." This would seem to infer that the author was then in some doubt whether to name it from Antonio or Shylock. As an individual, Shylock is altogether *the* character of the play, and exhibits more of mastership than all the others; so that, viewing the persons severally, we should say the piece ought to be named from him. But we have not far to seek for good reasons why it should rather be named as it is. For if the Jew is the more important individually, the Merchant is so dramatically. Antonio is the centre and main-spring of the action: without him, Shylock, however great in himself, had no business there. And the laws of dramatic combination, not any accident of individual prominence, are clearly what ought to govern in the naming of the play.

Not indeed that the Merchant is a small matter in himself; far from it: he is a highly interesting and attractive personage; nor am I sure but there may be timber enough in him for a good dramatic hero, apart from the Jew. Something of a peculiar charm attaches to him, from the state of mind in which we first see him. A dim, mysterious presage of evil weighs down his spirits, as though he felt afar off the coming-on of some great calamity. Yet this unwonted dejection, sweetened as it is with his habitual kindness and good-nature, has the effect of showing how dearly he is held by such whose friendship is the fairest earthly purchase of virtue. And it is considerable that upon tempers like his even the smiles of Fortune often have a strangely saddening effect. For such a man, even because he is good, is apt to be haunted with a sense of having more than he deserves; and this may not unnaturally inspire him with an indefinable dread of some reverse which shall square up the account of his present blessings. Thus his very happiness works, by subtle methods, to charge his heart with certain dark forebodings. So that such presentiments, whatever the disciples of positivism may say, are in the right line of nature:

> "Oft startled and made wise
> By their low-breathed interpretings,
> The simply-meek foretaste the springs
> Of bitter contraries."

But the sorrow can hardly be ungrateful to us, that has such noble comforters as Antonio's. Our nature is honoured in the feelings that spring up on both sides.

Wealth indeed seldom dispenses such warnings save to its most virtuous possessors. And such is Antonio. A kind-hearted and sweet-mannered man; of a large and liberal spirit; affable, generous, and magnificent in his dispositions; patient of trial, indulgent to weakness, free where he loves, and frank where he hates; in prosperity modest, in adversity cheerful; craving wealth for the uses of virtue, and as the sinews of friendship; — his character is one which we never weary of contemplating. The only blemish we perceive in him is his treatment of Shylock: in this, though evidently much more the fault of the times than of the man, we cannot help siding against him; than which we need not ask a clearer instance of poetical justice. Yet even this we blame rather as a wrong done to himself than to Shylock; inasmuch as the latter, notwithstanding he has had such provocations, avowedly grounds his hate mainly on those very things which make the strongest title to a good man's love. For the Jew's revenge fastens not so much on the man's abuse of him as on his kindness to others.

The friendship between the Merchant and his companions is such a picture as Shakespeare evidently delighted to draw. And so fair a sentiment is not apt to inhabit ignoble breasts. Bassanio, Gratiano, and Salarino are each admirable in their way, and give a pleasing variety to the scenes where they move. Bassanio, though something too lavish of purse, is a model of a gentleman; in whose character and behaviour all is order and propriety; with whom good manners are the proper outside and visibility of a fair mind, — the natural foliage and drapery of inward refinement and delicacy and rectitude. Well-bred, he has that in him which, even had his breeding been ill, would have raised him above it and made him a gentleman.

Gratiano and Salarino are two as clever, sprightly, and voluble persons as any one need desire to be with; the chief difference between them being, that the former *lets* his tongue run on from good impulses, while the latter *makes* it do so for good ends. If not so wise as Bassanio, they are more witty; and as much surpass him in strength, as they fall short of him in beauty, of character. It is observable that of the two Gratiano, while much the more prone to flood us with his talk, also shows less subjection of the individual to the common forms of social decorum; so that, if he behaves not quite so well as the others, he gives livelier proof that what good behaviour he has is his own; a growth from within, not a piece of imitation. And we are rather agreeably surprised, that one so talkative and rattle-tongued should therewithal carry so much weight of meaning; and he sometimes appears less sensible than he is, because of his galloping volubility. But he has no wish to be "reputed wise for saying nothing"; and he makes a merit of talking nonsense when, as is sometimes the case, nonsense is the best sort of sense: for, like a prime good fellow, as he is, he would rather incur the charge of folly than not, provided he can thereby add to the health and entertainment of his friends.

Lorenzo and Jessica, the runaway lovers, are in such a lyrical state of mind as rather hinders a clear view of their characters. Both are indeed overflowing with sweetness and beauty, but more, perhaps, as the result of nuptial inspiration than of inherent qualities. For I suppose the worst tempers are apt to run sweet while the honeymoon is upon them. However, as regards the present couple, it may be justly said that the instrument should be well-tuned and delicately strung to give forth such tones, be it touched ever so finely. Even Love, potent little god as he is, can move none but choice spirits to such delectable issues. Jessica's elopement, in itself and its circumstances, puts us to the alternative that either she is a bad child, or Shylock a bad father. And there is enough to persuade us of the latter; though not in such sort but that some share of the reproach falls to her. For if a young woman have so bad a home as to justify her in thus deserting and robbing it, the atmosphere of the place can hardly fail to leave *some* traces in her temper and character.

Lorenzo stands fair in our regard, negatively, because he does nothing unhandsome, positively, because he has such good men for his friends. And it is rather curious that what is thus done for him, should be done for Jessica by such a person as Launcelot Gobbo. For she and the clown are made to reflect each other's choicer parts: we think the better of her for having kindled something of poetry in such a clod, and of him for being raised above himself by such an object. And her conduct is further justified to our feelings by the odd testimony he furnishes of her father's badness; which testimony, though not of much weight in itself, goes far to confirm that of others. We see that the Jew is much the same at home as in the Rialto; that, let him be where he will, it is his nature to snarl and bite.

Such, in one view of the matter, is the dramatic propriety of this Launcelot. His part, though often faulted by those who can see but one thing at a time, materially aids the completeness of the work, in giving us a fuller view both of Jessica and of her father. But he has also a value in himself irrespective of that use: his own personal rights enter into the purpose of his introduction; and he carries in himself a part of the reason why he is so, and not otherwise: for Shakespeare seldom if ever brings in a person *merely* for the sake of others. A mixture of conceit and drollery, and hugely wrapped up in self, he is by no means a commonplace buffoon, but stands firm in his sufficiency of original stock. His elaborate nonsense, his grasping at a pun without catching it, yet feeling just as grand as if he did, is both ludicrous and natural. His jokes to be sure are mostly failures; nevertheless they are laughable, because he dreams not but they succeed. The poverty of his wit is thus enriched by his complacency in dealing it out. His part indeed amply pays its way, in showing how much of mirth may be caused by feebleness in a great attempt at a small matter. Besides, in him the mother element of the whole piece runs out into broad humour and travesty; his reasons for breaking with his master the Jew being, as it were, a variation in drollery upon the fundamental air of the play. Thus he exhibits under a comic form the general aspect of surrounding humanity; while at the same time his character is an integral part of that varied structure of human life which it belongs to the Gothic Drama to represent. On several accounts indeed he might not be spared.

In Portia Shakespeare seems to have aimed at a perfect scheme of an amiable, intelligent, and accomplished woman. And the result is a fine specimen of beautiful nature enhanced by beautiful art. Eminently practical in her tastes and turn of mind, full of native, homebred sense and virtue, Portia unites therewith something of the ripeness and dignity of a sage, a mellow eloquence, and a large, noble discourse; the whole being tempered with the best grace and sensibility of womanhood. As intelligent as the strongest, she is at the same time as feminine as the weakest of her sex: she talks like a poet and a philosopher, yet, strange to say, she talks, for all the world, just like a woman. She is as full of pleasantry, too, and as merry "within the limit of becoming mirth," as she is womanly and wise; and, which is more, her arch sportiveness always relishes as the free outcome of perfect moral health. Nothing indeed can be more fitting and well-placed than her demeanour, now bracing her speech with grave maxims of practical wisdom, now unbending her mind in sallies of wit, or of innocent, roguish banter. The sportive element of her composition has its happiest showing in her dialogue with Nerissa about the "parcel of wooers," and in her humorous description of the part she imagines herself playing in her purposed disguise. The latter is especially delightful from its harmonious contrast with the solid thoughtfulness which, after all, forms the staple and framework of her character. How charmingly it sets off the divine rapture of eloquence with which she discourses to the Jew of mercy!

> "I'll hold thee any wager,
> When we are both accoutred like young men,
> I'll prove the prettier fellow of the two,
> And wear my dagger with the braver grace;
> And speak between the change of man and boy
> With a reed voice; and turn two mincing steps
> Into a manly stride; and speak of frays,
> Like a fine-bragging youth; and tell quaint lies,
> How honourable ladies sought my love,
> Which I denying, they fell sick and died, —
> I could not do withal; — then I 'll repent,
> And wish, for all that, that I had not kill'd them:
> And twenty of these puny lies I'll tell;
> That men shall swear I've discontinu'd school
> Above a twelvemonth. I've within my mind
> A thousand raw tricks of these bragging Jacks,
> Which I will practise."

Partly from condition, partly from culture, Portia has grown to live more in the understanding than in the affections; for which cause she is a little more self-conscious than I exactly like: yet her character is hardly the less lovely on that account: she talks considerably of herself indeed, but always so becomingly, that we hardly wish her to choose any other subject; for we are pleasantly surprised that one so well aware of her gifts should still bear them so meekly. Mrs. Jameson, with Portia in her eye, intimates Shakespeare to have been about the only artist, except Nature, who could make women wise without turning them into men. And it is well worth the noting that, honourable as the issue of her course at the trial would be to a man, Portia shows no unwomanly craving to be in the scene of her triumph: as she goes there prompted by the feelings and duties of a wife, and for the saving of her husband's honour and peace of mind, — being resolved that "never shall he lie by Portia's side with an unquiet soul"; so she gladly leaves when these causes no longer bear in that direction. Then too, exquisitely cultivated as she is, humanity has not been so refined out of her, but that in such a service she can stoop from her elevation, and hazard a brief departure from the sanctuary of her sex.

Being to act for once the part of a man, it would seem hardly possible for her to go through the undertaking without more of self-confidence than were becoming in a woman: and the student may find plenty of matter for thought in the Poet's so managing as to prevent such an impression. For there is nothing like ostentation or conceit of intellect in Portia. Though knowing enough for any station, still it never once enters her head that she is too wise for the station which Providence or the settled order of society has assigned her. She would therefore neither hide her light under a bushel, that others may not see by it, nor perch it aloft in public, that others may see it; but would simply set it on a candlestick, that it may give light to all in her house. With her noble intellect she has gathered in the sweets of poetry and the solidities of philosophy, all for use, nothing for show; she has fairly domesticated them, has naturalized them in her sphere, and tamed them to her fireside, so that they seem as much at home there as if they had been made for no other place. And to all this mental enrichment she adds the skill

> "So well to know
> Her own, that what she wills to do or say
> Seems wisest, virtuousest, discreetest, best."

Portia's consciousness of power does indeed render her cool, collected, and firm, but never a whit unfeminine: her smooth command both of herself and of the matter she goes about rather heightens our sense of her modesty than otherwise: so that the impression we take from her is, that these high mental prerogatives are of no sex; that they properly belong to the common freehold of woman and man; and that the ladies of creation have just as good a right to them as the lords. Some of her speeches, especially at the trial, are evidently premeditated; for, as any good lawyer would do, she of course prepares herself in the case beforehand; but I should like to see the masculine lawyer that could premeditate any thing equal to them. It is to be noted withal that she goes about her work without the least misgiving as to the result; having so thoroughly booked herself both in the facts and the law of the case as to feel perfectly sure on that point. Hence the charming ease and serenity with which she moves amid the excitements of the trial. No trepidations of anxiety come in to disturb the preconcerted order and method of her course. And her solemn appeals to the Jew are made in the earnest hope of inducing him to accept a full and liberal discharge of the debt. When she says to him, "there 's thrice thy money offer'd thee," it is because she really feels that both the justice of the cause and the honour of her husband would be better served by such a payment than by the more brilliant triumph which awaits her in case the Jew should spurn her offer.

Thus her management of the trial, throughout, is a piece of consummate art; though of art in such a sense as presupposes perfect integrity of soul. Hence, notwithstanding her methodical forecast and preparation, she is as eloquent as an angel, and her eloquence, as by an instinctive tact, knows its time perfectly. One of her strains in this kind, her appeal to the Jew on the score of mercy, has been so often quoted, that it would long since have grown stale, if it were possible by any means to crush the freshness of unwithering youth out of it. And I hope it will not be taken as any abatement of the speaker's claim as a wise jurist, that she there carries both the head and the heart of a ripe Christian divine into the management of her cause. Yet her style in that speech is in perfect keeping with her habitual modes of thought and discourse: even in her most spontaneous expressions we have a reflex of the same intellectual physiognomy. For the mental aptitude which she displays in the trial seems to have been the germinal idea out of which her whole part was consistently evolved; as the Poet's method often was, apparently, first to settle what his persons were to do, and then to conceive and work out their characters accordingly.

It has been said that Shakespeare's female characters are inferior to his characters of men. Doubtless in some respects they are so; they would not be female characters if they were not; but then in other respects they are superior. Some people apparently hold it impossible for man and woman to be equal and different at the same time. Hence the false equality of the sexes which has been of late so often and so excruciatingly advocated. On this ground, the Poet could not have made his women equal to his men without unsexing and unsphering them; which he was just as far from doing as Nature is. The alleged inferiority, then, of his women simply means, I suppose, that they are women, as they ought to be, and not men, as he meant they should not be, and as we have cause to rejoice that they are not. He knew very well that in this matter equality and diversity are nowise incompatible, and that the sexes might therefore stand or sit on the same level without standing in the same shoes or sitting in the same seats. If, indeed, he had not known this, he could not have given *characters* of either sex, but only wretched and disgusting medlies and caricatures of both.

How nicely, on the one hand, Shakespeare discriminates things that really differ, so as to present in all cases the soul of womanhood, without a particle of effeminacy; and how perfectly, on the other hand, he reconciles things that seem most diverse, pouring into his women all the intellectual forces of the other sex, without in the least impairing or obscuring their womanliness; — all this is not more rare in poetry than it is characteristic of his workmanship. Thus Portia is as much superior to her husband in intellect, in learning, and accomplishment, as she is in wealth; but she is none the less womanly for all that. Nor, which is more, does she ever on that account take the least thought of inverting the relation between them. In short, her mental superiority breeds no kind of social displacement, nor any desire of it. Very few indeed of the Poet's men are more highly charged with intellectual power. While she is acting the lawyer in disguise, her speech and bearing seem to those about her in the noblest style of manliness. In her judge-like gravity and dignity of deportment; in the extent and accuracy of her legal knowledge; in the depth and appropriateness of her moral reflections; in the luminous order, the logical coherence, and the beautiful transparency of her thoughts, she almost rivals our Chief Justice Marshall. Yet to us, who are in the secret of her sex, all the proprieties, all the inward harmonies, of her character are exquisitely preserved; and the essential grace of womanhood seems to irradiate and consecrate the dress in which she is disguised.

Nor is it any drawback on her strength and substantial dignity of character, that her nature is all overflowing with romance: rather, this it is that glorifies her, and breathes enchantment about her; it adds that precious seeing to the eye which conducts her to such winning beauty and sweetness of deportment, and makes her the "rich-souled creature" that Schlegel describes her to be. Therewithal she may be aptly quoted as a mark-worthy instance how the Poet makes the several parts and persons of a drama cohere not only with one another but with the general circumstances wherein they occur. For so in Portia's character the splendour of Italian skies and scenery and art is reproduced; their spirit lives in her imagination, and is complicated with all she does and says.

If Portia is the beauty of this play, Shylock is its strength. He is a standing marvel of power and scope in the dramatic art; at the same time appearing so much a man of Nature's making, that we can hardly think of him as a creation of art. In the delineation Shakespeare had no less a task than to fill with individual life and peculiarity the broad, strong outlines of national character in its most revolting form. Accordingly Shylock is a true representative of his nation; wherein we have a pride which for ages never ceased to provoke hostility, but which no hostility could ever subdue; a thrift which still invited rapacity, but which no rapacity could ever exhaust; and a weakness which, while it exposed the subjects to wrong, only deepened their hate, because it kept them without the means or the hope of redress. Thus Shylock is a type of national sufferings, national sympathies, national antipathies. Himself an object of bitter insult and scorn to those about him; surrounded by enemies whom he is at once too proud to conciliate and too weak to oppose; he can have no life among them but money; no hold on them but interest; no feeling towards them but hate; no indemnity out of them but revenge. Such being the case, what wonder that the elements of national greatness became congealed and petrified into malignity? As avarice was the passion in which he mainly lived, the Christian virtues that thwarted this naturally seemed to him the greatest of wrongs.

With these strong national traits are interwoven personal traits equally strong. Thoroughly and intensely Jewish, he is not more a Jew than he is Shylock. In his hard, icy intellectuality, and his dry, mummy-like tenacity of purpose, with a dash now and then of biting sarcastic humour, we see the remains of a great and noble nature, out of which all the genial sap of humanity has been pressed by accumulated injuries. With as much elasticity of mind as stiffness of neck, every step he takes but the last is as firm as the earth he treads upon. Nothing can daunt, nothing disconcert him; remonstrance cannot move, ridicule cannot touch, obloquy cannot exasperate him: when he has not provoked them, he has been forced to bear them; and now that he does provoke them, he is hardened against them. In a word, he may be broken; he cannot be bent.

Shylock is great in every scene where he appears, yet each later scene exhibits him in a new element or aspect of greatness. For as soon as the Poet has set forth one side or phase of his character, he forthwith dismisses that, and proceeds to another. For example, the Jew's cold and penetrating sagacity, as also his malignant and remorseless guile, are finely delivered in the scene with Antonio and Bassanio, where he is first solicited for the loan. And the strength and vehemence of passion, which underlies these qualities, is still better displayed, if possible, in the scene with Antonio's two friends, Solanio and Salarino, where he first avows his purpose of exacting the forfeiture. One passage of this scene has always seemed to me a peculiarly idiomatic strain of eloquence, steeped in a mixture of gall and pathos; and I the rather notice it, because of the wholesome lesson which Christians may gather from it. Of course the Jew is referring to Antonio:

"He hath disgraced me, and hindered me half a million; laughed at my losses, mocked at my gains, scorned my nation, thwarted my bargains, cooled my friends, heated mine enemies; and what's his reason? I am a Jew. Hath not a Jew eyes? hath not a Jew hands, organs, dimensions, senses, affections, passions? fed with the same food, hurt with the same weapons, subject to the same diseases, healed by the same means, warmed and cooled by the same Winter and Summer, as a Christian is? If you prick us, do we not bleed? if you tickle us, do we not laugh? if you poison us, do we not die? and if you wrong us, shall we not revenge? if we are like you in the rest, we will resemble you in that. If a Jew wrong a Christian, what is his humility? revenge: if a Christian wrong a Jew, what should his sufferance be by Christian example? why, revenge. The villainy you teach me, I will execute; and it shall go hard but I will better the instruction."

I have spoken of the mixture of national and individual traits in Shylock. It should be observed further, that these several elements of character are so attempered and fused together, that we cannot distinguish their respective influence. Even his avarice has a smack of patriotism. Money is the only defence of his brethren as well as of himself, and he craves it for their sake as well as his own; feels indeed that wrongs are offered to them in him, and to him in them. Antonio has scorned his religion, balked him of usurious gains, insulted his person: therefore he hates him as a Christian, himself a Jew; hates him as a lender of money gratis, himself a griping usurer; hates him as Antonio, himself Shylock. Moreover, who but a Christian, one of Antonio's faith and fellowship, has stolen away his daughter's heart, and drawn her into revolt, loaded with his ducats and his precious, precious jewels? Thus his religion, his patriotism, his avarice, his affection, all concur to stimulate his enmity; and his personal hate thus reinforced overcomes for once his greed, and he grows generous in the prosecution of his aim. The only reason he will vouchsafe for taking the pound of flesh is, "if it will feed nothing else, it will feed my revenge"; a reason all the more satisfactory to him, forasmuch as those to whom he gives it can neither allow it nor refute it: and until they can rail the seal from off his bond, all their railings are but a foretaste of the revenge he seeks. In his eagerness to taste that morsel sweeter to him than all the luxuries of Italy, his recent afflictions, the loss of his daughter, his ducats, his jewels, and even the precious ring given him by his departed wife, all fade from his mind. In his inexorable and imperturbable hardness at the trial there is something that makes the blood to tingle. It is the sublimity of malice. We feel that the yearnings of revenge have silenced all other cares and all other thoughts. In his rapture of hate the man has grown superhuman, and his eyes seem all aglow with preternatural malignity. Fearful, however, as is his passion, he comes not off without moving our pity. In the very act whereby he thinks to avenge his own and his brethren's wrongs, the national curse overtakes him. In standing up for the letter of the law against all the pleadings of mercy, he has strengthened his enemies' hands, and sharpened their weapons, against himself; and the terrible Jew sinks at last into the poor, pitiable, heart-broken Shylock.

The inward strain and wrenching of his nature, caused by the revulsion which comes so suddenly upon him, is all told in one brief sentence, which may well be quoted as an apt instance how Shakespeare reaches the heart by a few plain words, when another writer would most likely pummel the ears with a high-strung oration. When it turns out that the Jew's only chance of life stands in the very mercy which he has but a moment before abjured; and when, as the condition of that mercy, he is required to become a Christian, and also to sign a deed conveying to his daughter and her husband all his remaining wealth; we have the following from him:

> "I pray you, give me leave to go from hence;
> I am not well : send the deed after me,
> And I will sign it."

Early in the play, when Shylock is bid forth to Bassanio's supper, and Launcelot urges him to go, because "my young master doth expect your reproach," Shylock replies, "So do I his." Of course he expects that reproach through the bankruptcy of Antonio. This would seem to infer that Shylock has some hand in getting up the reports of Antonio's "losses at sea"; which reports, at least some of them, turn out false in the end. Further than this, the Poet leaves us in the dark as to how those reports grew into being and gained belief. Did he mean to have it understood that the Jew exercised his cunning and malice in plotting and preparing them? It appears, at all events, that Shylock knew they were coming, before they came. Yet I suppose the natural impression from the play is, that he lent the ducats and took the bond, on a mere chance of coming at his wish. But he would hardly grasp so eagerly at a bare possibility of revenge, without using means to turn it into something more. This would mark him with much deeper lines of guilt. Why, then, did not Shakespeare bring the matter forward more prominently? Perhaps it was because the doing so would have made Shylock appear too steep a criminal for the degree of interest which his part was meant to carry in the play. In other words, the health of the drama as a work of *comic* art required his criminality to be kept in the background. He comes very near overshadowing the other characters too much, as it is. And Shylock's character is *essentially tragic;* there is none of the proper timber of comedy in him.

The Merchant of Venice is justly distinguished among Shakespeare's dramas, not only for the general felicity of the language, but also for the beauty of particular scenes and passages. For descriptive power, the opening scene of Antonio and his friends is not easily rivalled, and can hardly fail to live in the memory of any one having an eye for such things. Equally fine in its way is the scene of Tubal and Shylock, where the latter is so torn with the struggle of conflicting passions; his heart now sinking with grief at the account of his fugitive daughter's expenses, now leaping with malignant joy at the report of Antonio's losses. The trial-scene, with its tugging vicissitudes of passion, and its hush of terrible expectation, — now ringing with the Jew's sharp, spiteful snaps of malice, now made musical with Portia's strains of eloquence, now holy with Antonio's tender breathings of friendship, and dashed, from time to time, with Gratiano's fierce jets of wrath, and fiercer jets of mirth, — is hardly surpassed in tragic power anywhere; and as it forms the catastrophe proper, so it concentrates the interest of the whole play. Scarcely inferior in its kind is the night-scene of Lorenzo and Jessica, bathed as it is in love, moonlight, "touches of sweet harmony," and soul-lifting discourse, followed by the grave moral reflections of Portia, as she approaches her home, and sees its lights, and hears its music. The bringing in of this passage of ravishing lyrical sweetness, so replete with the most soothing and tranquillizing effect, close upon the intense dramatic excitement of the trial-scene, is such a transition as we shall hardly meet with but in Shakespeare, and aptly shows his unequalled mastery of the mind's capacities of delight. The affair of the rings, with the harmless perplexities growing out of it, is a well-managed device for letting the mind down from the tragic height whereon it lately stood, to the merry conclusion which the play requires. Critics, indeed, may easily quarrel with this sportive after-piece; but it stands approved by the tribunal to which Criticism itself must bow, — the spontaneous feelings of such as are willing to be made cheerful and healthy, without beating their brains about the *how* and *wherefore.* It is in vain that critics tell us we ought to "laugh by precept only, and shed tears by rule."

I ought not to close without remarking what a wide diversity of materials this play reconciles and combines. One can hardly realize how many things are here brought together, they are ordered in such perfect concert and harmony. The greatness of the work is thus hidden in its fine proportions. In many of the Poet's dramas we are surprised at the great variety of character: here, besides this, we have a remarkable variety of plot. And, admirable as may be the skill displayed in the characters individually considered, the interweaving of so many several plots, without the least confusion or embarrassment, evinces a still higher mastership. For, many and various as are the forms and aspects of life here shown, they all emphatically live together, as if they all had but one vital circulation.

THE MERRY WIVES OF WINDSOR.

The Merry Wives of Windsor, as we have it, was first printed in the folio of 1623. The play, however, was registered at the Stationers', January 18, 1602, as "an excellent and pleasant-conceited comedy of Sir John Falstaff and the Merry Wives of Windsor." In pursuance of this entry, an imperfect and probably fraudulent edition was published in the course of the same year, and was reprinted in 1619. In this quarto edition, the play is but about half as long as in the authentic copy of 1623, and some of the prose parts are printed so as to look like verse. It is in doubt whether the issue of 1602 was a fair reproduction of the play as originally written, or whether it was printed from a defective and mutilated transcript stealthily taken down by unskilful reporters at the theatre. On the former supposal, of course the play must have been rewritten and greatly improved, — a thing known to have been repeatedly done by the Poet; so that it is nowise unlikely in this case. But, as the question hardly has interest enough to pay the time and labour of discussing it, I shall dismiss it without further remark.

It is to be presumed that every reader of Shakespeare is familiar with the tradition which makes this comedy to have been written at the instance of Queen Elizabeth; who, upon witnessing the performance of *King Henry the Fourth*, was so taken with Falstaff, that she requested the Poet to continue the character through another play, and to represent him in love. This tradition is first heard of in 1702, eighty-six years after the Poet's death; but it was accepted by the candid and careful Rowe; Pope, also, Theobald, and others, made no scruple of receiving it, — men who would not be very apt to let such a matter pass unsifted, or help to give it currency, unless they thought there was good ground for it. Besides, the thing is not at all incredible in itself, either from the alleged circumstances of the case, or from the character of the Queen; and there are some points in the play that speak not a little in its support. One item of the story is, that the author, hastening to comply with her Majesty's request, wrote the play in the brief space of fourteen days. This has been taken by some as quite discrediting the whole story; but, taking the play as it stands in the copy of 1602, it does not seem to me that fourteen days is too brief a time for Shakespeare to have done the work in, especially with such a motive to quicken him.

This matter has a direct bearing in reference to the date of the writing. *King Henry the Fourth*, the First Part certainly, and probably the Second Part also, was on the stage before 1598. And in the title-page to the first quarto copy of *The Merry Wives*, we have the words, "As it hath been divers times acted by the Right Honourable my Lord Chamberlain's Servants, both before her Majesty and elsewhere." This would naturally infer the play to have been on the stage a considerable time before the date of that issue. And all the *clear* internal evidences of the play itself draw in support of the belief, that the Falstaff of Windsor memory was a continuation from the Falstaff of Eastcheap celebrity. And the whole course of blundering and exposure which Sir John here goes through is such, that I can hardly conceive how the Poet should have framed it, but that he was prompted to do so by some motive external to his own mind. That the free impulse of his genius, without suggestion or inducement from any other source, could have led him to put Falstaff through such a series of uncharacteristic delusions and collapses, is to me wellnigh incredible. So that I can only account for the thing by supposing the man as here exhibited to have been an after-thought sprung in some way from the manner in which an earlier and fairer exhibition of the man had been received.

All which brings the original composition of the play to a point of time somewhere between 1598 and 1601. On the other hand, the play, as we have it, contains at least one passage, inferring, apparently, that the work of revisal must have been done some time after the accession of King James, which was in March, 1603. That passage is the odd reason Mrs. Page gives Mrs. Ford for declining to share the honour of knighthood with Sir John: "These knights will *hack;* and so thou shouldst not alter the article of thy gentry"; which can scarce bear any other sense than as referring to the prodigality with which the King dispensed those honours in the first year of his English reign; knighthood being thereby in a way to grow so *hackneyed*, that it would rather be an honour not to have been dubbed. As for the reasons urged by Knight and Halliwell for dating the first writing as far back as 1593, they seem to me quite too far-fetched and fanciful to be worthy of notice; certainly not worth the cost of sifting, nor even of statement.

Much question has been made as to the particular period of his life in which Sir John prosecuted his adventures at Windsor, whether before or after the incidents of *King Henry the Fourth*, or at some intermediate time. And some perplexity appears to have arisen from confounding the order in which the several plays were written with the order of the events described in them. Now, at the close of the History, Falstaff and his companions are banished the neighborhood of the Court, and put under strong bonds of good behaviour. So that the action of the Comedy cannot well be referred to any point of time after that proceeding. Moreover we have Page speaking of Fenton as having "kept company with the wild Prince and Pointz." Then too, after Falstaff's experiences in the buck-basket and while disguised as "the wise woman of Brentford," we have him speaking of the matter as follows: "If it should come to the ear of the Court, how I have been transformed, and how my transformation hath been washed and cudgelled, they would melt me out of my fat drop by drop, and liquor fishermen's boots with me: I warrant they would whip me with their fine wits till I were as crestfallen as a dried pear." From which it would seem that he still enjoys at Court the odour of his putative heroism in killing Hotspur at the battle of Shrewsbury, with which the First Part of the History closes. The Second Part of the History covers a period of nearly ten years, from July, 1403, to March, 1413; in which time Falstaff may be supposed to have found leisure for the exploits at Windsor.

So that the action of the Comedy might well enough have taken place in one of Sir John's intervals of rest from the toils of war during the time occupied by the Second Part of the History. And this placing of the action is further sustained by the presence of Pistol in the Comedy; who is not heard of at all in the First Part of the History, but spreads himself with characteristic splendour in the Second. Falstaff's boy, Robin, also, is the same, apparently, who figures as his Page in the Second Part of the History. As for the Mrs. Quickly of Windsor, we can hardly identify her in any way with the Hostess of Eastcheap. For, as Gervinus acutely remarks, "not only are her outward circumstances different, but her character also is essentially diverse; similar in natural simplicity indeed, but at the same time docile and skilful, as the credulous wife and widow of Eastcheap never appears." To go no further, the Windsor Quickly is described as a *maid;* which should suffice of itself to mark her off as distinct from the Quickly of Boar's-head Tavern.

In truth, however, I suspect the Poet was not very attentive to the point of making the events of the several plays fadge together. The task of representing Sir John in love was so very different from that of representing him in wit and war, that he might well fall into some discrepancies in the process. And if he had been asked whereabouts in the order of Falstaff's varied exploits he meant those at Windsor to be placed, most likely he would have been himself somewhat puzzled to answer the question.

For the plot and matter of the Comedy, Shakespeare was apparently little indebted to any thing but his own invention. *The Two Lovers of Pisa*, a tale borrowed from the novels of Straparola, and published in Tarlton's *News out of Purgatory*, 1590, is thought to have suggested some of the incidents; and the notion seems probable. In that tale a young gallant falls in love with a jealous old doctor's wife, who is also young, and really encourages the illicit passion. The gallant, not knowing the doctor, takes him for confidant and adviser in the prosecution of his suit, and is thus thwarted in all his plans. The naughty wife conceals her lover, first in a basket of feathers, then between some partitions of the house, and again in a box of deeds and valuable papers. If the Poet had any other obligations, they have not been traced clearly enough to be worth noting.

As a specimen of pure comedy, *The Merry Wives of Windsor* by general concession stands unrivalled. I say *pure* comedy, for it has no such interminglings of high poetry and serious passion as mark the Poet's best comedies, and give them a semi-tragic cast. This play is not only full of ludicrous situations and predicaments, but is also rich and varied in comic characterization. Even Falstaff apart, who is an inexhaustible storehouse of laughter-moving preparations, there is comic matter enough in the characters and doings of the other persons to make the play a perpetual diversion. Though historically connected with the reign of Henry the Fourth, the manners and humours of the scene are those of the Poet's own time; and in this respect we need but compare it with Ben Jonson's *Every Man in his Humour*, to see "how much easier it was to vanquish the rest of Europe than to contend with Shakespeare."

The action of the piece proceeds throughout by intrigue; that is, a complication of cross-purposes wherein the several persons strive to outwit and circumvent one another. And the stratagems all have the appropriate merit of causing a pleasant surprise, and a perplexity that is grateful, because it stops short of confusion; while the awkward and grotesque predicaments, into which the persons are thown by their mutual crossing and tripping, hold attention on the alert, and keep the spirits in a frolic. Yet the laughable proceedings of the scene are all easy and free; that is, the comic situations are ingenious without being at all forced; the ingenuity being hidden in the naturalness with which every thing comes to pass. The play well illustrates, too, though in its own peculiar sort, the general order and method of Shakespeare's art; the surrounding parts falling in with the central one, and the subordinate plots drawing, as by a secret impulse, into harmony with the leading plot. For instance, while Falstaff undergoes repeated collapses from a hero into a butt, that others may laugh at his expense; the Welsh Parson and the French Doctor are also baulked of their revenge, just as they are getting over the preliminary pains and vexations; and, while pluming themselves with anticipated honours, are suddenly deplumed into "vlouting-stogs": Page, too, and his wife no sooner begin to exult in their success than they are taken down by the thrift of a counter stratagem, and left to the double shame of ignobly failing in an ignoble undertaking: and Ford's jealousy, again, is made to scourge himself with the very whip he has twisted for the scourging of its object. Thus all the more prominent persons have to chew the ashes of disappointment in turn; their plans being thwarted, and themselves made ridiculous, just as they are on the point of grasping their several fruitions. Falstaff, indeed, is the only one of them that rises by falling, and extracts grace out of his disgraces. For in him the grotesque and ludicrous is evermore laughing and chuckling over itself: he makes comedies extempore out of his own shames and infirmities; and is himself the most delighted spectator of the scenes in which he figures as chief actor.

This observation and enjoyment of the comical as displayed in himself, which forms one of Sir John's leading traits, and explains much in him that were else inexplicable, is here seen however labouring under something of an eclipse. The truth is, he is plainly out of his sphere; and he shows a strange lapse from his wonted sagacity in getting where he is: the good sense so conspicuous in his behaviour on other occasions ought to have kept him from supposing for a moment that he could inspire the passion of love in such a place; nor, as before observed, does it seem likely that the Poet would have shown him thus, but that he were moved thereto by something outside of his own mind. For of love in any right or even decent sense Sir John is essentially incapable. And Shakespeare evidently so regarded him: he therefore had no alternative but either to commit a gross breach of decorum or else to make the hero unsuccessful, — an alternative in which the moral sanity of his genius left him no choice. So that in undertaking the part of a lover the man must needs be a mark of interest chiefly for what is practised upon him. For, if we may believe Hazlitt, "wits and philosophers seldom shine in that character"; and, whether this be true or not, it is certain that "Sir John by no means comes off with flying colours." In fact, he is here the dupe and victim of his own heroism, and provokes laughter much more by what he suffers than by what he does.

But Falstaff, notwithstanding all these drawbacks, is still so far himself, that "nought but himself can be his conqueror." If he be overmatched, it is not so much by the strength or skill of his antagonists as from his being persuaded, seemingly against his judgment and for the pleasure of others, into a line of adventure where he is not qualified to shine, and where genius, wit, and understanding are commonly distanced by a full purse and a handsome person. His incomparable art in turning adversities into commodities; the good-humoured strategy whereby he manages to divert off all unpleasant feeling of his vices and frailties;

the marvellous agility and aptness of wit which, with a vesture of odd and whimsical constructions, at once hides the offensive and discovers the comical features of his conduct; the same towering impudence and effrontery which so lift him aloft in his more congenial exploits; and the overpowering eloquence of exaggeration with which he delights to set off and heighten whatever is most ludicrous in his own person or situation; — all these qualities, though not in their full bloom and vigour, are here seen in triumphant exercise.

On the whole, this bringing-forth of Sir John rather for exposure than for exhibition is not altogether grateful to those whom he has so often made to "laugh and grow fat." Though he still gives us wholesome shakings, we feel that it costs him too much: the rare exhilaration he affords us elsewhere, and even here, invests him with a sort of humorous reverence; insomuch that we can scarce help pitying even while we approve his merited, yet hardly merited, shames and failures. Especially it touches us something hard that one so wit-proud as Sir John should be thus dejected, and put to the mortification of owning that "ignorance itself is a plummet o'er me"; of having to "stand at the taunt of one that makes fritters of English"; and of asking, "Have I laid my brain in the sun, and dried it, that it wants matter to prevent so gross o'er-reaching as this?" and we would fain make out some excuse for him on the score of these slips having occurred at a time in his life when experience had not yet disciplined away the natural vanity which may sometimes lead a man of genius to fancy himself an object of the tender passion. And we are the more disposed to judge leniently of Falstaff, inasmuch as his merry persecutors are but a sort of decorous, respectable, commonplace people, who borrow their chief importance from the victim of their mischievous sport; and if they are not so bad as to make us wish him success, neither are they so good that we like to see them thrive at his expense. On this point Mr. Verplanck, it seems to me, has spoken just about the right thing: "Our choler would rise, despite of us, against Cleopatra herself, should she presume to make a dupe and tool of regal old Jack, the natural lord and master of all about him; and, though not so atrociously immoral as to wish he had succeeded with the Windsor gypsies, we plead guilty to the minor turpitude of sympathy, when he tells his persecutors, with brightening visage and exultant twinkle of eye, 'I am glad, though you have ta'en a special stand to strike at me, that your arrow hath glanced.'"

There is, however, another and perhaps a more instructive view to be taken of Sir John as here represented. I shall have occasion hereafter to note how, all through the period of *King Henry the Fourth*, he keeps growing worse and worse, while the Prince is daily growing better. Out of their sport-seeking intercourse he picks whatever is bad, whereas the other gathers nothing but the good. As represented in the Comedy he seems to be in the swiftest part of this worsening process. At the close of the First Part of the History, the Prince freely yields up to him the honour of Hotspur's fall; thus carrying home to him such an example of self-renouncing generosity as it would seem impossible for the most hardened sinner to resist. And the Prince appears to have done this partly in the hope that it might prove a seed of truth and grace in Falstaff, and start him in a better course of life. But the effect upon him is quite the reverse. Honour is nothing to him but as it may help him in the matter of sensual and heart-steeling self-indulgence. And the surreptitious fame thus acquired, instead of working in him for good, merely serves to procure him larger means and larger license for pampering his gross animal selfishness. His thoughts dwell not at all on the Prince's act of magnanimity, which would shame his egotism and soften his heart, but only on his own ingenuity and success in the stratagem that led to that act. So that the effect is just to puff him up more than ever with vanity and conceit of wit, and thus to give a looser rein and a sharper stimulus to his greed and lust; for there is probably nothing that will send a man faster to the Devil than that sort of conceit. The result is, that Falstaff soon proceeds to throw off whatever of restraint may have hitherto held his vices in check, and to wanton in the arrogance of utter impunity. As he then unscrupulously appropriated the credit of another's heroism; so he now makes no scruple of sacrificing the virtue, the honour, the happiness of others to his own mean and selfish pleasure.

But this total subjection of the mental to the animal nature cannot long proceed without betraying the succours of reason. When the bands of morality are thus spurned, a man rapidly sins his understanding into lameness; as its better forces must needs be quickly rotted in such a vapour-bath of sensuality. In this way an overweening pride of wit often results in causing a man to be deserted by his wits; this too in matters where he feels surest of them and has most need of them. In refusing to see what is right, he loses the power of seeing what is prudent and safe. He who persists in such a course will inevitably be drawn into signal lapses of judgment, however richly nature may have endowed him with that faculty: he will stumble over his own self-love; his very assurance will be tripping him when he least expects it. And so Falstaff's conceit and egotism, working together, as they do, with his greed and lust, have the effect of stuffing him with the most childish gullibility, at once laying him open to the arts of bamboozling, and inviting others to practise them upon him. He has grown to look with contempt upon honesty as a cheap and vulgar thing, and is well punished in that honest simplicity easily outwits him: nay, more; his fancied skill in sensual intrigue brings him to a pass where ignorance itself is a clean overmatch for him, and fairly earns the privilege of flouting at him.

Falstaff is fair-spoken when he chooses to be, can talk with judgment and good sense, and has at command the arts of a gentlemanly and dignified bearing. The two

Windsor wives, meeting him at a social dinner, and seeing him in his best suit of language and manners, think him honourable as well as pleasant, and are won to some notes of respect and affability towards him: "he would not swear; praised women's modesty; and gave such orderly and well-behaved reproof of all uncomeliness," that they would have sworn his disposition was at one with the truth of his words. And because they meet his fair deportment with some gentle returns of politeness, therefore he, in his conceit of wit, of rank, and of fame, thinks they are smitten with a passion for him. Fancying that they are hotly in love with him, he resolves on making love to them; not that he is at all touched with the passion, but with the cool intent of feigning a responsive flame for other and more selfish ends. Their husbands are known to be rich, and they are said to have the free use of their husbands' wealth. So his conclusion is, that they are "a region in Guiana, all gold and bounty: they shall be my East and West Indies, and I will trade to them both." In his spendthrift self-indulgence, notwithstanding all the supplies which his purse-taking habits and his late imputed service bring in, he has come to be hard-up for cash, insomuch that his rascal followers are for deserting him and turning to other resources. By driving a love-intrigue with the women, he expects to work the keys to the full coffers which they have at such command, and thus to replenish his low-ebbing means.

Thus we here have Sir John in the process of complacently feeding his glutton fancies with matter raked from the foulest gutters of baseness. The women, burning with anger and shame, knock their wits together for revenge; and the answer which they, in their shrewdly-concerted plan, return to his advances is to him a pledge of entire success: he is so transported, that he leaps clean out of his senses forthwith, and the giddiness of his newly-fired conceit fairly puts out the eyes of his understanding. His vanity is now quite omnivorous: once possessed with the monstrous idea of having become an object of love in such a place, nothing is too gross for him to swallow. The raw and unspiced stuffings of Master Brook convey to him no hint of mistrust: he drinks them in with unfaltering confidence; and opens his breast to this total stranger as freely as if he were his sworn and long-tried counsellor; the offered bribe of the man's money so falling in with the other baits of greed as to swamp his discretion utterly. After being cheated through the adventures of the buck-basket, where he was "stopped in with stinking clothes that fretted in their own grease," he appears indeed to have some smell of the gross trickery played upon him; and vows to himself that, if he be served such another trick, he will have his brains taken out, and buttered, and given to a dog for a new-year's gift. But still his vanity and thirst of money are too much for his startled prudence: upon the offer of a second device, that too of a very flimsy texture, and very thinly disguised, his paralysis of wit returns, and his suspicions sink afresh into their dreamless nap. In the hard blows and buffets there experienced, he has stronger arguments than before of the game practised on him; still the deep spell on his judgment continues unbroken: and now the very shame and grief of his past failures and punishments seem to co-operate with his palsy of reason in preparing him for a third hoax even more gross and palpable than the former two.

When at length the untrussed hero is made to see how matters have been carried with him, and to feel the chagrin of being so egregiously fooled, he is indeed cast down to the lowest notes of self-contempt; and though he so far rallies at last as to cover his retreat with marked skill, yet he leaves the path behind him strewn thick with the sweat-drops of his mortification. In his pride of wit and cleverness, he had looked with scorn upon plain common people as no better than blockheads; and had only thought to use them, and even his own powers of mind, for compassing the means of animal gratification. But he now stands thoroughly degraded in his own sight, and this too in the very points where he had built his conceit of superiority. He finds that all his wit and craft were not enough to prevent even Sir Hugh, the simple-minded Welsh parson, from making him a laughing-stock. We too, whose moral judgment may have been seduced from the right by the fascinations of his intellectual playing, are brought to estimate more justly the natural honours and safeguards of downright integrity and innocence; and to see that the deepest shrewdness stands in not thinking to be shrewd at all. Thus our judgment of the man is set right in the very point where it was most liable to be drawn astray. Gervinus regards this idea as being the soul of the piece. He thinks the Poet's leading purpose here was to teach that plain-thoughted, guileless honesty is a natural overmatch for studied cunning; and to show how self-seeking craft and intricacy are apt to be caught in the snares they have laid for others, while unselfish truth and simplicity are protected against them by those instinctive moral warnings of nature which crafty men despise. And he rightly observes that the play illustrates the point in repeated instances. Thus the policy and sharp practice of the Host to catch gain, of Ford to detect and expose the imagined sins of his wife, and of Mr. and Mrs. Page to mismatch their daughter, only bring to confusion the parties themselves; their crafty devices, like Falstaff's, being outwitted and cheated by the "*honest* knaveries" of their intended victims. Thus the several cases concur to enforce the moral, that "an egotist like Falstaff can suffer no severer defeat than from the honesty which he believes not, and from the simplicity which he esteems not."

I refrain from attempting a full analysis of Sir John's character, till I encounter him at the noontide of his glory, stealing, drinking, lying, recruiting, warring, and discoursing of wine, wit, valour, and honour, with Prince Hal at hand to wrestle forth the prodigies of his big-teeming brain.

Sir John's followers are here under a cloud along with him, being little more than the shadows of what they appear when their master is fully himself and in his proper element. Bardolph and Pistol are indeed the same men, or rather things, as in the History; but the redundant fatness of their several peculiarities is here not a little curtailed: the fire in Bardolph's nose waxes dim for lack of fuel; the strut is much dried out of Pistol's tongue from want of drink to generate loftiness: the low state of their master's purse, and the discords thence growing between him and them, have rather soured their tempers, and that sourness rusts and clogs the wheels of their inner man. Corporal Nym is not visibly met with in *King Henry the Fourth*, though the atmosphere smells at times as if he had been there; but we have him again in *King Henry the Fifth*, where he carries to a somewhat higher pitch the character of "a fellow that frights humour out of its wits."

I have before observed that the Mrs. Quickly of this play is plainly another individual than the Hostess of Eastcheap: the latter has known Sir John "these twenty-nine years, come peascod time," whereas to the former his person is quite unknown till she goes to him with a message from the Windsor wives. But she seems no very remote kin of the Hostess aforesaid: though clearly discriminated in character, yet they have a strong family likeness. Her chief action is in the capacity of a matchmaker and go-between; and her perfect impartiality towards all of Anne Page's suitors, both in the service she renders and the return she accepts, well exemplifies the indefatigable benevolence of that class of worthies towards themselves, and is so true to the life of a certain perpetual sort of people as almost to make one believe in the transmigration of souls.

"Mine Host of the Garter" is indeed a model of a host; up to any thing, and brimful of fun, so that it runs out at the ends of his fingers; and nothing delights him more than to uncork the wit-holders of his guests, unless, peradventure, it be to uncork his wine-holders for them. His exhilarating conceit of practical shrewdness, serving as oil to make the wheels of his mind run smooth and glib, is choicely characteristic both of himself individually and of the class he represents. — Sir Hugh Evans is an odd marriage of the ludicrous and the honourable. In his officious simplicity he moralizes the play much better, no doubt, than a wiser man would. The scene where, in expectation of the fight with Doctor Caius, he is full of "cholers," and "trempling of mind," and "melancholies," and has "a great dispositions to cry," and strikes up a lullaby to the palpitations of his heart without seeming to know it, while those palpitations in turn scatter his memory, and discompose his singing, is replete with a quiet delicacy of humour hardly to be surpassed. It is thought by some that both he and Caius may be delineations, slightly caricatured, of what the Poet had seen and conversed with; there being a certain portrait-like reality and effect about them, with just enough of the ideal to lift them into the region of art.

Hazlitt boldly pronounces Shakespeare "the only writer who was as great in describing weakness as strength." However this may be, I am pretty sure that, after Falstaff, there is not a greater piece of work in the play than Master Abraham Slender, cousin to Robert Shallow, Esquire, — a dainty sprout, or rather sapling, of provincial gentry, who, once seen, is never to be forgotten. In his consequential verdancy, his aristocratic boobyism, and his lack-brain originality, this pithless hereditary squireling is quite inimitable and irresistible; — a tall though slender specimen of most effective imbecility, whose manners and character must needs all be from within, because he lacks force of nature to shape or dress himself by any model. Mr. Hallam, whose judgment in such things is not often at fault, thinks Slender was intended as "a satire on the brilliant youth of the provinces," such as they were "before the introduction of newspapers and turnpike roads; awkward and boobyish among civil people, but at home in rude sports, and proud of exploits at which the town would laugh, yet perhaps with more courage and good-nature than the laughers."

Ford's jealousy is managed with great skill so as to help on the plot, bringing on a series of the richest incidents, and drawing the most savoury issues from the mellow, juicy old sinner upon whom he is practising. The means whereby he labours to justify his passion, spreading temptations and then concerting surprises, are quite as wicked as any thing Falstaff does, and have, besides, the further crime of exceeding meanness; but both their meanness and their wickedness are of the kind that rarely fail to be their own punishment. The way in which his passion is made to sting and lash him into reason, and the happy mischievousness of his wife in glutting his disease, and thereby making an opportunity to show him what sort of stuff it lives on, are admirable instances of the wisdom with which the Poet underpins his most fantastic creations.

The counter-plottings, also, of Page and his wife, to sell their daughter against her better sense, are about as far from virtue as the worst purposes of Sir John; though, to be sure, their sins are of a more respectable kind than to expose them to ridicule. But we are the more willing to forget their unhandsome practices therein, because of their good-natured efforts at last to make Falstaff forget his sad miscarriages, and to compose, in a well-crowned cup of social merriment, whatever vexations and disquietudes still remain. — Anne Page is but an average specimen of discreet, placid, innocent mediocrity, yet with a mind of her own, in whom we can feel no such interest as a rich father causes to be felt by those about her. In her and Fenton a slight dash of romance is given to the play; their love forming a barely audible undertone of poetry in the chorus of comicalities, as if on purpose that while the sides are shaken the heart may not be left altogether untouched.

MUCH ADO ABOUT NOTHING.

Much Ado about Nothing, together with *As You Like It*, *King Henry the Fifth*, and Ben Jonson's *Every Man in his Humour*, was registered in the Stationers' books August 4, 1600; all with a caveat "to be stayed." Why the plays were thus locked up from the press by an injunction, does not appear; perhaps to keep the right of publishing them in the hands of those who made the entry. *Much Ado about Nothing* was entered again on the 23d of the same month, and was issued in quarto in the course of that year, with "as it hath been sundry times publicly acted" in the title-page; which would naturally infer the play to have been written in 1599, or in the early part of 1600. All the internal marks of style and temper bear in favour of the same date; as in these respects it is hardly distinguishable from *As You Like It*. It has also been ascertained from Vertue's manuscripts, that in May, 1613, John Heminge the actor, and the Poet's friend, received £40, besides a gratuity of £20 from the King, for presenting six plays at Hampton Court, *Much Ado about Nothing* being one of them.

After the one quarto of 1600, the play is not met with again till it reappeared in the folio of 1623. Some question has been made whether the folio was a reprint of the quarto, or from another manuscript. Considerable might be urged on either side; but the arguments would hardly pay the stating; the differences of the two copies being so few and slight as to make the question a thing of little consequence. The best editors generally agree in thinking the quarto the better authority of the two. Remains but to add that, with the two original copies, the text of the play is so clear and well-settled as almost to foreclose controversy.

As with many of the author's plays, a part of the plot and story of *Much Ado about Nothing* was borrowed. But the same matter had been so often borrowed before, and run into so many variations, that we cannot affirm with certainty to what source Shakespeare was immediately indebted. Mrs. Lenox, an uncommonly deep person, instructs us that the Poet here "borrowed just enough to show his poverty of invention, and added enough to prove his want of judgment"; a piece of criticism so choice and happy, that it ought by all means to be kept alive; though it is indeed just possible that the Poet can better afford to have such things said of him than the sayer can to have them repeated.

So much of the story as relates to Hero, Claudio, and John, bears a strong resemblance to the tale of Ariodante and Ginevra in Ariosto's *Orlando Furioso.* The Princess Ginevra, the heroine of the tale, rejects the love-suit of Duke Polinesso, and pledges her hand to Ariodante. Thereupon Polinesso engages her attendant Dalinda to personate the Princess on a balcony by moonlight, while he ascends to her chamber by a ladder of ropes; Ariodante being by previous arrangement stationed near the spot, so as to witness the supposed infidelity of his betrothed. This brings on a false charge against Ginevra, who is doomed to die unless within a month a true knight comes to do battle for her honour. Ariodante betakes himself to flight, and is reported to have perished. Polinesso now appears secure in his treachery. But Dalinda, seized with remorse for her part in the affair, and flying from her guilty paramour, meets with Rinaldo, and declares to him the truth. Then comes on the fight, in which Polinesso is slain by the champion of innocence; which done, the lover reappears, to be made happy with his Princess.

Here, of course, the wicked Duke answers to the John

of the play. But there is this important difference, that the motive of the former in vilifying the lady is to drive away her lover, that he may have her to himself; whereas the latter acts from a spontaneous malignity of temper, that takes a sort of disinterested pleasure in blasting the happiness of others.

A translation, by Peter Beverly, of that part of Ariosto's poem which contains this tale, was licensed for the press in 1565; and Warton says it was reprinted in 1600. And an English version of the whole poem, by Sir John Harrington, came out in 1591; but the play discovers no special marks of borrowing from this source. And indeed the fixing of any obligations in this quarter is the more difficult, inasmuch as the matter seems to have been borrowed by Ariosto himself. For the story of a lady betrayed to peril and disgrace by the personation of her waiting-woman was an old European tradition; it has been traced to Spain; and Ariosto interwove it with the adventures of Rinaldo, as yielding an apt occasion for his chivalrous heroism. Neither does the play show any traces of obligation to Spenser, who wrought the same tale into the variegated structure of his great poem. The story of Phedon, relating the treachery of his false friend Philemon, is in Book ii. canto 4 of *The Faerie Queene;* which Book was first published in 1590.

The connection between the play and one of Bandello's novels is much more evident, from the close similarity both of incidents and of names. Fenicia, the daughter of Lionato, a gentleman of Messina, is betrothed to Timbreo de Cardona, a friend of Piero d'Aragona. Girondo, a disappointed lover of the lady, goes to work to prevent the marriage. He insinuates to Timbreo that she is disloyal, and then to make good the charge arranges to have his own hired servant in the dress of a gentleman ascend a ladder and enter the house of Lionato at night, Timbreo being placed so as to witness the proceeding. The next morning Timbreo accuses the lady to her father, and rejects the alliance. Fenicia sinks down in a swoon; a dangerous illness follows; and, to prevent the shame of her alleged trespass, Lionato has it given out that she is dead, and a public funeral is held in confirmation of that report. Thereupon Girondo becomes so harrowed with remorse, that he confesses his villainy to Timbreo, and they both throw themselves on the mercy of the lady's family. Timbreo is easily forgiven, and the reconciliation is soon followed by the discovery that the lady is still alive, and by the marriage of the parties. Here the only particular wherein the play differs from the novel, and agrees with Ariosto's plan of the story, is, that the lady's waiting-woman personates her mistress when the villain scales her chamber-window.

It does not well appear how the Poet could have come to a knowledge of Bandello's novel, unless through the original; no translation of that time having been preserved. But the Italian was then the most generally-studied language in Europe; educated Englishmen were probably quite as apt to be familiar with it as they are with the French in our day; Shakespeare, at the time of writing this play, was thirty-five years old; and we have many indications that he knew enough of Italian to be able to read such a story as Bandello's in that language.

The foregoing account may serve to show, what is equally plain in many other cases, that Shakespeare preferred, for the material of his plots, such stories as were most commonly known, that he might have some tie of popular association and interest to work in aid of his purpose. It is to be observed, further, that the parts of Benedick and Beatrice, of Dogberry and Verges, and of several other persons, are altogether original with him; so that he stands responsible for all the wit and humour, and for nearly all the character, of the play. Then too, as is usual with him, the added portions are so made to knit in with the borrowed matter by mutual participation and interaction as to give a new life and meaning to the whole.

So that in this case, as in others, we have the soul of

originality consisting in something far deeper and more essential than any mere sorting or linking of incidents so as to form an attractive story. The vital workings of nature in the development of individual character, — it is on these, and not on any thing so superficial or mechanical as a mere frame-work of incident, that the real life of the piece depends. On this point I probably cannot do better than by quoting the following remarks from Coleridge:

"The interest in the plot is on account of the characters, not *vice versa*, as in almost all other writers: the plot is a mere canvas, and no more. Take away from *Much Ado about Nothing* all that is not indispensable to the plot, either as having little to do with it, or, like Dogberry and his comrades, forced into the service, when any other less ingeniously-absurd watchmen and night-constables would have answered the mere necessities of the action; take away Benedick, Beatrice, Dogberry, and the reaction of the former on the character of Hero, — and what will remain? In other writers the main agent of the plot is always the prominent character: John is the main-spring of the plot in this play; but he is merely shown, and then withdrawn."

The style and diction of this play has little that calls for special remark. In this respect the workmanship, as before noted, is of about the same cast and grain with that of *As You Like It;* sustained and equal; easy, natural, and modest in dress and bearing; everywhere alive indeed with the exhilarations of wit or humour or poetry, but without the laboured smoothness of the Poet's earlier plays, or the penetrating energy and quick, sinewy movement of his later ones. Compared with some of its predecessors, the play shows a decided growth in what may be termed virility of mind: a wider scope, a higher reach, a firmer grasp, have been attained: the Poet has come to read Nature less through "the spectacles of books," and does not hesitate to meet her face to face, and to trust and try himself alone with her. The result of all which appears in a greater freshness and reality of delineation. Here the persons have nothing of a dim, equivocal hearsay air about them, such as marks in some measure his earlier efforts in comedy. The characters indeed are not pitched in so high a key, nor conceived in so much breadth and vigour, as in several of the plays written at earlier dates: the plan of the work did not require this, or even admit of it; nevertheless the workmanship on the whole discovers more ripeness of art and faculty than even in *The Merchant of Venice.*

One of the Poet's methods was, apparently, first to mark out or else to adopt a given course of action, and then to conceive and work out his characters accordingly, making them such as would naturally cohere with and sustain the action, so that we feel an inward, vital, and essential relation between what they are and what they do. Thus there is nothing arbitrary or mechanical in the sorting together of persons and actions: the two stand together under a living law of human transpiration, instead of being gathered into a mere formal and outward juxtaposition. That is, in short, the persons act so because they *are* so, and not because the author *willed* to put them through such a course of action: what comes from them is truly rooted in them, and is *generated* vitally out of the nature within them; so that their deeds are the veritable pulsations of their hearts. And so it is in this play. The course of action, as we have seen, was partly borrowed. But there was no borrowing in the characteristic matter. The personal figures in the old tale are in themselves unmeaning and characterless. The actions ascribed to them have no ground or reason in any thing that they are: what they do, or rather *seem* to do, — for there is no real doing in the case, — proceeds not at all from their own natures or wills, but purely because the author chose to have it so. So that the persons and incidents are to all intents and purposes put together arbitrarily, and not under any vital law of human nature. Any other set of actions might just as well be tacked on to the same persons; any other persons might just as well be put through the same course of action. This merely outward and formal connection between the incidents and characters holds generally in the old tales from which Shakespeare borrowed his plots; while in his workmanship the connection becomes inherent and essential; there being indeed no difference in this respect, whether he first conceives the characters, and then draws out their actions, or whether he first plans a course of action, and then shapes the characte from which it is to proceed.

Much Ado about Nothing has a large variety of interest, now running into grotesque drollery, now bordering upon the sphere of tragic elevation, now revelling in the most sparkling brilliancy. The play indeed is rightly named: we have several nothings, each in its turn occasioning a deal of stir and perturbation: yet there is so much of real flavour and spirit stirred out into effect, that the littleness of the occasions is scarcely felt or observed; the thoughts being far more drawn to the persons who make the much ado than to the nothing about which the much ado is made. The excellences, however, both of plot and character, are rather of the striking sort, involving little of the hidden or retiring beauty which shows just enough on the surface to invite a diligent search, and then enriches the seeker with generous returns. Accordingly the play has always been very effective on the stage; the points and situations being so shaped and ordered that, with fair acting, they tell at once upon an average audience; while at the same time there is enough of solid substance beneath to justify and support the first impression; so that the stage-effect is withal legitimate and sound as well as quick and taking.

The characters of Hero and Claudio, though reasonably engaging in their simplicity and uprightness, offer no very salient points, and are indeed nowise extraordinary. It cannot quite be said that one "sees no more in them than in the ordinary of Nature's sale-work"; nevertheless they derive their interest mainly from the events that befall them; the reverse of which is generally true in Shakespeare's delineations. Perhaps we may justly say that, had the course of love run smooth with them, its voice, even if audible, had been hardly worth the hearing.

Hero is indeed kind, amiable, and discreet in her behaviour and temper: she has just that air, nay, rather just that soul of bland and modest quietness which makes the unobtrusive but enduring charm of home, such as I have seen in many a priestess of the domestic shrine; and this fitly marks her out as the centre of silent or unemphatic interest in her father's household. She is always thoughtful, never voluble; and when she speaks, there is no sting or sharpness in her tongue: she is even proud of her brilliant cousin, yet not at all emulous of her brilliancy; keenly relishes her popping and sometimes caustic wit, but covets no such gift for herself, and even shrinks from the laughing attention it wins. As Hero is altogether gentle and womanly in her ways, so she offers a sweet and inviting nestling-place for the fireside affections. The soft down of her disposition makes an admirable contrast to the bristling and emphatic yet genuine plumage of Beatrice; and there is something very pathetic and touching in her situation when she is stricken down in mute agony by the tongue of slander; while the "blushing apparitions" in her face, and the lightning in her eyes, tell us that her stillness of tongue proceeds from any thing but weakness of nature, or want of spirit. Her well-governed intelligence is aptly displayed in the part she bears in the stratagem for taming Beatrice to the gentler pace of love, and in the considerate forbearance which abstains from teasing words after the stratagem has done its work.

Claudio is both a lighter-timbered and a looser-built vessel than Hero; rather credulous, unstable, inconstant, and very much the sport of slight and trivial occasions. A very small matter suffices to upset him, though, to be sure, he is apt enough to be set right again. All this, no doubt, is partly owing to his youth and inexperience; but in truth his character is mainly that of a brave and clever upstart, somewhat intoxicated with sudden success, and not a little puffed with vanity of the Prince's favour. Notwithstanding John's ingrained, habitual, and well-known malice, he is ready to go it blind whenever John sees fit to try his art upon him; and even after he has been duped into one strain of petulant folly by his trick, and has found out the falsehood of it, he is still just as open to a second and worse duping. All this may indeed pass as indicating no more in his case than the levity of a rather pampered and over-sensitive self-love. In his unreflective and headlong techiness, he fires up at the least hint that but seems to touch his honour, without pausing, or deigning to observe the plainest conditions of a fair and prudent judgment.

But, after all the allowance that can be made on this score, it is still no little impeachment of his temper, or his understanding, that he should lend his ear to the poisonous breathings of one whose spirits are so well known to "toil in frame of villainies." As to his rash and overwrought scheme of revenge for Hero's imputed sin, his best excuse therein is, that the light-minded Prince, who is indeed such another, goes along with him; while it is somewhat doubtful whether the patron or the favourite is more at fault in thus suffering artful malice to "pull the wool over his eyes." Claudio's finical and foppish attention to dress, so amusingly ridiculed by Benedick, is a well-conceived trait of his character; as it naturally hints that his quest of the lady grows more from his seeing the advantage of the match than from any deep heart-interest in her person. And his being sprung into such an unreasonable fit of jealousy towards the Prince at the masquerade is another good instance of the Poet's skill and care in small matters. It makes an apt preparation for the far more serious blunder upon which the main part of the action turns. A piece of conduct which the circumstances do not explain is at once explained by thus disclosing a certain irritable levity in the subject. On much the same ground we can also account very well for his sudden running into a match which at the best looks more like a freak of fancy than a resolution of love, while the same suddenness on the side of the more calm, discreet, and patient Hero is accounted for by the strong solicitation of the Prince and the prompt concurrence of her father. But even if Claudio's faults and blunders were greater than they are, still his behaviour at the last were enough to prove a real and sound basis of manhood in him. The clean taking-down of his vanity and self-love, by the exposure of the poor cheats which had so easily caught him, brings out the true staple of his character. When he is made to feel that on himself alone falls the blame and the guilt which he had been so eager to revenge on others, then his sense of honour acts in a right noble style, prompting him to avenge sternly on himself the wrong and the injury he has done to the gentle Hero and her kindred.

Critics have unnecessarily found fault with the Poet for the character of John, as if it lay without the proper circumference of truth and nature. They would prefer, apparently, the more commonplace character of a disappointed rival in love, whose guilt might be explained away into a pressure of violent motives. But Shakespeare saw deeper into human nature. And perhaps his wisest departure from the old story is in making John a morose, sullen, ill-conditioned rascal, whose innate malice renders the joy of others a pain, and the pain of others a joy, to him. The wanton and unprovoked doing of mischief is the natural luxury and pastime of such envious spirits as he is. To be sure, he assigns as his reason for plotting to blast Claudio's happiness, that the "young start-up hath all the glory of my overthrow"; but then he also adds, "If I can cross him any way, I bless myself every way"; which shows his true motive-spring to be a kind of envy-sickness. For this cause, any thing that will serve as a platform "to build mischief on" is grateful to him. He thus exemplifies in a small figure the same spontaneous malice which towers to such a stupendous height of wickedness in Iago. We may well reluct to believe in the reality of such characters; but, unhappily, human life discovers too many plots and doings that cannot be otherwise accounted for; nor need we go far to learn that men may "spin motives out of their own bowels." In pursuance of this idea, the Poet takes care to let us know that, in John's account, the having his sour and spiteful temper tied up under a pledge of fair and kindly behaviour is to be "trusted with a muzzle, and enfranchised with a clog"; that is, he thinks himself robbed of freedom when he is not allowed to bite.

Ulrici, regarding the play as setting forth the contrast between life as it is in itself and as it seems to those engaged in its struggles, looks upon Dogberry as embodying the whole idea of the piece. And, sure enough, the impressive insignificance of this man's action to the lookers-on is only equalled by its stuffed importance to himself: when he is really most absurd and ridiculous, then it is precisely that he feels most confident and grand; the irony that is rarefied into wit and poetry in others being thus condensed into broad humour and drollery in him. The German critic is not quite right however in thinking that his blundering garrulity brings to light the infernal plot; as it rather operates to keep that plot in the dark: he is too fond of hearing himself talk to make known what he has to say, in time to prevent the evil; and amidst his tumblings of conceit the truth leaks out at last rather in spite of him than in consequence ot any thing he does. Dogberry and his "neighbour Verges" are caricatures; but such caricatures as Shakespeare alone of English writers has had a heart to conceive and a hand to delineate; though perhaps Sir Walter comes near enough to him in that line to be named in the same sentence. And how bland, how benignant, how genial, how human-hearted, these caricatures are! as if the Poet felt the persons, with all their grotesque oddities, to be his own veritable flesh-and-blood kindred. There is no contempt, no mockery here; nothing that ministers an atom of food to any unbenevolent emotion: the subjects are made delicious as well as laughable; and delicious withal through the best and kindliest feelings of our nature. The Poet's sporting with them is the free, loving, whole-hearted play of a truly great, generous, simple, child-like soul. Compared to these genuine offspring of undeflowered genius, the ill-natured and cynical caricatures in which Dickens, for example, so often and so tediously indulges, seem the workmanship of quite another species of being. The part of Dogberry was often attempted to be imitated by other dramatists of Shakespeare's time; which shows it to have been a decided hit on the stage. And indeed there is no resisting the delectable humour of it: but then the thing is utterly inimitable; Shakespeare being no less unapproachable in this vein than in such delineations as Shylock and Lear and Cleopatra.

Benedick and Beatrice are much the most telling feature of the play. They have been justly ranked among the stronger and deeper of Shakespeare's minor characters. They are just about the right staple for the higher order of comic delineation; whereas several of the leading persons in what are called the Poet's comedies draw decidedly into the region of the Tragic. The delineation, however, of Benedick and Beatrice stays at all points within the proper sphere of Comedy. Both are gifted with a very piercing, pungent, and voluble wit; and pride of wit is with both a specially-prominent trait; in fact, it appears to be on all ordinary occasions their main actuating principle. The rare entertainment which others have from their displays in this kind has naturally made them quite conscious of their gift; and this consciousness has not less naturally led them to make it a matter of some pride. They study it and rely on it a good deal as their title or passport to approval and favour. Hence a *habit* of flouting and raillery has somewhat usurped the outside of their characters, insomuch as to keep their better qualities rather in the background, and even to obstruct seriously the outcome of what is best in them.

Whether for force of understanding or for solid worth of character, Benedick is vastly superior both to Claudio and to the Prince. He is really a very wise and noble fellow; of a healthy and penetrating intelligence, and with a sound underpinning of earnest and true feeling; as appears when the course of the action surprises or inspires him out of his pride of brilliancy. When a grave occasion comes, his superficial habit of jesting is at once postponed, and the choicer parts of manhood promptly assert themselves in clear and handsome action. We are thus given to know that, however the witty and waggish companion or makesport may have got the ascendency in him, still he is of an inward composition to forget it as soon as the cause of wronged and suffering virtue or innocence gives him a manly and generous part to perform. And when the blameless and gentle Hero is smitten down with cruel falsehood, and even her father is convinced of her guilt, he is the first to suspect that "the practice of it lies in John the bastard." With his just faith in the honour of the Prince and of Claudio, his quick judgment and native sagacity forthwith hit upon the right clew to the mystery. Much the same, all through, is to be said of Beatrice; who approves herself a thoroughly brave and generous character. The swiftness and brilliancy of wit upon which she so much prides herself are at once forgotten in resentment and vindication of her injured kinswoman. She becomes somewhat furious indeed, but it is a noble and righteous fury,—the fury of kindled strength too, and not of mere irritability, or of a passionate temper.

As pride of wit bears a main part in shaping the ordinary conduct of these persons; so the Poet aptly represents them as being specially piqued at what pinches or touches them in that point. Thus, in their wit-skirmish at the masquerade, what sticks most in Benedick is the being described as "the Prince's jester," and the hearing it said that, if his jests are "not marked, or not laughed at," it "strikes him into melancholy"; while, on the other side, Beatrice is equally stung at being told that "she had her good wit out of *The Hundred Merry Tales*." Their keen sensitiveness to whatever implies any depreciation or contempt of their faculty in this kind is exceedingly well conceived. Withal it shows, I think, that jesting, after all, is more a matter of art with them than of character.

As might be expected, the good repute of Benedick and Beatrice has been not a little perilled, not to say damaged, by their redundancy of wit. But it is the ordinary lot of persons so witty as they to suffer under the misconstructions of prejudice or partial acquaintance. Their very sparkling seems to augment the difficulty of coming to a true knowledge of them. How dangerous it is to be so gifted that way, may be seen by the impression these persons have had the ill luck to make on one whose good opinion is so desirable as Campbell's. "During one half of the play," says he, "we have a disagreeable female character in Beatrice. Her portrait, I may be told, is deeply drawn and minutely finished. It is; and so is that of Benedick, who is entirely her counterpart, except that he is less disagreeable." And again he speaks of Beatrice as an "odious woman." I am right sorry that so tasteful and genial a critic should have such hard thoughts of the lady. In support of his opinion he quotes Hero's speech, "Disdain and scorn ride sparkling in her eyes," &c.; but he seems to forget that these words are spoken with the intent that Beatrice shall hear them, and at the same time think she overhears them; that is, not as being true, but as being suited to a certain end, and as having just enough of truth to be effective for that end. And the effect which the speech has on Beatrice proves that it is not true as regards her character, however good it may be for the speaker's purpose. To the same end, the Prince, Claudio, and Leonato speak as much the other way, when they know Benedick is overhearing them; and what is there said in her favour is just a fair offset to what was before said against her. But indeed it is plain enough that any thing thus spoken really for the ear of the subject, yet seemingly in confidence to another person, ought not to be received in evidence against her.

But the critic's disparaging thoughts in this case are well accounted for in what himself had unhappily witnessed. "I once knew such a pair," says he; "the lady was a perfect Beatrice: she railed hypocritically at wedlock before her marriage, and with bitter sincerity after it. She and her Benedick now live apart, but with entire reciprocity of sentiments; each devoutly wishing that the other may soon pass into a better world." So that the writer's strong dislike of Beatrice is a most pregnant testimony to the Poet's truth of delineation; inasmuch as it shows how our views of his characters, as of those in real life, depend less perhaps on what they are in themselves than on our own peculiar associations. Nature's and Shakespeare's men and women seem very differently to different persons, and even to the same persons at different times. Regarded, therefore, in this light, the censure of the lady infers such a tribute to the Poet, that I half suspect the author meant it as such. In reference to the subject, however, my judgment goes much rather with that of other critics: That in the unamiable passages of their deportment Benedick and Beatrice are playing a part; that their playing is rather to conceal than to disclose their real feelings; that it is the very strength of their feelings which puts them upon this mode of disguise; and that the pointing of their raillery so much against each other is itself proof of a deep and growing mutual interest: though it must be confessed that the ability to play so well, and in that kind, is a great temptation to carry it to excess, or to use it where it may cause something else than mirth. This it is that justifies the repetition of the stratagem for drawing on a match between them; the same process being needed in both cases in order "to get rid of their reciprocal disguises, and make them straightforward and in earnest." And so the effect of the stratagem is to begin the unmasking which is so thoroughly completed by the wrongs and sufferings of Hero: they are thus disciplined out of their playing, and made to show themselves as they are: before we saw their art; now we see their virtue, — the real backbone of their characters; and it becomes manifest enough that, with all their superficial levity and caustic sportiveness, they yet have hearts rightly framed for the serious duties and interests of life.

It is very considerable, also, how their peculiar cast of self-love and their pride of wit are adroitly worked upon in the execution of the scheme for bringing them together. Both are deeply mortified at overhearing how they are blamed for their addiction to flouting, and at the same time both are highly flattered in being made each to believe that the other is secretly dying of love, and that the other is kept from showing the truth by dread of mocks and gibes. As they are both professed heretics on the score of love and marriage, so both are tamed out of their heresy in the glad persuasion that they have each proved too much for the other's pride of wit, and have each converted the other to the true faith. But indeed that heresy was all along feigned as a refuge from merry persecutions; and the virtue of the thing is, that in the belief that they have each conquered the other's assumed fastidiousness, they each lay aside their own. The case involves a highly curious interplay of various motives on either side; and it is not easy to say whether vanity or generosity, the self-regarding or the self-forgetting emotions, are uppermost in the process.

The wit of these two persons, though seeming at first view much the same, is very nicely discriminated. Beatrice, intelligent as she is, has little of reflection in her wit; but throws it off in rapid flashes whenever any object ministers a spark to her fancy. Though of the most piercing keenness and the most exquisite aptness, there is no ill-nature about it; it stings indeed, but does not poison. The offspring merely of the moment and the occasion, it catches the apprehension, but quickly slides from the memory. Its agility is infinite; wherever it may be, the instant one goes to put his hand upon it, he is sure to find it or feel it somewhere else. The wit of Benedick, on the other hand, springs more from reflection, and grows with the growth of thought. With all the pungency, and nearly all the pleasantry of hers, it has less of spontaneous volubility. Hence in their skirmishes she always gets the better of him; hitting him so swiftly, and in so many spots, as to bewilder his aim. But he makes ample amends when out of her presence, trundling off jests in whole paragraphs. In short, if his wit be slower, it is also stronger than hers: not so agile of movement, more weighty in matter, it shines less, but burns more; and as it springs much less out of the occasion, so it bears repeating much better. The effect of the serious events in bringing these persons to an armistice of wit is a happy stroke of art; and perhaps some such thing was necessary, to prevent the impression of their being jesters by trade. It proves at least that Beatrice is a witty woman, and not a mere female wit. To be sure, she is rather spicy than sweet; but then there is a kind of sweetness in spice, — especially such spice as hers.

I have already referred to the apt naming of this play. The general view of life which it presents answers well to the title. The persons do indeed make or have *much ado*; but all the while to us who are in the secret, and ultimately to them also, all this much ado is plainly *about nothing*. Which is but a common difference in the aspect of things as they appear to the spectators and the partakers; it needs but an average experience to discover that real life is full of just such passages: what troubled and worried us yesterday made others laugh then, and makes us laugh to-day: what we fret or grieve at in the progress, we still smile and make merry over in the result.

AS YOU LIKE IT.

The Comedy of As You Like It was registered at the Stationers', in London, on the 4th of August, 1600. Two other of Shakespeare's plays, and one of Ben Jonson's, were entered at the same time; all of them under an injunction, "to be stayed." In regard to the other two of Shakespeare's plays, the stay appears to have been soon removed, as both of them were entered again in the course of the same month, and published before the end of that year. In the case of *As you Like It*, the stay seems to have been kept up; perhaps because its continued success on the stage made the theatrical company unwilling to part with their interest in it.

This is the only contemporary notice of the play that has been discovered. As it was not mentioned in the list given by Francis Meres in 1598, we are probably warranted in presuming it had not been heard of at that time. The play has a line, "Who ever lov'd, that lov'd not at first sight?" apparently quoted from Marlowe's version of *Hero and Leander*, which was published in 1598. So that we may safely conclude the play to have been written some time between that date and the date of the forecited entry at the Stationers'; that is, when the Poet was in his thirty-sixth or thirty-seventh year. The play was never printed, that we know of, till in the folio of 1623, where it stands the tenth in the division of Comedies. The text is there presented in a very satisfactory state, with but few serious errors, and none that can fairly be called impracticable.

Before passing from this branch of the subject, perhaps I ought to cite a curious piece of tradition, clearly pointing to the play in hand. Gilbert Shakespeare, a brother of William, lived till after the Restoration, which occurred in 1660; and Oldys tells us of "the faint, general, and almost lost ideas" which the old man had, of having once seen the Poet act a part in one of his own comedies;

"wherein, being to personate a decrepit old man, he wore a long beard, and appeared so weak and drooping, that he was forced to be carried by another person to a table, at which he was seated among some company who were eating, and one of them sung a song." This could have been none other than the "goold old man" Adam, in and about whom we have so much noble thought; and we thus learn that his character, beautiful in itself, yet more so for this circumstance, was sustained by the Poet himself.

In regard to the originals of this play, two sources have been pointed out, — *The Cook's Tale of Gamelyn*, sometime attributed to Chaucer, but upon better advice excluded from his works; and a novel by Thomas Lodge entitled *Rosalynd; Euphues' Golden Legacy.* As the *Tale of Gamelyn* was not printed till more than a century later, it has been questioned whether Shakespeare ever saw it. Nor indeed can much be alleged as indicating that he ever did: one point there is, however, that may have some weight that way. An old knight, Sir John of Boundis, being about to die, calls in his wise friends to advise him touching the distribution of his property among his three sons. They advise him to settle all his lands on the eldest, and leave the youngest without any thing. Gamelyn, the youngest, being his favourite son, he rejects their advice, and bestows the largest portion upon him. The Poet goes much more according to their advice; Orlando, who answers to Gamelyn, having no share in the bulk of his father's estate. A few other resemblances, also, may be traced, wherein the play differs from Lodge's novel; though none of them are so strong as to force the inference that Shakespeare must have consulted the *Tale.* Nor, in truth, is the matter of much consequence, save as bearing upon the question whether the Poet was of a mind to be unsatisfied with such printed books as lay in his way. I would not exactly affirm him to have been "a hunter of manuscripts"; but indications are not wanting, that he sometimes had access to them: nor is it at all unlikely that one so greedy of intellectual food, so eager and so apt to make the most of all the means within his reach, should have gone beyond the printed resources of his time. Besides, there can be no question that Lodge was very familiar with the *Tale of Gamelyn:* he follows it so closely in a large part of his novel as to leave scarce any doubt that he wrote with the manuscript before him; and if he, who was also sometime a player, availed himself of such sources, why may not Shakespeare have done the same?

The practical use of such inquiries is, that they exhibit the Poet in the character where I like especially to view him, namely, as an earnest and diligent seeker after knowledge, and as building himself up in intelligence and power by much the same means as are found to serve in the case of other men. He himself tells us that "ignorance is the curse of God, knowledge the wing wherewith we fly to Heaven." Assuredly he was a great student as well as a great genius; as full of aptness to learn as of force to create. If he had great faculties to work with, he was also a greater worker in the use of them. Nor is it best for us to think of him as being raised by natural gifts above the common methods and processes of high intellectual achievement.

Lodge's *Rosalynd* was first printed in 1590; and its popularity appears in that it was reprinted in 1592, and again in 1598. Steevens pronounced it a "worthless original"; but this sweeping sentence is so unjust as to breed some doubt whether he had read it. Compared with the general run of popular literature then in vogue, the novel has no little merit; and is very well entitled to the honour of having contributed to one of the most delightful poems ever written. A rather ambitious attempt indeed at fine writing; pedantic in style, not a little blemished with the elaborate euphemism of the time, and occasionally running into absurdity and indecorum; nevertheless, upon the whole, it is a varied and pleasing narrative, with passages of great force and beauty, and many touches of noble sentiment, and sometimes informed with a pastoral sweetness and simplicity quite charming.

To make a full sketch of the novel, in so far as the Poet borrowed from it, would occupy too much space. Still it seems desirable to indicate, somewhat, the extent of the Poet's obligations in this case; which can be best done, I apprehend, by stating, as compactly as may be, a portion of the story.

Sir John of Bordeaux, being at the point of death, called in his three sons, Saladyne, Fernandine, and Rosader, and divided his wealth among them, giving nearly a third to Rosader the youngest. After a short period of hypocritical mourning for his father, Saladyne went to studying how he might defraud his brothers, and ravish their legacies. He put Fernandine to school at Paris, and kept Rosader as his foot-boy. Rosader bore this patiently for three years, and then his spirit rose against it. While he was deep in meditation on the point, Saladyne came along and began to jerk him with rough speeches. After some interchange of angry and insulting words, Rosader "seized a great rake, and let drive at him," and soon brought him to terms. Saladyne, feigning sorrow for what he had done, then drew the youth, who was of a free and generous nature, into a reconciliation, till he might devise how to finish him out of the way.

Now, Gerismond, the rightful King of France, had been driven into exile, and his crown usurped, by Torismond, his younger brother. To amuse the people, and keep them from thinking of the banished King, the usurper appointed a day of wrestling and tournament; when a Norman, of great strength and stature, who had wrestled down as many as undertook with him, was to stand against all comers. Saladyne went to the Norman secretly, and engaged him with rich rewards to despatch Rosader, in case Rosader should come within his grasp. He then pricked his brother on to the wrestling, telling him how much honour it would bring him, and that he was the only one to uphold the renown of the family. The youth, full of heroic thoughts, was glad of such an opportunity. When the time came, Torismond went to preside over the games, taking with him the Twelve Peers of France, his daughter Alinda, his niece Rosalynd, and all the most famous beauties of the Court. Rosalynd, "upon whose cheeks there seemed a battle between the graces," was the centre of attraction, "and made the cavaliers crack their lances with more courage." The tournament being over, the Norman offered himself as general challenger at wrestling. While he is in the full career of success, Rosader alights from his horse, and presents himself for a trial. He quickly puts an end to the Norman's wrestling; though not till his eyes and thoughts have got badly entangled with the graces of Rosalynd. On the other side, she is equally smitten with his handsome person and heroic bearing, insomuch that, the spectacle being over, she takes from her neck a jewel, and sends it to him by a page, as an assurance of her favour.

This outline, as far as it goes, almost describes, word for word, the course and order of events in the play. And so it is, in a great measure, through the other parts and incidents of the plot; such as the usurper's banishment of his niece, and the escape of his daughter along with her; their arrival in the Forest of Arden, where Rosalynd's father has taken refuge; their encounter with the shepherds, their purchase of the cottage, and their adventures in the pastoral life. So, too, in the flight of Rosader to the same Forest, taking along with him the old servant, who is called Adam Spencer, his carving of love-verses in the bark of trees, his meeting with the disguised Rosalynd, and the wooing and marrying that enrich the forest scenes.

Thus much may suffice to show that the Poet has here borrowed a good deal of excellent matter. With what judgment and art the borrowed matter was used by him can only be understood on a careful study of his workmanship. In no one of his comedies indeed has he drawn more freely from others; nor, I may add, is there any one wherein he has enriched his drawings more liberally from the glory of his own genius. To appreciate his wisdom as shown in what he left unused, one must read the whole of Lodge's novel. In that work we find no traces of Jaques, or Touchstone, or Audrey; nothing, indeed, that could yield the slightest hint towards either of those characters. It scarce need be said that these superaddings are enough of themselves to transform the whole into another nature; pouring through all its veins a free and lively circulation of the most original wit and humour and poetry. And by a judicious indefiniteness as to persons and places, the Poet has greatly idealized the work, throwing it at a romantic distance, and weaving about it all the witchery of poetical perspective; while the whole falls in so smoothly with the laws of the imagination, that the breaches of geographical order are never noticed save by such as cannot understand poetry without a map.

No one at all competent to judge in the matter will suppose that Shakespeare could have been really indebted to Lodge, or to whomsoever else, for any of the *characters* in *As You Like It.* He merely borrowed certain names and incidents for the bodying-forth of conceptions purely his own. The resemblance is all in the drapery and circumstances of the representation, not in the individuals. For instance, we can easily imagine Rosalind in an hundred scenes not here represented; for she is a substantive personal being, such as we may detach and consider apart from the particular order wherein she stands: but we can discover in her no likeness to Lodge's Rosalynd, save that of name and situation: take away the similarity here, and there is nothing to indicate any sort of relationship between the heroines of the play and the novel. And it is considerable that, though the Poet here borrows so freely, still there is no sign of any borrowing in the work itself: we can detect no foreign influences, no second-hand touches, nothing to suggest that any part of the thing had ever been thought of before; what he took being so thoroughly assimilated with what he gave, that the whole seems to have come fresh from Nature and his own mind: so that, had the originals been lost, we should never have suspected there were any.

Shakespeare generally preferred to make up his plots and stories out of such materials as were most familiar to his audience. Of this we have many examples; but the fact is too well known to need dwelling upon. Though surpassingly rich in fertility and force of invention, he was notwithstanding singularly economical and sparing in the use of it. Which aptly shows how free he was from every thing like a sensational spirit or habit of mind. Nature was every thing to him, novelty nothing, or next to nothing. The true, not the new, was always the soul of his purpose; than which nothing could better approve the moral healthiness of his genius. Hence, in great part, his noble superiority to the intellectual and literary fashions of his time. He understood these perfectly; but he deliberately rejected them, or rather struck quite above or beyond them. We rarely meet with any thing that savours of *modishness* in his workmanship. Probably the best judgment ever pronounced upon him is Ben Jonson's, "He was not of an age, but for all time." For even so it is with the permanences of our intellectual and imaginative being that he deals, and not with any transiencies of popular or fashionable excitement or pursuit. And as he cared little for the new, so he was all the stronger in that which does not grow old, and which lives on from age to age in the perennial, unwithering freshness of Truth and Nature. For the being carried hither and thither by the shifting mental epidemics of the day, what is it, after all, but a tacit confession of weakness or disease? proving, at the least, that one has not strength of mind enough to "feel the soul of Nature," or to live at peace with the solidities of reason. And because the attractions of mere novelty had no force with Shakespeare; because his mind dwelt far above the currents of intellectual fashion and convention; therefore his dramas stand "exempt from the wrongs of time"; and the study of them is, with but a single exception, just our best discipline in those forms and sources of interest which underlie and outlast all the flitting specialties of mode and custom, —

> "Truths that wake, to perish never;
> Which neither listlessness nor mad endeavour,
> Nor Man nor Boy,
> Nor all that is at enmity with joy,
> Can utterly abolish or destroy."

As You Like It is exceedingly rich and varied in character. The several persons stand out round and clear in themselves, yet their distinctive traits in a remarkable degree sink quietly into the feelings without reporting themselves in the understanding; for which cause the clumsy methods of criticism are little able to give them expression. Subtile indeed must be the analysis that should reproduce them to the intellect without help from the Dramatic Art.

Properly speaking, the play has no hero; for, though Orlando occupies the foreground, the characters are mainly co-ordinate; the design of the work precluding any subordination among them. Diverted by fortune from all their cherished plans and purposes, they pass before us in just that moral and intellectual dishabille which best reveals their indwelling graces of mind and heart. Schlegel remarks that "the Poet seems to have aimed, throughout, at showing that nothing is wanting, to call forth the poetry that has its dwelling in Nature and the human mind, but to throw off all artificial restraint, and restore both to their native liberty." This is well said; but it should be observed withal that the persons have already been "purified by suffering"; and that it was under the discipline of social restraint that they developed the virtues which make them go right without such restraint, as indeed they do, while we are conversing with them. Because they have not hitherto been altogether free to do as they would, therefore it is that they are good and beautiful in doing as they have a mind to now. Let us beware of attributing to Nature, as we call it, that goodness which proceeds from *habits* generated under Gospel culture and the laws of Christian society. After all, the ordinary conditions of social and domestic life give us far more than they take away. It requires a long schooling in the *prescriptions* of order and rectitude, to fit us for being left to ourselves. In some sense indeed it is a great enlargement of liberty to be rid of all the loves and duties and reverences which the Past may have woven about us; and many there are who seem to place freedom of mind in having nothing to look up to, nothing to respect outside of themselves. But human virtue does not grow in this way; and the stream must soon run dry if cut off from the spring. And I have no sympathy with those who would thus crush all tender and precious memories out of us, and then give the name of *freedom* to the void thus created in our souls. The liberty that goes by unknitting the bands of reverence and dissolving the ties that draw and hold men together in the charities of a common life, is not the liberty for me, nor is it the liberty that Shakespeare teaches. I am much rather minded to say, with a lawyer-poet of our time,

"If we lose
All else, we will preserve our household laws;
Nor let the license of these fickle times
Subvert the holy shelter which command
Of fathers, and undoubting faith of sons,
Rear'd for our shivering virtues."

It is true, however, that in this play the better transpirations of character are mainly conducted in the eye of Nature, where the passions and vanities that so much disfigure human life find little to stir them into act. In the freedom of their woodland resort, and with the native inspirations of the place to kindle and gladden them, the persons have but to live out the handsome thoughts which they have elsewhere acquired. Man's tyranny has indeed driven them into banishment; but their virtues are much more the growth of the place they are banished from than of the place they are banished to.

Orlando is altogether such a piece of young-manhood as it does one good to be with. He has no special occasion for heroism, yet we feel that there is plenty of heroic stuff in him. Brave, gentle, modest, and magnanimous; never thinking of his high birth but to avoid dishonouring it; in his noble-heartedness, forgetting, and causing others to forget, his nobility of rank; he is every way just such a man as all true men would choose for their best friend. His persecuting brother, talking to himself, describes him as "never school'd, and yet learned; full of noble device; of all sorts enchantingly beloved; and indeed so much in the heart of the world, and especially of my own people, who best know him, that I am altogether misprised"; and this description is amply justified by his behaviour. The whole intercourse between him and his faithful old servant Adam is replete on both sides with that full-souled generosity in whose eye the nobilities of Nature are always sure of recognition.

Shakespeare evidently delighted in a certain natural harmony of character wherein virtue is free and spontaneous, like the breathing of perfect health. And such is Orlando. He is therefore good without effort; nay, it would require some effort for him to be otherwise; his soul gravitating towards goodness as of its own accord: "In his proper motion he ascends; descent and fall to him is adverse." And perhaps the nearest he comes to being aware of his virtue is when his virtue triumphs over a mighty temptation; that is, when he sees his unnatural brother in extreme peril;

> "But kindness, nobler ever than revenge,
> And nature, stronger than his just occasion,"

made him risk his own life to save him; and even in this case the divine art of overcoming evil with good seems more an instinct than a conscious purpose with him. This is one of the many instances wherein the Poet delivers the highest results of Christian discipline as drawing so deeply and so creatively into the heart, as to work out with the freedom and felicity of native, original impulse.

I must dismiss Orlando with a part of his tilt of wit with Jaques, as that very well illustrates the composition of the man:

"*Jaq.* I thank you for your company; but, good faith, I had as lief have been myself alone.

Orlan. And so had I; but yet, for fashion's sake, I thank you too for your society.

Jaq. God b' wi' you: let's meet as little as we can.

Orlan. I do desire we may be better strangers.

Jaq. I pray you, mar no more trees with writing love-songs in their barks.

Orlan. I pray you, mar no more of my verses with reading them ill-favouredly.

Jaq. Rosalind is your love's name?

Orlan. Yes, just.

Jaq. I do not like her name.

Orlan. There was no thought of pleasing you when she was christened.

Jaq. What stature is she of?

Orlan. Just as high as my heart.

Jaq. You have a nimble wit: I think it was made of Atalanta's heels. Will you sit down with me? and we two will rail against our mistress the world and all our misery.

Orlan. I will chide no breather in the world but myself, against whom I know most faults."

The banished Duke exemplifies the best sense of nature as thoroughly informed and built up with Christian discipline and religious efficacy; so that the asperities of life do but make his thoughts run the smoother. How sweet, yet how considerative and firm, is every thing about his temper and moral frame! He sees all that is seen by the most keen-eyed satirist, yet is never moved to be satirical, because he looks with wiser and therefore kindlier eyes. The enmity of Fortune is fairly disarmed by his patience;

her shots are all wasted against his breast, garrisoned as it is with the forces of charity and peace: his soul is made storm-proof by gentleness and truth: exile, penury, the ingratitude of men, the malice of the elements, what are they to him? he has the grace to sweeten away their venom, and to smile the sting out of them. He loves to stay himself upon the compensations of life, and to feed his gentler affections by dwelling upon the good which adversity opens to him, or the evil from which it withdraws him; and so he rejoices in finding "these woods more free from peril than the envious Court." In his philosophy, so bland, benignant, and contemplative, the mind tastes the very luxury of rest, and has an antepast of measureless content.

Touchstone, though he nowhere strikes so deep a chord within us as the poor Fool in *King Lear*, is, I think, the most entertaining of Shakespeare's privileged characters. And he is indeed a mighty delectable fellow! wise too, and full of the most insinuative counsel. How choicely does his grave, acute nonsense moralize the scenes wherein he moves! Professed clown though he be, and as such ever hammering away with artful awkwardness at a jest, a strange kind of humorous respect still waits upon him notwithstanding. It is curious to observe how the Poet takes care to let us know from the first, that beneath the affectations of his calling some precious sentiments have been kept alive; that far within the Fool there is laid up a secret reserve of the man, ready to leap forth and combine with better influences as soon as the incrustations of art are thawed and broken up. This is partly done in the scene where Rosalind and Celia arrange for their flight from the usurper's Court. Rosalind proposes, —

> "But, cousin, what if we assay'd to steal
> The clownish Fool out of your father's Court?
> Would he not be a comfort to our travel?"

And Celia replies, —

> He'll go along o'er the wide world with me :
> Leave me alone to woo him."

Where we learn that some remnants, at least, of a manly heart in him have asserted their force in the shape of unselfish regards, strong as life, for whatever is purest and loveliest in the characters about him. He would rather starve or freeze, with Celia near him, than feed high and lie warm where his eye cannot find her. If, with this fact in view, our honest esteem does not go out towards him, then we, I think, are fools in a worse sense than he is.

So much for the substantial manhood of Touchstone, and for the Poet's human-heartedness in thus putting us in communication with it. As for the other points of his character, I scarce know how to draw a reader into them by any turn of analysis. Used to a life cut off from human sympathies; stripped of the common responsibilities of the social state; living for no end but to make aristocratic idlers laugh; one therefore whom nobody heeds enough to resent or be angry at any thing he says; — of course his habit is to speak all for effect, nothing for truth: instead of reflecting the natural force and image of things, his vocation is to wrest and transshape them from their true form and pressure. Thus a strange wilfulness and whimsicality has wrought itself into the substance of his mind. He takes nothing for what it is in itself, but only for the odd quirks of thought he can twist out of it. Yet his nature is not so "subdued to what it works in" but that, amidst the scenes and inspirations of the Forest, the Fool quickly slides into the man; the supervenings of the place so running into and athwart what he brings with him, that his character comes to be as dappled and motley as his dress. Even the new passion which there overtakes him has a touch of his wilfulness in it: when he falls in love, as he really does, nothing seems to inspire and draw him more than the unloveliness of the object; thus approving that even so much of nature as survives in him is not content to run in natural channels.

Jaques is, I believe, an universal favourite, as indeed he well may be, for he is certainly one of the Poet's happiest conceptions. Without being at all unnatural, he has an amazing fund of peculiarity. Enraptured out of his senses at the voice of a song; thrown into a paroxysm of laughter at sight of the motley-clad and motley-witted Fool; and shedding the twilight of his merry-sad spirit over all the darker spots of human life and character; he represents the abstract and sum-total of an utterly useless yet perfectly harmless man, seeking wisdom by abjuring its first principle. An odd choice mixture of reality and affectation, he does nothing but think, yet avowedly thinks to no purpose; or rather thinking is with him its own end. On the whole, if in Touchstone there is much of the philosopher in the Fool, in Jaques there is not less of the fool in the philosopher; so that the German critic, Ulrici, is not so wide of the mark in calling them "two fools."

Jaques is equally wilful, too, with Touchstone, in his turn of thought and speech, though not so conscious of it; and as he plays his part more to please himself, so he is proportionably less open to the healing and renovating influences of Nature. We cannot justly affirm, indeed, that "the soft blue sky did never melt into his heart," as Wordsworth says of his Peter Bell; but he shows more of resistance than all the other persons to the poetries and eloquences of the place. Tears are a great luxury to him: he sips the cup of woe with all the gust of an epicure. Still his temper is by no means sour: fond of solitude, he is nevertheless far from being unsocial. The society of good men, provided they be in adversity, has great charms for him. He likes to be with those who, though deserving the best, still have the worst: virtue wronged, buffeted, oppressed, is his special delight; because such moral discrepancies offer the most salient points to his cherished meditations. He himself enumerates nearly all the forms of melancholy except his own, which I take to be the melancholy of self-love. And its effect in his case is not unlike that of

Touchstone's art; inasmuch as he greatly delights to see things otherwise than as they really are, and to make them speak out some meaning that is not in them; that is, their plain and obvious sense is not to his taste. Nevertheless his melancholy is grateful, because free from any dash of malignity. His morbid habit of mind seems to spring from an excess of generative virtue. And how racy and original is everything that comes from him! as if it bubbled up from the centre of his being; while his perennial fulness of matter makes his company always delightful. The Duke loves especially to meet him in his "sullen fits," because he then overflows with his most idiomatic humour. After all, the worst that can be said of Jaques is, that the presence of men who are at once fortunate and deserving corks him up; which may be only another way of saying that he cannot open out and run over, save where things are going wrong.

It is something uncertain whether Jaques or Rosalind be the greater attraction: there is enough in either to make the play a continual feast; though her charms are less liable to be staled by use, because they result from health of mind and symmetry of character; so that in her presence the head and the heart draw together perfectly. I mean that she never starts any moral or emotional reluctances in our converse with her: all our sympathies go along with her freely, because she never jars upon them, or touches them against the grain.

For wit, this strange, queer, lovely being is fully equal to Beatrice, yet nowise resembling her. A soft, subtile, nimble essence, consisting in one knows not what, and springing up one can hardly tell how, her wit neither stings nor burns, but plays briskly and airily over all things within its reach, enriching and adorning them; insomuch that one could ask no greater pleasure than to be the continual theme of it. In its irrepressible vivacity it waits not for occasion, but runs on for ever, and we wish it to run on for ever: we have a sort of faith that her dreams are made up of cunning, quirkish, graceful fancies; her wits being in a frolic even when she is asleep. And her heart seems a perennial spring of affectionate cheerfulness: no trial can break, no sorrow chill, her flow of spirits; even her sighs are breathed forth in a wrappage of innocent mirth; an arch, roguish smile irradiates her saddest tears. No sort of unhappiness can live in her company: it is a joy even to stand her chiding; for, "faster than her tongue doth make offence, her eye doth heal it up."

So much for her choice idiom of wit. But I must not pass from this part of the theme without noting also how aptly she illustrates the Poet's peculiar use of humour. For I suppose the difference of wit and humour is too well understood to need any special exposition. But the two often go together; though there is a form of wit, much more common, that burns and dries the juices all out of the mind, and turns it into a kind of sharp, stinging wire. Now Rosalind's sweet establishment is thoroughly saturated with humour, and this too of the freshest and wholesomest quality. And the effect of her humour is, as it were, to *lubricate* all her faculties, and make her thoughts run brisk and glib even when grief has possession of her heart. Through this interfusive power, her organs of play are held in perfect concert with her springs of serious thought. Hence she is outwardly merry and inwardly sad at the same time. We may justly say that she laughs out her sadness, or plays out her seriousness: the sorrow that is swelling her breast puts her wits and spirits into a frolic; and in the mirth that overflows through her tongue we have a relish of the grief with which her heart is charged. And our sympathy with her inward state is the more divinely moved, forasmuch as she thus, with indescribable delicacy, touches it through a masquerade of playfulness. Yet, beneath all her frolicsomeness, we feel that there is a firm basis of thought and womanly dignity; so that she never laughs away our respect.

It is quite remarkable how, in respect of her disguise, Rosalind just reverses the conduct of Viola, yet with much the same effect. For, though she seems as much at home in her male attire as if she had always worn it, this never strikes us otherwise than as an exercise of skill for the perfecting of her masquerade. And on the same principle her occasional freedoms of speech serve to deepen our sense of her innate delicacy; they being manifestly intended as a part of her disguise, and springing from the feeling that it is far less indelicate to go a little out of her character, in order to prevent any suspicion of her sex, than it would be to hazard such a suspicion by keeping strictly within her character. In other words, her free talk bears much the same relation to her character as her dress does to her person, and is therefore becoming to her even on the score of feminine modesty. — Celia appears well worthy of a place beside her whose love she shares and repays. Instinct with the soul of moral beauty and female tenderness, the friendship of these more-than-sisters "mounts to the seat of grace within the mind."

> "We still have slept together;
> Rose at an instant, learn'd, play'd, eat together;
> And wheresoe'er we went, like Juno's swans,
> Still we went coupled and inseparable."

The general drift and temper, or, as some of the German critics would say, the ground-idea of this play, is aptly hinted by the title. As for the beginnings of what is here represented, these do not greatly concern us; most of them lie back out of our view, and the rest are soon lost sight of in what grows out of them; but the issues, of which there are many, are all exactly to our mind; we feel them to be just about right, and would not have them otherwise. For example, touching Frederick and Oliver, our wish is that they should repent, and repair the wrong they have done, in brief, that they should become good; which is precisely what takes place; and as soon as they do this, they naturally love those who were good before. Jaques, too, is so fitted to moralize the discrepancies of human life, so happy and at home, and withal so agreeable, in that exercise, that we would not he should follow the good Duke when in his case those discrepancies are composed. The same might easily be shown in respect of the other issues. Indeed I dare ask any genial, considerate reader, Does not every thing turn out just *as you like it?* Moreover there is an indefinable something about the play that puts us in a receptive frame of mind; that opens the heart, soothes away all querulousness and fault-finding, and makes us easy and apt to be pleased. Thus the Poet here disposes us to like things as they come, and at the same time takes care that they shall come as we like. The whole play indeed is *as you like it.*

Much has been said by one critic and another about the improbabilities in this play. I confess they have never troubled me; and, as I have had no trouble here to get out of, I do not well know how to help others out. Wherefore, if any one be still annoyed by these things, I will turn him over to the elegant criticism of the poet Campbell: "Before I say more of this dramatic treasure, I must absolve myself by a confession as to some of its improbabilities. Rosalind asks her cousin Celia, 'Whither shall we go?' and Celia answers, 'To seek my uncle in the Forest of Arden.' But, arrived there, and having purchased a cottage and sheep-farm, neither the daughter nor niece of the banished Duke seem to trouble themselves much to inquire about either father or uncle. The lively and natural-hearted Rosalind discovers no impatience to embrace her sire, until she has finished her masked courtship with Orlando. But Rosalind was in love, as I have been with the comedy these forty years; and love is blind; for until a late period my eyes were never couched so as to see this objection. The truth however is, that love is *wilfully* blind; and now that my eyes are opened, I shut them against the fault. Away with your best-proved improbabilities, when the heart has been touched and the fancy fascinated."

As a fitting pendent to this, I may further observe that the bringing of lions, serpents, palm-trees, rustic shepherds, and banished noblemen together in the Forest of Arden, is a strange piece of geographical license, which certain critics have not failed to make merry withal. Perhaps they did not see that the very grossness of the thing proves it to have been designed. The Poet keeps his geography true enough whenever he has cause to do so. He knew, at all events, that lions did not roam at large in France. By this irregular combination of actual things, he informs the whole with ideal effect, giving to this charming issue of his brain "a local habitation and a name," that it may link-in with our flesh-and-blood sympathies, and at the same time turning it into a wild, wonderful, remote, fairy-land region, where all sorts of poetical things may take place without the slightest difficulty. Of course Shakespeare would not have done thus, but that he saw quite through the grand critical humbug which makes the proper effect of a work of art depend upon our belief in the actual occurrence of the thing represented. But your "critic grave and cool," I suppose, is one who, like Wordsworth's "model of a child,"

> "Can string you names of districts, cities, towns,
> The whole world over, tight as beads of dew
> Upon a gossamer thread : he sifts, he weighs ;
> All things are put to question ; he must live
> Knowing that he grows wiser every day,
> Or else not live at all, and seeing too
> Each little drop of wisdom as it falls
> Into the dimpling cistern of his heart.
> O, give us once again the wishing-cap
> Of Fortunatus, and the invisible coat
> Of Jack the Giant-killer, Robin Hood,
> And Sabra in the forest with Saint George !
> The child, whose love is here, at least doth reap
> One precious gain, that he forgets himself."

As far as I can determine the matter, *As You Like It* is, upon the whole, my favourite of Shakespeare's comedies. Yet I should be puzzled to tell why; for my preference springs not so much from any particular points or features, wherein it is surpassed by several others, as from the general toning and effect. The whole is replete with a beauty so delicate yet so intense, that we feel it everywhere, but can never tell especially where it is, or in what it consists. For instance, the descriptions of forest scenery come along so unsought, and in such easy, quiet, natural touches, that we take in the impression without once noticing what it is that impresses us. Thus there is a certain woodland freshness, a glad, free naturalness, that creeps and steals into the heart before we know it. And the spirit of the place is upon its inhabitants, its genius within them: we almost breathe with them the fragrance of the Forest, and listen to "the melodies of woods and winds and waters," and feel

> "The Power, the Beauty, and the Majesty,
> That have their haunts in dale, or piny mountain,
> Or forest by slow stream, or pebbly spring."

Even the Court Fool, notwithstanding all the crystallizing process that has passed upon him, undergoes, as we have seen, a sort of rejuvenescence of his inner man, so that his wit catches at every turn the fresh hues and odours of his new whereabout. I am persuaded indeed that Milton had a special eye to this play in the lines, —

> "And sweetest Shakespeare, Fancy's child,
> Warbles his native wood-notes wild."

To all which add, that the kindlier sentiments here seem playing out in a sort of jubilee. Untied from set purposes and definite aims, the persons come forth with their hearts already tuned, and so have but to let off their redundant music. Envy, jealousy, avarice, revenge, all the passions that afflict and degrade society, they have left in the city behind them. And they have brought the intelligence and refinement of the Court without its vanities and vexations; so that the graces of art and the simplicities of nature meet together in joyous, loving sisterhood. A serene and mellow atmosphere of thought encircles and pervades the actors in this drama; as if on purpose to illustrate how

"One impulse from a vernal wood
May teach you more of man,
Of moral evil, and of good,
Than all the sages can."

Nature throws her protecting arms around them; Beauty pitches her tents before them; Heaven rains its riches upon them: with "no enemy but Winter and rough weather," Peace hath taken up her abode with them; and they have nothing to do but to "fleet the time carelessly, as they did in the golden world."

But no words of mine, I fear, will justify to others my own sense of this delectable workmanship. I can hardly think of any thing else in the whole domain of Poetry so inspiring of the faith that "every flower enjoys the air it breathes." The play, indeed, abounds in wild, frolicsome graces which cannot be described; which can only be seen and felt; and which the hoarse voice of Criticism seems to scare away, as the crowing of the cocks is said to have scared away the fairy spirits from their nocturnal pastimes. I know not how I can better dismiss the theme than with some lines from Wordsworth, which these scenes have often recalled to my thoughts:

"Nature never did betray
The heart that lov'd her; 't is her privilege
Through all the years of this our life to lead
From joy to joy: for she can so inform
The mind that is within us, so impress
With quietness and beauty, and so feed
With lofty thoughts, that neither evil tongues,
Rash judgments, nor the sneers of selfish men,
Nor greetings where no kindness is, nor all
The dreary intercourse of daily life,
Shall e'er prevail against us, or disturb
Our cheerful faith, that all which we behold
Is full of blessings."

TWELFTH NIGHT; OR, WHAT YOU WILL.

THE COMEDY of TWELFTH NIGHT; OR, WHAT YOU WILL, was never printed, that we know of, during the author's life. It first appeared in the folio of 1623: consequently that edition, and the reprint of it in 1632, are our only authorities for the text. Fortunately, in this instance, the original printing was very good for that time; the few errors have proved, for the most part, easy of correction; so that the text offers little matter of difficulty or disagreement among editors.

In default of positive information, this play was for a long time set down as among the last-written of the Poet's dramas. This opinion was based upon such slight indications, gathered from the work itself, as could have no weight but in the absence of other proofs. No contemporary notice of the play was discovered till the year 1828, when Mr. Collier, delving among the "musty records of antiquity" stored away in the Museum, lighted upon a manuscript *Diary*, written, as was afterwards ascertained, by one John Manningham, a barrister who was entered at the Middle Temple in 1597. Under date of February 2d, 1602, the author notes, "At our feast we had a play called *Twelfth Night, or What You Will*, much like *The Comedy of Errors*, or *Menechmi* in Plautus, but most like and near to that in the Italian called *Inganni*." The writer then goes on to state such particulars of the action, as fully identify the play which he saw with the one now under consideration. It seems that the benchers and members of the several Inns-of-Court were wont to enrich their convivialities with a course of wit and poetry. And the forecited notice ascertains that Shakespeare's *Twelfth Night* was performed before the members of the Middle Temple on the old Church festival of the Purification, formerly called Candlemas; — an important link in the course of festivities that used to continue from Christmas to Shrovetide. We thus learn that one of the Poet's sweetest plays was enjoyed by a gathering of his learned and studious contemporaries, at a time when this annual jubilee had rendered their minds congenial and apt, and when Christians have so much cause to be happy and gentle and kind, and therefore to cherish the convivial delectations whence kindness and happiness naturally grow.

As to the date of the composition, we have little difficulty in fixing this somewhere between the time when the play was acted at the Temple, and the year 1598. In Act iii., scene 2, when Malvolio is at the height of his ludicrous beatitude, Maria says of him, "He does smile his face into more lines than are in the new map, with the augmentation of the Indies." In 1598 was published an English version of *Linschoten's Discourse of Voyages*, with a map exactly answering to Maria's description. Nor is any such multilineal map known to have appeared in England before that time. Besides, that was the first map of the world, in which the *Eastern Islands* were included. So that the allusion can hardly be to any thing else; and the words *new map* would seem to infer that the passage was written not long after the appearance of the map in question.

Again: In Act iii., scene 1, the Clown says to Viola, "But, indeed, words are very rascals, since bonds disgraced them." This may be fairly understood as referring to an order issued by the Privy Council in June, 1600, and laying very severe restrictions upon stage performances. This order prescribes that "there shall be about the city two houses and no more, allowed to serve for the use of common stage plays"; that "the two several companies of players, assigned unto the two houses allowed, may play each of them in their several houses twice a-week, and no oftener"; and that "they shall forbear altogether in the time of Lent, and likewise at such time and times as any extraordinary sickness or infection of disease shall appear to be in or about the city." The order was directed to the principal magistrates of the city and suburbs, "strictly charging them to see to the execution of the same"; and it is plain, that if rigidly enforced it would have amounted almost to a total suppression of play-houses, as the expenses of such establishments could hardly have been met, in the face of so great drawbacks.

Therewithal it is to be noted that the Puritans were specially forward and zealous in urging the complaints which put the Privy Council upon issuing this stringent process; and it will hardly be questioned that the character of Malvolio was partly meant as a satire on that remarkable people. That the Poet should be somewhat provoked at their action in bringing about such tight restraints upon the freedom of his art, was certainly natural enough. Nor is it a small addition to their many claims on our gratitude, that their aptness to "think, because they were virtuous, there should be no more cakes and ale," had the effect of calling forth so rich and withal so good-natured a piece of retaliation. Perhaps it should be remarked further, that the order in question, though solicited by the authorities of the city, was not enforced; for even at that early date those magistrates had hit upon the method of stimulating the complaints of discontented citizens till orders were taken for removing the alleged grievances, and then of letting such orders sleep, lest the enforcing of them should hush those complaints, and thus take away all pretext for keeping up the agitation.

The story upon which the more serious parts of *Twelfth Night* were founded appears to have been a general favourite before and during Shakespeare's time. It is met with in various forms and under various names in the Italian, French, and English literature of that period. The earliest form of it known to us is in Bandello's collection of novels. From the Italian of Bandello it was transferred, with certain changes and abridgments, into the French of Belleforest, and makes one in his collection of *Tragical Histories*. From one or the other of these sources the tale was borrowed again by Barnabe Rich, and set forth as *The History of Apolonius and Silla;* making the second in his collection of tales entitled *Farewell to the Military Profession*, which was first printed in 1581.

Until the discovery of Manningham's *Diary*, Shakespeare was not supposed to have gone beyond these sources, and it was thought something uncertain to which of these he was most indebted for the raw material of his play. It is now held doubtful whether he drew from either of them. The passage I have quoted from that *Diary* notes a close resemblance of *Twelfth Night* to an Italian play "called *Inganni*." This has had the effect of directing attention to the Italian theatre in quest of his originals. Two comedies bearing the title of *Gl' Inganni* have been found, both of them framed upon the novel of Bandello, and both in print before the date of *Twelfth Night.* These, as also the three forms of the tale mentioned above, all agree in having a brother and sister, the latter in male attire, and the two bearing so close a resemblance in person and dress as to be indistinguishable; upon which circumstance some of the leading incidents are made to turn. In one of the Italian plays, the sister is represented as assuming the name of *Cesare;* which is so like *Cesario*, the name adopted by Viola in her disguise, that the one may well be thought to have suggested the other. Beyond this point, *Twelfth Night* shows no clear connection with either of those plays.

But there is a third Italian comedy, also lately brought to light, entitled *Gl' Ingannati*, which is said to have been first printed in 1537. Here the traces of indebtedness are much clearer and more numerous. I must content myself with abridging the Rev. Joseph Hunter's statement of the matter. In the Italian play, a brother and sister, named Fabritio and Lelia, are separated at the sacking of Rome in 1527. Lelia is carried to Modena, where a gentleman resides, named Flamineo, to whom she was formerly attached. She disguises herself as a boy, and enters his service. Flamineo, having forgotten his Lelia, is making suit to Isabella, a lady of Modena. The disguised Lelia is employed by him in his love-suit to Isabella, who remains utterly deaf to his passion, but falls desperately in love with the messenger. In the third Act the brother Fabritio arrives at Modena, and his close resemblance to Lelia in her male attire gives rise to some ludicrous mistakes. At one time, a servant of Isabella's meets him in the street, and takes him to her house, supposing him to be the messenger; just as Sebastian is taken for Viola, and led to the house of Olivia. In due time, the needful recognitions take place, whereupon Isabella easily transfers her affection to Fabritio, and Flamineo's heart no less easily ties up with the loving and faithful Lelia. In her disguise, Lelia takes the name of *Fabio;* hence, most likely, the name of Fabian, who figures as one of Olivia's servants. The Italian play has also a subordinate character called Pasquella, to whom Maria corresponds; and another named *Malevolti*, of which *Malvolio* is a happy adaptation. All which fully establishes the connection between the Italian comedy and the English. But it does not follow necessarily that the foreign original was used by Shakespeare; so much of the lighter literature of his time having perished, that we cannot affirm with any certainty what importations from Italy may or may not have been accessible to him in his native tongue.

As for the more comic portions of *Twelfth Night*, — those in which Sir Toby Belch, Sir Andrew Aguecheek, and the Clown figure so delectably, — we have no reason for believing that any part of them was borrowed; there being no hints or traces of any thing like them in the previous versions of the story, or in any other book or writing known to us. And it is to be observed, moreover, that the Poet's borrowings, in this instance as in others, relate only to the plot of the work, the poetry and character being all his own; and that, here as elsewhere, he used what he took merely as the canvas whereon to pencil out and express the breathing creatures of his mind. So that the whole workmanship is just as original, in the only right sense of that term, as if the story and incidents had been altogether the children of his own invention; and he but followed his usual custom of so ordering his work as to secure whatever benefit might accrue from a sort of pre-established harmony between his subject and the popular mind.

I am quite at a loss to conceive why *Twelfth Night* should ever have been referred to the Poet's latest period of authorship. The play naturally falls, by the internal notes of style, temper, and poetic grain, into the middle period of his productive years. It has no such marks of vast but immature powers as are often met with in his earlier plays; nor, on the other hand, any of "that intense idiosyncrasy of thought and expression, — that unparalleled fusion of the intellectual with the passionate," — which distinguishes his later ones. Every thing is calm and quiet, with an air of unruffled serenity and composure about it, as if the Poet had purposely taken to such matter as he could easily mould into graceful and entertaining forms; thus exhibiting none of that crushing muscularity of mind to which the hardest materials afterwards or elsewhere became as limber and pliant as clay in the hands of a potter. Yet the play has a marked severity of taste; the style, though by no means so great as in some others, is singularly faultless; the graces of wit and poetry are distilled into it with indescribable delicacy, as if they came from a hand at once the most plentiful and the most sparing: in short, the work is everywhere replete with "the modest charm of not too much"; its beauty, like that of the heroine, being of the still, deep, retiring sort, which it takes one long to find, forever to exhaust, and which can be fully caught only by the reflective imagination in "the quiet and still air of delightful studies." Thus all things are disposed in most happy keeping with each other, and tempered in the blandest proportion of Art; so as to illustrate how

> "Grace, laughter, and discourse may meet,
> And yet the beauty not go less;
> For what is noble should be sweet."

If the characters of this play are generally less interesting in themselves than some we meet with elsewhere in the Poet's works, the defect is pretty well made up by the felicitous grouping of them. Their very diversities of temper and purpose are made to act as so many mutual affinities; and this too in a manner so spontaneous that we see not how they could possibly act otherwise. For broad comic effect, the cluster of which Sir Toby is the centre — all of them drawn in clear yet delicate colours — is inferior only to the unparalleled assemblage that makes rich the air of Eastcheap. Of Sir Toby himself — that most whimsical, madcap, frolicsome old toper, so full of antics and fond of sprees, with a plentiful stock of wit, which is kept in motion by an equally plentiful lack of money — it is enough to say, with our Mr. Verplanck, that "he certainly comes out of the same associations where the Poet saw Falstaff hold his revels"; and that, though "not Sir John, nor a fainter sketch of him, yet he has an odd sort of a family likeness to him." Sir Toby has a decided *penchant* for practical jokes; though rather because he takes a sort of disinterested pleasure in them, than because he loves to see himself in the process of engineering them through: for he has not a particle of ill-nature in him. Though by no means a coward himself, he nevertheless enjoys the exposure of cowardice in others; yet this again is not so much because such exposure feeds his self-esteem, as because he delights in the game for its own sake, and for the nimble pastime it yields to his faculties: that is, his impulses seem to rest in it as an ultimate object, or a part of what is to him the *summum bonum* of life. And it is much the same with his addiction to vinous revelry, and to the moister kind of minstrelsy; an addiction that proceeds in part from his keen gust of fun, and the happiness he finds in making sport for others as well as for himself: he will drink till the world turns round, but not unless others are at hand to enjoy the turning along with him.

Sir Andrew Aguecheek, the aspiring, lackadaisical, self-satisfied echo and sequel of Sir Toby, fitly serves the double purpose of a butt and a foil to the latter, at once drawing him out and setting him off. Ludicrously proud of the most petty, childish irregularities, which, however, his natural fatuity keeps him from acting, and barely suffers him to affect, on this point he reminds us of that impressive imbecility, Abraham Slender; yet not in such sort as to encroach at all on Slender's province. There can scarcely be found a richer piece of diversion than Sir Toby's practice in dandling Sir Andrew out of his money, and paying him off with the odd hope of gaining Olivia's hand. And the funniest of it is, that while Sir Toby understands him thoroughly he has not himself the slightest suspicion or inkling of what he is; he being as confident of his own wit as others are of his want of it. Nor are we here touched with any revulsions of moral feeling, such as might disturb our enjoyment of their fellowship; on the contrary, we sympathize with Sir Toby's sport, without any reluctances of virtue or conscience. To our sense of the matter, he neither has nor ought to have any scruples or compunctions about the game he is hunting. For, in truth, his dealing with Sir Andrew is all in the way of fair exchange. He gives as much pleasure as he gets. If he is cheating Sir Andrew out of his money, he is also cheating him into the proper felicity of his nature, and thus paying him with the equivalent best suited to his capacity. It suffices that, in being stuffed with the preposterous delusion about Olivia, Sir Andrew is rendered supremely happy at the time; while he manifestly has not force enough to remember it with any twinges of shame or self-reproach. And we feel that, while clawing his fatuous crotchets and playing out his absurdities, Sir Toby is really doing Sir Andrew no wrong, since the latter is then most himself, is in his happiest mood, and in the most natural freedom of his indigenous gifts and graces. All which quite precludes any division of our sympathies, and just makes our comic enjoyment of their intercourse simply perfect.

Malvolio, the self-love-sick Steward, has hardly had justice done him, his bad qualities being indeed of just the kind to defeat the recognition of his good ones. He represents a perpetual class of people, whose leading characteristic is moral demonstrativeness, and who are never satisfied with a law that leaves them free to do right, unless it also give them the power to keep others from doing wrong. To quote again from Mr. Verplanck, Malvolio embodies "a conception as true as it is original and droll; and its truth may still be frequently attested by comparison with real Malvolios, to be found everywhere from humble domestic life up to the high places of learning, of the State, and even of the Church." From the central idea of the character it follows in course that the man has too much conscience to mind his own business, and is too pure to tolerate mirth in others, because too much swollen and stiffened with self-love to be merry himself. His highest exhilaration is when he contemplates the image of his self-imputed virtues: he lives so entranced with the beauty of his own inward parts, that he would fain hold himself the wrong side out, to the end that all the world may duly appreciate and admire him. Naturally, too, the more he hangs over his own moral beauty, the more pharisaical and sanctimonious he becomes in his opinion and treatment of others. For the glass which magnifies to his view whatever of good there may be in himself, also serves him as an inverted telescope to *minify* the good of those about him; and, which is more, the self-same spirit that prompts him to invert the instrument upon other men's virtues, naturally moves him to turn the big end upon their faults and the small end upon his own. Of course, therefore, he is never without food for censure and reproof save when he is alone with himself, where, to be sure, his intense consciousness of virtue just breathes around him "the air of Paradise." Thus his continual frothing over with righteous indignation all proceeds from the yeast of pride and self-importance working mightily within him. Maria, whose keen eye and sure tongue seldom fail to hit the white of the mark, describes him as not being "any thing constantly, but a time-pleaser." And it is remarkable that the emphasized moral rigidity of such men is commonly but the outside of a mind secretly intent on the service of the time, and caring little for any thing but to trim its sails to the winds of self-interest and self-advancement. Yet Malvolio is really a man of no little talent and accomplishment, as he is also one of marked skill, fidelity, and rectitude in his calling; so that he would be a right worthy person all round, but for his inordinate craving

> "to be dress'd in an opinion
> Of wisdom, gravity, profound conceit;
> As who should say, *I am Sir Oracle,*
> *And when I ope my lips, let no dog bark.*"

This overweening moral coxcombry is not indeed to be reckoned among the worst of crimes; but perhaps there is no other one fault so generally or so justly offensive, and therefore none so apt to provoke the merciless retaliations of mockery and practical wit.

Maria, the little structure packed so close with mental spicery, has read Malvolio through and through; she knows him without and within; and she never speaks of him, but that her speech touches the very pith of the theme; as when she describes him to be one "that cons State without book, and utters it by great swaths; the best-persuaded of himself, so crammed, as he thinks, with excellences, that it is his ground of faith that all who look on him love him." Her quaint stratagem of the letter has and is meant to have the effect of disclosing to others what her keener insight has long since discovered; and its working lifts her into a model of arch, roguish mischievousness, with wit to plan and art to execute whatsoever falls within the scope of such a character. Her native sagacity has taught her how to touch him in just the right spots to bring out the reserved or latent notes of his character. Her diagnosis of his inward state is indeed perfect; and when she makes the letter instruct him, — "Be opposite with a kinsman, surly with servants; let thy tongue tang arguments of State; put thyself into the trick of singularity," — her arrows are so aimed as to cleave the pin of his most characteristic predispositions.

The scenes where the waggish troop, headed by this "noble gull-catcher" and "most excellent devil of wit," bewitch Malvolio into "a contemplative idiot," practising upon his vanity and conceit till he seems ready to burst with an ecstasy of self-consequence, and they "laugh themselves into stitches" over him, are almost painfully diverting. It is indeed sport to see him "jet under his advanced plumes"; and during this part of the operation our hearts freely keep time with theirs who are tickling out his buds into full-blown thoughts: at length, however, when he is under treatment as a madman, our delight in his exposure passes over into commiseration of his distress, and we feel a degree of resentment towards his ingenious persecutors. The Poet, no doubt, meant to push the joke upon him so far as to throw our sympathies over on his side, and make us take his part. For his character is such that perhaps nothing but excessive reprisals on his vanity and conceit could make us do justice to his real worth.

The shrewd, mirth-loving Fabian, who in greedy silence devours up fun, tasting it too far down towards his knees to give any audible sign of the satisfaction it yields him, is an apt and willing agent in putting the stratagem through. If he does nothing towards inventing or cooking up the repast, he is at least a happy and genial partaker of the banquet that others have prepared. — Feste, the jester, completes this illustrious group of laughing and laughter-moving personages. Though not, perhaps, quite so wise a fellow as Touchstone, of *As-You-Like-It* memory, nor endowed with so fluent and racy a fund of humour, he nevertheless has enough of both to meet all the demands of his situation. If, on the one hand, he never launches the ball of fun, neither, on the other, does he ever fail to do his part towards keeping it rolling. On the whole, he has a sufficiently facile and apposite gift at jesting out philosophy, and moralizing the scenes where he moves; and whatever he has in that line is perfectly original with him. It strikes me, withal, as a rather note-worthy circumstance that both the comedy and the romance of the play meet together in him, as in their natural home. He is indeed a right jolly fellow; no note of mirth springs up but he has answering susceptibilities for it to light upon; but he also has at the same time a delicate vein of tender pathos in him; as appears by the touchingly-plaintive song he sings, which, by the way, is one of

> "The very sweetest Fancy culls or frames,
> Where *tenderness* of heart is strong and deep."

I am not supposing this to be the measure of his lyrical invention, for the song probably is not of his making; but the selection marks at least the setting of his taste, or rather the tuning of his soul, and thus discovers a choice reserve of feeling laid up in his breast.

Such are the scenes, such the characters that enliven Olivia's mansion during the play: Olivia herself, calm, cheerful, of "smooth, discreet, and stable bearing," hovering about them; sometimes unbending, never losing her dignity among them; often checking, oftener enjoying their merry-makings, and occasionally emerging from her seclusion to be plagued by the Duke's message and bewitched by his messenger: and Viola, always perfect in her part, yet always shrinking from it, appearing among them from time to time on her embassies of love; sometimes a partaker, sometimes a provoker, sometimes the victim of their mischievous sport.

All this array of comicalities, exhilarating as it is in itself, is rendered doubly so by the frequent changes and playings-in of poetry breathed from the sweetest spots of romance, and which "gives a very echo to the seat where Love is thron'd"; ideas and images of beauty creeping and stealing over the mind with footsteps so soft and delicate that we scarce know what touches us, — the motions of one that had learned to tread

> "As if the wind, not he, did walk,
> Nor press'd a flower, nor bow'd a stalk."

Upon this portion of the play Hazlitt has some spirited remarks: "We have a friendship for Sir Toby; we patronize Sir Andrew; we have an understanding with the Clown, a sneaking kindness for Maria and her rogueries; we feel a regard for Malvolio, and sympathize with his gravity, his smiles, his cross-garters, his yellow stockings, and imprisonment: but there is something that excites in us a stronger feeling than all this."

Olivia is a considerable instance how much a fair and candid setting-forth may do to render an ordinary person attractive, and shows that for the homebred comforts and fireside tenour of life such persons after all are apt to be the best. Nor, though something commonplace in her make-up, such as the average of cultivated womanhood is always found to be, is she without bright and penetrative thoughts, whenever the occasion calls for them. Her reply to the Steward, when, by way of scorching the Clown, he "marvels that her ladyship takes delight in such a barren rascal," gives the true texture of her mind and moral frame: "O, you are sick of self-love, Malvolio, and taste with a distempered appetite. To be generous, guiltless, and of free disposition, is to take those things for bird-bolts that you deem cannon-bullets. There is no slander in an allowed Fool, though he do nothing but rail; nor no railing in a known discreet man, though he do nothing but reprove." Practical wisdom enough to make the course of any household run smooth! The instincts of a happy, placid temper have taught Olivia that there is as little of Christian virtue as of natural benignity in stinging away the spirit of kindness with a tongue of acid and acrimonious pietism. Her firm and healthy pulse beats in sympathy with the sportiveness in which the proper decorum of her station may not permit her to bear an active part. And she is too considerate, withal, not to look with indulgence on the pleasantries that are partly meant to divert her thoughts, and air off a too vivid remembrance of her recent sorrows. Besides, she has gathered, even under the discipline of her own afflictions, that as, on the one hand, "what Nature makes us mourn she bids us heal," so, on the other, the free hilarities of wit and humour, even though there be something of nonsense mixed up with them, are a part of that "bland philosophy of life" which helps to knit us up in the unions of charity and peace; that they promote cheerfulness of temper, smooth down the lines of care, sweeten away the asperities of the mind, make the eye sparkling and lustrous; and, in short, do much of the very best stitching in the embroidered web of friendship and fair society. So that she finds abundant motive in reason, with no impediment in religion, to refrain from spoiling the merry passages of her friends and servants by looking black or sour upon them.

Olivia is manifestly somewhat inclined to have her own way. But then it must also be acknowledged that her way is pretty apt to be right. This wilfulness, or something that borders upon it, is shown alike in her impracticability to the Duke's solicitations, and in her pertinacity in soliciting his messenger. And it were well worth the while to know, if we could, how one so perverse in certain spots can manage notwithstanding to be so agreeable as a whole. Then too, if it seems rather naughty in her that she does not give the Duke a better chance to try his power upon her, she gets pretty well paid in falling a victim to the eloquence which her obstinacy stirs up. Nor is it altogether certain whether her conduct springs from a pride that will not listen where her fancy is not taken, or from an unambitious modesty that prefers not to "match above her degree." Her "beauty truly blent, whose red and white Nature's own sweet and cunning hand laid on," saves the credit of the fancy-smitten Duke in such an urgency of suit as might else breed some question of his manliness; while her winning infirmity, as expressed in the tender violence with which she hastens on "a contract and eternal bond of love" with the astonished and bewildered Sebastian, "that her most jealous and too doubtful soul may live at peace," shows how well the sternness of the brain may be tempered into amiability by the meekness of womanhood.

Manifold indeed are the attractions which the Poet has shed upon his heroes and heroines; yet perhaps the learned spirit of the man is more wisely apparent in the home-keeping virtues and unobtrusive beauty of his average characters. And surely the contemplation of Olivia may well suggest the question, whether the former be not sometimes too admirable to be so instructive as those whose graces walk more in the light of common day. At all events, the latter may best admonish us,

> "How Verse may build a princely throne
> On humble truth."

Similar thoughts might aptly enough be suggested by the Duke, who, without any very splendid or striking qualities, manages somehow to be a highly agreeable and interesting person. His character is merely that of an accomplished gentleman, enraptured at the touch of music, and the sport of thick-thronging fancies. It is plain that Olivia has only enchanted his imagination, not won his heart; though he is not himself aware that such is the case. This fancy-sickness — for it appears to be nothing else — naturally renders him somewhat capricious and fantastical, "unstaid and skittish in his motions"; and, but for the exquisite poetry which it inspires him to utter, would rather excite our mirth than enlist our sympathy. To use an illustration from another play, Olivia is not so much his Juliet as his Rosaline; and perhaps a secret persuasion to that effect is the real cause of her rejecting his suit. Accordingly, when he sees her placed beyond his hope, he has no more trouble about her; but turns, and builds a true affection where, during the preoccupancy of his imagination, so many sweet and tender appeals have been made to his heart.

In Shakespeare's delineations as in nature, we may commonly note that love, in proportion as it is deep and genuine, is also inward and reserved. To be voluble, to be fond of spreading itself in discourse, or of airing itself in the fineries of speech, seems indeed quite against the instinct of that passion; and its best eloquence is when it ties up the tongue, and *steals* out in other modes of expression, the flushing of the cheeks and the mute devotion of the eyes. In its purest forms, it is apt to be a secret even unto itself, the subjects of it knowing indeed that something ails them, but not knowing exactly what. So that the most effective love-making is involuntary and unconscious. And I suspect that, as a general thing, if the true lover's passion be not returned before it is spoken, it stands little chance of being returned at all.

Now, in Orsino's case, the passion, or whatever else it may be, is too much without to be thoroughly sound within. Like Malvolio's virtue, it is too glass-gazing, too much enamoured of its own image, and renders him too apprehensive that it will be the death of him, if disappointed of its object. Accordingly he talks too much about it, and his talking about it is too ingenious withal; it makes his tongue run glib and fine with the most charming divisions of poetic imagery and sentiment; all which shrewdly infers that he lacks the genuine thing, and has mistaken something else for it. Yet, when we hear him dropping such riches as this, —

> "O, when mine eyes did see Olivia first,
> Methought she purg'd the air of pestilence!"

and this, —

> "She that hath a heart of that fine frame
> To pay this debt of love but to a brother,
> How will she love when the rich golden shaft
> Hath kill'd the flock of all affections else
> That live in her!" —

we can hardly help wishing that such were indeed the true vernacular of that passion. But it is not so, and on the whole it is much better than so: for love, that which is rightly so called, uses a diviner language even than that; and this it does when, taking the form of religion, it sweetly and silently embodies itself in deeds. And this is the love that Southey had in mind when he wrote, —

> "They sin who tell us love can die."

In Viola, divers things that were else not a little scattered are thoroughly composed; her character being the unifying power that draws all the parts into true dramatic consistency. Love-taught herself, it was for her to teach both Orsino and Olivia how to love: indeed she plays into all the other parts, causing them to embrace and cohere within the compass of her circulation. And yet, like some subtile agency, working most where we perceive it least, she does all this without rendering herself a special prominence in the play.

It is observable that the Poet has left it uncertain whether Viola was in love with the Duke before assuming her disguise, or whether her heart was won afterwards by reading "the book even of his secret soul" while wooing another. Nor does it much matter whether her passion were the motive or the consequence of her disguise, since in either case such a man as Olivia describes him to be might well find his way to tougher hearts than Viola's. But her love has none of the skittishness and unrest which mark the Duke's passion for Olivia: complicated out of all the elements of her being, it is strong without violence; never mars the innate modesty of her character; is deep as life, tender as infancy, pure, peaceful, and unchangeable as truth.

Mrs. Jameson — who, with the best right to know what belongs to woman, unites a rare talent for taking others along with her, and letting them see the choice things which her apprehensive eye discerns, and who, in respect of Shakespeare's heroines, has left little for others to do but quote her words — remarks that "in Viola a sweet consciousness of her feminine nature is for ever breaking through her masquerade: she plays her part well, but never forgets, nor allows us to forget, that she is playing a part." And, sure enough, every thing about her save her dress "is semblative a woman's part": she has none of the assumption of a pert, saucy, waggish manhood, which so delights us in Rosalind in *As You Like It;* but she has that which, if not better in itself, is more becoming in her, — "the inward and spiritual grace of modesty" pervading all she does and says. Even in her railleries with the comic characters there is all the while an instinctive drawing-back of female delicacy, touching our sympathies, and causing us to feel most deeply what she is, when those with whom she is playing least suspect her to be other than she seems. And the same is true concerning her passion, of which she never so speaks as to compromise in the least the delicacies and proprieties of her sex; yet she lets fall many things from which the Duke easily gathers the drift and quality of her feelings directly he learns what she is. But the great charm of her character lies in a moral rectitude so perfect and so pure as to be a secret unto itself; a clear, serene composure of truth, mingling so freely and smoothly with the issues of life, that while, and perhaps even because she is herself unconscious of it, she is never once tempted to abuse or to shirk her trust, though it be to play the attorney in a cause that makes so much against herself. In this respect she presents an instructive contrast to Malvolio, who has much virtue indeed, yet not so much but that the counter-pullings have rendered him intensely conscious of it, and so drawn him into the vice, at once hateful and ridiculous, of moral pride. The virtue that fosters conceit and censoriousness is like a dyspeptic stomach, the owner of which is made all too sensible of it by the conversion of his food to wind, — a wind that puffs him up. On the other hand, a virtue that breathes so freely as not to be aware of its breathing is the right moral analogue of a thoroughly eupeptic state; as "the healthy know not of their health, but only the sick."

Sundry critics have censured, some of them pretty sharply, the improbability involved in the circumstance of Viola and Sebastian resembling each other so closely as to be mistaken the one for the other. Even so just and liberal a critic as Hallam has stumbled at this circumstance, so much so as quite to disconcert his judgment of the play. The improbability is indeed palpable enough; yet I have to confess that it has never troubled me, any more than certain things not less improbable in *As You Like It*. But even if it had, still I should not hold it any just ground for faulting the Poet, inasmuch as the circumstance was an accepted article in the literary faith of his time. But indeed this censure proceeds from that old heresy which supposes the proper effect of a work of art to depend on the imagined reality of the matter presented; that is, which substitutes the delusions of insanity for the half-voluntary illusions of a rational and refining pleasure.

Of Sebastian himself the less need be said, forasmuch as the leading traits of his character, in my conception of it, have been substantially evolved in what I have said of his sister. For the two are really as much alike in the inward texture of their souls as in their visible persons; at least their mutual resemblance in the former respect is as close as were compatible with proper manliness in the one, and proper womanliness in the other. Personal bravery, for example, is as characteristic of him as modesty is of her. In simplicity, in gentleness, in rectitude, in delicacy of mind, and in all the particulars of what may be termed complexional harmony and healthiness of nature, — in these they are as much twins as in birth and feature. Therewithal they are both alike free from any notes of a pampered self-consciousness. Yet in all these points a nice discrimination of the masculine and feminine proprieties is everywhere maintained. In a word, there is no confusion of sex in the delineation of them: as like as they are, without and within, the man and the woman are nevertheless perfectly differentiated in all the essential attributes of each.

The conditions of the plot did not require nor even permit Sebastian to be often or much in sight. We have indeed but little from him, but that little is intensely charged with significance; in fact, I hardly know of another instance in Shakespeare where so much of character is accomplished in so few words. The scene where he is first met with consists merely of a brief dialogue between him and Antonio, the man who a little before has recovered him from the perils of shipwreck. He there has neither time nor heart for any thing but gratitude to his deliverer, and sorrow at the supposed death of his sister: yet his expression of these is so ordered as to infer all the parts of a thorough gentleman; the efficacies of a generous nature, of good breeding, of liberal culture, and of high principle, all concurring in one result, and thus filling up the right idea of politeness as "benevolence guided by intelligence."

The society delineated in this play is singularly varied and composite; the names of the persons being a mixture of Spanish, Italian, and English. Though the scene is laid in Illyria, the period of the action is undefined, and the manners and costumes are left in the freedom of whatever time we may choose antecedent to that of the composition, provided we do not exceed the proper limits of imaginative reason.

This variety in the grouping of the persons, whether so intended or not, very well accords with the spirit in which, or the occasion for which, the title indicates the play to have been written. Twelfth Day, anciently so called as being the twelfth after Christmas, is the day whereon the Church has always kept the feast of "The Epiphany, or the Manifestation of Christ to the Gentiles." So that, in preparing a Twelfth-Night entertainment, the idea of fitness might aptly suggest, that national lines and distinctions should be lost in the paramount ties of a common Religion; and that people the most diverse in kindred and tongue should draw together in the sentiment of "one Lord, one Faith, one Baptism"; their social mirth thus relishing of universal Brotherhood.

The general scope and plan of *Twelfth Night, as a work of art*, is hinted in its second title; all the comic elements being, as it were, thrown out simultaneously, and held in a sort of equipoise; so that the readers are left to fix the preponderance where it best suits their several bent or state of mind, and each, within certain limits and conditions, may take the work in *what sense he will.* For, where no special prominence is given to any one thing, there is the wider scope for individual aptitude or preference, and the greater freedom for each to select for virtual prominence such parts as will best knit in with what is uppermost in his thoughts.

The significance of the title is further traceable in a peculiar spontaneousness running through the play. Replete as it is with humours and oddities, they all seem to spring up of their own accord; the comic characters being free alike from disguises and pretensions, and seeking merely to let off their inward redundancy; caring nothing at all whether everybody or nobody sees them, so they may have their whim out, and giving utterance to folly and nonsense simply because they cannot help it. Thus their very deformities have a certain grace, since they are genuine and of Nature's planting: absurdity and whimsicality are indigenous to the soil, and shoot up in free, happy luxuriance, from the life that is in them. And by thus setting the characters out in their happiest aspects, the Poet contrives to make them simply ludicrous and diverting, instead of putting upon them the constructions of wit or spleen, and thereby making them ridiculous or contemptible. Hence it is that we so readily enter into a sort of fellowship with them; their foibles and follies being shown up in such a spirit of good-humour, that the subjects themselves would rather join with us in laughing than be angered or hurt at the exhibition. Moreover the high and the low are here seen moving in free and familiar intercourse, without any apparent consciousness of their respective ranks: the humours and comicalities of the play keep running and frisking in among the serious parts, to their mutual advantage; the connection between them being of a kind to be felt, not described.

Thus the piece overflows with the genial, free-and-easy spirit of a merry Twelfth Night. Chance, caprice, and intrigue, it is true, are brought together in about equal portions; and their meeting and crossing and mutual tripping cause a deal of perplexity and confusion, defeating the hopes of some, suspending those of others: yet here, as is often the case in actual life, from this conflict of opposites order and happiness spring up as the final result: if what we call accident thwart one cherished purpose, it draws on something better, blighting a full-blown expectation now, to help the blossoming of a nobler one hereafter: and it so happens in the end that all the persons but two either have *what they will*, or else grow willing to have what comes to their hands.

Such, I believe, as nearly as I know how to deliver it, is the impression I hold of this charming play; an impression that has survived, rather say, has kept growing deeper and deeper through many years of study, and after many, many an hour spent in quiet communion with its scenes and characters. In no one of his dramas, to my sense, does the Poet appear to have been in a healthier or happier frame of mind, more free from the fascination of the darker problems of humanity, more at peace with himself and all the world, or with Nature playing more kindly and genially at his heart, and from thence diffusing her benedictions through his whole establishment. So that, judging from this transpiration of his inner poetic life, I should conclude him to have had abundant cause for saying, —

> "Eternal blessings on the Muse,
> And her divine employment; —
> The blameless Muse who trains her sons
> For hope and calm enjoyment."

ALL'S WELL THAT ENDS WELL.

All's Well that Ends Well was first published in the folio of 1623, and is among the worst-printed plays in that volume. In many places the text, as there given, is in a most unsatisfactory state; and in not a few I fear it must be pronounced incurably at fault. A vast deal of study and labour has been spent in trying to rectify the numerous errors; nearly all the editors and commentators, from Rowe downwards, have strained their faculties upon the work: many instances of corruption have indeed yielded to critical ingenuity and perseverance, and it is to be hoped that still others may; but yet there are several passages which give little hope of success, and seem indeed too hard for any efforts of corrective sagacity and skill. This is not the place for citing examples of textual difficulty: so I must be content with referring to Dyce's elaborate annotation on the play.

Why the original printing of this play should thus have been exceptionally bad, is a matter about which we can only speculate; and as in such cases speculation can hardly lead to any firm result, probably our best way is to note the textual corruption as a fact, and there let it rest. Still it may be worth the while to observe on this head, that in respect of plot and action the piece is of a somewhat forbidding, not to say repulsive nature; and though it abounds in wisdom, and is not wanting in poetry, and has withal much choice delineation of character, and contains scenes which stream down with the Poet's raciest English, yet it is not among the plays which readers are often drawn to by mere recollections of delight: one does not take to it heartily, and can hardly admire it without something of effort: even when it wins our approval, it seems to do so rather through our sense of right than through our sense of pleasure: in short, I have to confess that the perusal is more apt to inspire an apologetic than an enthusiastic tone of mind. It may be a mere fancy of mine; but I have often thought that the extreme badness of the printing may have been partly owing to this cause; that the Poet may have left the manuscript in a more unfinished and illegible state, from a sense of something ungenial and unattractive in the subject-matter and action of the play.

No direct and certain contemporary notice of *All's Well that Ends Well* has come down to us. But the often-quoted list of Shakespeare's plays set forth by Francis Meres in his *Palladis Tamia*, 1598, includes a play called *Love's Labour's Won*, — a title nowhere else given to any of the Poet's pieces. Dr. Farmer, in his *Essay on the Learning of Shakespeare*, 1767, first gave out the conjecture, that the two titles belonged to one and the same play; and this opinion has since been concurred or acquiesced in by so many competent critics, that it might well be allowed to pass without further argument. There is no other of the Poet's dramas to which that title applies so well, while, on the other hand, it certainly fits this play quite as well as the one it now bears. The whole play is emphatically *love's labour:* its main interest throughout turns on the unwearied and finally-successful struggles of affection against the most stubborn and disheartening obstacles. It may indeed be urged that the play entitled *Love's Labour's Won* has been lost; but this, considering what esteem the Poet's works were held in, both in his time and ever since, is so very improbable as to be hardly worth dwelling upon. There was far more likelihood that other men's dross would be fathered upon him than that any of his gold would be lost. And, in fact, contemporary publishers were so eager to make profit of his reputation, that they forged his name to various plays which most certainly had no touch of his hand.

The Rev. Joseph Hunter has spent a deal of learning and ingenuity in trying to make out that the play referred to by Meres as *Love's Labour's Won* was *The Tempest.* Among Shakespeare's dramas he could hardly have pitched upon a more unfit subject for such a title. There is no *love's labour* in *The Tempest.* For, though a lover does indeed there labour awhile in piling logs, this is nowise from love, but simply because he cannot help himself. Nor does he thereby *win* the lady, for she was won before, — "at the first sight they have chang'd eyes"; — and the labour was imposed for the testing of his love, not for the gaining of its object; and was all the while refreshed with the "sweet thoughts" that in heart she was already his; while in truth the father was overjoyed at the "fair encounter of two most rare affections," and was quite as intent on the match as the lovers were themselves. In short, there is no external evidence whatever in favour of Mr. Hunter's notion, while the internal evidence makes utterly against it.

There is, then, no reasonable doubt that *All's Well that*

Ends Well was originally written before 1598. For myself, I have no doubt that the first writing was several years before that date; as early at least as 1592 or 1593. Coleridge, in his *Literary Remains*, holds the play to have been "originally intended as the counterpart of *Love's Labour's Lost*"; and a comparison of the two naturally leads to that conclusion without any help from the title. This inward relation of the plays strongly infers them both to have been written about the same time, or in pretty near succession. Now *Love's Labour's Lost* was published in 1598, and in the title-page is said to have been "newly corrected and augmented," which fairly supposes the first writing of that play also to have been several years before, since some considerable time would naturally pass before the Poet saw cause for revising his workmanship. And the diversities of style in that play fully concur herewith in arguing a considerable interval between the original writing and the revisal.

It is abundantly certain, from internal evidence, that the play now in hand also underwent revisal, and this too after a much longer interval than in the case of *Love's Labour's Lost*. Here the diversities of style are much more strongly marked than in that play. Accordingly it was Coleridge's decided opinion, first given out in his lectures in 1813, and again in 1818, though not found in his *Literary Remains*, that "*All's Well that Ends Well* was written at two different and rather distant periods of the Poet's life." This we learn from Mr. Collier, who heard those lectures, and who adds that Coleridge "pointed out very clearly two distinct styles, not only of thought, but of expression." The same judgment has since been enforced by Tieck and other able critics; and the grounds of it are so manifest in the play itself, that no observant reader will be apt to question it. Verplanck tells us he had formed the same opinion before he learned through Mr. Collier what Coleridge thought on the subject; and his judgment of the matter is given with characteristic felicity as follows: "The contrast of two different modes of thought and manners of expression, here mixed in the same piece, must be evident to all who have made the shades and gradations of Shakespeare's varying and progressive taste and mind at all a subject of study." *

I have elsewhere observed at some length † on the Poet's diversities of style, marking them off into three periods, severally distinguished as earlier, middle, and later styles. Outside of the play itself, we have in this case no help towards determining at what time the revisal was made, or how long a period intervened between this and the original writing. To my taste, the better parts of the workmanship relish strongly of the Poet's later style, — perhaps I should say quite as strongly as the poorer parts do of his earlier. This would bring the revisal down to as late a time as 1603 or 1604: which date accords, not only with my own sense of the matter, but with the much better judgment of the critics I have quoted. I place the finished *Hamlet* at or near the close of the Poet's middle period; and I am tolerably clear that in this play he discovers a mind somewhat more advanced in concentrated fulness, and a hand somewhat more practised in sinewy sternness, than in the finished *Hamlet*. I will quote two passages by way of illustrating the Poet's different styles as seen in this play.

* The point is further amplified and illustrated by the same critic in a passage equally happy, as follows : "Much of the graver dialogue, especially in the first two Acts, reminds the reader, in taste of composition, in rhythm, and in a certain quaintness of expression, of *The Two Gentlemen of Verona*. The comic part is spirited and laugh-provoking, yet it consists wholly in the exposure of a braggart coxcomb, — one of the most familiar comic personages of the stage, and quite within the scope of a boyish artist's knowledge of life and power of satirical delineation. On the other hand, there breaks forth everywhere, and in many scenes entirely predominates, a grave moral thoughtfulness, expressed in a solemn, reflective, and sometimes in a sententious brevity of phrase and harshness of rhythm, which seem to me to stamp many passages as belonging to the epoch of *Measure for Measure*, or of *King Lear*. We miss, too, the gay and fanciful imagery which shows itself continually, alike amidst the passion and the moralizing of the previous comedies."

† Page 190 of this volume.

The first is from the dialogue of Helena and the King, in Act ii., scene 1, where she persuades him to make trial of her remedy:

"The great'st Grace lending grace,
Ere twice the horses of the Sun shall bring
Their fiery torcher his diurnal ring;
Ere twice in murk and occidental damp
Moist Hesperus hath quench'd his sleepy lamp;
Or four-and-twenty times the pilot's glass
Hath told the thievish minutes how they pass;
What is infirm from your sound parts shall fly,
Health shall live free, and sickness freely die."

Here we have the special traits of Shakespeare's youthful style, — an air of artifice and studied finery, a certain self-conscious elaborateness and imitative rivalry, — which totally disappear in, for instance, the blessing the Countess gives her son as he is leaving for the Court:

"Be thou blest, Bertram! and succeed thy father
In manners, as in shape! thy blood and virtue
Contend for empire in thee, and thy goodness
Share with thy birthright! Love all, trust a few,
Do wrong to none; be able for thine enemy
Rather in power than use, and keep thy friend
Under thy own life's key; be check'd for silence,
But never tax'd for speech. What Heaven more will,
That thee may furnish, and my prayers pluck down,
Fall on thy head!"

I the rather quote this latter, because of its marked resemblance to the advice Polonius gives his son in *Hamlet.* Mr. White justly observes that "either the latter is an expansion of the former, or the former a reminiscence of the latter"; and I fully concur with him that the second part of the alternative is the more probable. It is hardly needful to add that the passage here quoted breathes a higher and purer moral tone than the resembling one in *Hamlet;* but this I take to be merely because the venerable Countess is a higher and purer source than the old politician. For a broader and bulkier illustration of the point in hand, the student probably cannot do better than by comparing in full the dialogue from which the first of the forecited passages is taken with the whole of the second scene in Act i. These seem to me at least as apt and telling examples as any, of the Poet's rawest and ripest styles so strangely mixed in this play; and the difference is here so clearly pronounced, that one must be dull indeed not to perceive it.

As regards the notion of Mr. Hunter before referred to, it is indeed true, as he argues, that the play twice bespeaks its present title; but both instances occur in just those parts which relish most of the Poet's later style. And the line in the epilogue, — "*All is well ended*, if this suit *be won*," — may be fairly understood as intimating some connection between the two titles which the play is supposed to have borne.

The only known source from which the Poet could have borrowed any part of this play is a story in Boccaccio, entitled *Giletta di Nerbona.* In 1566 William Paynter published an English version of this tale in his *Palace of Pleasure.* Here it was, no doubt, that Shakespeare got his borrowed matter; and the following outline will show the nature and extent of his obligations.

Isnardo, Count of Rousillon, being sickly, kept in his house a physician named Gerardo of Nerbona. The Count had a son named Beltramo, and the physician a daughter named Giletta, who were brought up together. The Count dying, his son was left in the care of the King and sent to Paris. The physician also dying some while after, his daughter, who had loved the young Count so long that she knew not when her love began, sought occasion of going to Paris, that she might see him; but, being diligently looked to by her kinsfolk, because she was rich and had many suitors, she could not see her way clear. Now the King had a swelling on his breast, which through ill treatment was grown to a fistula; and, having tried all the best physicians and being only rendered worse by their efforts, he resolved to take no further counsel or help. Giletta, hearing of this, was very glad, as it suggested an apt reason for visiting Paris, and offered a chance of compassing her secret and cherished wish. Arming herself with such knowledge in the healing art as she had gathered from her father, she rode to Paris and repaired to the King, praying him to show her his disease. He consenting, as soon as she saw it she told him that, if he pleased, she would within eight days make him whole. He asked how it was possible for her, being a young woman, to do that which the best physicians in the world could not; and, thanking her for her good-will, said he was resolved to try no more remedies. She begged him not to despise her knowledge because she was a young woman, assuring him that she ministered physic by the help of God, and with the cunning of Master Gerardo of Nerbona, who was her father. The King, hearing this, and thinking that peradventure she was sent of God, asked what might follow, if she caused him to break his resolution, and did not heal him. She said, "Let me be kept in what guard you list, and if I do not heal you let me be burnt; but, if I do, what recompense shall I have?" He answered that, since she was a maiden, he would bestow her in marriage upon a gentleman of right good worship and estimation. To this she agreed, on condition that she might have such a husband as herself should ask, without presumption to any member of his family; which he readily granted. This done, she set about her task, and before the eight days were passed he was entirely well; whereupon he told her she deserved such a husband as herself should choose, and she declared her choice of Beltramo, saying she had loved him from her childhood. The King was very loth to grant him to her; but, because he would not break his promise, he had him called forth, and told him what had been done. The Count, thinking her stock unsuitable to his nobility, disdainfully said, "Will you, then, sir, give me a physician to wife?" The King pressing him to comply, he answered, "Sire, you may take from me all that I have, and give my person to whom you please, because I am your subject;

but I assure you I shall never be contented with that marriage." To which he replied, "Well, you shall have her, for the maiden is fair and wise, and loveth you entirely; and verily you shall lead a more joyful life with her than with a lady of a greater House"; whereupon the Count held his peace. The marriage over, the Count asked leave to go home, having settled beforehand what he would do. Knowing that the Florentines and the Senois were at war, he was no sooner on horseback than he stole off to Tuscany, meaning to side with the Florentines; by whom being honorably received and made a captain, he continued a long time in their service.

His wife, hoping by her well-doing to win his heart, returned home, where, finding all things spoiled and disordered by reason of his absence, she like a sage lady carefully put them in order, making all his people very glad of her presence and loving to her person. Having done this, she sent word thereof to the Count by two knights, adding that, if she were the cause of his forsaking home, he had but to let her know it, and she, to do him pleasure, would depart thence. Now he had a ring which he greatly loved, and kept very carefully, and never took off his finger, for a certain virtue which he knew it had. When the knights came, he said to them churlishly, "Let her do what she list; for I purpose to dwell with her when she shall have this ring on her finger, and a son of mine in her arms." The knights, after trying in vain to change his purpose, returned to the lady, and told his answer; at which she was very sorrowful, and bethought herself a good while how she might accomplish those two things. She then called together the noblest of the country, and told them what she had done to win her husband's love; that she was loth he should dwell in perpetual exile on her account; and therefore would spend the rest of her life in pilgrimages and devotion; praying them to let him know she had left, with a purpose never to return. Then, taking with her a maid and one of her kinsmen, she set out in the habit of a pilgrim, well furnished with silver and jewels, told no one whither she was going, and rested not till she came to Florence. She put up at the house of a poor widow; and the next day, seeing her husband pass by on horseback, she asked who he was. The widow told her this, and also that he was marvellously in love with a neighbour of hers, a gentlewoman who was poor, but of right honest life and report, and dwelt with her mother, a wise and honest lady. After hearing this, she was not long in deciding what to do. Going secretly to the house, and getting a private interview with the mother, she told her whole story, and how she hoped to thrive in her undertaking, if the mother and daughter would lend their aid. In recompense she proposed to give the daughter a handsome marriage portion; and the mother replied, "Madam, tell me wherein I may do you service; if it be honest, I will gladly perform it; and, that being done, do as it shall please you." So an arrangement was made, that the daughter should encourage the Count, and signify her readiness to grant his wish, provided he would first send her the ring he prized so highly, as a token of his love. Proceeding with great subtlety as she was instructed, the daughter soon got the ring; and at the time fixed for the meeting the Countess supplied her place; the result of which was, that she became the mother of two fine boys, and so was prepared to claim her dues as a wife upon the seemingly-impossible terms which the Count himself had proposed.

Meanwhile her husband, hearing of her departure, had returned to his country. In due time the Countess also took her journey homeward, and arrived at Montpellier, where, hearing that the Count was about to have a great party at his house, she determined to go thither in her pilgrim's weeds. Just as they were on the point of sitting down to the table, she came to the place where her husband was, and fell at his feet weeping, and said, "My lord, I am thy poor unfortunate wife, who, that thou mightest return and dwell in thy house, have been a great while begging about the world. Therefore I now beseech thee to observe the conditions which the two knights that I sent to thee did command me to do; for behold, here in my arms, not only one son of thine, but twain, and likewise the ring: it is now time, if thou keep promise, that I should be received as thy wife." The Count knew the ring, and the children also, they were so like him, and desired her to rehearse in order how all these things came about. When she had told her story, he knew it to be true; and, perceiving her constant mind and good wit, and the two fair young boys, to keep his promise, and to please his people, and the ladies that made suit to him, he caused her to rise up, and embraced and kissed her, and from that day forth loved and honoured her as his wife.

From this sketch it will be seen that the Poet anglicized Beltramo into Bertram, changed Giletta to Helena, and closely followed Boccaccio in the main features of the plot so far as regards these persons and the widow and her daughter. Beyond this, the novel yields no hints towards the play, while the latter has several judicious departures from the matter of the former. Giletta is rich, and has a fine establishment of her own; which so far reduces the social inequality between her and the Count: Helena is poor and dependent, so that she has nothing to stand upon but her nobility of nature and merit. Beltramo, again, has no thought of going to Florence till after his compelled marriage; so that his going to the war is not from any free stirring of virtue in him, but purely to escape the presence of a wife that has been forced upon him. With Bertram, the unwelcome marriage comes in only as an additional spur to the execution of a purpose already formed. Before Helena makes her appearance at the Court, his spirit is in revolt against the command which would make him

> "stay here the forehorse to a smock,
> Creaking his shoes on the plain masonry,
> Till honour is bought up, and no sword worn
> But one to dance with."

He therefore resolves to "steal away" to the war along with other brave and enterprising spirits; and we have some lords of the Court ministering fuel to this noble fire burning within him. These stirrings of native gallantry, this brave thirst of honourable distinction, go far to redeem him from the rank dishonours of his conduct, as showing that he is not without some strong and noble elements of manhood. Here we have indeed no little just ground of respect; and that his purpose is but quickened into act by the thought of finding a refuge in such manly work from the thraldom of a hated marriage, operates as further argument in the same behalf. And this purpose, springing as it does from the free promptings of his nature, has the further merit, that it involves a deliberate braving of the King's anger; thus showing that he will even peril his head rather than leave what is best in him to "fust unused." All which plainly infers that he has at least the right virtues of a soldier. And the promise thus held out from the start is made good in the after-performance. He proves a gallant, a capable, a successful warrior, and returns with well-won laurels. In all these points, the play is a manifest improvement on the tale. And I suspect the Poet took care to endow his hero with this streak of nobility, because he felt that there was some danger lest Helena's pursuit of Bertram should rather have the effect of lowering her than of elevating him in our thoughts.

But the crowning innovation upon the matter of the tale lies in the characters of Lafeu, the Countess, the Clown, and Parolles, and in the comic proceedings; all which, so far as is known, are entirely of the Poet's invention. And it is quite remarkable what an original cast is given to his development of the borrowed characters by the presence of these; and how in the light of their mutual interaction the conduct of all becomes, not indeed right or just, but consistent and clear. Helena's native force and rectitude of mind are approved from the first in her just appreciation of Parolles; and her nobility of soul and beauty of character are reflected all along in the honest sagacity of Lafeu and the wise motherly affection of the Countess, who never see or think of her but to turn her advocates and wax eloquent in her behalf. The thoughtful and benevolent King also, on becoming acquainted with her, is even more taken with her moral and intellectual beauty than with her service in restoring him to health. The Countess regards her as "a maid too virtuous for the contempt of empire"; and, on hearing Bertram's "dreadful sentence" against her, she is prompt to declare, "He was my son, but I do wash his name out of my blood, and thou art all my child"; and it is her very heart that speaks, —

"What angel shall
Bless this unworthy husband? he cannot thrive,
Unless her prayers, which Heaven delights to hear,
And loves to grant, reprieve him from the wrath
Of greatest justice."

To the King she is "all that is virtuous"; "young, wise, fair"; "virtue and she is her own dower." Lafeu remembers her at the close as "a sweet creature," and as one

"Whose beauty did astonish the survey
Of richest eyes; whose words all ears took captive;
Whose dear perfection hearts that scorn'd to serve
Humbly call'd mistress."

Thus she walks right into all hearts that have any doors for the entrance of virtue and loveliness. And her modest, self-sacrificing worth is brought home to our feelings by the impression she makes on the good; while in turn our sense of their goodness is proportionably heightened by their noble sensibility to hers.

Parolles, again, is puffed up into a more consequential whiffet than ever, by being taken into the confidence of a haughty young nobleman; while, on the other side, the stultifying effects of Bertram's pride are seen in that it renders him the easy dupe of a most base and bungling counterfeit of manhood. It was natural and right, that such a shallow, paltry word-gun should ply him with impudent flatteries, and thereby gain an ascendency over him, and finally draw him into the crimes and the shames that were to whip down his pride; and it was equally natural that his scorn of Helena should begin to relax, when he was brought to see what a pitiful rascal, by playing upon that pride, had been making a fool of him. He must first be mortified, before he can be purified. The springs of moral health within him have been overspread by a foul disease; and the proper medicine is such an exposure of the latter as shall cause him to feel that he is himself a most fit object of the scorn which he has been so forward to bestow. Accordingly the embossing and untrussing of his favourite is the starting of his amendment: he begins to distrust the counsels of his cherished passion, when he can no longer hide from himself into what a vile misplacing of trust they have betrayed him. Herein, also, we have a full justification, both moral and dramatic, of the game so mercilessly practised on Parolles: it is avowedly undertaken with a view to rescue Bertram, whose friends know full well that nothing can be done for his good, till the fascination of that crawling reptile is broken.

Finally, Helena's just discernment of character, as shown in the case of Parolles, pleads an arrest of judgment in behalf of Bertram. And the fact that with all her love for him she is not blind to his faults, is a sort of pledge that she sees through them into a worth which they hide from others. For, indeed, she has known him in his childhood, before his heart got pride-bound with conceit of rank and titles; and therefore may well have a reasonable faith, that beneath the follies and vices which have overcrusted his character, there is still an undercurrent of sense and virtue, a wisdom of nature, not dead but asleep, whereby he may yet be recovered. So that, in effect, we are not unwilling to see him through her eyes, and, in the strength of her well-approved wisdom, to take it upon trust that he has good qualities which we are unable of ourselves to discover.

Thus the several parts are drawn into each other, and thereby made to evolve a manifold rich significance; insomuch that the characters of Helena and Bertram, as Shakespeare conceived them, cannot be rightly understood apart from the others with which they are dramatically associated.

It is indeed curious to observe how much care the Poet takes that his heroine may come safe and sweet through the perils of her course. For instance, at the very outset, when she first learns of the King's disease, in the dialogue about her father, the Countess says in her hearing, "Would, for the King's sake, he were living! I think it would be the death of the King's disease"; and Lafeu replies, "The King very lately spoke of him admiringly and mourningly." This serves as a pregnant hint to her for what she afterwards undertakes. She now remembers the special instructions of her father touching that disease; and the hint combining with her treasured science, her loyalty, and affection, works her into the strong confidence of being able to help the King. Thus the main point of her action is put into her mind incidentally by the speech of others. And she goes to Paris, with the full approval and blessing of her foster-mother, *mainly* with the view of securing to one whom she highly reveres the benefit of her father's skill. It is true, a still deeper and dearer hope underlies and supports her action; which hope however springs and grows, not because she foresees at all how things are to turn, but merely from a pious trust, which is in her case both natural and just, that her father's "good receipt" will somehow, "for her legacy, be sanctified by the luckiest stars in heaven."

The same delicate care for her honour, as if this were indeed sacred and precious in the Poet's regard, is shown at various other points. It is very note-worthy how, all along, she shapes her action from step to step, not by any long-headed planning, but merely as events suggest and invite her onward. Helena is indeed brave, wise, prudent, sagacious, quick and clear of perception, swift and steadfast in resolution, prompt, patient, and persevering in action; but there is nothing of a crafty or designing mind in what she does. She displays no special forecast, no subtle or far-sighted scheming; though quick and apt at seizing and using opportunities, she does not make or even seek them. So it is in the strange proceedings at Florence, whereby she manages to fulfil the hard conditions imposed by her husband. Here, as elsewhere, she has her fine penetrative faculties all wide-awake, but there is no contriving or forcing of occasions: when she sees a way open before her, she strikes into it promptly, and pursues it with quiet yet energetic constancy; and whatever apt occasions emerge to her view, she throws herself into them at once, and, with a sort of divine tact, turns them to the best possible account in furtherance of her cherished hope. In this way the Poet manages to bring her character off clean and fragrant in our thoughts, by making us feel that in whatever blame might else attach to her acts, the circumstances only are responsible, while to her belongs the credit of using those circumstances purely, wisely, and well.

It is further observable, and a very material point too, that Helena seems to think the better of Bertram for his behaviour towards her: she takes it as evidence at least of honesty in him, and of a certain downrightness of character, that shrinks from a life of appearances, and knows not how to affect what he does not feel. So far from blaming his indifference, she rather blames herself as having brought him into a false position. She loves him simply because she cannot help it; she wants him to love her for the same reason; and the point she aims at is so to act and be and appear, that he cannot help loving her. She knows right well that the choice must be mutual, else marriage is rather a sacrilege than a sacrament; and the great question is, how she may win him to reciprocate her choice: nothing less than this will suffice her; and she justly takes it as her part to *inspire* him with the feeling, understanding perfectly that neither talk nor force can be of any use to that end. Even a love that springs from a sense of duty is not what she wants: her own love did not spring from that source. So she "would not have him till she does deserve him," yet knows not how that desert should ever be: still she cannot put off the faith that love will sooner or later triumph, if worthily shown by deeds. He is much noted as a fine instance of manly beauty: all are taken with his handsome person. It is not, probably ought not to be, in womanhood, to be proof against such attractions. In the sweetness of their youthful intercourse, this has silently got the mastery of her thoughts, and penetrated her being through and through:

> "'Twas pretty, though a plague,
> To see him every hour; to sit and draw
> His archèd brows, his hawking eye, his curls,
> In our heart's table."

And now she must needs strive with all her might, by loving ways, by kind acts, by self-sacrificing works, to catch his heart, as he has caught hers. Then too a holy instinct of womanhood teaches her that a man must be hard indeed, to resist the wedded mother of his children, and most of all, to keep his heart untouched by the power of a wife when burdened with a mother's precious wealth. Therewithal she rightly apprehends the danger Bertram is in from the wordy, cozening squirt, the bedizened, scoundrelly dandiprat, who has so beguiled his youth and ignorance. She must bless and sweeten him out of that contagion into the religion of home; and she feels that nothing but an honourable love of herself can save him. This she aims at, and finally accomplishes.

Coleridge incidentally speaks of Helena as "Shakespeare's loveliest character." And Mrs. Jameson, from whose judgment I shall take no appeal, sets her down as exemplifying that union of strength and tenderness which Foster, in one of his *Essays*, describes as being "the utmost and rarest endowment of humanity"; — a character, she adds, "almost as hard to delineate in fiction as to find in real life." Without either questioning or subscribing these statements, I have to confess that, for depth, sweetness, energy, and solidity of character, all drawn into one, Helena is not surpassed by more than two or three of Shakespeare's heroines. Her great strength of mind is well shown in that, absorbed as she is in the passion that shapes her life, hardly any of the Poet's characters, after Hamlet, deals more in propositions of general truth, as distinguished from the utterances of individual sentiment and emotion. We should suppose that all her thoughts, being struck out in such a glowing heat, would so cleave to the circumstances as to have little force apart from them; yet much that she says holds as good in a general application as in her own particular. Which rightly infers that she sees things in their principles; that is, her thoughts touch the pith of whatever matter she takes in hand; while at the same time broad axiomatic notes of discourse drop from her with an ease which shows that her mind is thoroughly at home in them. For this cause, her feelings, strong as they are, never so get the upper hand as to beguile her into any self-delusion; as appears in the unbosoming of herself to the Countess, where we have the greatest reluctance of modesty yielding to a holy regard for truth. It is there manifest that she has taken a full and just measure of her situation: she frankly avows the conviction that she "loves in vain," and that she "strives against hope"; that she "lends and gives where she is sure to lose"; nevertheless she resolves to "venture the well-lost life of hers on his Grace's cure," and leave the result in other hands.

In her condition, both there and afterwards, there is much indeed to move our pity; yet her behaviour and the grounds of it are such that she never suffers any loss of our respect; one reason of which is, because we see that her sound faculties and fine feelings are keenly alive to the nature of what she undertakes. Thus she passes unharmed through the most terrible outward dishonours, firmly relying on her rectitude of purpose; and we dare not think any thing to her hurt, because she looks her danger square in the face, and nobly feels secure in that apparelling of strength. Here, truly, we have something very like the sublimity of moral courage. And this precious, peerless jewel in a setting of the most tender, delicate, sensitive womanhood! It is a clear triumph of the inward and essential over the outward and accidental; her character being radiant of a moral and spiritual grace which the lowest and ugliest situation cannot obscure.

There certainly needs no scruple that the delineation is one of extraordinary power: perhaps, indeed, it may stand as Shakespeare's masterpiece in the conquest of inherent difficulties. And it is observable that here, for once, he does not carry his point without evident tokens of exertion. He does not outwrestle the resistance of the matter without letting us see that he is wrestling Of course the hardness of the task was to represent the heroine as doing what were scarce pardonable in another; yet as acting on such grounds, from such motives, and to such issues, that the undertaking not only is, but is felt to be, commendable in her. Lamb puts it just right: "With such exquisite address is the dangerous subject handled, that Helena's forwardness loses her no honour: delicacy dispenses with its laws in her favour; and nature, in her single case, seems content to suffer a sweet violation." And the Poet seems to have felt that something like a mysterious, supernatural impulse, together with all the reverence and authority of the old Countess, and also the concurring voice of all the wise and good about her in hearty approval of her course and eloquent admiration of her virtue, — that all these were needful to bring her through with dignity and honour. Nor, perhaps, after all, could any thing but success fully vindicate her undertaking; for such a thing, to be proper, must be practicable: and who could so enter into her mind as to see its practicability till it is done? At the last we accept it as a sort of inspiration, — authenticated to us as such in the result, — when she frames her intent in the meditation, —

> "Impossible be strange attempts to those
> That weigh their pains in sense, and do suppose
> What hath not been can't be."

Before leaving the subject, I am moved to add that, though Helena is herself all dignity and delicacy, some of her talk with Monsieur Words the puppy in the first scene is neither delicate nor dignified: it is simply a foul blot, and I can but regret the Poet did not throw it out in the revisal; sure I am that he did not retain it to please himself.

Almost everybody falls in love with the Countess. And, truly, one so meek and sweet and venerable, who can help loving her? or who, if he can resist her, will dare to own it? I can almost find it in my heart to adore the beauty of youth; yet this blessed old creature is enough to persuade me that age may be more beautiful still. Her generous sensibility to native worth amply atones for her son's mean pride of birth: all her honours of rank and place she would gladly resign, to have been the mother of the poor orphan left in her charge. Feeling as she does the riches of that orphan's soul, — a feeling that bespeaks like riches in herself, — all the factitious distinctions of life sink to nothing in her regard; and the only distinction worth having is that which grows by building honour out of one's own virtue, and not by inheriting it from the virtue of others. So, in her breast, "adoption strives with nature"; and, weighing the adopted and the native together in her motherly judgment, she finds "there's nothing here too good for him but only she"; and "which of them both is dearest to her, she has no skill in sense to make distinction." Withal she is a charming instance of youth carried on into age; so that Helena justly recognizes her as one "whose aged honour cites a virtuous youth." Thus her Winter inherits a soft warm robe of precious memories woven out of her Spring: when she first learns of the heroine's state of mind, the picture of her own May revives to her eye, the treasure of her maiden years blooms afresh; she remembers that "this thorn doth to our rose of youth rightly belong"; and has more than ever a mother's heart towards the silent sufferer, because she holds fast her old faith that

> "It is the show and seal of nature's truth,
> Where love's strong passion is impress'd in youth."

Well might Campbell say of her, that "she redeems nobility by reverting to nature."

Johnson delivers his mind touching the young Count as follows: "I cannot reconcile my heart to Bertram; — a man noble without generosity, and young without truth; who marries Helena as a coward, and leaves her as a profligate: when she is dead by his unkindness, sneaks home to a second marriage; is accused by a woman he has wronged, defends himself by falsehood, and is dismissed to happiness." A terrible sentence indeed! and its vigour, if not its justice, is attested by the frequency with which it has been quoted.

Now, in the first place, the Poet did not mean we should reconcile our hearts to Bertram, but that he should not unreconcile them to Helena; nay, that her love should appear the nobler for the unworthiness of its object. Then, he does not marry her as a coward, but merely because he has no choice; nor does he yield till he has shown all the courage that were compatible with discretion. She is forced upon him by a stretch of prerogative which seems strange indeed to us, but which in feudal times was generally held to be just and right, so that resistance to it was flat rebellion. And, as before observed, Bertram's purpose of stealing away to the war was bravely formed without any reference to Helena, and from a manly impulse or ambition to be doing something that might show him not unworthy of his House and his social inheritance. The King presses him with the hard alternative of taking Helena as his wife,

> "Or I will throw thee from my care for ever
> Into the staggers and the cureless lapse
> Of youth and ignorance ; both my revenge and hate
> Loosing upon thee, in the name of justice,
> Without all terms of pity."

Nor, when thus driven to make a show of mastering his aversion, is there any thing mean or cringing in the way he does it: his language is not only reluctant and reserved, but is even made severe with a dash of irony:

> "When I consider
> What great creation and what dole of honour
> Flies where you bid it, I find that she, which late
> Was in my nobler thoughts most base, is now
> *The praisèd of the King.*"

Marriage, in truth, is a thing that he has not begun to think of; the passion that rightly leads to it is yet dormant in him; to the proper charms of woman he is insensible, his heart being all set on other things. Then, again, he does not leave Helena as a profligate, but rather to escape from what is to him an unholy match, as being on his side without love; and his profligacy is not so much the cause as the consequence of his flight and exile. In the midst of his manlier work, he is surprised into a passion unfelt by him before; and the tie which has been strained upon him, and which his heart still disowns, is partly to blame for the profligate intrigue into which he plunges, because it shuts off the conditions of an honourable love. — Finally, he is not dismissed to happiness, but rather left where he cannot be happy, unless he shall have dismissed his faults. And, surely, he may have some allowance, because of the tyranny laid upon him, — this too in a sentiment where nature pleads loudest for freedom, and which, if free, yields the strongest motives to virtue; if not, to vice.

As for his falsehood, or rather string of falsehoods, this is indeed a pretty dark passage. The guilty passion with which he is caught betrays him into a course of action still more guilty: he is entangled, almost before he knows it, in a net of vile intrigue, from which there is no escape but by lying his way out; and the more he struggles to get free the more he gets engaged. It seems an earnest of "the staggers and the cureless lapse of youth" with which the King has threatened him. But he pays a round penalty in the shame that so quickly overtakes him; which shows how careful the Poet was to make due provision for his amendment. His original fault, as already noted, was an overweening pride of birth: yet in due time he unfolds in himself better titles to honour than ancestry can bestow; and, this done, he naturally grows more willing to recognize similar titles in another. It is to be noted further, that Bertram is all along a man of few words; which may be one reason why Parolles, who is all words, as his name imports, *burrs* upon him and works his infection into him with such signal success. His habitual reticence springs mainly from real, inward strength of nature; but partly also from that same unsocial pride which lays him so broadly open to the arts of sycophancy, and thus draws him, as if spellbound, under the tainted breath of that strange compound of braggart, liar, and fop.

Thus Shakespeare purposely represents Bertram as a very mixed character, in whom the evil gains for some time a most unhopeful mastery; and he takes care to provide, withal, the canon whereby he would have him judged: "The web of our life is of a mingled yarn, good and ill together: our virtues would be proud, if our faults whipp'd them not; and our crimes would despair, if they were not cherished by our virtues." A pregnant and subtile reflection indeed, which may sound strange to many; but the truth and wisdom of it are well approved by the grave and saintly Hooker, who was "not afraid to affirm it boldly," that proud men sometimes "receive a benefit at the hands of God, and are assisted with His grace, when with His grace they are not assisted, but permitted, and that grievously, to transgress; whereby, as they were in overgreat liking of themselves supplanted, so the dislike of that which did supplant them may establish them afterwards the surer."

Captain Parolles is verily Shakespeare's most illustrious *pronoun* of a man. Several critics have somehow found it in their hearts to speak of him and Falstaff together. A foul sin against Sir John! who, whatever else he may deserve, certainly does not deserve that. Schlegel, however, justly remarks that the scenes where our captain figures contain matter enough for an excellent comedy. It is indeed a marvel that one so inexpressibly mean, and withal so fully aware of his meanness, should not cut his own acquaintance. But the greatest wonder about him is, how the Poet could so run his own intellectuality into such a windbag, without marring his windbag perfection. The character of Parolles is interpreted with unusual fulness in the piercing comments of the other persons. He seems indeed to have been specially "created for men to breathe themselves upon." Thus one describes him as "a most notable coward, an infinite and endless liar, an hourly promise-breaker, the owner of no one good quality"; and again, as having "outvillained villainy so far, that the rarity redeems him." And he is at last felt to be worth feeding and keeping alive for the simple reason of his being such a miracle of bespangled, voluble, impudent good-for-nothingness, that contempt and laughter cannot afford to let him die. But the roundest and happiest delivery of him comes from the somewhat waggish but high-spirited and sharp-sighted Lord Lafeu, who finds him "my good window of lattice," and one whose "soul is in his clothes"; and who says to him, "I did think thee, for two ordinaries, to be a pretty wise fellow; thou didst make tolerable vent of thy travel: it might pass: yet the scarfs and the bannerets about thee did manifoldly dissuade me from believing thee a vessel of too great a burden." The play is choicely seasoned throughout with the good-humoured old statesman's spicery; and our captain is the theme that draws most of it out.

That the goddess whom Bertram worships does not whisper in his ear the unfathomable baseness of this "lump of counterfeit ore," is a piece of dramatic retribution at once natural and just. Far as the joke is pushed upon Parolles, we never feel like crying out, *Hold, enough!* for, "that he should know what he is, and be that he is," seems an offence for which infinite shames were hardly a sufficient indemnification. And we know right well that such a hollow, flaunting, strutting roll of effrontery and poltroonery cannot possibly have soul enough to be inwardly hurt by the utmost pressure of disgrace and scorn. And yet, strange as it may seem, Parolles represents a class of actual men; how truly, is well shown in that the delineation, in its main features, but especially as of "one that lies three thirds, and uses a known truth to pass a thousand nothings with," might almost be mistaken for a portrait of a very noted character of our time, — a man too — which is strangest of all — whose success with the voters has even beaten that of his dramatic prototype with Bertram.

Verplanck thinks, as he well may, that the Poet's special purpose in this play was to set forth the precedence of innate over circumstantial distinctions. Gervinus also takes the same view: "The idea that merit goes before rank is the soul of this piece and of the relation between Bertram and Helena." And this high moral centre is not only pronounced strongly in verbal discourse, but, which is still better, is silently placed in the characters themselves and in the facts of the play. Yet observe with what a catholic spirit the Poet teaches this great lesson; frankly recognizing the noble man in the nobleman, and telling us, in effect, that none know so well how to prize the nobilities of nature as those who, like the King and the Countess of this play, have experienced the nothingness of all other claims. To be sure, their generous superiority to adventitious distinctions is partly because of a certain regenerative efficacy flowing from the heroine: pride of birth is sweetly rebuked in her presence; a subtile inspiration from her seems to steal away whatever prejudice of rank they may have, and to cheat them into full sympathy with truth and virtue; and, with the exception of Bertram and the bescarfed coxcomb that spaniels him, all from the King downwards are won to the free worship of untitled merit directly they begin to converse with this meek and modest incarnation of Nature's eloquence.

MEASURE FOR MEASURE.

Measure for Measure, in its vein of thought and complexion of character, is the deepest of Shakespeare's comedies, — deeper even than some of his tragedies. The foundation principles of ethics are here explored far as the plummet of thought can sound; the subtleties and intricacies of the human heart are searched with an insight which the sharpest and most inquisitive criticism may strive in vain to follow. The mind almost loses itself in attempting to trace out through their course the various and complicated lines of reflection here suggested.

We have no authentic contemporary notice of the play whatever, till it appeared in the folio of 1623. I say *authentic* notice; because the item which, some years ago, Mr. Peter Cunningham claimed to have found among some old records preserved at Somerset House, and which makes the play to have been acted at Court in December, 1604, has been lately set aside as a fabrication. Though printed much better than *All's Well that Ends Well*, still the text set forth in the folio gives us but too much cause to regret the lack of earlier copies; there being several passages that are, to all appearance, incurably defective or corrupt.

The strongly-marked peculiarities of the piece in language, cast of thought, and moral temper, have invested it with great psychological interest, and bred a strange desire among critics to connect it in some way with the author's mental history, — with some supposed crisis in his feelings and experience. Hence the probable date of the writing was for a long time argued more strenuously than the subject would otherwise seem to justify; and, as often falls out in such cases, the more the critics argued the point, the further they were from coming to an agreement. And, in truth, the plain matter-of-fact critics have here succeeded much better in the work than their more philosophical brethren; which aptly shows how little the brightest speculation can do in questions properly falling within the domain of facts.

In default of other data, the critics in question based their arguments upon certain probable allusions to contemporary matters; especially on those passages which express the Duke's fondness for "the life remov'd," and his aversion to being greeted by crowds of people. Chalmers brought forward also the very pertinent fact of a long-sleeping statute having been revived in 1604, which punished with death all divorced or divorcing persons who married again while their former husbands or wives were living. This circumstance, he thinks, might well have suggested what is said by the Duke:

> "We have strict statutes and most biting laws, —
> The needful bits and curbs to headstrong steeds, —
> Which for this fourteen years we have let sleep;
> Even like an o'ergrown lion in a cave,
> That goes not out to prey."

Chalmers had the sagacity to discover also a sort of portrait-like resemblance in the Duke to King James the First. As the King was indeed a much better theologian than statesman or ruler, the fact of the Duke's appearing rather more at home in the cowl and hood than in his ducal robes certainly lends some colour to this discovery.

The King's unamiable repugnance to being gazed upon by throngs of admiring subjects is thus spoken of by a contemporary writer: "In his public appearance, especially in his sports, the accesses of the people made him so impatient, that he often dispersed them with frowns, that we may not say, with curses." And his churlish bearing towards the crowds which, prompted by eager loyalty, flocked forth to hail his accession, is noted by several historians. But he was a pretty free encourager of the Drama, as well as of other liberal preparations; and, with those who had tasted, or who sought, his patronage, it was natural that these symptoms of weakness should pass for tokens of a wise superiority to the dainties of popular applause. All which renders it not unlikely that the Poet may have had an eye to the King in the passages cited by Malone in support of his conjecture:

"I love the people,
But do not like to stage me to their eyes:
Though it do well, I do not relish well
Their loud applause and aves vehement;
Nor do I think the man of safe discretion
That does affect it."

"So play the foolish throngs with one that swoons;
Come all to help him, and so stop the air
By which he should revive: and even so
The general, subject to a well-wish'd king,
Quit their own part, and in obsequious fondness
Crowd to his presence, where their untaught love
Must needs appear offence."

The allusion here being granted, Malone's inference, that the play was made soon after the King's accession, and before the effect of his unlooked-for austerity on this score had spent itself, was natural enough. Nor is the conjecture of Ulrici and others without weight, "that Shakespeare was led to the composition of the play by the rigoristic sentiments and arrogant virtue of the Puritans." And in this view several points of the main action might have been aptly suggested at the time in question: for the King had scarcely set foot in England but he began to be worried by the importunities of that remarkable people; who had been feeding upon the hope, that by the sole exercise of his prerogative he would work through a radical change in the constitution of the Church, and so bring her into accordance with their ideas: — all this on the principle, of course, that a minority however small, with the truth, was better than a majority however large, without it.

The accession of King James to the English throne was in March, 1603. So that the forecited arguments would conclude the writing of the play to have been nearly synchronous with the revisal of *All's Well that Ends Well*, and with the production of *King Lear*, perhaps also of *Macbeth;* at least, within the same period of four or five years. The characteristics of style and temper draw to the same conclusion as regards the date of the writing.

There is no doubt that for some particulars in the plot and story of *Measure for Measure* the Poet was ultimately indebted to Cinthio, an Italian novelist of the sixteenth century. The original story makes the eighty-fifth in his *Hundred Tales.* A youth named Ludovico is there overtaken in the crime of seduction: Juriste, a magistrate highly reputed for wisdom and justice, passes sentence of death upon him; and Ludovico's sister, a virgin of rare gifts and graces, goes to pleading for his life. Her beauty and eloquence have the same effect on Juriste as Isabella's on Angelo. His proposals are rejected with scorn and horror; but the lady, overcome by the pathetic entreaties of her brother, at last yields to them under a solemn promise of marriage. His object being gained, the wicked man then commits a double vow-breach, neither marrying the sister nor sparing the brother. She appeals to the Emperor, by whom Juriste is forced to marry her, and then sentenced to death; but is finally pardoned at the lady's suit, who is now as earnest and eloquent for her husband as she had been for her brother. Her conduct touches him with remorse, and at length proves as effective in reforming his character as it was in redeeming his life.

As early as 1578, this tale was dramatized after a sort by George Whetstone, and was published as *The History of Promos and Cassandra.* Whetstone was a writer of learning and talent, but not such that even the instructions of a Shakespeare could have made him capable of dramatic excellence; and, as he had no such benefit, his performance is insipid and worthless enough. The drama is in Two Parts, and is written in verse, with alternate rhymes. In his conduct of the story Whetstone varies somewhat from the original; as the following abstract will show:

In the city of Julio, then under the rule of Corvinus, King of Hungary, there was a law that for incontinence the man should suffer death, and the woman be marked out for infamy by her dress. Through the indulgence of magistrates, this law came to be little regarded. The government falling at length into the hands of Lord Promos, he revived the statute, and, a youth named Andrugio being convicted of the fault in question, resolved to visit the penalties in their utmost rigour upon both the parties. Andrugio had a sister of great virtue and accomplishment, named Cassandra, who undertook to sue for his life. Her good behaviour, great beauty, and "the sweet order of her talk" wrought so far with the governor as to induce a short reprieve. Being inflamed soon after with a criminal passion, he set down the spoil of her honour as the ransom. She spurned his suit with abhorrence. Unable, however, to resist the pleadings of her brother, she at last yielded to the man's proposal, on condition of his pardoning her brother and then marrying her. This he vowed to do; but, his end once gained, instead of keeping his vow, he ordered the jailer to present Cassandra with her brother's head. As the jailer knew what the governor had done, he took the head of a felon just executed, and set Andrugio at liberty. Cassandra, supposing the head to be her brother's, was at the point to kill herself for grief, but spared that stroke, to be avenged on the traitor. She devised to make her case known to the King; who forthwith hastened to do justice on Promos, ordering that, to repair the lady's honour, he should marry her, and then, for his crime against the State, lose his head. No sooner was Cassandra a wife than all her rhetoric of eye, tongue, and action was tasked to procure the pardon of her husband; but the King, tendering the public good more than hers, denied her suit. At length, Andrugio, overcome by his sister's grief, made himself known; for he had all the while been about the place in disguise; whereupon the King, to honour the virtues of Cassandra, pardoned both him and Promos.

In 1592, Whetstone published his *Heptameron of Civil Discourses*, containing a prose version of the same tale. It is observable that he deviates from Cinthio in bringing Andrugio off alive; and as Shakespeare does the same with Claudio, we may well conclude that he drew directly from Whetstone, not from the original author. Beyond the mere outline of the story, it does not appear that the Poet borrowed any thing more than a few slight hints and casual expressions. And a comparison of the two pieces would nowise reduce his claims; it being not less creditable to have lifted the story out of the mire into such a region of art and poetry than to have invented it. Then too, even as regards the story, Shakespeare varies from Whetstone much more materially than the latter does from Cinthio: representing the illicit meeting of Claudio and Juliet as taking place under the shield of a solemn betrothment; which very much lessens their fault, as marriage bonds were already upon them; and proportionably heightens Angelo's wickedness, as it brings on him the guilt of making the law responsible for his own arbitrary rigour. But the main *original* feature in the plot of *Measure for Measure* is the part of Mariana, which puts a new life into the whole, and purifies it almost into another nature; as it prevents the soiling of Isabella's womanhood, supplies an apt reason for the Duke's mysterious conduct, and yields a pregnant motive for Angelo's pardon, in that his life is thereby bound up with that of a wronged and innocent woman, whom his crimes are made the occasion of restoring to her rights and happiness; so that her virtue may be justly allowed to reprieve him from death.

In the comic parts of Whetstone's drama there is all the grossness of *Measure for Measure*, without any thing that the utmost courtesy of language can call wit or humour. So that, if the Poet here received no help, neither can he have any excuse, from the workmanship of his predecessor. But he probably saw that some such matter was required by the scheme of the play and the laws of dramatic proportion. And as in these parts the truth and character are all his own, so he can hardly be blamed for not anticipating the delicacy or squeamishness of later times, there being none such in the most refined audiences of his day; while, again, his choice of a subject so ugly in itself is amply screened from censure by the lessons of virtue and wisdom which he used it as an opportunity for delivering. To have trained and taught a barbarous tale of cruelty and lust into such a fruitage of poetry and humanity, may well offset whatever of offence there may be in the play to modern taste.

I have already referred to certain characteristics of style and temper which this play shares with several others probably written about the same time, and which, as before observed, have been thought to mark some crisis in the Poet's life. It cannot well be denied that the plays in question have something of a peculiar spirit, which might aptly suggest that some passage of bitter experience must have turned the milk of his genius for a time into gall, and put him upon a course of harsh and indignant thought. The point is well stated by Hallam: "There seems to have been a period of Shakespeare's life when his heart was ill at ease, and ill content with the world or his own conscience: the memory of hours misspent, the pang of affection misplaced or unrequited, the experience of man's worser nature, which intercourse with ill-chosen associates peculiarly teaches, — these, as they sank down into the depths of his great mind, seem not only to have inspired into it the conception of Lear and Timon, but that of one primary character, the censurer of mankind."* And Verplanck speaks in a similar strain of "that portion of the author's life which was memorable for the production of the additions to the original *Hamlet*, with their melancholy wisdom; probably of *Timon*, with its indignant and hearty scorn, and rebukes of the baseness of civilized society; and above all of *Lear*, with its dark pictures of unmixed, unmitigated guilt, and its terrible and prophet-like denunciations."

These words certainly carry much weight, and may go far to warrant the belief of the writers, that the Poet was smitten with some rude shock of fortune which untuned the melody of his soul, and wrenched his mind from its once smooth and happy course, causing it to recoil upon itself and brood over its own thoughts. Yet there are considerable difficulties besetting a theory of this kind. For, in some other plays referred by these critics to the same period, there is so much of the Poet's gayest and happiest workmanship as must greatly embarrass if not quite upset such a theory. But, whatever may have caused the peculiar tone and the cast of thought in the forenamed plays, it is pretty certain that the darkness was not permanent;

* "This type," continues the writer, "is first seen in the philosophic melancholy of Jaques, gazing with an undiminished serenity, and with a gayety of fancy, though not of manners, on the follies of the world. It assumes a graver cast in the exiled Duke of the same play, and one rather more severe in the Duke of *Measure for Measure*. In all these, however, it is merely a contemplative philosophy. In Hamlet this is mingled with the impulses of a perturbed heart under the pressure of extraordinary circumstances: it shines no longer, as in the former characters, with a steady light, but plays in fitful coruscations amid feigned gayety and extravagance In Lear, it is the flash of sudden inspiration across the incongruous imagery of madness: in Timon, it is obscured by the exaggerations of misanthropy."

the clear azure, soft sunshine, and serene sweetness of *The Tempest* and *The Winter's Tale* being unquestionably of a later date. And, surely, in the life of so earnest and thoughtful a man as Shakespeare, there might well be, nay, there must have been, times when, without any special woundings or bruisings of fortune, his mind got fascinated by the appalling mystery of evil that haunts our fallen nature.

That such darker hours, however occasioned, were more frequent at one period of the Poet's life than at others, is indeed probable. And it was equally natural that their coming should sometimes engage him in heart-tugging and brain-sweating efforts to scrutinize the inscrutable workings of human guilt, and thus stamp itself strongly upon the offspring of his mind. Thus, without any other than the ordinary progress of thoughtful spirits, we should naturally have a middle period, when the early enthusiasm of hope had passed away, and before the deeper, calmer, but not less cheerful tranquillity of resignation had set in. For so it is apt to be in this life of ours: the angry barkings of fortune, or what seem such, have their turn with us; "the fretful fever and the stir unprofitable" work our souls full of discord and perturbation; but after a while these things pass away, and are followed by a more placid and genial time; the experienced insufficiency of man for himself having charmed our wrestlings of thought into repose, and our spirits having undergone the chastening and subduing power of life's sterner discipline.

In some such passage, then, I should rather presume the unique conception of *Measure for Measure* to have been formed in the Poet's mind. I say unique, because this is his only instance of comedy where the wit seems to foam and sparkle up from a fountain of bitterness; where even the humour is made pungent with sarcasm; and where the poetry is marked with tragic austerity. In none of his plays does he discover less of leaning upon pre-existing models, or a more manly negligence, perhaps sometimes carried to excess, of those lighter graces of manner which none but the greatest minds may safely despise. His genius is here out in all its colossal individuality, and he seems to have meant it should be so; as if he felt quite sure of having now reached his mastership; so that henceforth, instead of leaning on those who had gone before, he was to be himself a leaning-place for those who should follow.

Accordingly the play abounds in fearless grapplings and strugglings of mind with matters too hard to consist with much facility and gracefulness of tongue. The thought is strong, and in its strength careless of appearances, and seems rather wishing than fearing to have its roughnesses seen: the style is rugged, irregular, abrupt, sometimes running into an almost forbidding sternness, but everywhere throbbing with life: often a whole page of meaning is condensed and rammed into a clause or an image, so that the force thereof beats and reverberates through the entire scene: with little of elaborate grace or finish, we have bold, deep strokes, where the want of finer softenings and shadings is more than made up by increased energy and expressiveness; the words going right to the spot, and leaving none of their work undone. Thus the workmanship is in a very uncommon degree what I sometimes designate as *steep*, meaning thereby *hard to get to the top of.* Hence it is perhaps, in part, that so many axioms and "brief sententious precepts" of moral and practical wisdom from this play have wrought themselves into the currency and familiarity of household words, and live for instruction or comfort in the memory of many who know nothing of their original source. As a strong instance in point, take Isabella's meaty apothegm, —

> "Man, proud man,
> Drest in a little brief authority, —
> Most ignorant of what he's most assur'd, —
> Plays such fantastic tricks before high Heaven
> As make the angels weep; who, *with our spleens,*
> *Would all themselves laugh mortal.*"

Which means that, if the angels had our disposition to

splenetic or satirical mirth, the sight of our human arrogance strutting through its absurd antics would cast them into such an ecstasy of ridicule, that they would laugh themselves clean out of their immortality; this celestial prerogative being quite incompatible with such ebullitions of spleen.

Whether from the nature of the subject, or the mode of treating it, or both, *Measure for Measure* is generally regarded as one of the least attractive, though most instructive, of Shakespeare's plays. Coleridge, in those fragments of his critical lectures which now form our best text-book of English criticism, says, "This play, which is Shakespeare's throughout, is to me the most painful — rather say the only painful — part of his genuine works." From this language, sustained as it is by other high authorities, I probably should not dissent; but when, in his *Table Talk*, he says that "Isabella herself contrives to be unamiable, and Claudio is detestable," I can by no means go along with him.

It would seem indeed as if undue fault had sometimes been found, not so much with the play itself as with some of the persons, from trying them by a moral standard which cannot be fairly applied to them, or from not duly weighing all the circumstances, feelings, and motives under which they are represented as acting. Thus Ulrici speaks of Claudio as being guilty of seduction. Which is surely wide of the mark; it being clear enough that, according to the usages then and there established, he was, as he considered himself to be, virtually married, though not admissible to all the rights of the married life. Hence we have the Duke assuring Mariana that there would be no crime in her meeting with Angelo, because he was her "husband on a pre-contract." And it is well known that in ancient times the ceremony of betrothment conferred the marriage tie, though not the nuptials, so that the union of the parties was thenceforth firm in the eye of the law itself. So again Hallam, speaking of Isabella: "One is disposed to ask whether, if Claudio had been really executed, the spectator would not have gone away with no great affection for her; and at least we now feel that her reproaches against her miserable brother, when he clings to life like a frail and guilty being, are too harsh." As to the first branch of this indictment, I might have ventured to ask the writer how his affection would have stood towards the heroine, if she had yielded to Angelo's proposal. As to the second branch, though I do indeed feel that Claudio were rather to be pitied than blamed, whatever course he had taken in so terrible an alternative, yet the conduct of his sister strikes me as every way creditable to her. Her reproaches were indeed too harsh, if they sprang from want of love; but such is evidently not the case. The truth is, she is in a very hard struggle between affection and principle: she needs, and she hopes, to have the strain upon her womanly fortitude lightened by the manly fortitude of her brother; and her harshness of reproof discovers the natural workings of a tender and deep affection, in an agony of disappointment at being urged, by one for whom she would die, to an act which she shrinks from with noble horror, and justly considers worse than death. So that we here have the keen anguish of conflicting feelings venting itself in a severity which, though unmerited, serves to disclose the more impressively her nobleness of character.

Again, the same critic, referring to the part of Mariana as indispensable to "a satisfactory termination" of the story, objects, that "it is never explained how the Duke had become acquainted with this secret, and, being acquainted with it, how he had preserved his esteem and confidence in Angelo." But, surely, we are given to understand at the outset that the Duke has not preserved the esteem and confidence in question. In his first scene with Friar Thomas, among his reasons for the action he has on foot, he makes special mention of this one:

> "Lord Angelo is precise;
> *Stands at a guard with envy;* scarce confesses
> That his blood flows, or that his appetite
> Is more to bread than stone: *hence shall we see,*
> *If power change purpose, what our* SEEMERS *be.*"

Which clearly infers that his main purpose in assuming the disguise of a monk is to unmask the deputy, and demonstrate to others what has long been known to himself. And he throws out other hints of a belief or suspicion that Angelo is angling for emolument or popularity, and baiting his hook with great apparent strictness and sanctity of life; thus putting on sheep's clothing, in order to play the wolf with more safety and success. As to the secret concerning Mariana, it seems enough that the Duke knows it, that the knowledge justifies his distrust, and that when the time comes he uses it for a good purpose; the earlier part of the play thus preparing quietly for what is to follow, and the later explaining what went before. In truth, the Duke is better able to understand the deputy's character than to persuade others of it: this is one of his motives for the stratagem. And a man of his wisdom, even if he have no available facts in the case, might well suspect an austerity so theatrical as Angelo's to be rather an art than a virtue: he could not well be ignorant that, when men are so forward to air their graces and *make* their light shine, they can hardly be aiming at any glory but their own.

It is to be supposed, withal, that Angelo has been wont to set himself up as an example of ghostly rectitude, and to reflect somewhat on the laxity of the Duke's administration. These reproofs the Duke cannot answer without laying himself open to the retort of being touched with jealousy. Then too Angelo is nervously apprehensive of reproach; is ever on the watch, and "making broad his phylacteries," lest malice should spy some holes in his conduct; for such is the meaning of "standing at a guard with envy": whereas "virtue is bold, and goodness never fearful" in that kind. The Duke knows that such an ostentatious strictness, however it may take with the multitude, is among the proper symptoms of a bad conscience; that such high professions of righteousness are seldom used but as a mask to cover some secret delinquencies from the public eye. Angelo had entered into a solemn engagement of marriage, his motive being the lady's wealth; her wealth being lost, so that she could no longer hold him through his secret sin of covetousness, he had cruelly deserted her; this great wrong he had still more cruelly made use of to purchase a brighter semblance of virtue, blasting her good name with alleged discoveries of crime, and thus fattening his own reputation with the life-blood of his innocent and helpless victim. Here was an act of extreme heartlessness and turpitude, too bad to be believed of one so ensconced in solemn plausibilities. The matter had come privately to the Duke's knowledge; but his tongue was tied by the official delicacies of his position.

A certain class of offences had caused a law to be passed of such overstrained severity that it broke down in the trial; so it fell into disuse, and became a dead letter, — a perch to birds of prey, and not their terror. From its extreme rigour, this law was extremely odious; and, as is always the case with laws so hated, the attempt to enforce it drew on a commensurate reaction of licentiousness; the law thus stimulating the evil it was meant to repress, — a mistaken plaster inflaming the sore. Angelo had been secretly guilty of a far worse sin than the one this law was aimed against, but had managed to fence himself about with practical impunity; nay, his crafty, sanctimonious selfishness had even turned that sin to an increase of honour, and so made it a basis of pride. As the slumbering law does not touch his case, he is earnest to have it revived and put to work: so the Duke, being somewhat divided between the pleadings of justice and mercy, concludes to let him try his hand. In the discharge of his new office, which he conceives his great moral strictness to have gained for him, Angelo thinks to build his reputation still higher by striking at a conspicuous object. In the prosecution of his scheme, he soon goes to attempting a vastly deeper breach of the very law he is enforcing than that of the man whom he has found obnoxious to its penalties. Claudio's offence was done when the law was sleeping. Angelo has just awakened it, yet he proceeds against Claudio as if the latter had transgressed while the law was vigilant. Angelo's transgression has no such excuse, since he has himself already given new life and force to the law. Nevertheless he persists in his design, and hardens himself to the point of resolving to "give his sensual race the rein." The hitherto unsuspected evil within he is now fully aware of, but looks it squarely in the face, and rushes headlong into the double crime of committing in its worst form the sin and at the same time punishing the lighter form of it with death in another. Thus it turns out that

> "This outward-sainted deputy —
> Whose settled visage and deliberate word
> Nips youth i' the head, and follies doth emmew
> As falcon doth the fowl — is yet a devil;
> His filth within being cast, he would appear
> A pond as deep as Hell."

Yet Angelo is at first not so properly a hypocrite as a self-deceiver. For it is very considerable that he wishes to be, and sincerely thinks he is, what he affects and appears to be; as is plain from his consternation at the wickedness which opportunity awakens into conscious action within him. He thus typifies that sort of men of whom Bishop Butler says, "they try appearances upon themselves as well as upon the world, and with at least as much success; and choose to manage so as to make their own minds easy with their faults, which can scarce be done without management, rather than to mend them." Even so Angelo for self-ends imitates sanctity, and then gets taken in by his own imitation. This "mystery of iniquity" locks him from all true knowledge of himself. He must be worse before he will be better. The refined hypocrisies which so elude his eye, and thus nurse his self-righteous pride, must put on a grosser form, till he cannot choose but see himself as he is. The secret devil within must blaze out in a shape too palpable to be ignored. And so, as often happens where the subtleties of self-deceit are thus cherished, he at length proceeds a downright conscious hypocrite, this too of the deepest dye.

Angelo's original fault lay in forgetting or ignoring his own frailty. As a natural consequence, his "darling sin is pride that apes humility." And his conceit of virtue, — "my gravity, wherein (let no man hear me) I take pride," — while it keeps him from certain vices, is itself a far greater vice than any it keeps him from; insomuch that his interviews with Isabella may almost be said to *elevate* him into lust. They at least bring him to a just vision of his inward self. The serpent charms of self-deceit which he has so hugged are now broken. For even so — and how awful is the fact! — men often wound themselves so deeply with medicines, that Providence has no way for them, apparently, but to make wounds medicinal, or, as Hooker says, "to cure by vice where virtue hath stricken." So indeed it must be where men turn their virtues into food of spiritual pride; which is the hardest of all sores to be cured, "inasmuch as that which rooteth out other vices causeth this." And perhaps the array of low and loathsome vices, which the Poet has clustered about Angelo in the persons of Lucio, Pompey, and Mrs. Overdone, was necessary, to make us feel how unspeakably worse than any or all of these is Angelo's pride of virtue. It can hardly be needful to add, that in Angelo these fearful traits of character are depicted with a truth and sternness of pencil, such as could scarce have been achieved but in an age fruitful in living examples of them.

The placing of Isabella, "a thing ensky'd and sainted," and who truly *is* all that Angelo seems, side by side with such a breathing, shining mass of pitch, is one of those dramatic audacities wherein none perhaps but a Shakespeare could safely indulge. Of her character the most prolific hint that is given is what she says to the disguised Duke, when he is urging her to fasten her ear on his advisings touching the part of Mariana: "I have spirit to do any thing that appears not foul in the truth of my spirit." That is, she cares not what face her action may wear to the world, nor how much reproach it may bring on her from others, if it will only leave her the society, which she has never parted from, of a clean breast and a pure conscience.

Called from the cloister, where she is on the point of taking the veil of earthly renouncement, to plead for her brother's life, she comes forth a saintly anchoress, clad in the austerest sweetness of womanhood, to throw the light of her virgin soul upon the dark, loathsome scenes and characters around her. With great strength of intellect and depth of feeling she unites an equal power of imagination, the whole being pervaded, quickened, and guided by a still, intense religious enthusiasm. And because her virtue is securely rooted and grounded in religion, therefore she never thinks of it as her own, but only as a gift from the Being whom she adores, and who is her only hope for the keeping of what she has. Which suggests the fundamental point of contrast between her and Angelo, whose virtue, if such it may be called, is nothing, nay, worse than nothing, because it is a virtue of his own making, is without any inspiration from the one Source of all true good, and so has no basis but pride, which is itself a bubble. Accordingly her character appears to me among the finest, in some respects the very finest, in Shakespeare's matchless cabinet of female excellence.

The power and pathos with which she pleads for her brother are well known. At first she is timid, distrustful of her powers, shrinking with modest awe of the law's appointed organ; and she seems drawn unawares into the heights of moral argument and the most sweetly-breathing strains of Gospel wisdom. Much of what she says has become domesticated wherever the English language is spoken, and would long since have grown stale, if it were possible to crush the freshness of immortal youth out of it. The dialogues between her and Angelo are extremely subtile and suggestive on both sides, fraught with meanings to reward the most searching ethical study, but which I cannot stay to trace out, and which the closest criticism would fail to exhaust. At the opening of their interview, she is in a struggle between wishing and not wishing, and therefore not in a mood to "play with reason and discourse." With her settled awe of purity, she cannot but admit the law to be right, yet she sees not how, in the circumstances, mercy can be wrong. At this thought her heart presently kindles, her eloquence springs to work, and its tones grow deeper, clearer, more penetrating, as point after point catches her mental eye. Thenceforth it is a keen encounter of mind with mind; but on his side it is the conscious logic of an adroit and practised lawyer, who has full mastery of his case, and is prompt in all the turns of legal ingenuity; while on her side it is the logic of nature's finest moral instincts spontaneously using the forces of a quick, powerful, and well-balanced intellect as their organ of expression. She perceives at once how subtile and acute of apprehension he is; so, lest her speech should have too much edge, she veils the matter in figures of a somewhat enigmatical cast, because she knows that he will instantly take the sense. Her instinctive knowledge of the human heart guides her directly to his secret springs of action. With a tact that seems like inspiration, she feels out his assailable points, and still surprises and holds him with new and startling appeals to his innermost feelings. At length, when, his wicked purpose being formed, he goes to talking to her in riddles, she quickly understands him, but thinks he is only testing her: her replies leave him in doubt whether craft or innocence speaks in her: so she draws him on to speaking plainer and plainer, till at last he makes a full and explicit avowal of his inhuman baseness. He is especially caught, be it observed, "in the strong toil" of her moral grace; at least he is pleased to think so: and as he has been wont to pride himself on being a saint, so he now takes refuge in the thought, "O cunning enemy, that to catch a saint, with saints dost bait thy hook!"

It is not to be denied, indeed, that Isabella's chastity is rather too demonstrative and self-pronounced; but this is because of the unblushing and emphatic licentiousness of her social environment. Goodness cannot remain undemonstrative amidst such a rank demonstrativeness of its opposite: the necessity it is under of fighting against so much and such aggressive evil forces it into stress, and so into taking a full measure of itself. Isabella, accordingly, is deeply conscious and mindful of her virtue, which somewhat mars the beauty of it, I admit; but in the circumstances it could not be otherwise: with such a strong stew of corruption boiling and bubbling all about her, it was not possible that purity in her case should retain that bland, unconscious repose which is indeed its greatest charm. From the prevailing rampancy of vice, a certain air of oversternness and rigidity has wrought itself into her character, displacing somewhat of its proper sweetness and amiability: but, in the right view of things, this loss is well made up in that she is the more an object of reverence; albeit I have to confess that she would touch me rather more potently, if she had a little more of loveliness and a little less of awfulness. And it is remarkable that even Lucio, light-minded libertine as he is, whose familiar sin it is to jest with maids, "tongue far from heart," cannot approach her, but that his levity is at once awed into soberness, and he regards her as one "to be talk'd with in sincerity, as with a saint."

The Duke has been rather hardly dealt with by critics. Shakespeare — than whom it would not be easy to find a better judge of what belongs to wisdom and goodness — seems to have meant him for a wise and good man: yet he represents him as having rather more skill and pleasure in strategical arts and roundabout ways than is altogether in keeping with such a character. Some of his alleged reasons for the action he goes about reflect no honour on him; but it is observable that the sequel does not approve them to have been his real ones: his conduct, as the action proceeds, infers better motives than his speech offered at the beginning; which naturally suggests that there may have been more of purpose than of truth in his speaking. His first dialogue with Angelo is, no doubt, partly ironical. A liberal, thoughtful, and merciful prince, but with more of whim and caprice than exactly suits the dignity of his place, humanity speaks richly from his lips; yet in his actions the philosopher and the divine are better shown than the statesman and ruler. Therewithal he seems to take a very questionable delight in moving about as an unseen providence, by secret counsels leading the wicked designs of others to safe and just results. It is indeed true, as Heraud observes regarding him, that so "Divine Providence, while it deputes its authority to the office-bearers of the world, is still present both with them and it, and ever ready to punish the evil-doer": still I doubt of its being just the thing for the world's office-bearers to undertake the functions of Providence in that particular. Probably the Duke should not be charged with a fanaticism of intrigue; but he comes something nearer to it than befits a mind of the first order. Schlegel thinks "he has more pleasure in overhearing his subjects than in governing them in the usual way of princes"; and sets him down as an exception to the proverb, "A cowl does not make a monk": and perhaps his princely virtues are somewhat obscured by the disguise which so completely transforms him into a monk. Whether he acts upon the wicked principle with which that fraternity is so often reproached, or not, it is pretty certain that some of his means can be justified by nothing but the end. But perhaps, in the vast complexity of human motives and affairs, a due exercise of fairness and candour will find cause enough for ascribing to him the merit of honestly pursuing the good and true according to the best lights he has. Hereabouts Schlegel makes the following just remark: "Shakespeare, amidst the rancour of religious parties, delights in painting monks, and always represents their influence as beneficial; there being in his plays none of the black and knavish specimens which an enthusiasm for Protestantism, rather than poetical inspiration, has put some modern poets upon delineating. He merely gives his monks an inclination to be busy in the affairs of others, after renouncing the world for themselves; though in respect of pious frauds he does not make them very scrupulous."

As to the Duke's pardoning of Angelo, though Justice seems to cry out against the act, yet in the premises it were still more unjust in him to do otherwise; the deception he has practised on Angelo in substituting Mariana having plainly bound him to the course he finally takes in that matter. For the same power whereby he works through this deception might easily have prevented Angelo's crime; and to punish the offence after thus withholding the means of prevention were clearly wrong: not to mention how his proceedings here involve an innocent person; so that he ought to spare Angelo for her sake, if not for his own. Coleridge indeed strongly reprehends this act, on the ground that "cruelty, with lust and damnable baseness, cannot be forgiven, because we cannot conceive them as being morally repented of." But it seems to me hardly prudent or becoming thus to set bounds to the grace of repentance, or to say what amount of sin must necessarily render a man incapable of being reformed. All which may in some measure explain the Duke's severity to the smaller crime of Lucio, after his clemency to the greater one of Angelo.

I must not leave the gentle Duke without remarking how, especially in the earlier portions of the play, his tongue drops the very manna of moral and meditative wisdom. His discourse in reconciling Claudio to the quick approach of death condenses the marrow of all that philosophy and divinity can urge, to wean us mortals from the "many deceiving promises of life."

Lucio is one of those mixed characters, such as are often generated amidst the refinements and pollutions of urban society, in whom low and disgusting vices, and a frivolity still more offensive, are blended with engaging manners and some manly sentiments. Thus he appears a gentleman and a blackguard by turns; and, which is more, he does really unite something of these seemingly-incompatible qualities. With a true eye and a just respect for virtue in others, yet, so far as we can see, he cares not a jot to have it in himself. And while his wanton, waggish levity seems too much for any generous sentiment to consist with, still he shows a strong and steady friendship for Claudio, and a heart-felt reverence for Isabella; as if on purpose to teach us that "the web of our life is of a mingled yarn, good and ill together." And perhaps the seeming "snow-broth blood" of Angelo puts him upon affecting a more frisky circulation than he really has. For an overacted austerity is not the right way to win others out of a too rollicking levity.

Dr. Johnson rather oddly remarks that "the comic scenes are natural and pleasing": not that the remark is not true enough, but that it appears something out of character in him. And if these scenes please, it is not so much from any fund of mirthful exhilaration, or any genial gushings of wit and humour, as for the remorseless, unsparing freedom, not unmingled with touches of scorn, with which the deformities of mankind are anatomized. The contrast between the right-hearted, well-meaning Claudio, a generous spirit walled in with overmuch infirmity, and Barnardine, a frightful petrification of humanity, "careless, reckless and fearless of what is past, present, or to come," is in the Poet's boldest manner.

Nevertheless the general current of things is far from

musical, and the issues greatly disappointing. The drowsy Justice which we expect and wish to see awakened, and set in living harmony with Mercy, apparently relapses at last into a deeper sleep than ever. Our loyalty to Womanhood is not a little wounded by the humiliations to which poor Mariana stoops, at the ghostly counsels of her spiritual guide, that she may twine her life with that of the execrable hypocrite who has wronged her sex so deeply. That, amid the general impunity, the mere telling of some ridiculous lies to the disguised Duke about himself, should draw down a disproportionate severity upon Lucio, the lively, unprincipled, fantastic jester and wag, who might well be let pass as a privileged character, makes the whole look more as if done in mockery of justice than in honour of mercy. Except, indeed, the noble unfolding of Isabella, scarce any thing turns out to our wish; nor are we much pleased at seeing her diverted from the quiet tasks and holy contemplations where her heart is so much at home; although, as Gervinus observes, "she has that two-sided nature, the capacity to enjoy the world, according to circumstances, or to dispense with it."

The title of this play is apt to give a wrong impression of its scope and purpose. *Measure for Measure* is itself equivocal; but the subject-matter here fixes it to be taken in the sense, not of the old Jewish proverb, "An eye for an eye, and a tooth for a tooth," but of the divine precept, "Whatsoever ye would that men should do to you, do ye even so to them." Thus the title falls in with one of Portia's appeals to Shylock, "We do pray for mercy, and that same prayer doth teach us all to render the deeds of mercy." The moral centre of the play properly stands in avoidance of extremes, —

> "the golden mean and quiet flow
> Of truths that soften hatred, temper strife.

THE TEMPEST.

The Tempest is on all hands regarded as one of Shakespeare's perfectest works. Some of his plays, I should say, have beams in their eyes; but this has hardly so much as a mote; or, if it have any, my own eyes are not clear enough to discern it. I dare not pronounce the work faultless, for this is too much to affirm of any human workmanship; but I venture to think that whatever faults it may have are such as criticism is hardly competent to specify. In the characters of Ariel, Miranda, and Caliban, we have three of the most unique and original conceptions that ever sprang from the wit of man. We can scarce imagine how the Ideal could be pushed further beyond Nature; yet we here find it clothed with all the truth and life of Nature. And the whole texture of incident and circumstance is framed in keeping with that Ideal; so that all the parts and particulars cohere together, mutually supporting and supported.

The leading sentiment naturally inspired by the scenes of this drama is, I believe, that of delighted wonder. And such, as appears from the heroine's name, Miranda, who is *the* potency of the drama, is probably the sentiment which the play was meant to inspire. But the grace and efficacy in which the workmanship is steeped are so ethereal and so fine, that they can hardly be discoursed in any but the poetic form: it may well be doubted whether Criticism has any fingers delicate enough to grasp them. So much is this the case, that it seemed to me quite doubtful whether I should do well to undertake the theme at all. For Criticism is necessarily obliged to substitute, more or less, the forms of logic for those of art; and art, it scarce need be said, can do many things that are altogether beyond the reach of logic. On the other hand, the charm and verdure of these scenes are so unwithering and inexhaustible, that I could not quite make up my mind to leave the subject untried. Nor do I know how I can better serve my countrymen than by engaging and helping them in the study of this great inheritance of natural wisdom and unreproved delight. For, assuredly, if they early learn to be at home and to take pleasure in these productions, their whole after-life will be the better and the happier for it.

The Tempest is one of the plays that were never printed till in the folio of 1623; where, for reasons unknown to us, it stands the first in the volume; though, as we shall presently see, it was among the last of the Poet's writing.

It has been ascertained clearly enough that the play was written somewhere between 1603 and 1613. On the one hand, the leading features of Gonzalo's Commonwealth, as described in the play, were evidently taken from Florio's translation of Montaigne. As the passage is curious in itself, and as it aptly illustrates the Poet's method of appropriating from others, I will quote it:

"*Gon.* Had I plantation of this isle, my lord,
And were the King on 't, what would I do?
I' the Commonwealth I would by contraries
Execute all things: for no kind of traffic
Would I admit; no name of magistrate;
Letters should not be known; riches, poverty,
And use of service, none; contract, succession,
Bourn, bound of land, tilth, vineyard, none;
No use of metal, corn, or wine, or oil;
No occupation; all men idle, all;
And women too, — but innocent and pure;
No sovereignty; —
Seb. Yet he would be King on 't.
Ant. The latter end of his Commonwealth forgets the beginning.
Gon. All things in common Nature should produce
Without sweat or endeavour: treason, felony,
Sword, pike, knife, gun, or need of any engine,
Would I not have; but Nature should bring forth,
Of its own kind, all foison, all abundance,
To feed my innocent people."

In Montaigne's Essay *Of the Cannibals*, as translated by Florio, we have the following: "It is a nation, would I answer Plato, that hath no kind of traffic, no knowledge of letters, no intelligence of numbers, no name of magistrate, nor of politic superiority; no use of service, of riches, or of poverty; no contracts, no successions, no dividences; no occupation, but idle; no respect of kindred, but common; no apparel, but natural; no manuring of lands; no use of wine, corn, or metal: the very words that import lying, falsehood, treason, dissimulation, covetousness, envy, detraction, and pardon, were never heard amongst them."

Here the borrowing is too plain to be questioned; and this fixes the writing of *The Tempest* after 1603. On the other hand, Malone ascertained from some old records that the play was acted by the King's players "before Prince Charles, the Princess Elizabeth, and the Prince Palatine, in the beginning of 1613."

For any nearer fixing of the date we have nothing firm to go upon but probabilities. Some of these, however, are pretty strong. I must rest with noting one of them:

Some hints towards the play were derived, apparently, from a book published by one Jourdan in 1610, and entitled, *A Discovery of the Bermudas, otherwise called the Isle of Devils.* The occasion was as follows: A fleet of nine ships, with some five hundred people, sailed from England in May, 1609. Among the officers were Sir George Somers, Sir Thomas Gates, and Captain Newport. The fleet was headed by the *Sea-Venture*, called the Admiral's Ship. On the 25th of July they were struck by a terrible tempest, which scattered the whole fleet, and parted the *Sea-Venture* from the rest. Most of the ships, however, reached Virginia, left the greater part of their people there, and sailed again for England, where Gates arrived in August or September, 1610, having been sent home by Lord Delaware. Jourdan's book, after relating their shipwreck, continues thus: "But our delivery was not more strange in falling so happily upon land, than our provision was admirable. For the Islands of the Bermudas, as every one knoweth that hath heard or read of them, were never inhabited by any Christian or Heathen people, but ever reputed a most prodigious and enchanted place, affording nothing but gusts, storms, and foul weather. Yet did we find the air so temperate, and the country so abundantly fruitful, that, notwithstanding we were there for the space of nine months, we were not only well refreshed, but out of the abundance thereof provided us with some reasonable quantity of provision to carry us for Virginia, and to maintain ourselves and the company we found there." About the same time, the Council of Virginia also put forth a narrative of "the disasters which had befallen the fleet, and of their miraculous escape," wherein we have the following: "These Islands of the Bermudas have ever been accounted an enchanted pile of rocks, and a desert inhabitation of devils; but all the fairies of the rocks were but flocks of birds, and all the devils that haunted the woods were but herds of swine."

In this account and these extracts there are several points which clearly connect with certain things in the play. To mark those points, or to trace out that connection, seems hardly worth the while. It may be well to add that the Poet's *still-vexed Bermoothes* seems to link his work in some way with Jourdan's narrative. So that 1610 is as early a date as can well be assigned for the writing of *The Tempest.* The supernatural in the play was no doubt the Poet's own creation; but it would have been in accordance with his usual method to avail himself of whatever interest might spring from the popular notions touching the Bermudas. In his marvellous creations the people would see nothing but the distant marvels with which their fancies were prepossessed.

Concurrent with all this is the internal evidence of the play itself. The style, language, and general cast of thought, the union of richness and severity, the grave, austere beauty of character which pervades it, and the organic compactness of the whole structure, all go to mark it as an issue of the

Poet's ripest years. Coleridge regarded it as "certainly one of Shakespeare's latest works, judging from the language only." Campbell the poet considers it his very latest. "*The Tempest*," says he, "has a sort of sacredness as the last work of a mighty workman. Shakespeare, as if conscious that it would be his last, and as if inspired to typify himself, has made his hero a natural, a dignified, and benevolent magician, who could conjure up 'spirits from the vasty deep,' and command supernatural agency by the most seemingly-natural and simple means. Shakespeare himself is Prospero, or rather the superior genius who commands both Prospero and Ariel. But the time was approaching when the potent sorcerer was to break his staff, and bury it fathoms in the ocean 'deeper than did ever plummet sound.' That staff has never been and will never be recovered." But I suspect there is more of poetry than of truth in this; at least I can find no warrant for it: on the contrary, we have fair ground for believing that at least *Coriolanus*, *King Henry the Eighth*, and perhaps *The Winter's Tale* were written after *The Tempest.* Mr. Verplanck, rather than give up the notion so well put by Campbell, suggests that the Poet may have *revised The Tempest* after all his other plays were written, and inserted the passage where Prospero abjures his "rough magic," and buries his staff, and drowns his book. But I can hardly think that Shakespeare had any reference to himself in that passage: for, besides that he did not use to put his own feelings and purposes into the mouth of his characters, the doing so in this case would infer such a degree of self-exultation as, it seems to me, his native and habitual modesty would scarce permit.

No play or novel has been discovered to which Shakespeare could have been at all indebted for the plot or matter of *The Tempest.* There is indeed an old ballad called *The Inchanted Island*, which was once thought to have contributed something towards the play: but it is now generally held to be more modern than the play, and probably founded upon it; the names and some of the incidents being varied, as if on purpose to disguise its connection with a work that was popular on the stage.

There has been considerable discussion as to the scene of *The Tempest*. A wide range of critics from Mr. Chalmers to Mrs. Jameson have taken for granted that the Poet fixed his scene in the Bermudas. For this they have alleged no authority but his mention of "the still-vex'd Bermoothes." Ariel's trip from "the deep nook to fetch dew from the still-vex'd Bermoothes" does indeed show that the Bermudas were in the Poet's mind; but then it also shows that his scene was not there; for it had been no feat at all worth mentioning for Ariel to fetch dew from one part of the Bermudas to another. An aerial voyage of some two or three thousand miles was the least that so nimble a messenger could be expected to make any account of. Besides, in less than an hour after the wrecking of the King's ship, the rest of the fleet are said to be upon the Mediterranean, "bound sadly home for Naples." On the other hand, the Rev. Mr. Hunter is very positive that, if we read the play with a map before us, we shall bring up at the island of Lampedusa, which "lies midway between Malta and the African coast." He makes out a pretty fair case, nevertheless I must be excused; not so much that I positively reject his theory as that I simply do not care whether it be true or not. But if we must have any supposal about it, the most reasonable as well as the most poetical one seems to be, that the Poet, writing without a map, placed his scene upon an island of the mind; and that it suited his purpose to transfer to his ideal whereabout some of the wonders of trans-Atlantic discovery. I should almost as soon think of going to history for the characters of Ariel and Caliban, as to geography for the size, locality, or whatsoever else, of their dwelling-place. And it is to be noted that the old ballad just referred to seems to take for granted that the island was but an island of the mind; representing it to have disappeared upon Prospero's leaving it:

> "From that day forth the isle has been
> By wandering sailors never seen:
>   Some say 'tis buried deep
> Beneath the sea, which breaks and roars
> Above its savage rocky shores,
>   Nor e'er is known to sleep."

Coleridge says "*The Tempest* is a specimen of the purely romantic drama." The term *romantic* is here used in a technical sense; that is, to distinguish the Shakespearian from the Classic Drama. In this sense, I cannot quite agree with the great critic that the drama is *purely* romantic. Highly romantic it certainly is, in its wide, free, bold variety of character and incident, and in all the qualities that enter into the picturesque; yet not romantic in such sort, I think, but that it is at the same time equally classic; classic, not only in that the unities of time and place are strictly observed, but as having the other qualities which naturally go with those laws of the classic form; in its severe beauty and majestic simplicity, its interfusion of the lyrical and the ethical, and in the mellow atmosphere of serenity and composure which envelopes it: as if on purpose to show the Poet's mastery not only of both the Classic and Romantic Drama, but of the common Nature out of which both of them grew. This union of both kinds in one without hindrance to the distinctive qualities of either, — this it is, I think, that chiefly distinguishes *The Tempest* from the Poet's other dramas. Some have thought that in this play Shakespeare specially undertook to silence the pedantic cavillers of his time by showing that he could keep to the rules of the Greek stage, if he chose to do so, without being any the less himself. But it seems more likely that he was here drawn into such a course by the leadings of his own wise spirit than by the cavils of contemporary critics; the form appearing too cognate with the matter to have been dictated by any thing external to the work itself.

There are some points that naturally suggest a comparison between *The Tempest* and *A Midsummer-Night's Dream*. In both the Poet has with equal or nearly equal success carried Nature, as it were, beyond herself, and peopled a purely ideal region with the attributes of life and reality; so that the characters touch us like substantive, personal beings, as if he had but described, not created them. But, beyond this, the resemblance ceases: indeed no two of his plays differ more widely in all other respects.

The Tempest presents a combination of elements apparently so incongruous that we cannot but marvel how they were brought together; yet they blend so sweetly, and co-operate so smoothly, that we at once feel at home with them, and see nothing to hinder their union in the world of which we are a part. For in the mingling of the natural and the supernatural we here find no gap, no break; nothing disjointed or abrupt; the two being drawn into each other so harmoniously, and so knit together by mutual participations, that they seem strictly continuous, with no distinguishable line to mark where they meet and join. It is as if the gulf which apparently separates the two worlds had been abolished, leaving nothing to prevent a free circulation and intercourse between them.

Prospero, standing in the centre of the whole, acts as a kind of subordinate Providence, reconciling the diverse elements to himself and in himself to one another. Though armed with supernatural might, so that the winds and waves obey him, his magical and mysterious powers are tied to truth and right: his "high charms work" to none but just and beneficent ends; and whatever might be repulsive in the magician is softened and made attractive by the virtues of the man and the feelings of the father: Ariel links him with the world above us, Caliban with the world beneath us, and Miranda — "thee, my dear one, thee my daughter" — with the world around and within us. And the mind acquiesces freely in the miracles ascribed to him; his thoughts and aims being so at one with Nature's inward harmonies, that we cannot tell whether he shapes her movements or merely falls in with them; that is, whether his art stands in submission or command. His sorcery indeed is the sorcery of knowledge, his magic the magic of virtue. For what so marvellous as the inward, vital necromancy of good which transmutes the wrongs that are done him into motives of beneficence, and is so far from being hurt by the powers of Evil, that it turns their assaults into new sources of strength against them? And with what a smooth tranquillity of spirit he everywhere speaks and acts! as if the discipline of adversity had but served

> "to elevate the will,
> And lead him on to that transcendent rest
> Where every passion doth the sway attest
> Of Reason seated on her sovereign hill."

Shakespeare and Bacon, the Prince of poets and the Prince of philosophers, wrought out their mighty works side by side, and nearly at the same time, though without any express recognition of each other. And why may we not regard Prospero as prognosticating in a poetical form those vast triumphs of man's rational spirit which the philosopher foresaw and prepared? For it is observable that, before Prospero's coming to the island, the powers which cleave to his thoughts and obey his "so potent art" were at perpetual war, the better being in subjection to the worse, and all being turned from their rightful ends into a mad, brawling dissonance: but he teaches them to know their places; and, "weak masters though they be," without such guidance, yet under his ordering they become powerful, and work together as if endowed with a rational soul and a social purpose; their insane gabble turning to speech, their savage howling to music; so that

> "the isle is full of noises,
> Sounds, and sweet airs, that give delight, and hurt not."

Wherein is boldly figured the educating of Nature up, so to speak, into intelligent ministries, she lending man hands because he lends her eyes, and weaving her forces into vital union with him.

> "You by whose aid —
> Weak masters though ye be — I have bedimm'd
> The noontide Sun, call'd forth the mutinous winds,
> And 'twixt the green sea and the azure vault
> Set roaring war: to the dread rattling thunder
> Have I given fire, and rifted Jove's stout oak
> With his own bolt: the strong-bas'd promontory
> Have I made shake; and by the spurs pluck'd up
> The pine and cedar."

In this bold imagery we seem to have a kind of prophecy of what human science and skill have since achieved in taming the great forces of Nature to man's hand, and harnessing them up into his service. Is not all this as if the infernal powers should be appeased and soothed by the melody and sweetness of the Orphean harp and voice? And do we not see how the very elements themselves grow happy and merry in serving man, when he by his wisdom and eloquence has once charmed them into order and concert? Man has but to learn Nature's language and obey her voice, and she clothes him with plenipotence. The mad warring of her forces turns to rational speech and music when he holds the torch of reason before them and makes it shine full in their faces. Let him but set himself steadfastly to understand and observe her laws, and her mighty energies hasten to wait upon him, as docile to his hand as the lion to the eye and voice of Lady Una. So that we may not unfairly apply to Prospero what Bacon so finely interprets of Orpheus, as "a wonderful and divine person skilled in all kinds of harmony, subduing and drawing all things after him by sweet and gentle methods and modulations."

All this, to be sure, is making the work rather an allegory than a drama, and therein of course misrepresents its quality. For the connecting links in this strange intercourse of man and Nature are "beings individually determined," and affect us as persons, not as propositions.

Ariel and Caliban are equally preternatural, though in opposite directions. Ariel's very being is spun out of melody and fragrance; at least, if a feeling soul and an intelligent will are the warp, these are the woof of his exquisite texture. He has just enough of human-heartedness to know how he would feel were he human, and a proportionable sense of gratitude, which has been aptly called "the memory of the heart": hence he needs to be often reminded of his obligations, but is religiously true to them so long as he remembers them. His delicacy of nature is nowhere more apparent than in his sympathy with right and good: the instant he comes within their touch he follows them without reserve; and he will suffer any torments rather than "act the earthy and abhorr'd commands" that go against his moral grain. And what a merry little personage he is withal! as if his being were cast together in an impulse of play, and he would spend his whole life in one perpetual frolic.

But the main ingredients of Ariel's zephyr-like constitution are shown in his leading inclinations; as he naturally has most affinity for that of which he is framed. Moral ties are irksome to him; they are not his proper element: when he enters their sphere, he feels them to be holy indeed; but, were he free, he would keep out of their reach, and follow the circling seasons in their course, and always dwell merrily in the fringes of Summer. Prospero quietly intimates his instinctive dread of the cold by threatening to make him "howl away twelve Winters." And the chief joy of his promised release from service is, that he will then be free to live all the year through under the soft rule of Summer, with its flowers and fragrances and melodies. He is indeed an arrant little epicure of perfume and sweet sounds, and gives forth several songs which "seem to sound in the air, and as if the person playing them were invisible."

A part of Ariel's unique texture is well shown in the scene where he relents at the sufferings of the shipwrecked lords, and remonstrates with his master in their behalf:

"*Ariel.* The King,
His brother, and yours, abide all three distracted;
And the remainder mourning over them,
Brimful of sorrow and dismay; but chiefly
He that you term'd *the good old lord, Gonzalo:*
His tears run down his beard, like Winter's drops
From eaves of reeds: your charm so strongly works 'em,
That, if you now beheld them, your affections
Would become tender.
Pros. Dost thou think so, spirit?
Ariel. Mine would, sir, were I human."

Another mark-worthy feature of Ariel is, that his power does not stop with the physical forces of Nature, but reaches also to the hearts and consciences of men; so that by his music he can kindle or assuage the deepest griefs of the one, and strike the keenest pangs of remorse into the other. This comes out in the different effects of his art upon Ferdinand and the guilty King, as related by the men themselves:

"Where should this music be? i' the air or th' earth?
It sounds no more: — and, sure, it waits upon
Some god o' the island. Sitting on a bank,
Weeping again the King my father's wreck,
This music crept by me upon the waters,
Allaying both their fury and my passion
With its sweet air: thence I have follow'd it,
Or it hath drawn me rather: — but it is gone.
No, it begins again."

Such is the effect on Ferdinand: now mark the contrast when we come to the King:

"O, it is monstrous, monstrous!
Methought the billows spoke, and told me of it;
The winds did sing it to me; and the thunder,
That deep and dreadful organ-pipe, pronounc'd
The name of Prosper: it did bass my trespass.
Therefore my son i' the ooze is bedded; and
I'll seek him deeper than e'er plummet sounded,
And with him there lie mudded."

In the planting of love, too, Ariel beats old god Cupid

all to nothing. For it is through some witchcraft of his that Ferdinand and Miranda are surprised into a mutual rapture; so that Prospero notes at once how "at the first sight they have chang'd eyes," and "are both in either's power." All which is indeed just what Prospero wanted; yet he is himself fairly startled at the result: that fine issue of nature outruns his thought; and the wise old gentleman takes care forthwith lest it work too fast:

> "This swift business
> I must uneasy make, lest too light winning
> Make the prize light."

I must note one more trait in Ariel. It is his fondness of mischievous sport, wherein he reminds us somewhat of Fairy Puck in *A Midsummer-Night's Dream.* It is shown in the evident gust with which he relates the trick he has played on Caliban and his confederates, when they were proceeding to execute their conspiracy against the hero's life:

> "As I told you, sir, they were red-hot with drinking;
> So full of valour, that they smote the air
> For breathing in their faces; beat the ground
> For kissing of their feet; yet always bending
> Towards their project. Then I beat my tabor;
> At which, like unback'd colts, they prick'd their ears,
> Advanc'd their eyelids, lifted up their noses
> As they smelt music: so I charm'd their ears,
> That, calf-like, they my lowing follow'd through
> Tooth'd briers, sharp furzes, pricking goss, and thorns,
> Which enter'd their frail shins: at last I left them
> I' the filthy-mantled pool beyond your cell,
> There dancing up to th' chins."

Of Ariel's powers and functions as Prospero's prime minister, no logical forms, nothing but the Poet's art, can give any sort of an idea. No painter, I am sure, can do any thing with him; still less can any sculptor. Gifted with the ubiquity and multiformity of the substance from which he is named, before we can catch and define him in any one shape, he has passed into another. All we can say of him on this score is, that through his agency Prospero's thoughts forthwith become things, his volitions events. And yet, strangely and diversely as Ariel's nature is elemented and composed, with touches akin to several orders of being, there is such a self-consistency about him, he is so cut out in individual distinctness, and so rounded-in with personal attributes, that contemplation freely and easily rests upon him as an object. In other words, he is by no means an abstract idea personified, or any sort of intellectual diagram, but a veritable *person;* and we have a personal feeling towards the dear creature, and would fain knit him into the living circle of our human affections, making him a familiar playfellow of the heart, to be cherished with "praise, blame, love, kisses, tears, and smiles."

If Caliban strikes us as a more wonderful creation than Ariel, it is probably because he has more in common with us, without being in any proper sense human. Perhaps I cannot hit him off better than by saying that he represents, both in body and soul, a sort of intermediate nature between man and brute, with an infusion of something that belongs to neither; as though one of the transformations imagined by the Developmentists had stuck midway in its course, where a breath or vapour of essential Evil had knit itself vitally into his texture. Caliban has all the attributes of humanity from the moral downwards, so that his nature touches and borders upon the sphere of moral life; still the result but approves his exclusion from such life, in that it brings him to recognize moral law only as making for self; that is, he has intelligence of seeming wrong in what is done to him, but no conscience of what is wrong in his own doings. It is a most singular and significant stroke in the delineation, that sleep seems to loosen the fetters of his soul, and lift him above himself: then indeed, and then only, "the muddy vesture of decay" doth not so "grossly close him in," but that some proper spirit-notices come upon him; as if in his passive state the voice of truth and good vibrated down *to* his soul, and stopped there, being unable to kindle any answering tones within: so that in his waking hours they are to him but as the memory of a dream.

> "Sometime a thousand twangling instruments
> Will hum about mine ears ; and sometime voices,
> That, if I then had wak'd after long sleep,
> Will make me sleep again : and then, in dreaming,
> The clouds methought would open, and show riches
> Ready to drop upon me ; that, when I wak'd,
> I cried to dream again."

Thus Caliban is part man, part demon, part brute, each being drawn somewhat out of itself by combination with the others, and the union of all preventing him from being either; for which cause language has no generic term that fits him. Yet this strange, uncouth, but life-like confusion of natures Prospero has educated into a sort of poet. This, however, has nowise tamed, it has rather increased, his innate malignity and crookedness of disposition; education having of course but *educed* what was in him. Even his poetry is, for the most part, made up of the fascinations of ugliness; a sort of inverted beauty; the poetry of dissonance and deformity; the proper music of his nature being to curse, its proper laughter to snarl. Schlegel finely compares his mind to a dark cave, into which the light of knowledge falling neither illuminates nor warms it, but only serves to put in motion the poisonous vapours generated there.

Now it is by exhausting the resources of instruction on such a being that his innate and essential deficiency is best shown. For, had he the germs of a human soul, they must needs have been drawn forth by the process that has made him a poet. The magical presence of spirits has indeed cast into the caverns of his brain some faint reflection of a better world, but without calling up any answering emotions or aspirations; he having no susceptibilities to catch and take in the epiphanies that throng his whereabout.

So that, paradoxical as it may seem, he exemplifies the twofold triumph of art over nature, and of nature over art; that is, art has triumphed in making him a poet, and nature, in still keeping him from being a man; though he has enough of the human in him to evince in a high degree the swelling of intellectual pride.

But what is most remarkable of all in Caliban is the perfect originality of his thoughts and manners. Though framed of grossness and malignity, there is nothing vulgar or commonplace about him. His whole character indeed is developed from within, not impressed from without; the effect of Prospero's instructions having been to make him all the more himself; and there being perhaps no soil in his nature for conventional vices and knaveries to take root and grow in. Hence the almost classic dignity of his behaviour compared with that of the drunken sailors, who are little else than a sort of low, vulgar conventionalities organized, and as such not less true to the life than consistent with themselves. In his simplicity, indeed, he at first mistakes them for gods who "bear celestial liquor," and they wax merry enough at the "credulous monster"; but, in his vigour of thought and purpose, he soon conceives such a scorn of their childish interest in whatever trinkets and gewgaws meet their eye, as fairly drives off his fit of intoxication; and the savage of the woods, half-human though he be, seems nobility itself beside the savages of the city.

In fine, if Caliban is, so to speak, the organized sediment and dregs of the place, from which all the finer spirit has been drawn off to fashion the delicate Ariel, yet having some parts of a human mind strangely interwoven with his structure; every thing about him, all that he does and says, is suitable and correspondent to such a constitution of nature. So that all the elements and attributes of his being stand and work together in living coherence, thus rendering him no less substantive and personal to our apprehension than he is original and peculiar in himself.

Such are the objects and influences amidst which the clear, placid nature of Miranda has been developed. Of the world whence her father was driven, its crimes and follies and sufferings, she knows nothing; he having studiously kept all such notices from her, to the end, apparently, that nothing might thwart or hinder the plastic efficacies that surrounded her. And here all the simple and original elements of her being, love, light, grace, honour, innocence, all pure feelings and tender sympathies, whatever is sweet and gentle and holy in womanhood, seem to have sprung up in her nature as from celestial seed: "the contagion of the world's slow stain" has not visited her; the chills and cankers of artificial wisdom have not touched nor come nigh her: if there were any fog or breath of evil in the place that might else dim or spot her soul, it has been sponged up by Caliban, as being more congenial with his nature; while he is simply "a villain she does not love to look on." Nor is this all. The aerial music beneath which her soul has expanded with answering sweetness seems to rest visibly upon her, linking her as it were with some superior order of beings: the spirit and genius of the place, its magic and mystery, have breathed their power into her face; and out of them she has unconsciously woven herself a robe of supernatural grace, in which even her mortal nature seems half hidden, so that we are in doubt whether she belongs more to Heaven or to Earth. Thus both her native virtues and the efficacies of the place seem to have crept and stolen into her unperceived, by mutual attraction and assimilation twining together in one growth, and each diffusing its life and beauty over and through the others. It would seem indeed as if Wordsworth must have had Miranda in his eye, (or was he but working in the spirit of that Nature which she so rarely exemplifies?) when he wrote,

"The floating clouds their state shall lend
To her; for her the willow bend:
Nor shall she fail to see

Even in the motions of the storm
Grace that shall mould the maiden's form
By silent sympathy.

The stars of midnight shall be dear
To her ; and she shall lean her ear
In many a secret place
Where rivulets dance their wayward round,
And beauty born of murmuring sound
Shall pass into her face."

Yet, for all this, Miranda not a whit the less touches us as a creature of flesh and blood,

"A being breathing thoughtful breath,
A traveller between life and death."

Nay, rather she seems all the more so, inasmuch as the character thus coheres with the circumstances, the virtues and poetries of the place being expressed in her visibly; and she would be far less real to our feelings, were not the wonders of her whereabout thus vitally incorporated with her innate and original attributes.

It is observable that Miranda does not perceive the working of her father's art upon herself. For, when he casts a spell of drowsiness over her, so that she cannot choose but sleep, on being awaked by him she tells him, "The strangeness of your story put heaviness in me." So his art conceals itself in its very potency of operation; and seems the more like nature for being preternatural. It is another noteworthy point, that while he is telling his strange tale he thinks she is not listening attentively to his speech, partly because he is not attending to it himself, his thoughts being busy with the approaching crisis of his fortune, and drawn away to the other matters which he has in hand, and partly because in her trance of wonder at what he is relating she seems abstracted and self-withdrawn from the matter of his discourse. His own absent-mindedness on this occasion is aptly and artfully indicated by his broken and disjointed manner of speech. That his tongue and thought are not beating time together appears in that the latter end of his sentences keeps forgetting the beginning.

These are among the fine strokes and delicate touches whereby the Poet makes, or rather permits, the character of his persons to transpire so quietly as not to excite special notice at the time. That Miranda should be so rapt at her father's tale as to seem absent and wandering, is a charming instance in point. For indeed to her the supernatural stands in the place of Nature; and nothing is so strange and wonderful as what actually passes in the life and heart of man: miracles have been her daily food, her father being the greatest miracle of all; which must needs make the common events and passions and perturbations of the world seem to her miraculous. All which is wrought out by the Poet with so much art and so little appearance of art, that Franz Horn is the only critic, so far as I know, that seems to have thought of it.

I must not dismiss Miranda without remarking the sweet union of womanly dignity and childlike simplicity in her character, she not knowing or not caring to disguise the innocent movements of her heart. This, too, is a natural result of her situation. The instance to which I refer is when Ferdinand, his manhood all alive with her, lets her hear his soul speak; and she, weeping at what she is glad of, replies, —

> "Hence, bashful cunning!
> And prompt me, plain and holy innocence! —
> I am your wife, if you will marry me;
> If not, I'll die your maid: to be your fellow
> You may deny me; but I'll be your servant,
> Whether you will or no."

Equally fine is the circumstance that her father opens to her the story of his life, and lets her into the secret of her noble birth and ancestry, at a time when she is suffering with those that she saw suffer, and when her eyes are jewelled with "drops that sacred pity hath engender'd"; as if on purpose that the ideas of rank and dignity may sweetly blend and coalesce in her mind with the sympathies of the woman.

In Ferdinand is portrayed one of those happy natures, such as we sometimes meet with, who are built up all the more strongly in truth and good by contact with the vices and meannesses of the world. Courage, piety, and honour are his leading characteristics; and these virtues are so much at home in his breast, and have such an easy, natural ascendant in his conduct, that he thinks not of them, and cares only to prevent or remove the stains which affront his inward eye. The meeting of him and Miranda is replete with magic indeed, — a magic higher and more potent even than Prospero's; the riches that nestle in their bosoms at once leaping forth and running together in a stream of poetry which no words of mine can describe. So much of beauty in so few words, and those few so plain and simple, — "O, wondrous skill and sweet wit of the man!"

Shakespeare's genius is specially venerable in that he makes piety and honour go hand in hand with love. It seems to have been a fixed principle with him, if indeed it was not rather a genial instinct, that where the heart is rightly engaged, there the highest and tenderest thoughts of religion do naturally cluster and converge. For indeed the love that looks to marriage is itself a religion: its first impulse is to invest its object with poetry and consecration: to be "true to the kindred points of Heaven and home," is both its inspiration and its law. It thus involves a sort of regeneration of the inner man, and carries in its hand the baptismal fire of a nobler and diviner life.

And so it is in this delectable instance. In Ferdinand, as in all generous natures, "love betters what is best." Its first springing in his breast stirs his heavenward thoughts and aspirations into exercise: the moment that kindles his heart towards Miranda also kindles his soul in piety to God; and he knows not how to commune in prayer with the Source of good, unless he may couple her welfare with his own, and breathe her name in his holiest service. Thus his love and piety are kindred and coefficient forces, as indeed all true love and piety essentially are. However thoughtless we may be of the Divine help and guardianship for ourselves, we can hardly choose but crave them for those to whom our souls are knit in the sacred dearness of household ties. And so with this noble pair, the same power that binds them to each other in the sacraments of love also binds them both in devout allegiance to the Author of their being; whose presence is most felt by them in the sacredness of their mutual truth.

So much for the illustration here so sweetly given of the old principle, that whatsoever lies nearest a Christian's heart, whatsoever he tenders most dearly on Earth, whatsoever draws in most intimately with the currents of his soul, that is the spontaneous subject-matter of his prayers; our purest loves thus sending us to God, as if from an instinctive feeling that unless God be sanctified in our hearts, our hearts cannot retain their proper life.

In regard to what springs up between Ferdinand and Miranda, it is to be noted that Prospero does little but furnish occasions. He indeed thanks the quaint and delicate Ariel for the kindling touch that so quickly puts them "both in either's power"; for it seems to him the result of a finer inspiration than his art can reach; and so he naturally attributes it to the magic of his airy minister; whereas in truth it springs from a source far deeper than the magic of either, — a pre-established harmony which the mutual recognition now first quickens into audible music. After seeing himself thus outdone by the Nature he has been wont to control, and having witnessed such a "fair encounter of two most rare affections," no wonder that Prospero longs to be a man again, like other men, and gladly returns to

"The homely sympathy that heeds
The common life; our nature breeds;
A wisdom fitted to the needs
Of hearts at leisure."

The strength and delicacy of imagination displayed in the characters already noticed are hardly more admirable than the truth and subtilty of observation shown in others.

In the delineation of Antonio and Sebastian, short as it is, we have a volume of wise science, which Coleridge remarks upon thus: "In the first scene of the second Act, Shakespeare has shown the tendency in bad men to indulge in scorn and contemptuous expressions, as a mode of getting rid of their own uneasy feelings of inferiority to the good, and also of rendering the transition of others to wickedness easy, by making the good ridiculous. Shakespeare never puts habitual scorn into the mouths of other than bad men, as here in the instance of Antonio and Sebastian."

Nor is there less of judgment in the means used by Prospero for bringing them to a better mind; provoking in them the purpose of crime, and then taking away the performance; that so he may lead them to a knowledge of themselves, and awe or shame down their evil by his demonstrations of good. For such is the proper effect of bad designs thus thwarted, showing the authors at once the wickedness of their hearts and the weakness of their hands; whereas, if successful in their schemes, pride of power would forestall and prevent the natural shame and remorse of guilt. And we little know what evil it lieth and lurketh in our hearts to will or to do, till occasion invites or permits; and Prospero's art here stands in presenting the occasion till the wicked purpose is formed, and then removing it as soon as the hand is raised. In the case of Antonio and Sebastian, the workings of magic are so mixed up with those of Nature, that we cannot distinguish them; or rather Prospero here causes the supernatural to pursue the methods of Nature.

And the same deep skill is shown in the case of the good old Lord Gonzalo, whose sense of his own infelicities seems lost in his care to minister comfort and diversion to others. Thus his virtue spontaneously opens the springs of wit and humour in him amid the terrors of the storm and shipwreck; and he is merry while others are suffering, and merry even from sympathy with them; and afterwards his thoughtful spirit plays with Utopian fancies; and if "the latter end of his Commonwealth forgets the beginning," it is all the same to him, his purpose being only to beguile the anguish of supposed bereavement. It has been well said that "Gonzalo is so occupied with duty, in which alone he finds pleasure, that he scarce notices the gnat-stings of wit with which his opponents pursue him; or, if he observes, firmly and easily repels them."

The comic portions and characters of this play are in Shakespeare's raciest vein; yet they are perfectly unique and singular withal, being quite unlike any other of his preparations in that kind, as much so as if they were the growth of a different planet.

The presence of Trinculo and Stephano in the play has sometimes been regarded as a blemish. I cannot think it so. Their part is not only good in itself as comedy, but is in admirable keeping with the rest. Their follies give a zest and relish to the high poetries amidst which they grow. Such things go to make up the mysterious whole of human life; and they often help on our pleasure while seeming to hinder it: we may think they were better left out, but, were they left out, we should somehow feel the want of them. Besides, this part of the work, if it does not directly yield a grateful fragrance, is vitally connected with the parts that do. For there is perhaps no one of the Poet's dramas of which it can be more justly affirmed that all the parts draw together in organic unity, so that every thing helps every other thing.

Such are the strangely-assorted characters that make up this charming play. This harmonious working together of diverse and opposite elements, — this smooth concurrence of heterogeneous materials in one varied yet coherent impression, — by what subtile process this is brought about, is perhaps too deep a problem for Criticism to solve.

I cannot leave the theme without remarking what an atmosphere of wonder and mystery overhangs and pervades this singular structure; and how the whole seems steeped in glories invisible to the natural eye, yet made visible by the Poet's art: so that the effect is to lead the thoughts insensibly upwards to other worlds and other forms of being. It were difficult to name any thing else of human workmanship so thoroughly transfigured with

> "the gleam,
> The light that never was on sea or land,
> The consecration and the poet's dream."

The celestial and the earthly are here so commingled,— commingled, but not confounded,— that we see not where the one begins or the other ends: so that in the reading we seem transported to a region where we are strangers, yet old acquaintances; where all things are at once new and familiar; the unearthly visions of the spot hardly touching us with surprise, because, though wonderful indeed, there is nothing about them but what readily finds or creates some answering powers and sympathies within us. In other words, they do not surprise us, because they at once kindle us into fellowship with them. That our thoughts and feelings are thus at home with such things, and take pleasure in them,— is not this because of some innate aptitudes and affinities of our nature for a supernatural and celestial life?

> "Point not these mysteries to an art
> Lodg'd above the starry pole?"

THE WINTER'S TALE.

In Shakespeare's time there lived in London one Simon Forman, M. D., to whom we are indebted for our earliest notice of The Winter's Tale. He was rather an odd genius, I should think; being an adept in occult science and the arts of magic, and at the same time an ardent lover of the stage; thus symbolizing at once with the most conservative and the most radical tendencies of the age: for, strange as it may seem, the Drama then led the van of progress; Shakespeare being even a more audacious innovator in poetry and art than Bacon was in philosophy. Be this as it may, Forman evidently took great delight in the theatre, and he kept a diary of what he witnessed there. Not many years ago, the manuscript of this diary was discovered by Mr. Collier in the Ashmolean Museum, and a portion of its contents published. Forman was at the Globe theatre on Wednesday, the 15th of May, 1611, and under that date he records "how Leontes the King of Sicilia was overcome with jealousy of his wife with the King of Bohemia, his friend that came to see him, and how he contrived his death, and would have had his cup-bearer poison him, who gave the King warning thereof, and fled with him to Bohemia. Also, how he sent to the oracle of Apollo, and the answer of Apollo was that she was guiltless; and except the child was found again that was lost, the King should die without issue: for the child was carried into Bohemia, and there laid in a forest, and brought up by a shepherd; and the King of Bohemia's son married that wench, and they fled into Sicilia, and by the jewels found about her she was known to be Leontes' daughter, and was then sixteen years old."

This clearly identifies the performance seen by Forman as *The Winter's Tale* of Shakespeare. It is altogether probable that the play was then new, and was in its first course of exhibition. For Sir George Buck became Master of the Revels in October, 1610, and was succeeded in that office by Sir Henry Herbert in 1623, who passed *The Winter's Tale* without examination, on the ground of its being an "old play formerly allowed by Sir George Buck." As the play had to be licensed before it could be performed, this ascertains its first performance to have been after October, 1610. So that *The Winter's Tale* was most likely presented for official sanction some time between that date and the 15th of May following, when Forman saw it at the Globe. To all this must be added the internal characteristics of the play itself, which is in the Poet's ripest and most idiomatic style of art. It is not often that the date of his workmanship can be so closely remarked. *The Winter's Tale* was never printed, so far as we know, till it appeared in the folio of 1623.

In the plot and incidents of this play, Shakespeare followed very closely the *Pandosto*, or, as it was sometimes called, the *Dorastus and Fawnia*, of Robert Greene. This novel appears to have been one of the most popular books of the time; there being no less than fourteen old editions of it known, the first of which was in 1588. Greene was a scholar, a man of some genius, Master of Arts in both the Universities, and had indeed much more of learning than of judgment in the use and application of it. For it seems as if he could not write at all without overloading his pages with classical allusion, nor hit upon any thought so trite and commonplace, but that he must run it through a series of aphoristic sentences twisted out of Greek and Roman lore. In this respect, he is apt to remind one of his fellow-dramatist, Thomas Lodge, whose *Rosalynd* contributed so much to the Poet's *As You Like It:* for it was then much the fashion for authors to prank up their matter with superfluous erudition. Like all the surviving works of Greene, *Pandosto* is greatly charged with learned impertinence, and in the annoyance thence resulting one is apt to overlook the real merit of the performance. It is better than Lodge's *Rosalynd* for this reason, if for no other, that it is shorter. I must condense so much of the tale as may suffice to indicate the nature and extent of the Poet's obligations.

Pandosto, King of Bohemia, and Egistus, King of Sicilia, had passed their boyhood together, and grown into a mutual friendship which kept its hold on them long after coming to their crowns. Pandosto had for his wife a very wise and beautiful lady named Bellaria, who had made him the father of a prince called Garinter in whom both himself and his people greatly delighted. After many years of separation, Egistus "sailed into Bohemia to visit his old friend," who, hearing of his arrival, went with a great train of lords and ladies to meet him, received him very lovingly, and wished his wife to welcome him. No pains were spared to honour the royal visitor and make him feel at home. Bellaria, "to show how much she liked him whom her husband loved," treated Egistus with great confidence, often going herself to his chamber to see that nothing should be amiss. This honest familiarity increased from day to day, insomuch that when Pandosto was busy with State affairs they would walk into the garden and pass their time in pleasant devices. After a while, Pandosto began to have doubtful thoughts, considering the beauty of his wife, and the comeliness and bravery of his friend. This humour growing upon him, he went to watching them, and fishing for proofs to confirm his suspicions. At length his mind got so charged with jealousy that he felt quite certain of the thing he feared, and studied for nothing so much as revenge. He resolved to work by poison, and called upon his cup-bearer, Franion, to execute the scheme, and pressed him to it with the alternative of preferment or death. The minister, after trying his best to dissuade the King, at last gave his consent, in order to gain time, then went to Egistus, and told him the secret, and fled with him to Sicilia. Full of rage at being thus baffled, Pandosto then let loose his fury against the Queen, ordering her forthwith into close prison. He then had his suspicion proclaimed as a certain truth; and though her character went far to discredit the charge, yet the sudden flight of Egistus caused it to be believed. And he would fain have made war on Egistus, but that the latter not only was of great strength and prowess, but had many kings in his alliance, his wife being daughter to the Emperor of Russia.

Meanwhile the Queen in prison gave birth to a daughter;

which put the King in a greater rage than ever, insomuch that he ordered both the mother and the babe to be burnt alive. Against this cruel sentence his nobles stoutly remonstrated; but the most they could gain was, that he should spare the child's life; his next device being to put her in a boat and leave her to the mercy of the winds and waves. At the hearing of this hard doom, the Queen fell down in a trance, so that all thought her dead; and on coming to herself she at last gave up the babe, saying, "Let me kiss thy lips, sweet infant, and wet thy tender cheeks with my tears, and put this chain about thy little neck, that if fortune save thee, it may help to succour thee."

When the day of trial came, the Queen, standing as a prisoner at the bar, and seeing that nothing but her death would satisfy the King, "waxed bold, and desired that she might have law and justice," and that her accusers might be brought before her face. The King replied that their word was enough, the flight of Egistus confirming what they had said; and that it was her part "to be impudent in forswearing the fact, since she had passed all shame in committing the fault." At the same time he threatened her with a cruel death; which she met by telling him that her life had ever been such as no spot of suspicion could stain, and that, if she had borne a friendly countenance towards Egistus, it was only as he was her husband's friend: "therefore, if she were condemned without further proof, it was rigour, and not law." The judges said she spoke reason, and begged that her accusers might be openly examined and sworn; whereupon the King went to browbeating them, the very demon of tyranny having got possession of him. The Queen then told him that, if his fury might stand for law, it was of no use for the jury to give their verdict; and therefore she begged him to send six of his noblemen to "the Isle of Delphos," to inquire of Apollo whether she were guilty or not. This request he could not refuse. The messengers using all haste soon came back with the sealed answer of Apollo. The court being now assembled again, the scroll was opened and read in their presence, its contents being much the same as in the play. As soon as Apollo's verdict was known, the people raised a great shout, rejoicing and clapping their hands, that the Queen was clear. The repentant King then besought his nobles to intercede with the Queen in his behalf, at the same time confessing how he had tried to compass the death of Egistus; and while he was doing this word came that the young Prince was suddenly dead; at the hearing of which the Queen fell down, and could never be revived: the King also sank down senseless, and lay in that state three days; and there was nothing but mourning in Bohemia. Upon reviving, the King was so frenzied with grief and remorse that he would have killed himself, but that his peers being present stayed his hand, entreating him to spare his life for the people's sake. He had the Queen and Prince very richly and piously entombed; and from that time repaired daily to the tomb to bewail his loss.

Up to this point, the play, so far as the mere incidents are concerned, is little else than a dramatized version of the tale: henceforth the former diverges more widely from the latter, though many of the incidents are still the same in both.

The boat with its innocent freight was carried by wind and tide to the coast of Sicilia, where it stuck in the sand. A poor shepherd, missing one of his sheep, wandered to the seaside in search of it. As he was about to return he heard a cry, and, there being no house near, he thought it might be the bleating of his sheep; and going to look more narrowly he spied a little boat from which the cry seemed to come. Wondering what it might be, he waded to the boat, and found the babe lying there ready to die of cold and hunger, wrapped in an embroidered mantle, and having a chain about the neck. Touched with pity he took the infant in his arms, and as he was fixing the mantle there fell at his feet a very fair rich purse containing a great sum of gold. To secure the benefit of this wealth, he carried the babe home as secretly as he could, and gave her in charge to his wife, telling her the process of the discovery. The shepherd's name was Porrus, his wife's Mopsa; the precious foundling they named Fawnia. Being themselves childless, they brought her up tenderly as their own daughter. With the gold Porrus bought a farm and a flock of sheep, which Fawnia at the age of ten was set to watch; and, as she was likely to be his only heir, many rich farmers' sons came to his house as wooers; for she was of singular beauty and excellent wit, and at sixteen grew to such perfection of mind and person that her praises were spoken at the Sicilian Court. Nevertheless she still went forth every day with the sheep, veiling her face from the Sun with a garland of flowers; which attire became her so well, that she seemed the goddess Flora herself for beauty.

King Egistus had an only son, named Dorastus, a Prince so adorned with gifts and virtues, that both King and people had great joy of him. He being now of ripe age, his father sought to match him with some princess; but the youth was little minded to wed, as he had more pleasure in the exercises of the field and the chase. One day, as he was pursuing this sport, he chanced to fall in with the lovely shepherdess, and while he was rapt in wonder at the vision one of his pages told him she was Fawnia, whose beauty was so much talked of at the Court.

The story then goes on to relate the matter of their courtship; how the Prince resolved to forsake his home and inheritance, and become a shepherd, for her sake, as she could not think of matching with one above her degree; how, forecasting the opposition and dreading the anger of his father, he planned for escaping into Italy, in which enterprise he was assisted by an old servant of his named Capnio, who managed the affair so shrewdly, that the Prince made good his escape, taking the old shepherd along with him; how, after they got to sea, the ship was seized by a tempest and carried away to Bohemia; and how at length the several parties met together at the Court of Pandosto, which drew on a disclosure of the facts, and a happy marriage of the fugitive lovers.

I must add one more item from the novel, as it aptly shows what advantage is sometimes to be gained by tracing the Poet in his reading. In the play, the Shepherd on finding the babe is made to exclaim, "What have we here? Mercy on 's, a bairn; a very pretty bairn! a boy, or a child, I wonder?" For some hundred years, editorial ingenuity has been strained to the utmost to explain why *child* should be thus used in opposition to *boy;* and nothing would do but to surmise an obsolete custom of speech which made *child* signify *girl.* The simple explanation is, that *boy* is a misprint for *god.* For this felicitous restoration we are indebted to Mr. R. G. White, of New York, who was guided to it by the corresponding passage of the novel: "The shepherd, who before had never seen so fair a babe nor so rich jewels, thought assuredly that it was *some little god*, and began with great devotion to knock on his breast. The babe, who writhed with the head to seek for the pap, began again to cry, whereby the poor man knew *it was a child.*" That we are not gods, is indeed evident enough when we cry. Of course the man's devotion turned all to pity as soon as he caught that little but most unequivocal note of humanity.

From the foregoing sketch, it would seem that the Poet must have written with the novel before him, and not merely from general recollection. Here, again, as in case of *As You Like It*, to appreciate his judgment and taste, one needs to compare his workmanship in detail with the original, and to note what he left unused. The free sailing between Sicily and Bohemia he retained, inverting, however, the local order of the persons and incidents, so that Polixenes and Florizel are Bohemian Princes, whereas their prototypes, Egistus and his son, are Sicilians. The reason of this inversion does not appear. Of course, the Poet could not have done it with any view to disguise his obligations; as his purpose evidently was, to make the popular interest of the tale tributary to his own success and profit. The most original of men, he was also the most free from pride and conceit of originality. In this instance, too, as in others, the instinctive rectitude of his genius is manifest in that, the subject once chosen, and the work begun, he thenceforth lost himself in the inspiration of his theme; all thoughts of popularity and pay being swallowed up in the supreme regards of Nature and Truth. For so, in his case, however prudence might dictate the plan, poetry was sure to have command of the execution. If he was but human in electing what to do, he became divine as soon as he went to doing it. And it is further considerable that, with all his borrowings in this play, the Poet nowhere drew more richly or more directly from his own spring. The whole life of the work is in what he gave, not in what he took; the mechanism of the story being used but as a skeleton to underpin and support the eloquent contexture of life and beauty. In the novel, Paulina and the Clown are wanting altogether; while Capnio yields but a slight hint, if indeed it be so much, towards the part of Antolycus. And, besides the great addition of life and matter in these persons, the play has several other judicious departures from the novel.

In Leontes all the revolting features of Pandosto, save his jealousy, and the headstrong insolence and tyranny thence proceeding, are purged away; so that while the latter has neither intellect nor generosity to redeem his character, jealousy being the least of his faults, the other has a liberal stock of both. And in Bellaria the Poet had little more than a bare framework of incident wherein to set the noble, lofty womanhood of Hermione, — a conception far, far above the reach of such a mind as Greene's. In the matter of the painted statue, Shakespeare, so far as is known, was altogether without a model, as he is without an imitator; the boldness of the plan being indeed such as nothing but entire success could justify, and wherein it is hardly possible to conceive of anybody but Shakespeare's having succeeded. And yet here it is that we are to look for the idea and formal cause of Hermione's character, while her character, again, is the shaping and informing power of the whole drama. For this idea is really the living centre and organic law in and around which all the parts of the work are vitally knit together. But, indeed, the Poet's own most original and inimitable mode of conceiving and working out character is everywhere dominant.

So much has been said about the anachronisms of this play, that it seems needful to add a word concerning them. We have already seen that the making of seaports and landing of ships in Bohemia were taken from Greene. Mr. Verplanck conjectures that by Bohemia Shakespeare meant simply the land of the Boii, an ancient people several tribes of whom settled in the maritime parts of France: but I hardly think he would have used the name with so much license at a time when the boundaries of that country were so well fixed and so widely known. For the events of the Reformation had made Bohemia an object of special interest to the people of England, and there was much intercourse between the English and Bohemian Courts. I have no notion indeed that this breach of geography was a blunder: it was meant, no doubt, for the convenience of thought; and such is its effect, until one goes to viewing the parts of the work with reference to ends not contemplated in the use here made of them. And the same is to be said touching several points of chronological confusion; such as the making Whitsun pastorals, Christian burial, Julio Romano, the Emperor of Russia, and Puritans singing psalms to hornpipes, all contemporary with the Oracle of Delphi; wherein actual things are but marshalled into an ideal order, so as to render Memory subservient to Imagination. In these and such points, it is enough that the materials be apt to combine among themselves, and that they agree in working out the issue proposed, the end thus regulating the use of the means. For a work of art, as such, should be itself an object for the mind to rest upon, not a directory to guide it to something else. So that here we may justly say "the mind is its own place"; and, provided the work be true to this intellectual whereabout, breaches of geography and history are of little consequence. And Shakespeare knew full well, that in poetical workmanship Memory stands absolved from the laws of time, and that the living order of art has a perfect right to overrule and supersede the chronological order of facts. In a word, history and chronology have no rights which a poet, as such, is bound to respect. In his sphere, things draw together and unite in virtue of other affinities than those of succession and coexistence. A work of art must indeed aim to be understood and felt; and so far as historical order is necessary to this, so far it may justly claim a prerogative voice. But still such a work must address itself to the mind and heart of man as man, and not to particular men as scholars or critics. That Shakespeare did this better than anybody else is the main secret of his supremacy. And it implies a knowledge far deeper than books could give, — the knowledge of a mind so intuitive of Nature, and so at home with her, as not to need the food of learning, because it fed directly on that which is the original food of learning itself.

Hence the conviction which I suppose all true Shakespearians to have, that no amount of scholastic advantages and acquirements could really do any thing towards explaining the mystery of his works. To do what he did at all, he must have had a native genius so strong and clear and penetrative, as to become more than learned without the aid of learning. What could the hydrants of knowledge do for a mind which thus dwelt at its fountain? Or why should he need to converse with Wisdom's messengers, whose home was in the very court and pavilion of Wisdom herself? Shakespeare is always weakest when a fit of learning takes him. But then he is stronger without learning than any one else is with it, and, perhaps, than he would have been with it himself; as the crutches that help the lame are but an incumbrance to the whole.

Perhaps I ought to add, touching the forecited anachronisms, that the Poet's sense of them may be fairly regarded as apparent in the naming of the piece. He seems to have judged that, in a dramatic *tale* intended for the delight of the fireside during a long, quiet Winter's evening, such things would not be out of place, and would rather help than mar the entertainment and life of the performance. Thus much indeed is plainly hinted more than once in the course of the play; as in Act v. scene 2, where, one of the Gentlemen being asked, "What became of Antigonus, that carried hence the child?" he replies, "Like an *old tale* still, which will have matter to rehearse, though credit be asleep, and not an ear open."

Much the same is to be said touching the remarkable freedom which the Poet here takes with the conditions of time; there being an interval of sixteen years between the third and fourth Acts, which is with rather un-Shakespearian awkwardness bridged over by the Chorus introducing Act iv. This freedom, however, was inseparable from the governing idea of the piece, nor can it be faulted but upon such grounds as would exclude all dramatized fiction from the stage. It is to be noted also that while the play thus divides itself into two parts, these are skilfully woven together by a happy stroke of art. The last scene of the third Act not only finishes the action of the first three, but by an apt and unforced transition begins that of the other two; the two parts of the drama being smoothly drawn into the unity of a continuous whole by the introduction of the old Shepherd and his son at the close of the one and the opening of the other. This natural arrangement saves the imagination from being disturbed by any yawning or obtrusive gap of time, notwithstanding the lapse of so many years in the interval. On this point, Gervinus remarks that, "while Shakespeare has in other dramas permitted a twofold action united by a common idea, he could not in this instance have entirely concentrated the two actions; he could but unite them indistinctly by a leading idea in both; though the manner in which he has outwardly united them is a delicate and spirited piece of art.

In the delineation of Leontes there is an abruptness of change which strikes us, at first view, as not a little a-clash with nature: we cannot well see how one state of mind grows out of another: his jealousy shoots in comet-like, as something unprovided for in the general ordering of his character. Which causes this feature to appear as if it were suggested rather by the exigencies of the stage than by the natural workings of human passion. And herein the Poet seems at variance with himself; his usual method being to unfold a passion in its rise and progress, so that we go along with it freely from its origin to its consummation. And, certainly, there is no accounting for Leontes' conduct, but by supposing a predisposition to jealousy in him, which, however, has been hitherto kept latent by his wife's clear, firm, serene discreetness, but which breaks out into sudden and frightful activity as soon as she, under a special pressure of motives, slightly overacts the confidence of friendship. There needed but a spark of occasion to set this secret magazine of passion all a-blaze.

The Pandosto of the novel has, properly speaking, no character at all: he is but a human figure going through a set of motions; that is, the person and the action are put together arbitrarily, and not under any law of vital correspondence. Almost any other figure would fit the motions just as well. It is true, Shakespeare had a course of action marked out for him in the tale. But then he was bound by his own principles of art to make the character such as would rationally support the action, and cohere with it. For such is the necessary law of moral development and transpiration. Nor is it by any means safe to affirm that he has not done this. For it is to be noted that Polixenes has made a pretty long visit, having passed, it seems, no less than nine changes of the Moon at the home of his royal friend. And he might well have found it not always easy to avoid preferring the Queen's society to the King's; for she is a most irresistible creature, and her calm, ingenuous modesty, itself the most dignified of all womanly graces, is what, more than any thing else, makes her so. What secret thoughts may have been gathering to a head in the mind of Leontes during that period, is left for us to divine from the after-results. And I believe there is a jealousy of friendship, as well as of love. Accordingly, though Leontes invokes the Queen's influence to induce a lengthening of the visit, yet he seems a little disturbed on seeing that her influence has proved stronger than his own.

> "*Leon.* Is he won yet?
> *Herm.* He'll stay, my lord.
> *Leon.* At my request he would not.
> Hermione, my dear'st, thou never spok'st
> To better purpose.
> *Herm.* Never?
> *Leon.* Never, but once.
> *Herm.* What! have I twice said well? when was 't before?
> I pr'ythee tell me.
> *Leon.* Why, that was when
> Three crabbed months had sour'd themselves to death,
> Ere I could make thee open thy white hand,
> And clap thyself my love: then didst thou utter,
> *I'm yours forever.*"

There is, I think, a relish of suppressed bitterness in this last speech, as if her long reluctance had planted in him a germ of doubt whether, after all, her heart was really in her words of consent. For the Queen is a much deeper character than her husband. It is true, these notices, and various others, drop along so quiet and unpronounced, as hardly to arrest the reader's attention. Shakespeare, above all other men, delights in just such subtile insinuations of purpose; they belong indeed to his usual method of preparing for a given issue, yet doing it so slyly as not to preclude surprise when the issue comes.

So that in his seeming abruptness Leontes, after all, does but exemplify the strange transformations which sometimes occur in men upon sudden and unforeseen emergencies. And it is observable that the very slightness of the Queen's indiscretion, the fact that she goes but a little, a very little too far, only works against her, causing the King to suspect her of great effort and care to avoid suspicion. And on the same principle, because he has never suspected her before, therefore he suspects her all the more vehemently now: that his confidence has hitherto stood unshaken, he attributes to extreme artfulness on her part; for even so, to an ill-disposed mind perfect innocence is apt to give an impression of consummate art. A passion thus groundless and self-generated might well be full-grown as soon as born. The more greedy and craving, too, that it has nothing real to eat; it therefore proceeds at once to "make the meat it feeds on," causing him to magnify whatever he sees, and to imagine many things that are not. That jealousy, however, is not the habit of his mind, appears in that it finds him unprepared, and takes him by surprise; insomuch that he forthwith loses all self-control, and runs right athwart the rules of common decency and decorum, so that he becomes an object at once of pity, of hatred, and scorn.

I think the Poet hardly anywhere shows a keener and juster insight of nature than in the behaviour of this man while the distemper is upon him. He is utterly reason-proof, and indeed acts as one literally insane. For the poison infects not only his manners, but his very modes of thought: in fact, all his rational and imaginative forces, even his speech and language, seem to have caught the disease. And all the loathsome filth which had settled to the bottom of his nature is now shaken up to the surface, so that there appears to be nothing but meanness and malignity and essential coarseness in him. Meanwhile an instinctive shame of his passion and a dread of vulgar ridicule put him upon talking in dark riddles and enigmas: hence the confused, broken, and disjointed style, an odd jumble of dialogue and soliloquy, in which he tries to jerk out his thoughts, as if he would have them known, and yet not have them known. I believe men generally credit themselves with peculiar penetration when they are in the act of being deluded, whether by themselves or by others. Hence, again, the strange and even ludicrous conceit in which Leontes wraps himself. "Not noted, is 't," says he, referring to the Queen's imaginary crime, —

> "not noted, is 't,
> But of the finer natures? by some severals
> Of head-piece extraordinary? lower messes,
> Perchance, are to this business purblind."

Thus he mistakes his madness for a higher wisdom, and clothes his delusion with the spirit of revelation; so that Camillo rightly says, —

> "You may as well
> Forbid the sea for to obey the Moon
> As or by oath remove or counsel shake
> The fabric of his folly, whose foundation
> Is pil'd upon his faith."

I must note one more point of the delineation. When Leontes sends his messengers to Delphos, he avows this as his reason for doing so:

> "Though I am satisfied, and need no more
> Than what I know, yet shall the Oracle
> Give rest to th' minds of others."

Which means simply that he is not going to let the truth of the charge stand in issue, and that he holds the Divine authority to be a capital thing, provided he may use it, and need not obey it; that is, if he finds the god agreeing with him in opinion, then the god's judgment is infallible; if not, then, in plain terms, he is no god. And they who have closely observed the workings of jealousy, know right well that in all this Shakespeare does not one whit "overstep the modesty of Nature."

The Poet manages with great art to bring Leontes off

from the disgraces of his passion, and repeal him home to our sympathies, which had been freely drawn to him at first by his generosity of friendship. To this end, jealousy is represented as his only fault, and this as a sudden freak, which passes on directly into a frenzy, and whips him quite out of himself, temporarily overriding his characteristic qualities, but not combining with them; the more violent for being unwonted, and the shorter-lived for being violent. In his firm, compact energy of thought and speech, after his passion has cleared itself, and in his perennial flow of repentance after his bereavement, are displayed the real tone and texture of his character. We feel that, if his sin has been great, his suffering is also great, and that if he were a greater sinner, his suffering would be less. Quick, impulsive, headstrong, he admits no bounds to anger or to penitence; condemns himself as vehemently as he does others; and will spend his life in atoning for a wrong he has done in a moment of passion: so that we are the more willing to forgive him, inasmuch as he never forgives himself.

The old poets seem to have contemplated a much wider range of female excellence than it has since grown customary to allow; taking for granted that whatsoever we feel to be most divine in man might be equally so in woman; and so pouring into their conceptions of womanhood a certain *manliness* of soul, wherein we recognize an union of what is lovely with what is honourable, — such a combination as would naturally inspire any right-minded man at the same time with tenderness and with awe. Their ideas of delicacy did not preclude strength: in the female character they were rather pleased than otherwise to have the sweetness of the violet blended with the grandeur of the oak; probably because they saw and felt that woman might be big-hearted and brave-minded, and yet be none the less womanly; and that love might build all the higher and firmer for having its foundations laid deep in respect.

This largeness of heart and liberality of thought often comes out in their writings, and that too whether in dealing with ideal or with actual women; which suggests that in what they chose to create they were a good deal influenced by what they were accustomed to see. For in a thing that works so much from the sympathies, it could hardly be but that they reflected the mind and spirit of their age. Of this the aptest illustration that my reading has lighted upon is in Ben Jonson's lines on the Countess of Bedford, describing "what kind of creature I could most desire to honour, serve, and love":

'I meant to make her fair, and free, and wise,
Of greatest blood, and yet more good than great;
I meant the day-star should not brighter rise,
Nor lend like influence from his lucent seat:
I meant she should be courteous, facile, sweet,
Hating that solemn vice of greatness, pride;
I meant each softest virtue there should meet,
Fit in that softer bosom to reside:
Only a learned and a manly soul
I purpos'd her; that should with even powers
The rock, the spindle, and the shears control
Of Destiny, and spin her own free hours."

That Shakespeare fully shared in this magnanimous bravery of sentiment, we need no further proof than is furnished in the heroine of this play. We can scarce call Hermione sweet or gentle, though she is both; she is a *noble* woman, — one whom, even in her greatest anguish, we hardly *dare* to pity. The whole figure is replete with classic grace, is shaped and finished in the highest style of classic art. As she acts the part of a statue in the play, so she has a statue-like calmness and firmness of soul. A certain austere sweetness pervades her whole demeanour, and seems, as it were, the essential form of her life. It is as if some masterpiece of ancient sculpture had warmed and quickened into life from its fulness of beauty and expression.

Appearing at first as the cheerful hostess of her husband's

friend, and stooping from her queenly elevation to the most winning affabilities, her behaviour rises in dignity as her sorrow deepens. With an equal sense of what is due to the King as her husband, and to herself as a woman, a wife, and a mother, she knows how to reconcile all these demands; she therefore resists without violence, and submits without weakness. And what her wise spirit sees to be fit and becoming, that she always has strength and steadiness of character to do: hence, notwithstanding the insults and hardships wantonly put upon her, she still preserves the smoothnesses of peace; is never betrayed into the least sign of anger or impatience or resentment, but maintains, throughout, perfect order and fitness and proportion in act and speech: the charge, so dreadful in itself, and so cruel in its circumstances, neither rouses her passions, as it would Paulina's, nor stuns her sensibilities, as in the case of Desdemona; but, like the sinking of lead in the ocean's bosom, it goes to the depths without ruffling the surface of her soul. Her situation is indeed full of pathos, — a pathos the more deeply-moving to others, that it stirs no tumults in her; for her nature is manifestly fitted up and furnished with all tender and gentle and womanly feelings; only she has the force of mind to control them, and keep them all in the right place and degree. "They are the patient sorrows that touch nearest." And so, under the worst that can befall, she remains within the region of herself, calm and serenely beautiful, stands firm, yet full of grace, in the austere strengths of reason and conscious rectitude. And when, at her terrible wrongs and sufferings, all hearts are shaken, all eyes wet, but her own, the impression made by her stout-hearted fortitude is of one whose pure, tranquil, deep-working breast is the home of sorrows too big for any eye-messengers to report:

"Calm pleasures there abide, majestic pains."

The delineation keeps the same tone and texture through all its parts, but the sense of it is specially concentrated in what she says when the King winds up his transport of insane fury by ordering her off to prison:

"Good my lords,
I am not prone to weeping, as our sex
Commonly are; the want of which vain dew
Perchance shall dry your pities; but I have
That honourable grief lodg'd here which burns
Worse than tears drown. 'Beseech you all, my lords,
With thoughts so qualified as your charities
Shall best instruct you, measure me; — and so,
The King's will be perform'd! — 'Beseech your Highness,
My women may be with me; for, you see,
My plight requires it. — Do not weep, good fools;
There is no cause: when you shall know your mistress
Has deserv'd prison, then abound in tears,
As I come out. — . . . . Adieu, my lord:
I never wish'd to see you sorry; now
I trust, I shall."

And her character is answerably reflected in the minds of the King's chief counsellors, whose very swords seem stirring with life in the scabbards, and yearning to leap forth and vindicate the honour of their glorious Queen, but that awe of the crown restrains them.

Her last speech at the trial is, I am apt to think, the solidest piece of eloquence in the language. It is like a piece of the finest statuary marble, chiselled into perfect form; so compact of grain, that you cannot crush it into smaller space; while its effect is as wholesome and bracing as the atmosphere of an iced mountain when tempered by the Summer sun. The King threatens her with death, and she replies, —

"Sir, spare your threats:
The bug which you would fright me with I seek.
To me can life be no commodity:
The crown and comfort of my life, your favour,
I do give lost; for I do feel it gone,
But know not how it went: my second joy,
And first-fruits of my body, from his presence
I 'm barr'd, like one infectious: my third comfort,
Starr'd most unluckily, is from my breast,

> The innocent milk in its most innocent mouth,
> Hal'd out to murder: myself on every post
> Proclaim'd a strumpet; with immodest hatred,
> The child-bed privilege denied, which 'longs
> To women of all fashion: lastly, hurried
> Here to this place, i' the open air, before
> I have got strength of limit. Now, my liege,
> Tell me what blessings I have here alive,
> That I should fear to die. Therefore, proceed.
> But yet hear this; mistake me not: My life,
> I prize it not a straw; but for mine honour,
> Which I would free, if I shall be condemn'd
> Upon surmises, all proofs sleeping else
> But what your jealousies awake, I tell you
> 'Tis rigour, and not law."

Noble simplicity of the olden time, when the best and purest of women, with the bravest men in presence, thought no shame to hear themselves speaking such plain honest words as these!

The Queen's long concealing of herself has been censured by some as repugnant to nature. Possibly they may think it somewhat strained and theatrical, but it is not so: the woman is but true to herself, in this matter, and to the solid and self-poised repose in which her being dwells. So that the thing does not seem repugnant to nature as individualized by her reason and will; nor is her character herein more above or out of nature than the proper ideal of art abundantly warrants. For to her keen sensibility of honour the King's treatment is literally an *infinite* wrong; nor does its cruelty more wound her affection, than its meanness alienates her respect; and one so strong to bear injury might well be equally strong to remember it. Therewithal she knows full well that, in so delicate an instrument as married life, if one string be out of tune the whole is ajar, and will yield no music: for her, therefore, all things must be right, else none are so. And she is both too clear of mind and too upright of heart to put herself where she cannot be precisely what the laws of propriety and decorum require her to seem. Accordingly, when she does forgive, the forgiveness is simply *perfect;* the breach that has been so long a-healing is at length *completely* healed; for to be whole and entire in whatever she does, is both an impulse of nature and a law of conscience with her. When the King was wooing her, she held him off three months, which he thought unreasonably long; but the reason why she did so is rightly explained when, for his inexpressible sin against her, she has locked herself from his sight sixteen years, leaving him to mourn and repent. Moreover, with her severe chastity of principle, the reconciliation to her husband must begin there where the separation grew. Thus it was for Perdita to restore the parental unity which her being represents, but of which she had occasioned the breaking.

Such is Hermione, in her "proud submission," her "dignified obedience," with her Roman firmness and integrity of soul, heroic in strength, heroic in gentleness, the queenliest of women, the womanliest of queens. She is perhaps the Poet's best illustration of the great principle, which I fear is not so commonly felt as it should be, that the highest beauty always has an element or shade of the terrible in it, so that it awes you while it attracts.

> "If I prove honey-mouth'd, let my tongue blister,
> And never to my red-look'd anger be
> The trumpet any more."
>
> "Good Queen, my lord, good Queen; I say, good Queen,
> And would by combat make her good, so were I
> A man, the worst about you."
>
> "For ever
> Unvenerable be thy hands, if thou
> Tak'st up the Princess by that forcèd baseness
> Which he has put upon 't."

Such are some of the words that boil over from the stout heart of Paulina, — the noblest and most amiable termagant we shall anywhere find, — when, with the new-born babe in charge, she confronts the furious King. He threatens to have her burnt, and she replies instantly, —

"I care not :
It is an heretic that makes the fire,
Not she which burns in 't."

If her faults were a thousand times greater than they are, I could pardon them all for this one little speech; which proves that Shakespeare was, I will not say a Protestant, but a true Christian, intellectually at least, and far deeper in the spirit of his religion than a large majority of the Church's official organs were in his day, or, let me add, have been any day since. And this was written, be it observed, at a time when the embers of the old ecclesiastical fires were not yet wholly extinct, and when many a priestly b[illegible] was deploring the lay ascendency which kept them from being rekindled.

Paulina makes a superb counterpart to Hermione, heightening the effect of her character by the most emphatic contrast, and at the same time reflecting it by her intense and outspoken sympathy. Without any of the Queen's dignified calmness and reserve, she is alive to all her inward beauty and greatness: with a head to understand and a heart to reverence such a woman, she unites a temper to fight, a generosity to die for her. But no language but her own can fitly measure the ardour with which she loves and admires and even adores her "dearest, sweetest mistress," whose power has indeed gone all through her, so that every part of her nature cannot choose but speak it, when the occasion kindles her. Loud, voluble, violent, and viraginous, with a tongue sharper than a sword, and an eloquence that fairly blisters where it hits, she has, therewithal, too much honour and magnanimity and kind feeling either to use them without good cause, or to forbear using them at all hazards when she has such cause. Mrs. Jameson classes her, and justly, no doubt, among those women — and she assures us there are many such — who seem regardless of the feelings of those for whom they would sacrifice their life.

"I thought she had some great matter there in hand; for she hath privately, twice or thrice a day, ever since the death of Hermione, visited that removed house." Such is the speech of one gentleman to another, as the royal party and all the Court are going to Paulina's house to see the mysterious workmanship of Julio Romano. Nothing could better suggest the history of that quiet, placid intercourse, with its long record of patient, self-rewarding service; a fellowship in which little needed to be said, for each knew what was in the other's mind by a better language than words. It is such an idea of friendship as it does the heart good to rest upon. Just think of those two great manly souls, enshrined in womanly tenderness, thus communing together in secret for sixteen long years! And what a powerful charm of love and loyalty must have been cast upon Paulina's impulsive tongue, that she should keep so reticent of her dear cause through all that time! To play the woman after that fashion would not hurt any of us.

During the first three Acts the interest of this play is mainly tragic; the scene is densely crowded with incidents; the action hurried, abrupt, almost spasmodic; the style quick and sharp, flashing off point after point in brief, sinewy strokes; and all is rapidity and despatch: what with the insane fury of the King, the noble agony of the Queen, the enthusiasm of the Court in her behalf, and the King's violence towards both them and her, the mind is kept on the jump: all which, if continued to the end, would generate rather a tumult and hubbub in the thoughts, than that inward music which the title of the play promises; not to say, that such a prolonged hurry of movement would at length become monotonous and wearisome. Far otherwise the latter half of the play. Here the anticipations proper to a long, leisurely winter evening are fully met; the general effect is soothing and composing; the tones, dipped in sweetness, fall gently on the ear, disposing the mind to be still and listen and contemplate; thus making the play, as Coleridge describes it, "exquisitely respondent to the title." It would seem, indeed, that in these scenes the Poet had spo cially endeavoured how much of silent effect he could produce, without diverging from the dramatic form. To this end, he provides resting-places for thought; suspending or retarding the action by musical pauses and periods of lyrical movement, and breathing in the mellowest strains of poetical harmony, till the eye is "made quiet by the power of beauty," and all tumult of mind is hushed in the very intensity of feeling.

In the last two Acts we have a most artful interchange and blending of romantic beauty and comic drollery. The lost Princess and the heir-apparent of Bohemia, two of the noblest and loveliest beings that ever fancy conceived, occupy the centre of the picture, while around them are clustered rustic shepherds and shepherdesses amid their pastimes and pursuits, the whole being enlivened by the tricks and humours of a merry pedler and pickpocket. For simple purity and sweetness, the scene which unfolds the loves and characters of the Prince and Princess is not surpassed by any thing in Shakespeare. Whatsoever is enchanting in romance, lovely in innocence, elevated in feeling, and sacred in faith, is here concentrated; forming, all together, one of those things which we always welcome as we do the return of Spring, and over which our feelings may renew their youth for ever. So long as flowers bloom and hearts love, they will do it in the spirit of this scene.

It is a pastoral frolic, where free thoughts and guileless hearts rule the hour, all as true and as pure as the tints and fragrances with which field and forest and garden have beautified the occasion. The neighbouring swains and lasses have gathered in, to share and enhance the sport. The old Shepherd is present, but only as a looker-on, having for the nonce resigned the command to his reputed daughter. Under their mutual inspiration, the Prince and Princess are each in the finest rapture of fancy, while the surrounding influences of the rustic festival are just enough to enfranchise their inward music into modest and delicate utterance. He has tastefully decked her person with flowers, till no traces of the shepherdess can be seen, and she seems herself a multitudinous flower; having also attired himself "with a swain's wearing," so that the prince is equally obscured.

> "These your unusual weeds to each part of you
> Do give a life : no shepherdess ; but Flora,
> Peering in April's front. This your sheep-shearing
> Is as a meeting of the petty gods,
> And you the queen on 't."

Thus he opens the play. And when she repeats her fears of the event:

> "Thou dearest Perdita,
> With these forc'd thoughts, I pr'ythee, darken not
> The mirth o' the feast : or I 'll be thine, my fair,
> Or not my father's ; for I cannot be
> Mine own, nor any thing to any, if
> I be not thine : to this I am most constant,
> Though destiny say no."

The King and Camillo steal upon them in disguise, and while they are present we have this:

> "*Perdita.* Come, take your flowers :
> Methinks I play as I have seen them do
> In Whitsun pastorals : sure, this robe of mine
> Does change my disposition.
> *Florizel.* What you do
> Still betters what is done. When you speak, sweet,
> I 'd have you do it ever : when you sing,
> I 'd have you buy and sell so ; so give alms ;
> Pray so ; and, for the ordering your affairs,
> To sing them too : when you do dance I wish you
> A wave o' the sea, that you might ever do
> Nothing but that ; move still, still so, and own
> No other function. Each your doing is
> So singular in each particular,
> Crowning what you have done i' the present deed,
> That all your acts are queens.
> *Perdita.* O Doricles !
> Your praises are too large : but that your youth,
> And the true blood that peeps so fairly through 't,
> Do plainly give you out an unstain'd shepherd,
> With wisdom I might fear, my Doricles,
> You woo'd me the false way.

Florizel. I think you have
As little skill to fear as I have purpose
To put you to 't. But come; our dance, I pray.
Polix. This is the prettiest low-born lass that ever
Ran on the green-sward: nothing she does or seems
But smacks of something greater than herself, —
Too noble for this place.
Camil. He tells her something
That makes her blood look out: Good sooth, she is
The queen of curds and cream.
Polix. 'Pray you, good shepherd, what fair swain is this
Which dances with your daughter?
Shep. They call him Doricles; and boasts himself
To have a worthy feeding: I but have it
Upon his own report, and I believe it;
He looks like sooth. He says he loves my daughter:
I think so too; for never gaz'd the Moon
Upon the water, as he 'll stand, and read,
As 't were, my daughter's eyes: and, to be plain,
I think there is not half a kiss to choose
Who loves another best.
Polix. She dances featly.
Shep. So she does any thing, though I report it,
That should be silent."

Perdita, notwithstanding she occupies so little room in the play, fills a large space in the reader's thoughts, almost disputing precedence with the Queen. And her mother's best native qualities reappear in her, sweetly modified by pastoral associations; her nature being really much the same, only it has been developed and seasoned in a different atmosphere; a nature too strong indeed to be displaced by any power of circumstances or supervenings of art, but at the same time too delicate and susceptive not to take a lively and lasting impress of them. So that, while she has thoroughly assimilated, she nevertheless clearly indicates, the food of place and climate, insomuch that the dignities of the princely and the simplicities of the pastoral character seem striving which shall express her goodliest. We can hardly call her a poetical being; she is rather poetry itself, and every thing lends and borrows beauty at her touch. A playmate of the flowers, when we see her with them, we are at a loss whether they take more inspiration from her or she from them; and while she is the sweetest of poets in making nosegays, the nosegays become in her hands the richest of crowns. If, as Schlegel somewhere remarks, the Poet is "particularly fond of showing the superiority of the innate over the acquired," he has surely nowhere done it with finer effect than in this unfledged angel.

There is much to suggest a comparison of Perdita and Miranda; yet how shall I compare them? Perfectly distinct indeed as individuals, still their characters are strikingly similar; only Perdita has perhaps a sweeter gracefulness, the freedom, simplicity, and playfulness of nature being in her case less checked by external restraints; while Miranda carries more of a magical and mysterious charm woven into her character from the supernatural influences of her whereabout. So like, yet so different, it is hard saying which is the better of the two, or rather one can hardly help liking her best with whom he last conversed. It is an interesting fact also, for such it seems to be, that these two glorious delineations were produced very near together, perhaps both the same year; and this too when Shakespeare was in his highest maturity of poetry and wisdom; from which it has been not unjustly argued that his experience both in social and domestic life must have been favourable to exalted conceptions of womanhood. The Poet, though in no sort a bigot, was evidently full of loyal and patriotic sentiment; and I have sometimes thought that the government of Elizabeth, with the grand national enthusiasm which clustered round her throne and person, may have had a good deal to do in shaping and inspiring this part of his workmanship. Be that as it may, with but one great exception, I think the world now finds its best ideas of moral beauty in Shakespeare's women.

Florizel's character is in exquisite harmony with that of the Princess. To be sure, it may be said that if he is worthy of her, it is mainly her influence that makes him so. But then it is to be observed, on the other hand, that as in such cases men find only what they bring the faculties for finding, so the meeting with her would not have elicited such music from him, had not his nature been originally responsive to hers. For he is manifestly drawn and held to her by a powerful instinct of congeniality. And none but a living abstract and sum-total of all that is manly could have so felt the perfections of such a woman. The difference between them is, that she was herself before she saw him, and would have been the same without him; whereas he was not and could not be himself, as we see him, till he caught inspiration from her; so that he is but right in saying, —

> "I bless the time
> When my good falcon made her flight across
> Thy father's ground."

Nevertheless it is a clear instance of the pre-establish·d harmony of souls: but that his spirit were akin to hers, he could not have recognized his peer through such a disguise of circumstances. For any one to be untouched and unsweetened by the heavenly purity of their courtship, were indeed a sin almost too great to be forgiven.

Shakespeare knew, — none better, — that in order to be a lover in any right sense of the term, one must first be a man. He therefore does not leave the Prince without an opportunity to show that he is such. And it is not till after the King has revealed himself, and blown up the mirth of the feast by his explosion of wrath, that the Prince displays his proper character in this respect. I need not stay to remark how well the Poet orders the action for that purpose; suffice it to say that the Prince then fully makes good his previous declaration:

> "Were I crown'd the most imperial monarch,
> Thereof most worthy; were I the fairest youth
> That ever made eye swerve; had force and knowledge
> More than was ever man's; I would not prize them,

> Without her love; for her employ them all;
> Commend them or condemn them to her service,
> Or to their own perdition."

The minor characters of this play are both well conceived and skilfully disposed, the one giving them a fair personal, the other a fair dramatic interest. The old Shepherd and his clown of a son are near, if not in, the Poet's happiest comic vein. Autolycus, the "snapper-up of unconsidered trifles," is the most amiable and ingenious rogue we should desire to see; who cheats almost as divinely as those about him love, and whose thieving tricks the very gods seem to crown with thrift in reward of his wit. His self-raillery and droll soliloquizing give us the feeling that his sins are committed not so much for lucre as for fun. — The Poet was perhaps a little too fond of placing his characters in situations where they have to be false in order to be the truer; which no doubt sometimes happens; yet, surely, in so delicate a point of morality, some care is needful, lest the exceptions become too much for the rule. And something too much of this there may be in the honest, upright, yet deceiving old lord, Camillo. I speak this under correction; for I know it is not safe to fault Shakespeare's morals; and that they who affect a better morality than his are very apt to turn out either hypocrites or moral coxcombs. As for the rest, this Camillo, though little more than a staff in the drama, is nevertheless a pillar of State; his integrity and wisdom making him a light to the counsels and a guide to the footsteps of the greatest around him. Fit to be the stay of princes, he is one of those venerable relics of the past which show us how beautiful age can be, and which, linking together different generations, form at once the salt of society and the strength of government.

I have never seen this play on the stage; but I can well understand how the scene with the painted statue, if fairly delivered, might be surpassingly effective. The illusion is all on the understandings of the spectators; and they seem to feel the *power* without the *fact* of animation, or to have a *sense* of mobility in a *vision* of fixedness. And such is the magic of the scene, that we almost fancy them turning into marble, as they fancy the marble turning into flesh.

END OF VOL. I.